ENVIRONMENTAL PSYCHOLOGY

FOR DESIGN

DAK Kopec

NEWSCHOOL
OF ARCHITECTURE
AND DESIGN

FAIRCHILD
PUBLICATIONS, INC.
NEW YORK

Executive Editor: Olga T. Kontzias

Acquisitions Editor: Joseph Miranda

Assistant Acquisitions Editor: Jaclyn Bergeron

Art Director: Adam B. Bohannon

Production Manager: Ginger Hillman

Associate Production Editor: Beth Cohen

Project Editor: Jason Moring

Development Editor: Donna Frassetto

Photo Researcher: Matthew McHenry

Copy Editor: Vivian Gomez

Interior Design and Layout: Susan Day

Cover Design: Susan Day

Cover Photos (from left): Larry Williams/Corbis;
G. Schuster/Corbis; Tor Eigeland; Corbis; Luca Babini/Corbis;
Henry Diltz/Corbis; Craig Lovell/Corbis

Library of Congress Catalog Card Number: 2005933566

ISBN: 1-56367-424-6

GST R 133004424

Printed in China

TP 11

This book is dedicated to my family for all of their support and to my mentors, Jan Bast of the Design Institute of San Diego and Michael Stepner and Gil Cooke of the NewSchool of Architecture & Design.

CONTENTS

EXTENDED CONTENTS

PREFACE

The built environment has been part of the human experience since the dawn of civilization, from the first mobile villages to today's megalopolises. Modern-day people spend the vast majority of their lives within built environments; they live, learn, work, shop, and recreate both in and surrounded by built structures. These are environments that people mold to fit their needs according to the conditions, events, and trends that shape their world, such as the design trends of the late 1950s that were spawned by both the atomic age and the Cold War. Although several fields address environmental modification, environmental psychology is well positioned to study the psychosocial responses to phenomena such as these.

Despite the best efforts of those in the design profession to conceive of and mold environments in ways that complement people's behavioral needs and desires, most of their approaches have been haphazard and have given little consideration to a design's effects on the population it is intended to serve. The unintended consequences of a building and its design—such as issues related to comfort, privacy, crowding, or even maintenance—affect users in ways that may range from relatively insignificant to profound.

Designing the built environment for human habitation can be a daunting task because it is much more than a conglomeration of aesthetic or artistic perspectives. Environments built for human habitation must be carefully designed to fulfill the needs of the intended occupants. A collaborative approach between designers and environmental psychologists can create an artistic statement as well as satisfy the needs and preferences of the intended users. This allows designers, environmental psychologists, and occupants to reach a consensus of opinion.

Environmental psychology is the study of human behaviors in relation to their environments and vice versa. The science of environmental psychology traces its roots to the early 20th century, but it was 1943 when Egon Brunswik first used the term and a new discipline was born. Environmental psychology was not a field-specific study until 1968, when the first Ph.D. program was developed at the City University of New York. Although a great deal of research validates the importance of the symbiotic relationship between humans and the environment, the practical value of this research may elude students of practitioner-oriented fields, most of whom dedicate their lives to the implementation of design rather than to design research.

The core focus of this book is on the practice and principles of environmental psychology. The writing is specifically geared to the practicing designer. In an effort to bridge the gap between research and practice among the design fields and environmental psychology, this book introduces the discipline of environmental psychology to students in a way that will inspire them to embrace the concepts and incorporate them into their daily practices. This book considers the historical context of human habitation; initial research regarding the relationship between environments and human behaviors; and individual differences related to age, gender, and cultural background. Through brief discussions of scientific research, philosophical perspectives, and illustrations of design in practice, this book incorporates fundamental environmental psychology concepts into the practice of the design fields.

This book is intended for professional designers and students who are pursuing formal or informal education with the intent of putting their knowledge into practice within design fields that contribute to the built environment. These fields include interior design, architecture, city planning, and landscape design, among others. Because environmental components affect behavioral manifestations (educational test scores, social problems in and out of school, domestic abuse and violence, longevity and illness progression among the elderly, and much more), students of service industries and of social work who recognize and wish to understand the impact of the environment on human behaviors may also benefit from this book. However, as we begin to bridge the gaps among scientific research, theory, and practice, we must also retain the roots and traditions of scientific inquiry.

Design students, being very visual and creative, often have difficulty understanding discussions of multiple research studies. This book discusses in a meaningful and practical way environmental concepts, issues, and resolutions, including the fundamental principles that are grounded in research conducted within the design and social science fields that guide environmental psychology; it also examines various factors that influence human behaviors within the built environment.

This book contains several pedagogical features. It begins with a concise introduction of the principles and concepts that are discussed in the text and concludes with an appendix, a comprehensive glossary, and an index. Key terms are boldfaced throughout each chapter and defined in chapter terminology lists to facilitate reading and comprehension. Each chapter begins by introducing the main concepts that will be discussed in it; contains illustrated examples of some of the main concepts with succinct and relevant information and explanations; and concludes with a summary that highlights the information discussed. Discussion questions and learning activities that reinforce what students learn, a glossary of the terms introduced in the chapter, and references to material cited throughout the chapter are provided.

Acknowledgments

Several very good textbooks approach the field of environmental psychology from a more scientific perspective than this volume: *Environmental Psychology, 5th Edition*, by Paul A. Bell, Thomas C. Greene, Jeffery D. Fisher, and Andrew Baum; *Environmental Psychology: Practices and Principles, 3rd Edition*, by Robert Gifford; and *The Handbook of Environmental Psychology*, edited by Robert Bechtel and Arza Churchman. Without the amalgamation of data and research that these and other authors have contributed to the field, this specialized textbook could not have been developed.

More broadly, I salute all the researchers who dedicate themselves to environmental psychology and environmental design and without whom there would be no knowledge to bring into practice. I also applaud the excellent work of InformeDesign.com, an Internet research tool administered through the University of Minnesota and sponsored by the American Society of Interior Designers. This website provides excellent and easy-to-use information that can benefit all designers.

In addition, I would like to thank the following reviewers, selected by Fairchild Books, for their helpful comments and suggestions during the preparation of the manuscript: Jan Bast, Design Institute of San Diego; Robert Bechtel, University of Arizona; Dan Beert, Bellevue Community College; Duncan Case, University of Nebraska; Naz Kaya, University of Georgia; Katrina Lewis, Kansas State University; Setha Low, City University of New York; Joan McLain-Kark, Virginia Tech; Jack Nasar, Ohio State University; and Suzanne Scott, University of Wisconsin.

Finally, I would like to thank the following people who have contributed to this book in a variety of ways: Jimma Alegado, Katherine Bahk, Brandy Beardslee, Karen Blackerby, Alla Carrasco, Jen-Yi Chan, Annabel Fogal, Katsura Furumi, Linda Gram, Christin Handlin, Sara Harstrom, Zack Hegg, Theresa Holt, Peter Karrol, Bronwen Keller, Maggie Kennison, Lisa Levenson, Michael Lohr, Jane Mead, Ricardo Miramontes, Jennifer Lawson Molinets, Kathryn Murray, April Prunty, Catherine Reith, Paul Norman Reyes, Greg Robe, Kris Stoyak, Kristin L. Thorpe, and Kimberly Yackel.

INTRODUCTION

The human–environment relationship can be examined from a broad range of perspectives, all of which acknowledge that environments have components that people use to classify and therefore to comprehend their surroundings. These components relate to people's environmental preferences, and the way in which people interpret them directly relates to their levels of stimulation. Environmental psychology may be defined as the study of symbiotic relationships between humans and their environments: A stimulus causes an action, which causes an event, which in turn causes another action, and so on. Understanding the relationship between stimulation and human responses is an important component of good design.

The field of psychology studies cognition and perception among many components of the human mind. Environmental psychology combines the study of the psych with that of environmental components. Research that began in the early 20th century continues to prove that design has a greater effect on people than previously conceived. By influencing the beneficial secretion and absorption of neurochemicals through environmental characteristics, design can positively affect the physical and psychological health and well-being of an environment's occupants and users. It is the design professional's responsibility to assess each client individually to fully comprehend and satisfy each client's needs.

People respond to the world around them based on who they are. The manner in which people perceive, understand, and make choices about their environments; cope with environmental stressors; and connect emotionally with a place depends in part on their psychological health. This is affected by their physical health, surroundings, and feelings relative to issues of personal control such as autonomy, safety, privacy, territory, and crowding.

Technology has evolved much more rapidly than the human psych. The human species is a component of the natural world, which itself is intrinsic to the human experience and therefore is fundamental to human well-being. Human nature is composed of animal instincts, socialized roles, and personal characteristics and preferences. Human cognition and perception are influenced by physiology, culture, imagination, and life experience. Human beings are most satisfied in environments where they feel a connection between what they see and who they are. Understanding the relationships of subjective attributes, such as beauty and color, to the built environment will help design professionals to better perceive, conceptualize, plan, and create spaces that will enable people to interact more effectively with their various environments and more easily find their way in the world.

Stress response is the body's natural self-preservation system, a fundamental biological short-term safeguard. However, when we are in a constant stressful state, we lose the ability to think, behave, and function normally, and our subordinate body systems begin to shut down. Understanding how architectural and landscape design affect people's fears and subsequent behaviors can help planners and designers to create more comfortable spaces that will ensure the occupants' physical and psychological safety. Environmental design practices can serve to reduce criminality and increase community safety by creating orderly, clearly defined spaces that maximize the occupants' field of observation and sense of ownership, which serves to strengthen community spirit.

The totality of the built environment—geographic location and climate; purpose and function; image and style; occupants and visitors; the impact of the design on the community at large; and even construction materials, methods, and code requirements—must be carefully considered throughout the planning and design process. By anticipating user population levels and constituencies, design professionals can instigate many proactive initiatives to help minimize stress and maximize user satisfaction in all settings.

Successful environments promote satisfaction and enjoyment for all parties concerned. Planners and designers can ensure positive experiences by creating enjoyable environments that utilize appropriate locations and structural images; maximize positive factors and variables as well as control negative ones; and consist of pleasant easily maintained and defended spaces that comfortably and efficiently support various activities of daily life, work, and/or recreation as required.

Before people are born they inhabit safe, nurturing, cohesive, and responsive physical environments from which they spontaneously receive everything they need. They spend the rest of their lives attempting to create physical constructs that are equally satisfying. Life in general is stressful because it is uncertain, messy, tiresome, inconvenient, dangerous, and terminal; in certain communities it can also be competitive, crowded, fast-paced, dirty, and toxic. Thoughtful planning and design initiatives grounded in environmental psychology can serve to lessen, minimize, and even preclude these conditions.

ENVIRONMENTAL
PSYCHOLOGY
FOR DESIGN

ONE

Overview of Environmental Psychology

The environment that surrounds us has influenced our behaviors and actions as well as the evolution of our species since the dawn of time. Whether due to fear, necessity, or naturally occurring challenges such as droughts, floods, and extreme temperatures, we have always adapted to myriad environmental conditions. Early humans examined weather patterns, interpreted animal behaviors, and identified fertile soils among their efforts to improve their understanding of and relationship to the natural world. By doing so, they conducted the first environmental studies, the results of which prompted certain human response behaviors, such as stockpiling food and water, seeking shelter and high ground, and planting and harvesting crops.

We humans are inextricably woven into the fabric of our environments, and we affect those environments just as they affect us. Over the millennia most human societies have, in essence, evolved from small groups of nomadic hunter-gatherer clans to villages and cities. There is evidence in some parts of the world today of the ways humans used to live (Figure 1.1a and b). The !Kung of the Kalahari Desert, for example, continue to live a nomadic lifestyle. However, in the past 100 years alone, our relationship to the various environments we occupy has undergone more radical changes than ever before. There are few places where a person can escape the signs and symptoms of human attempts to dominate the planet; increased population has engendered the largest cities in human history, and many small cities are now the size of the largest ancient cities. For example, the population of the modern city of Bakersfield, California, is roughly equivalent to that of ancient Rome (250,000). We continue to develop technology that enables our sedentary lifestyle, and overpopulation coupled with higher personal expectations has increased the time we spend with people who are not family members. Although these changes may seem benign, we are seeing more violent behaviors in our schools, hospitals, and neighborhoods. Various factors that affect either our physical or social environments, or both, cause these behaviors.

Our symbiotic relationship with our environment causes researchers to struggle with the timeless question of which came first: the behavior or the environment. The following example illustrates the cause-and-effect relationship between humans and their surroundings. Imagine yourself chewing gum as you walk down the street. You want to spit it out, but you see no garbage cans. The absence of a garbage can in the environment causes you to spit the gum onto the ground—a behavioral action—and you have now influenced the environment by littering. You unknowingly step on the gum and track it into a friend's house. Your friend reacts with hostility, so you take offense and storm out of the house.

As this simplified example illustrates, it is important to avoid engaging in deterministic behaviors (i.e., acting on the notion that preceding events and conditions determine every succeeding event). We must remember to avoid attributing an **effect** (result) entirely to a single cause because social and biological factors also contribute to that effect. Gary Evans[1] corroborated this position when he linked environmental conditions to social manifestations that influence social conditions, as in the example on page 5. The field of environmental psychology is one that embraces multiple factors and rejects the single-variable approach.

3

a

b

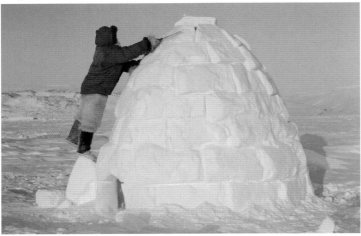

Figure 1.1a and b: Early human civilizations regarded territorial expanses as their homes. For these people, their ancestral lands were far more important than dwellings that merely provided shelter. In many instances, early houses were portable, such as the yurt (a) or temporary, such as the igloo (b).

Governing Perspectives in Psychology

Psychology as a field has different governing perspectives. To understand the practice of environmental psychology, a person must first understand the points of reference from which the field gains much of its information.

- The *cognitive perspective* contends that cognition—the process by which an organism gains knowledge or becomes aware of events or objects in its environment and uses that knowledge for comprehension and problem-

solving—develops as a result of the relationship organisms have with their environments. It includes the processes people use to think, decide, and learn. For example, many children learn which parent is likely to say yes or no when they ask for something and therefore can usually figure out which parent to approach and how to ask.

- The *humanistic perspective* is based on the notions of free will (the idea that we control our own destinies) and the desire for self-actualization (the idea that we aspire for more than basic survival). Its main premise is that a person's primary motivation in life is to fulfill his or her potential.

- The *learning* or *behavioral perspective* suggests that our future behaviors are dictated by what we learn from past experiences of pleasure or pain. For example, by touching a hot stove burner and discovering that burner = hot = pain, we learn to avoid contact with stove burners.

- The *neurobiological perspective* deduces that our actions are hardwired as a result of neurological or biological activity, and therefore our behaviors result from both our genetic makeup and our physiological reactions to our environments. For example, because external stressors such as noise can stimulate the secretion of adrenaline, which causes a faster heart rate and increased blood pressure, many people need to control the occurrence and levels of these stressors within their environments.

- The *sociocultural perspective* states that social conditions, such as status, gender norms, and expectations, operate in conjunction with cultural traits, such as ethnicity, heritage, and tradition, to produce certain behaviors.

Because no one perspective is more correct than another, the field of environmental psychology tends to incorporate them all into a holistic analysis. Consider the scenario depicted in Figure 1.2. A man is at work in an office building that has caught fire. He deduces from a loud bell and the faint smell of smoke that he should head for the fire exit. This is the *cognitive perspective*. Meanwhile, the sight, smell, and taste of smoke cause his body to release chemicals, initiating the fight-or-flight response. This is the *neurobiological perspective*. As he works his way down the stairs, he starts to panic as he recalls being burned as child. This is the *learning* or *behavioral perspective*. However, he was raised to believe that as a man, it is his obligation to help women and children prompting him to stop and help. This is the *sociocultural perspective*. His decision to act on that learned obligation, however, is a choice. This is the *humanistic perspective*.

A purist may contend that the man's reactions are based exclusively on just one of the perspectives described in the preceding example. An environmental psychologist, because of the multivariable **paradigm** (theoretical framework) characteristic of this field, would view this situation in stages and incorporate each of the five perspectives when analyzing the aggregate of behaviors in response to the environment.

The *neurobiological perspective* is based on physical science, which is always consistent; therefore, an action can be performed repeatedly and yield similar results over time. In the design fields, physical science stemming from neurobiological perspectives

has tremendous implications. Neurochemical secretion, absorption, and interaction that are attributed to environmental design and conditions provide the impetus for certain behaviors. For example, the **neurotransmitter** (neural chemical) serotonin is associated with mood. The body's natural response to overstimulation is to absorb serotonin to cope with it; however, this absorption can cause too little serotonin to be present in the brain, which can lead to depression. An environmental modification for an overstimulated person may include reducing environmental stimuli by decreasing lighting levels in the home and limiting visual complexity (Figure 1.3), for example, by reducing the number of such items as knickknacks, artwork, and reading material.

In contrast, the social sciences are based on the social world and systems—culture, religious beliefs, and traditions—and tend to study the social perspectives that lead to certain outcomes. The social sciences are not as precise as the physical sciences because human beings are not uniform and social trends are fluid; however, they do provide a high probability of accuracy. Human beliefs and notions

The role of neurotransmitters is discussed in more detail in Chapter 2.

Figure 1.2 (left): This scenario can be viewed from several different psychological perspectives, none of which is more correct than another.

Figure 1.3 (above): Notice the lack of elements on the coffee table, around the fireplace, and on the floor as well as the clean, simple lines of the architectural features and furnishings, all of which decrease the visual complexity of the room. Also note the use of interior greenery and the natural backdrop view via the large window. Greenery has been shown to reduce stress levels and to facilitate attention restoration (see Chapter 2).

change with the passage of time; for example, during the Victorian era people behaved and dressed more conservatively than they did during the roaring twenties. Such social trends make it difficult for social scientists to make absolute statements; they can predict with some certainty how most of the population will respond but cannot state that every person will absolutely respond in a given way. Design is highly contingent on social evolution, and scientific research into perceptions, preferences, interpretations, and worldviews must be constantly examined to provide designs that will be embraced by the general populace. A home with both formal and informal living rooms was considered highly desirable in the 1960s and 1970s but is much less so today. This typifies how design trends evolve over time and emphasizes the importance of social science as a collaborative component of design (Figure 1.4a–d).

As previously mentioned, while some fields rely

Figure 1.4a–d: Among these examples are homes with a great deal of complexity, such as those of the Victorian style (a). As society evolved, the art deco style emerged in the 1920s (b); although this style had a great deal of ornamentation, the clean lines allowed the complexity to be subdued. The mid-20th-century designs displayed even greater simplicity (c); detail and craftsmanship had been replaced by mass-produced components. Today, modern styles merge detailed elements with assembly-line philosophies, as seen in the example of the Tuscan-style home (d).

a

c

b

d

on a single or purist approach, environmental psychology is multimodal: It utilizes both social and physical science perspectives and views human behaviors in relation to the environment as deriving from a combination of social, cultural, and biological factors. In essence, environmental psychology incorporates cognitive, humanistic, learning or behavioral, neurobiological, and sociocultural perspectives.

History of the Field

The principles of observation and assessment—that is, observing the role of stimuli and tracking the subsequent reactions—are at the core of every science. However, even today most social science fields, including the various disciplines of psychology, tend to neglect the role of the environment when considering behavioral responses.

A great number of social science fields carried out the early study of environmental phenomena. Psychologists in the 1800s examined the effects of environmental perception, as related to light, sound, weight, and pressure, among other variables, on learning and behavior.[2] A 1916 study examined how external distractions affect work performance.[3] These pioneer studies were soon followed by another that examined the influence of workers' hours and the effects of ventilation on their productivity.[4] In 1929, an influential study examined the relationship between where students sat in a classroom and the grades they received.[5]

Among the most famous analyses conducted of the human–environment relationship were the 1924 Hawthorne studies that analyzed the effects of lighting on workers' performances.[6] The researchers involved in these studies hypothesized that increased lighting would correlate with increased worker production. To test this premise, the researchers placed a group of workers in a room where they were to perform their job duties. Each day, the researchers brightened the room by using a higher-wattage light bulb. As hypothesized, worker performance increased with brighter lighting; however, to cross-check their results, the researchers decided to decrease the brightness, the idea being that worker production should decrease with lower lighting levels. This did not happen; instead, worker production continued to increase, as a result of other variables.

Because of these findings, many scientists regarded the Hawthorne studies as a failure. However, these studies taught us the importance of controls in research, and they produced the following three important findings:

1. The effect of the physical environment is buffered by perceptions, beliefs, preferences, experiences, and personality (a new bulb must be an improvement; consequently, this must be a better environment).
2. One environmental variable turned out to be more important than the subtler variations (the employees felt special).
3. The physical environment changed the social dynamics (the study room layout facilitated more social contact).

These and other early studies illustrated that the environment we occupy dramatically influences how we perceive the world around us, how we see ourselves in relation to the greater social hierarchy, and how the environment affects our social behaviors. Understanding this symbiotic relationship is essential to the success of any environmental psychologist.

Egon Brunswik, considered by many to be the founder of environmental psychology, is credited with first using this term in 1943 to describe the field of human–environment relations.[7] Other researchers who have contributed to the study of the human–environment relationship come from the fields of behavioral geography and urban sociology. Kurt Lewin, a social ecologist, regarded the environment as a significant variable in the determination of behaviors and is credited with the idea of integrating information obtained from research with that of social practices, otherwise known as *action research*.[8] Another notable contributor to the study of human–environment relations was Roger Barker, who is widely regarded as an ecological psychologist. Barker and his colleagues formed the Midwest Psychological Field Station in Oskaloosa, Kansas, in 1947. They observed that two children in the same place behaved more similarly than one child in two places and concluded that the surrounding environment exerted a great deal of control over behavior. Eventually, Barker and his colleagues would research this phenomenon, ultimately concluding that our environments create behavior settings.

You can learn more about behavior settings in Chapter 2.

Other important names in environmental psychology include Abraham Maslow, William Ittelson, and Harold Proshansky. Maslow conducted a study with photographs of people and found that observers responded more positively to the people photographed when the observers were in beautiful rooms and more negatively when the observers were in ugly rooms.[9] Although this research may seem trivial, when we consider the behaviors that likely manifest from a positive environmental experience, we may theorize that beautiful environments invoke happy or pleasant feelings whereas ugly rooms invoke annoyance or discomfort. Ittelson and Proshansky not only conducted extensive research relative to theory, methodology, and application in real-world settings, but also developed the first Ph.D. program in environmental psychology in 1968 at the City University of New York (CUNY), which awarded the first doctorate in environmental psychology in 1975. Their 1974 text, entitled *Introduction to Environmental Psychology*, written with Leanne Rivlin and Gary Winkel, was the first textbook in this new field.

Academic Programs and Posteducational Opportunities

The discipline of environmental psychology is virtually unknown to the mainstream population. No proactive media campaigns educate the public about the field, its research focus, and the importance of these studies to the human race. Only a handful of schools in the United States offer stand-alone degrees in environmental psychology. The vast majority of students who matriculate with a degree find themselves in academia (because the degree is available almost exclusively at the graduate level), with only a small percentage working for a design firm or as independent consultants. Because the discipline itself is quite broad with only a few opportunities for higher education, individual interests within the field further separate those individuals who study environmental psychology.

Most institutions house their environmental psychology courses in the schools of architecture, design, psychology, human or social ecology, or even arts and sciences. This limits the uniformity of what is taught within the field; clearly, a clinical psychologist will teach an environmental psychology course differently from an architect. It is important that practicing designers appreciate that each approach is valuable because it contributes a different perspective.

Not all environmental psychologists share an interest in a particular area of specialization, but they do share the belief that the environment plays a crucial role in human behavior. The various subspecialties or concentrations within environmental psychology have given rise to terms such as *design psychology* or *neuroarchitecture*.

The American Psychological Association (APA), the governing body of psychological sciences, recognizes environmental psychology under Division 34, Population and Environment.[10] Its website lists the following areas of research interest:

- human response to built and natural settings
- impact of technological and natural hazards
- environmental perception and cognition
- design and planning issues

For people who enter the fields of environmental and behavioral psychology, common subspecialties or concentrations include, but are not limited to, the following:

- diversity, exclusion, and the environment
- housing issues and policy
- the meanings and experiences of the home and homelessness
- conflicts and contradictions in urban planning
- neighborhood and community participation
- open space planning and use
- human mobility and transportation
- design, use, and evaluation of public institutions
- participatory research and design
- gender and space
- political ecology and development
- environmental justice
- supportive environments for people with disabilities
- elderly people and the environment

The scope and practices of environmental psychology have a direct and symbiotic relationship with design fields. But the field itself studies the human–environment relationship at three levels of analysis[11] as follows:

1. fundamental psychological processes of perception, cognition, and personality as they filter and structure each individual's experience of the environment;
2. social management of space related to personal space, territoriality, crowding, and privacy; and
3. the effect of the physical setting on complex but common behaviors in everyday life (such as working, learning, and participating in daily activities in the home or community) and our relationship with the natural world.

Environmental psychology may be defined as the study of symbiotic relationships between humans and their environments. It is this holistic approach that separates environmental psychologists from other professionals within the design and social science fields.

Scope of Practice

Just as physicians use medications and surgery and counselors or therapists use methods of introspection and behavior modification, environmental psychologists use methods of environmental modification and design to diminish undesirable behaviors and enhance preferred behaviors, as discussed in subsequent chapters. The driving force behind the research in this field is the combination of social and biological factors. Social factors derive from our unique cultural, religious, social, and personal experiences; biological factors derive from our brains and bodies as part of the natural process of moving from one environment to another. The premise behind the research and practice of environmental psychology is a holistic consideration of biological, social, and environmental causal agents (Figure 1.5).

Environmental psychology can solve problems related to the principles of learning, motivation, perception, attitude formation, and social interaction, to name a few. Environmental psychologists are poised to explain why humans engage in particular behaviors in relation to their environments.

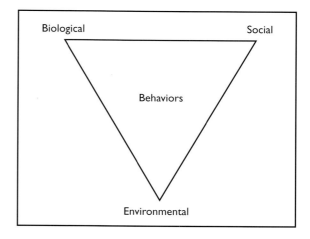

Figure 1.5: By looking at situations holistically and taking biological, social, and environmental factors into account, we can begin to understand why people engage in particular behaviors.

For the purposes of this book, the disciplines that can benefit the most from this work include architecture, city planning, interior design, and landscape design. According to Bell et al., "Designers need to consider how buildings affect the people using them by understanding both how design influences people and how we can modify the design to facilitate the function for which the setting is intended."[12]

Environmental Psychology Today

Environmental psychology is rooted in scientific methods related to the acquisition of theory, pursuit of knowledge, and practical application. In the minds of many practitioners, however, theory and knowledge can become blurred; therefore, many theories are transmitted as if they were knowledge rather than ideas that guide research. Knowledge is the truth that has been obtained from research. Think of a matador waving a red cape to entice a bull to charge. The theory that the color red invokes the bull's aggression was generally accepted until research proved that most animals are color-blind and that the movements of the cape are what cause the bull's arousal. However, matadors continue to use red capes because of other important variables affecting the practice: **culture** (the values, norms, and artifacts of a group of people) and **tradition** (a custom or practice that has been passed down from generation to generation). Humans

You can learn more about the biological factors that influence environmental design in Chapter 3.

tend to embrace these variables unless and until they prove harmful or inconvenient; in other words, they will maintain cultural and traditional behaviors as long as the results are not negative to their health and well-being.

Although practice can be based on theory, researchers who contribute to the practice of environmental psychology are obligated to pursue scientific truths. But change is always a constant in the human–environment relationship; whenever life is involved in the research, the end result will change because people change. Consider architectural preferences. The predominating New England home in the 1700s was highly segmented (it had many small rooms), but its main feature was that the kitchen was blocked from general view by a door. Contemporary studies indicate that women who work outside the home prefer kitchens that are open to the dining and living rooms.[13] Therefore, research conducted in the 1700s would yield very different truths from identical research conducted in the late 20th and early 21st centuries.

Incorporating the practice of environmental psychology within the design fields offers unique opportunities. Designers can make use of tools such as user **needs assessments**, known within the field as **predesign research (PDR)**, to evaluate a client's requirements prior to construction or occupancy. Early needs assessments were conducted primarily by academicians, who focused on settings such as housing, college dorms, and residential institutions.[14] An **occupancy evaluation** (assessment conducted during occupation) is another useful tool that was developed as a result of research by social scientists, designers, and planners interested in understanding building users' experiences.[15] Evaluating a future development for the intended users is not a novel idea; many architects have adopted it, calling it *behavior-based architectural programming*, and in medicine and psychology the same formative evaluation is called an *intake assessment*. Research methods include reviewing current literature, observing similar populations in similar environments, surveying individuals via personal interviews or written surveys, and developing focus groups. When this preliminary research has been factored in, the completed development tends to have fewer problems. Ideally, a needs assessment should be augmented by an occupancy evaluation of a similar environment. As a final evaluation of the project, a **postoccupancy evaluation (POE)** should be performed to assess the human–environment relationship because design ideas and concepts may not be applicable in an actual setting. For example, an office's air-conditioning system may be blocked if the employees were to pile storage boxes atop strategically placed furnishings.

Environmental psychologists are trained to use the methods and tools necessary for quick and cost-effective needs assessments and to follow up with a POE to verify if user needs were adequately addressed; in this manner, environmental psychologists can help architects, city planners, and interior and landscape designers to develop environments best suited to users' specific needs. The POE evaluates an overall product and is usually the final phase of the design process, enabling the designer to learn from previous mistakes and ensure better plans for future projects. The scenario described in Box 1.1 illustrates the value of a user needs assessment or predesign research.

Since they are able to understand the thought and emotional processes that produce or shape human desires, environmental psychologists help people understand the differences between temporary and long-standing needs. They also ascertain the primary, secondary, and tertiary functions of people's homes so that those homes can be designed to fulfill people's needs. Methods include taking a person on a tour of various homes in the area, encouraging a person to visit the homes of colleagues who will most likely make up his or her future peer group, and introducing issues that will arise in the future if the person proceeds with initial choices. Another effective method is to have a client host a design party, during which the architect, environmental psychologist, and interior or landscape designer solicit ideas and opinions from the guests. A design party works well because some clients trust their peers more than the people they hire, and the local people often have a fair idea about what works and what does not in their particular area. The outcome for the design firm that incorporates this extra step is greater client satisfaction over more time because this process will linger in the client's mind, and satisfied clients bring more referrals.

Box 1.1 Needs Assessment (Predesign Research)

SCENARIO

A business executive who has been transferred to New England commissions a design firm to build her new home. The designer conducts a needs assessment to ascertain the executive's desires—a Spanish-style villa complete with a courtyard for entertaining, high ceilings, tile floors, and so on (Figure 1.6). Realizing the design's impracticality in such a harsh environment, the designer then tries to suggest an alternative design style, but the executive insists that such a villa has been a dream since childhood. Further investigation reveals that the executive, born and raised in Southern California, has the design styles of that region as a primary point of reference and is drawing upon that which is most familiar and comfortable to her.

COMMENTARY

This scenario raises three issues, all of which the designer must discuss with the client. First, the executive has had insufficient time to acclimate to and embrace her new environment. Second, her feelings of insecurity about the unfamiliar surroundings are the source of her attempts to create a comfort zone. Third, a Spanish-style home will be an issue in the winter. As the executive gets to know the new environment, her design preferences will slowly change. She will start to embrace the New England style, want to fit in more with her new surroundings, and eschew the extra costs associated with architecture inappropriate to the New England climate.

Figure 1.6: People often make choices from a single perspective and neglect their greater surroundings. Therefore, they make poor choices that are incongruent to their environment. In this example, the Spanish-style architecture the executive insisted on is inappropriate for the cold climate of the Northeastern United States.

Practical Application

Because environmental psychology is a science that examines human behaviors in relation to the environment, much of the research has broad practical applicability within the human experience. In 1954, Maslow unveiled a model depicting a hierarchy of needs, based on natural instincts present in all animals (Figure 1.7). Almost from its inception, the model has come under scrutiny, with critics claiming that it lacks a scientific basis, an integrated conceptual structure, and supportive research evidence and that the concepts lack validity. Maslow, a humanist psychologist, proposed that all humans have fundamental needs and that they move up the

Self-actualization
—
Love

Safety

Physiological

Figure 1.7: It has long been recognized that design satisfies the self-actualization portion of Maslow's hierarchy of needs. However, recent research indicates that design can also affect the physiological and safety needs.

Figure 1.8: Children are physically aroused by their activities and subconsciously aroused by their environments. Visual stimulants in rooms intended for children are often designed to facilitate learning or play.

hierarchy as each need is met. When an individual's environment is not right (and many times this is the case), he or she will not proceed up the hierarchy, and this failure to advance causes psychological and emotional dysfunction.

If we were to accept Maslow's notion of the hierarchy of needs, along with the premise that the environment serves no other purpose than to fulfill hedonistic desires, the traditional human–environment relationship would be at the top of the pyramid as an aspect of self-actualization. However, human–environment research proves that our environments have a tremendous impact on how we feel, respond, and cope in daily life. Because the environment plays an intricate role in the overall physiological health and responses of the human psych, concern for our surroundings is a component not only of self-actualization but also of safety and of physiological needs.

For example, a child who feels crowded and vulnerable within an environment may experience child-related stress.[16] Feelings of crowding can lead to the fight-or-flight response, which is characterized by sympathetic nervous system activation that secretes chemicals into the bloodstream and mobi-

lizes a behavioral response.[17] If a child is repeatedly subjected to such a response due to an environmental condition, a physician may prescribe medication and a counselor or therapist may pursue behavior-modification techniques; however, an environmental psychologist, using the methods most compatible with natural human behaviors and responses, will modify the child's environment by eliminating sources of stimulation in the child's environment as the first step.

Human–environment interactions are based on our psychological processes in relation to our surroundings. Our environments are made up of physical stimuli (noise, light, and temperature), physical structures (dimensions, furniture, and hallways), and symbolic artifacts (the meaning or image of a setting). The fundamental psychological processes of arousal, overload, affect, adaptation, and personal control are integral to human–environment interactions (Figure 1.8).

- **Arousal** can be defined as excitement or stimulation to action or physiological readiness for activity.
- **Overload** is the negative mental state that results from excessive stimulation and arousal.
- **Affect** encompasses emotional reactions to the environment.
- **Adaptation** describes the process of adjustment to environmental conditions.
- **Personal control** is the ability to control an environment or a situation.

These interactions lead to outcomes that fall into categories of performance, health or stress, satisfaction, and interpersonal relationships. The positive relationship between human performance and the attention given to the individual, as well as the effects of room size and external stimuli such as noise, affect performance. For example, if a teacher pays more attention to student X, student X should do better in school. However, this one-dimensional approach assumes that variable Y influences human performance, which equals the behavioral output. The field of environmental psychology has evolved to approach behavioral science research in a multidimensional manner. This means that student X, when factored with situation Y and personality Z, may develop behavioral response XYZ.

In other words, if a teacher gives added attention to a student who has eaten a proper breakfast, received enough sleep, and is not stressed at home, and we decrease the density within the classroom, increase natural full-spectrum lighting, and decrease external stimuli such as noise, then the student's academic performance will be optimized. The level of optimization, however, is contingent on all factors.

Environmental psychologists study a range of issues related to the human–environment experience and, as a result, can predict with some certainty many emotional and physical reactions to environmental attributes. They analyze environmental cues that contribute to perceptions about a community, including infrastructure quality, the condition of city-owned buildings, the types and condition of local businesses, the availability and maintenance of green spaces, and owner-to-renter ratios. Other cues come from advertising methods and placement and ad messages themselves. For example, signs on poles or roofs along a commercial street indicate a drive-through community; signs situated just above head level along sidewalks indicate a walkable one. Ad messages indicate behaviors within a community and can inspire stereotypical or negative images when limited to certain areas; however, distributing the same ads equally throughout the community invalidates the image. For instance, the parents of teenage girls may decide to not buy a home in an area plastered with anti–teen pregnancy campaign ads because the ads would invoke a site-specific judgmental reaction: "Our daughters would be at risk in this neighborhood." But if those ads were all over town, the parents would tend to consider teen pregnancy as a common rather than a personal concern.

Large-scale gathering areas, such as corporate offices, schools, and resorts, are ideal settings for analyzing the environment to identify factors that contribute to or detract from desired behaviors (Figure 1.9). For example, occupants of corporate offices who use cubicle spaces or open office plans tend to exhibit greater levels of stress, lower productivity, and higher turnover rates than do occupants of offices with private work spaces. Environmental psychologists examine not only environmental components related to physical attributes, such as lighting, room size, acoustics, ancillary rooms

Figure 1.9: Open office plans subject employees to visual, auditory, and olfactory invasions by other workers. This example depicts different employees' working styles, which may not be compatible. The employee on the right probably works best amid chaos, whereas the employee on the left probably works best in an organized environment. In open office spaces, one or both of these employees will be at a disadvantage as their working styles are compromised.

a

Figure 1.10a and b: The home at the top is a safe haven as evidenced by the many personal artifacts, as well as a quiet, contemplative environment as evidenced by the books and the lack of a television (a). The home below has a design that is well suited for social gatherings, as evidenced by the open sofa arrangement allowing easy entry and exit, the large open spaces for standing around and talking, and the potential for background music with a piano in a subordinate part of the room (b). It would be much easier to imagine a cocktail party in Client B's home than in Client A's home.

b

(lunchrooms or lounges), wall and floor coverings, placement of work/study stations and equipment, and the use of color, but also the various relationships among employees, supervisors, and management to analyze the links between behaviors and outcomes.

For home environments, environmental psychologists analyze occupant desires and behaviors to develop homes that facilitate them (Figure 1.10a and b).

Environmental psychology is especially important in the initial planning and development of residential properties. For example, if a home's adult occupants work 9-to-5 jobs, the worst position for the kitchen is southwest; the occupants are already stressed from the day's activities, the evening sun adds glare and heat while they prepare dinner, and cooking heats the room further. These combined factors create in the occupants an agitated state and a greater propensity for verbal hostility. Environmental psychology can serve to create supportive environments for people challenged by physical, psychological, and age-related illnesses and injuries, and the stress and anxiety related to daily life or end-of-life issues, as detailed in subsequent chapters.

Summary Review

The environment plays an intricate role in the overall physiological and psychological health of humans. The science of environmental psychology is dedicated to the examination of the human environment experience as it relates to physical attributes and social components of human action and interaction processes. To accomplish this, environmental psychologists identify factors that either contribute to or detract from desired behaviors, and they analyze the links between behaviors and outcomes. This information enables them to predict emotional and physical reactions to environmental attributes in open spaces and within the built environment.

Psychology as a field has different governing perspectives from which the field gains much of its information. They include cognitive, humanistic, learning or behavioral, neurobiological, and sociocultural perspectives. While each of these perspectives can more than adequately explain behaviors,

most environmental psychologists will draw upon one or more to gain a better understanding of the environment–behavior relationship.

From a historical perspective, the relationship between humans and their environments dates back to early civilization, when early humans analyzed various aspects of the environment that promoted survival. However, science did not begin to study the human–environment relationship until the latter half of the 19th century, and the first Ph.D. program dedicated exclusively to environmental psychology appeared only in the late 1960s.

Egon Brunswik, Kurt Lewin, Russell Barker, and countless others have contributed to the field's research, which has demonstrated broad applicability to practicing design professionals. User needs assessments or PDRs and POEs provide tools that researchers can use to better measure the effectiveness of an environment for its occupants. As a field specialty, environmental psychology course work is generally integrated into the curricula of various departments such as design, family studies, and psychology. Each segment of study strengthens the field of environmental psychology.

Discussion Questions

1. Discuss the differences in the native architecture of three different climates, and discuss the climate-related reasons that led to the dominating architectural style of each region.
2. Consider your daily routine and analyze one aspect of it from three different psychological perspectives (cognitive, humanistic, learning or behavioral, neurobiological, or sociocultural). For example, you wake up to music rather than an alarm sound, or you must have a cup of coffee to begin your day.
3. Conceive and discuss a situation wherein social, biological, and environmental variables come together to influence a behavior.
4. Discuss an example of how you modified your environment to achieve greater relaxation or productivity.
5. Discuss ways in which behavioral psychology research is incorporated into everyday life. For example, a better understanding of how ergonomics benefits a person's life.

6. Describe why an environmental psychologist with a background in architecture may take a different approach to analyzing an environment than would a designer with no background in environmental psychology.

7. Discuss how Hollywood uses the environment as a nonverbal character. Explain how set design can affect a movie's mood, style, and message. Use one movie as an example and recast the set in another style (e.g., Bladerunner performed on the set of Mary Poppins).

Learning Activities

1. List three environmental factors that cannot be controlled by humans, and develop a way to modify inhabitable structures to compensate for those factors.

2. List three environmental factors that can be manipulated by humans. Develop an ethical argument as to whether it is better to manipulate environmental factors or to modify structures.

3. Develop a list of at least ten questions that would elicit detailed responses from a potential client in your current city about how he or she uses his or her home. Be sure the questions are open-ended and worded in such a way that they do not require any architectural knowledge but will still tell you what the client needs and wants in a home.

4. Imagine yourself in a culturally and geographically different region of the world and identify the setting. Will the questions developed for the preceding activity still work? Explain your position in an essay.

5. Host a small party at your home with the intention of designing a home. Ask your guests questions and record their responses. Develop a design according to the consensus of input and see what materializes.

6. From your own experience, either observed or personal, describe how a building or place has initiated a negative emotional response—not due to events that have occurred, but due to the architectural layout or environmental conditions such as noise, temperature, and lighting.

7. Describe how the experience of the building or place you identified in activity 6 has affected your design process or changed your ideas of good building design.

Terminology

adaptation The process of adjustment to environmental conditions

affect A person's emotional reaction to the environment

arousal Excitement or stimulation to action or physiological readiness for activity

culture The values, norms, and artifacts of a group of people

effect Resulting state or condition

needs assessment Survey conducted prior to construction or occupancy to determine environmental conditions and user needs

neurotransmitter Chemical substance that transmits nerve impulses across synapses

occupancy evaluation Survey of a planned development conducted during the formative stages to determine the needs of the intended users

overload The negative mental state that results when a person experiences excessive information, stimulation, and arousal

paradigm Philosophical or theoretical conceptual framework

personal control The ability to control the environment or situation

postoccupancy evaluation (POE) Survey conducted after a space is occupied to determine if user needs were met

predesign research (PDR) *See needs assessment*

tradition A custom or practice that has been passed down from generation to generation

References

1. Evans, G. W. (2004). The environment of childhood poverty. *American Psychologist, 59 (2)*, 77–92.

2. Bell, P. A., Greene, T. C., Fisher, J. D., and Baum, A. (2001). *Environmental psychology* (5th ed.). Orlando, FL: Harcourt College Publishers.

3. Morgan, J. J. (1916). The overcoming of distraction and other resistances. *Archives of Psychology No. 35, 24 (4)*, 1–84.

4. Vernon, H. M. (1919). *The influences of hours of*

work and of ventilation on output in tinplate man-ufacture. Publisher unknown.

5. Griffith, C. R. (1929). A comment upon the psychology of the audience. *Psychological Monographs, 30 (136)*, 36–47.

6. Snow, C. E. (1927). Research on industrial il-lumination (1923). *The Tech Engineering News, 8*, 257–282.

7. Brunswik, E. (1943). Organismic achievement and environmental probability. *Psychological Review, 50*, 255–272.

8. Lewin, K. (1943). Defining the "field at a given time." *Psychological Review, 50*, 292–310.

9. Maslow, A. H., and Mintz, N. L. (1956). Ef-fects of aesthetic surroundings: Initial effects of three aesthetic conditions upon perceiving "energy" and "well-being" in faces. *Journal of Psychology, 41*, 247–254.

10. American Psychological Association. (Nov. 10, 2003). Division 34, Population and Envi-ronment. Retrieved January 5, 2005 from http://web.uvic.ca/~apadiv34.

11. Gifford, R. (2002). *Environmental psychology: Practice and principles* (3rd ed.). Canada: Opti-mal Books.

12. See note two.

13. Hasell, M. J., Peatross, F. D., and Bono, C. A. (1993). Gender choice and domestic space: preferences for kitchens in married house-holds. *Journal of Architectural and Planning Re-search, 10*, 1–22.

14. Preiser, W. F. E. (1994). Built environmental evaluation: Conceptual basis, benefits and uses. *Journal of Architectural and Planning Re-search, 11 (2)*, 91–107.

15. Zeisel, J. (1975). *Sociology and architectural de-sign.* New York: Russell Sage Foundation, So-cial Science Frontiers series.

16. Jewett, J., and Peterson, K. (1997). *Stress and young children.* Champaign, IL: Educational Resources Information Center (ERIC) Clear-inghouse on Elementary and Early Childhood Education (EECE). Retrieved January 5, 2005 from http://ceep.crc.uiuc.edu/.

17. Taylor, S. E., Cousino-Klein, L., Lewis, B. P., Gruenewald, T. L., Gurung, R. A.R., and Up-degraff, J. A. (2000). Biobehavioral responses to stress in females: Tend-and-befriend, not fight-or-flight. *Psychological Review, 107 (3)*, 411–429.

TWO

Foundational Theories
of Environmental Psychology

The relationship between humans and their environments cannot be considered in absolute terms. Although there is some probability that an event or a behavior will occur most of the time with most people, it will not occur all of the time with all people. Consequently, environmental psychologists tend to speak in terms of theories that help to conceptualize the human–environment relationship. Theoretical concepts do not provide answers but rather guide research; this generates knowledge, which in turn informs practice. This chapter explores various theories that help explain the human–environment relationship and environmental perception. These theories are applied throughout the text as a means of developing successful designs for human occupation.

Theories of the Human–Environment Relationship

Much of the research conducted on the human–environment relationship has been based on four major theories: integration (also called *integral*), stimulation, control, and behavior-setting. The integration theory maintains that a combination of design features will influence people to behave and act in the most appropriate manners. The stimulation theory appears to have the broadest and most diverse implications related to environments. Consider the differing stimulation needs of a casino and a surgical recovery ward: The casino benefits from maximized environmental stimulation, whereas the surgical recovery ward does not. The stimulation theory overlaps both the control and behavior-setting theories. Most built environments have controls—some of which have more than others, for example, prisons. Designs that support behavior settings also establish **behavioral controls**, such as being automatically quiet and refraining from other potentially disturbing behaviors in a library. The way humans behave in other environments depends on social controls, as described by social learning theories that claim we learn socially acceptable actions and behaviors by observing others.

Social Learning Theories

Social or observational learning theories differ from human–environment theories because they declare that we learn by first observing others and eventually reproducing their actions. As outlined by Julian Rotter,[1, 2] the **social learning theory** emphasizes the following three precepts:

- People are intrinsically motivated to seek reinforcement, such as positive stimulation, and avoid unpleasant stimulation.
- Personality represents an interaction of the individual with the environment (for example, the stimuli that a person is aware of and responds to) and is a relatively stable framework for responding to situations in a particular way.
- To understand behavior, we must consider an individual's life history and learning experiences as well as the environment because our subjective interpretation of the environment determines our behavior.

Albert Bandura, another proponent of the social learning theory,[3, 4] agreed that personality is an interaction among the environment, behavior, and the person's psychological processes and that the environment and a person's behavior induce each other (a concept called *reciprocal determinism*). Bandura's theory, however, also stresses the importance of observational learning, or *modeling*, as a primary means of obtaining reinforcement because people naturally observe, process, and imitate the behaviors, attitudes, and emotional reactions of others to gain approval, acceptance, or rewards. Behavior modeling is intrinsic to all *behavior settings* (see Behavior-Setting Theories on page 22), fundamental to child development, widely used in training programs, and crucial to the success of commercial advertising, including marketing displays (by promoting an idea such as, "If I buy that car, then I'll be popular too").

For further discussion of behavior modeling see Chapter 14.

Integration (Integral) Theories

Robert Gifford uses the term **integral theories** to describe a group of models used to understand the complexity of the human–environment relationship.[5] Isidor Chein's integral framework[6] described the following five major elements that work in harmony, or integrate, to facilitate a particular behavior:

1. *Global environment.* Generalized characteristics of an environment.
2. *Instigators.* Stimuli that trigger particular behaviors.
3. *Goal objects and noxients.* Situations that cause satisfaction or produce unpleasantness.
4. ***Supports and constraints.*** Environmental aspects that facilitate or restrict behaviors.
5. *Directors.* Features that tell us where to go and what to do.

Figure 2.1 uses a casino to illustrate the five elements. Understanding a person's environment in this context will allow for a greater understanding of his or her behavior.[7]

Also considered to be part of the integration theories are interactional, transactional, and organismic theories. The **interactional theory**, the simplest form of integration theory, declares that people and the environment are separate entities that constantly interact.[8] It is based on **deterministic** ideas; in other words, it is based on the philosophical notion that circumstances have an absolute causal relationship to events. Many people subscribe to a system of **separatism** that presup-

poses that one entity must dominate another. For example, as a mother molds her child's behaviors to be in sync with the dominant society, most humans mold the environment to suit their needs, regardless of the long-term consequences.

The **transactional theory** is a method of inquiry that concentrates on patterns of relationships and contends that the human–environment relationship is mutually supportive. Nature provides a simple analogy, as illustrated in Figure 2.2. Similarly, design affects the user just as the user affects the design. For example, an architect designing a residence for a large and boisterous family might raise the ceilings in high-activity areas because the echoing will inspire the inhabitants to speak more distinctly, play music more softly, and so on. Ironically, humans seem to have little difficulty understanding the transactional relationship between the environment and other life forms, but when it comes to their own species most cling to an interactional perspective.

The **organismic theory**[9] states that social, societal, and individual characteristics intertwine with the environment in a complex symbiosis. The organismic theory professes that multiple contributing factors (e.g., people's experiences that day, their current health and state of minds, and the mood or disposition of others around them) combine with the environment to induce a particular behavior. For example, a man who does not ordinarily recycle containers may do so if he is dating a woman who does and he wishes to please her, if litter in his neighborhood annoys him, and if recycling bins are available. It is important to note that design can influence the man's recycling *behavior* by providing convenient bins, but it cannot influence his *motivation* for recycling.

Control Theories

Having a sense of control over our world and our place in it is crucial to our well-being. James Averill suggested that we have three types of control over our environments:

1. *Behavioral control.* The ability to change the environmental event.
2. *Cognitive control.* The ability to change the way in which we conceive of an environment.
3. *Decisional control.* The ability to choose a response.

Figure 2.1: For most of us, the word *casino* evokes an image of flashing lights and crowded gaming tables, and these generalized characteristics make a casino a *global environment*. Within it are *instigators* designed to entice people to gamble; slot machines generally serve this purpose (because even a novice can figure out how to use them), and the nickel slot becomes a *goal object* as an inexpensive way for nongamblers to pass the time as they wait for friends who enjoy gambling. However, the explosion of lights and noises that announces big payoffs can be a *noxient* if it is perceived to be unpleasant or painful. Casino environments are equipped with many built-in *supports* (e.g., cash machines, roaming attractive cocktail servers offering free drinks, and numerous gaming tables and machines), as well as security systems that act as *constraints* against cheating and stealing. A well-designed casino provides good *directors* (e.g., signs and pathways) to cash machines and gaming devices, and poor directors to areas where people can cash out or exit the facility. A casino is an environment that incorporates a global environment, instigators, goal objects, noxients, supports, constraints, and directors.

Figure 2.2: A tree bears fruit, a bird eats the fruit, the bird then flies miles away and defecates, a seed takes root, a new tree grows, and more fruit is produced; the tree gives to the bird (by producing food), and the bird gives back to the tree (by assisting procreation). This method of inquiry is needed to understand the pattern of actions or *transactional* relationship that is required for the propagation of the tree.

There is also primary and secondary control, with primary control being overt in given situation, and secondary control being more accommodating to the reality of a given situation.[10]

Personal control within an environment relates to both our freedom of action and the level and type of stimulation to which we are subjected; moreover, our actual or perceived influence or control over our environments directly affects our feelings within and about it. Most people have the ability to adapt to various levels of stimulation, have more actual control in certain settings than in others (e.g., at home as opposed to at work), and attempt to establish personal control using the psychological mechanisms of personal space and territoriality.[11] When this ability is compromised—for example, we feel that our freedom is constrained, or even anticipate a restricting factor, when we exceed our threshold—we usually try to reassert control over the situation or setting, a phenomenon referred to as **psychological reactance** or simply *reactance*.[12] However, when people believe they cannot control distressing factors within their environments, or they experience repeated failed efforts to establish or regain control, they may create physical or psychological barriers (i.e., engage in social withdrawal behaviors) and eventually give up, succumbing to *learned helplessness*.[13] Learned helplessness results from being put in a situation where there is no possibility of escape from harm or pain. Eventually, the person succumbs to fatalism and resignation: the person is powerless and decides there is no point in trying to improve the situation.

Personal space and territoriality are discussed in more detail in Chapter 4.

Behavior-Setting Theories

Some behaviors are considered appropriate in certain environments but not in others (e.g., it is socially acceptable to dress and act provocatively at a nightclub but not at a house of worship). Roger Barker[14] conceived the behavior-setting theory, which he defined as public places or occasions that evoke particular patterns of behaviors. The theory proposes that behavior must be studied in its natural context. These **behavior settings** are small-scale social systems composed of people and physical objects arranged in a way to carry out routine actions within a specified time and place. Examples include public places, such as schools, theaters, nightclubs, and places of worship, as well as occasions that shape behaviors, such as graduations, weddings, and funerals.

Through **operant conditioning** (the act of reinforcing desired behavior), we learn at an early age the behaviors expected of us within various environments and act accordingly; in this manner, different settings and situations prompt us to behave in specific manners. An important behavior-setting theory perspective is that of **synomorphy**, the principle that physical and social aspects of an environment should fit well together.[15] However, behavior settings are not permanent, but rather evolve according to the support and constraints of society over time.[16] For example, during the Soviet regime in Russia, which opposed many practices of religion, many ancient churches were used as bathhouses, gymnasiums, warehouses, and so on.

Most behavior settings are public environments that contain the following three components:

1. physical properties
2. social components
3. the environmental setting

A novice designer attempting to develop a behavior setting through design alone would be fulfilling only one of Barker's criteria if he or she did not consider the social components or the environmental setting. In this case, the designer would be engaging in a concept known as **architectural determinism**,[17] a direct and absolute relationship between the designed environment and a particular behavior. Many academicians do not subscribe to architectural determinism—which, at an extreme level, contends that it is the environment alone that causes behavior X—but certain design components of an overall environment do serve as learned-behavior cues. For example, a picture of a holy icon may or may not signify a holy site, but the picture commands respect from those who worship that icon.

Neurobiological research may one day firmly establish *architectural determinism* as the cause of certain behaviors. For example, casinos, cruise ships, and disorderly neighborhoods are all environments in which our senses are bombarded with environmental stimuli, prompting our natural human desire to minimize the stimulation. If we do so by ingesting a neurological depressant such as alcohol, has the environment created a situation that promotes alcoholism? Research shows that behaviors can indeed be activated by *environmental cues* without conscious thought.[18] The behavior manifested is often unconscious and the person is unaware of the potential influence of the stimulus in shaping his or her behavior. Because people differ in their everyday motivations, differences arise over time in the way such unconscious behaviors manifest. Clearly, more research is needed to assess the ethical implications of developing environments that elicit or instigate certain behaviors.

Stimulation Theories

Every living thing on earth reacts to sensory stimulation. **Stimulation theories** serve to conceptualize and explain the environment as a source of sensory information derived from sight, sound, touch, taste, and smell.[19] At a chocolate factory, for example, a line worker may call upon each of the five senses in relation to the production of chocolate candy. He would be surrounded by assorted visual stimuli, as well as the numerous sounds of machinery and production, the various chocolate smells, the feel of individual candies, and the taste of an occasional morsel (for quality control purposes, of course). Whereas this factory affects all five senses, most environments stimulate only sight, sound, and smell. Examining the different levels of sensory information deriving from an environment enables us to assess that environment's level of stimulation.

Each of our five senses can be overstimulated (hyperstimulated) or understimulated (hypostimulated). An important concept to understand is that of **threshold**, the point at which too much or too little stimulation is available. At one end of the threshold spectrum is the absolute minimal intensity of stimulus we can perceive and at the other is the maximum amount of stimulation we can cope with effectively. Once accustomed to a certain level of stimuli, we will no longer consciously notice it until it changes. Our level of perception will often dictate how much the stimulation must change before it is noticed.

Related theories that help to explain the relationship between stimulation and human behaviors include the **arousal perspective**, environmental

Box 2.1 What Research Tells Us: Human Behavior and Neuroimaging

In October 2004, P. Read Montague, Ph.D., director of the Human Neuroimaging Laboratory at Baylor College of Medicine in Houston, demonstrated a connection between neuroscience and consumer preferences that could have economic implications. Dr. Montague's team demonstrated that modern neuroscience techniques related to magnetic resonance imaging (MRI) can identify individual differences in decision-making behavior.

Study participants were asked to taste both Pepsi and Coca-Cola while blindfolded. With no reference point, the subjects showed no discernible preference; however, when shown product labels before they drank, 75 percent of the participants indicated a preference for Coke. Although the ventral putamen, the part of the brain involved in reward-related learning, showed activity when participants drank either brand, activity in the hippocampus and dorsolateral prefrontal cortex areas of the brain associated with recalling emotions and cultural memories, occurred only with Coke. The Coca-Cola label itself stimulated a significant and measurable increase in neural activity associated with memory, cultural knowledge, and self-image, whereas exposure to the Pepsi label produced no such increases. According to Dr. Montague, "There's a huge effect of the Coke label on brain activity related to the control of actions, the dredging up of memories and self-image. There is a response in the brain [that] leads to a behavioral effect." Dr. Montague's research suggests that pleasure is related to prior exposures and to the effectiveness of advertising and brand-name recognition. His research also suggests that values associated with particular brands can be powerful enough to physically alter consumers' brains and thus change their perceptions of a product. Although this study looked specifically at product valuation, many architects have extended the research into architectural and space-planning valuation. The goal of neuroscience research into design should mimic that of consumer science: Discover what drives neural valuation.

Source: McClure, S. M., Li, J., Tomlin, D., Cypert, K. S., Montague, L. M., and Montague, P. R. (2004). Neural correlates of behavioral preference for culturally familiar drinks. *Neuron, 44* (2), 279–287.

load or overstimulation, and adaptation. According to the arousal perspective, the environment itself causes an autonomic physiological response related to increased heart rate, blood pressure, respiration, adrenaline (epinephrine) secretion, and neural activity within the brain. In this way, architectural determinism does play a role in environmental design. Arousal has been described as being somewhere along a continuum between sleep and excitement.[20] In the cliché, "It sparked my curiosity (or imagination or interest)," the "spark" is arousal, which prompts the person to pursue the next step (satisfying that curiosity). The level of arousal we experience is often directly correlated to the level of stimulation provided by the environment. An excited child is overaroused, and a bored child is underaroused. Optimum arousal is an important factor in successful learning and productivity. While overarousal can lead to cognitive chaos ("I have so many ideas flooding my head that I don't know where to start"), underarousal can lead to inaction ("My mind is blank, and I don't know where to start") or even apathy ("I can't think, and I don't care"). Simply stated, arousal is a component of the human psych and is dependent on stimulation. Design cannot affect arousal directly, but it can serve to modify stimulation levels that affect arousal.

The terms *overstimulation* and **environmental load** are often used interchangeably. This concept assumes that humans have a limited ability to process incoming information, and in many cases when they experience too much information it leads to *overload*.[21, 22] However, as briefly mentioned, just as we can be overstimulated, we can also be understimulated. Anxiety and other psychological problems can occur when individuals are deprived of sensory stimuli.[23] Although there is much controversy about the effects of understimulation, at least one study showed a negative connection between understimulation and development of children.[24] When considering environmental load, designers must be knowledgeable about the greater environment in relation to lesser ones. For example, children attending a preschool in New York City are likely to be subjected to high amounts of urban clamor and may therefore benefit from a lower level of stimulation in their school environment, whereas children attending a preschool in rural Maine will likely require a variety of environmental stimuli in their school setting because their greater environment presents low levels of stimulation.

The **adaptation level theory** states that as a person becomes accustomed to a component or variable within an environment, its influence will be reduced. The survival mechanism of the human psych can adapt to a wide variety of stimulation levels, but there are both positive and negative implications. If a person's optimal level of stimulation is high, when thrust into average levels of stimulation he or she will experience the negative effects of understimulation and vice versa. Say there are two business executives, one from New York City and the other from Spokane, who have relocated to San Diego and are experiencing the negative effects of stress but for different reasons. The former New Yorker desires more intensity, which is why the laid-back environment becomes a source of stress. However, the Spokane native is used to a more conservative style and pace of life than exists in San Diego, which is why the faster paced environment becomes a source of stress. Although these people experienced stress related to over- and understimulation, the adaptation level theory states that both of them will adapt to the stimulation levels of their new environment.

The adaptation level theory can be applied to preferences in design styles. Imagine the reaction of Catherine the Great of Russia if she were to find herself in a Frank Lloyd Wright home (Figure 2.3a and b). How would she perceive the design? Considering the opulent display of wealth and artistry in both the Hermitage and Summer Palace, she would probably view Wright's clean lines and blending of design materials with the environment as boring and mundane. However, in time she might adapt to a different way of thinking and change her thoughts regarding the design style.

The *attention restoration theory*, developed by Rachel and Stephen Kaplan,[25] is based on concepts related to voluntary and involuntary attention. This theory maintains that situations requiring mental effort cause us to engage in **directed attention** (voluntary, intention- or goal-based attention), which requires more exertion over time. Like overworked muscles, directed attention can fail, thus creating **attentional deficit**, or an inability to concentrate (i.e., we need more time and energy to understand, retain, and recall information). Recovery requires rest, but excessive attentional fatigue may not be restorable by sleep. Periodic episodes of **effortless attention** (involuntary, interest-based attention), such as a walk in the woods or along the beach, serve as powerful and effective means of restoring attentional capacity. The word *effortless* is key; navigating a crowded beach where a person must avoid hazards in the sand and surf requires directed attention. When we need physical, psychological, and energy restoration, we are drawn to nature, and the presence of nature in our

Figure 2.3a and b: Catherine the Great's Summer Palace, located just outside Saint Petersburg in Russia, is an opulent display of wealth. Detailed craftsmanship, inlaid precious metals and gemstones, and a myriad of mosaics made from woods, amber, and other precious stones are found throughout the palace (a). Frank Lloyd Wright adopted an architectural style that attempted to blend the built environment with the natural environment. Rather than opulent displays of wealth, he embraced subtle nuances and natural elements in his designs (b).

environment has a profound effect on reducing levels of stress, thereby helping to restore attentional capacity.[26–30] The attention restoration theory asserts that **restorative experiences** occur in settings where we can function primarily in the involuntary mode (i.e., when we can observe or surround ourselves with stimuli that are involuntarily interesting), as shown in Figure 2.4.

Arousal, environmental load, and adaptation—three aspects of stimulation theories—interact dynamically. Consider a man who has spent his whole life in a high-stimulus environment. He has not only adapted to a high level of stimulation, but also probably finds it arousing and pleasurable; therefore, it would take a great deal of stimulation to overload him, but he also would be very susceptible to stress related to understimulation. Understanding how stimulation affects an individual, and the source of that stimulation, is important for design professionals. People who are overstimulated in the workplace will probably desire homes with few environmental stimuli, people who thrive on stimulation will probably want high-stimulus homes as an adjunct to their high-stimulus careers, and people who are understimulated by their careers may want higher levels of stimulation in their homes.

There are differing aspects of stimulation that affect the design process. By understanding these fundamental psychological processes and their behavioral outcomes designers can enhance the environment (Table 2.1).

Figure 2.4: People often seek restorative environments when they need rest, and vacation settings are characteristically high in such stimuli. Views are often so prized that people are willing to pay an additional premium to enjoy this restorative environment.

Table 2.1 Fundamental Psychological Processes and Their Behavioral Outcomes

PSYCHOLOGICAL STATE	PROCESS	BEHAVIORAL OUTCOME
Arousal	Behaviors are linked to physiological responses.	Ranges from hyper- to hypostimulation
Overload	Too much stimulation	Fight, flight, or withdrawal
Affect	Memory, sensation preferences	Emotional reaction to the environment
Adaptation	Adjustment to stimulation levels	Desire for certain levels of stimulation
Personal control	Influence over external stimulation	Ranges from successful coping to learned helplessness

Theories of Environmental Perception

The human–environment experience is complex, and researchers have attempted to explain the relationship from various perspectives to better comprehend how individuals perceive their environments.

Brunswik's Probabilistic Lens Model

Egon Brunswik is among a group of researchers termed functionalists.[31] Brunswik, as all functionalists, theorized that the environment contains an abundance of cues and that perceivers must be able to make sense of the most important ones if they are to function effectively. His probabilistic lens model,[32, 33] a theoretical framework that considers the human–environment relationship holistically, can be used to analyze a subjective interpretation of an environment's beauty or usefulness.

Brunswik considered the process of perception as being similar to a lens through which stimuli are perceived and become focused; however, in the lens model, environmental cues have only a certain probability of being useful (a concept called *probabilism*). The probabilistic lens model uses sets of predetermined objective criteria that lead to *actual* beauty and a different set of subjective (judgment-based) criteria that lead to *perceived* beauty. Consider the example in Figure 2.5.

Brunswik's theory differentiates between distal cues, which are characteristics of the setting, and proximal cues, which are the observer's subjective impressions (Table 2.2). It relies on the concept of *ecological validity*, that is, the relationship between

Figure 2.5: This sitting room has been designed with two facing sofas to promote and support conversation. Judge the sociability of this arrangement. The acceptability of this judgment will depend on how well you use the cues that are available to you, such as the color of room, the space between the sofas, the presence of a coffee table, and so on. According to the lens model, your final judgment will be based on summing up how well each of the cues allows you to predict the level of socialization that will occur in that room. However, your failure to take into account a sufficient number of cues and their probabilistic weighting can lead to many errors in judgment. For instance, although the room you are evaluating may have all of the components that lead to socialization, when it is occupied by two men, the presence of freshly cut flowers on the coffee table, perfume scent in the air, and a pink color scheme will most likely decrease the probability of socialization.

Table 2.2 Brunswik's Lens Model

THE SETTING	SELECTED DISTAL CUES	SELECTED PROXIMAL CUES	THE JUDGMENT
	Seating Arrangement	Crowded	
	Artwork	Elegance	
Actual Beauty	Floor Covering	Beauty	Perceived Beauty
	Furnishings	Comfortable	
	Lighting	Spaciousness	

Distal cues are related to actual beauty, while proximal cues are related to perceived beauty. Therefore, the goal of a designer is to positively relate the distal cues to the proximal cues. For example, does the seating arrangement foster perceptions of crowding or spaciousness?

Source: Gifford, R. (2002). *Environmental psychology: principles and practice* (3rd ed.), p. 28.

Figure 2.6: According to *Gibson's affordances*, elements in design may be developed for one purpose but may afford other unintended uses. A solid horizontal surface, such as the one at the top of this front wall, may be intended as a barrier but can also offer a place to sit on or lean against.

an environment and its cues that leads to an accurate perception of the environment. Because our understanding of an environment is affected by our perceptions of and familiarity with its individual components, Brunswik suggests that problems arise when we encounter environments that contain components or patterns that are unfamiliar to us. In these environments, we may come to incorrect conclusions, for example, about size, height, color, or angle.

The lens model further suggests that observers infer personality judgments about occupants based on environmental cues. The accuracy of those judgments is based on *cue validity*—whether the cue provides good information—and *cue utilization*—how the observer weights the cues.[34] Going back to the earlier example, how would you characterize a person who prefers a pink sitting room with flowers on the coffee table and scented with perfume? For most of us, pink suggests an environment belonging to a woman with strong feminine characteristics. However, depending on the *cue validity* and *cue utilization*, that conclusion may be incorrect.

Gibson's Affordances

James J. Gibson's *affordance* is a perspective that takes an ecological approach to perception. It suggests that, rather than perceiving individual features within an environment, we organize those features into recognizable patterns based on the arrangements of cues that provide immediate perceptual information.[35, 36] He further suggests that humans (among other organisms) actively explore their environments and perceive objects in a variety of ways. As such, we experience different objects differently; the functional properties of those objects as they are encountered are termed *affordances*. In Gibson's theory, the world is composed of substances, surfaces, and textures, the arrangement of which provides cognitive affordances, or instantly recognizable functions, of environmental features. See figure 2.6 as an example.

In contrast to Brunswik, Gibson believes that, rather than perceiving individual features or cues, humans respond to an ecologically structured environment. We do this by examining environments for those components that are useful or meaningful to us. For example, a flower garden may afford a quiet place to meditate, a source for freshly cut flowers, and a place to work; it also affords many insects with a home and a source for food. Many architects and designers strive to create environments that afford more than shelter. They attempt to develop environments that suit the unique needs of individuals while considering issues of sustainability, or conserving the earth's natural resources.

Although many design elements afford instantly recognizable functions, some environmental components are so similar that cognitive processes (the act recalling what has been learned or is known) are needed for people to make sense of what they are seeing.[37] A tired child who is touring a museum with his mother sits on an antique chair because he perceives that it has a good surface for sitting and knows that it will afford him rest. According to Gibson's affordances, the child is correct. However, the mother knows from the chair's appearance and placement that it is on display and not intended for use. Her son, not yet properly socialized, cannot make the same cognitive connection.

Berlyne's Collative Properties

Daniel Berlyne was one of the first psychologists to develop a model of aesthetics. His theory states that we respond to aesthetics based on their collative stimulus properties—that is, properties such as novelty, complexity, incongruity, and surprise that elicit comparative or investigative responses, which in turn cause perceptual conflict with other present or past stimuli.[38, 39]

- *Novelty* is anything new, an innovative idea, or something used in a different way. For example, a few years ago in South America, I first saw glass bottles built into a physical structure much as glass block is used.
- *Incongruity* refers to design features that seem out of place or out of context. Architects often violate neighborhood congruity by incorporating modern buildings into neighborhoods dominated by early–20th century styles, and designers often confuse incongruity, which is perceived negatively, with novelty, which is perceived positively.
- *Complexity* refers to the variety of items in the environment. In Washington State, for example, the dense Western forests' abundance of plant and animal life forms, rock formations, and streams and springs appear very complex compared with the central desert plains.
- *Surprise* reveals the unexpected, such as a home built around a large tree or a bathtub situated in a great room.

These properties are sometimes referred to as *collative properties*, meaning that they create a perceptual conflict; how we resolve that conflict leads to an aesthetic evaluation.

Berlyne believed that these properties influence the perceiver's aesthetic judgments through the following two psychological dimensions:

- *Hedonic tone* refers to those design elements, such as multiple gold-plated showerheads, that serve no purpose other than to provide beauty and pleasure.
- *Uncertainty-arousal* refers to subjective uncertainty, that is, simultaneous feelings of excite-

a

b

Figure 2.7a and b: Many environments developed for children utilize *Berlyne's collative properties*. In this rendering, the tunnel-like structure in the form of coral within a larger structure displays *surprise* and *incongruity* as well as *hedonic tone*; hedonic means that it serves no purpose other than to attract attention and provide pleasure. Its unusual features beg exploration, therefore evoking *uncertainty-arousal*. Its lines are *complex*, and the overall structure is a *novelty* (a). Constructing a building around an existing tree incorporates all six of *Berlyne's collative properties*. The tree growing through this ecoresort's dining room is a *novelty*, while the rest of the room appears as expected; the presence of a tree growing through the floor and ceiling is *incongruent*, and the tree itself adds *complexity* to the room. A person's first glimpse of this scene would no doubt inspire *surprise* and *uncertainty-arousal*; for those who would be attracted to an ecoresort, an element of *hedonic tone* is presented by the opportunity to dine in luxury (b).

ment and discomfort evoked by environments that seem both complex and simple or ordered and chaotic (Figure 2.7a and b).

Berlyne's collative properties cannot be applied without an understanding of a person's attitude, or predisposition, toward what is being perceived. Our attitudes are often rooted in our **worldview**, a perspective or philosophy that incorporates a general belief. Because such beliefs are often held by a certain culture or generation, a group of people may hold a similar attitude. For example, the attitude of many Asian people toward a particular building or location is based on their worldview that Chi or *qi* (life energy) must be allowed to flow smoothly.

Differences in attitude and worldviews have important consequences for design. For example, a garden complete with pathways constructed within a residence as part of the overall design may be perceived as novel by some observers, surprising by others, incongruent with others' expectations of home décor, and highly complex, and most who view it will probably consider it hedonistic.

Berlyne also examines the distinction between diversive and specific exploration. Diversive exploration occurs when a person is understimulated and seeks arousing stimuli in the environment. For example, a person who finds an environment too quiet may respond by turning up the stereo. Specific exploration occurs when a person is aroused by a particular stimulus and investigates it to reduce the uncertainty or to satisfy the curiosity of arousal. This is the case when a person hears water and explores the environment in search of the source.

Pleasure–Arousal–Dominance Hypothesis

Albert Mehrabian and James A. Russell postulated that humans have three primary emotional responses to an environment—pleasure (positive feelings), arousal (excitement or challenge), and dominance (control over the setting or situation)—based on the perspective that emotion is a mediator between our environments and personalities (preexisting influences) and our behavior (outcome).[40] Russell later rejected dominance as a primary response; his modified pleasure–arousal hypothesis claims that we are most attracted to set-

tings that are *moderately* arousing and *maximally* pleasurable, but that, in unpleasant environments, moderately arousing settings are the *least* desirable.

Russell's revised model is represented by a circumplex (i.e., a circular ordering or pattern of environmental evaluations) consisting of polarized emotional dimensions: arousing–not arousing and pleasurable–not pleasurable. Using this model, an observer can evaluate an environment by plotting its characteristics along each of the continuums, as illustrated in Figure 2.8.

Variables that affect a person's response to these dimensions include, but are not limited to, environmental factors (light, temperature, and objects or cues) and individual personality characteristics (introvert–extrovert and internal–external locus of control). The interaction of environmental and personal variables manifests in emotions, which affect work performance, interpersonal relations, and other behaviors.

The studies of Russell, Mehrabian, and others indicate that the emotional impact of an environment is systematically related to behavior in it. Because the opposite of dominance is vulnerability (which leads to uncertainty), the original **pleasure–arousal–dominance hypothesis** is wholly applicable to environmental design because people need to feel they have at least some measure of control over their circumstances.[41] Meeting all

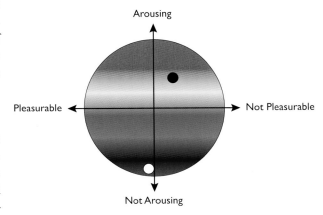

Figure 2.8: By the placement of the black dot, we can see that the person is aroused, but not in a pleasurable way. The corresponding emotion is most likely to be anger. The person indicated by the white dot is more happy than not, but is not very aroused. The probable emotion here is boredom.

Locus of control is discussed in more detail in Chapter 3.

three emotional needs will result in user or consumer satisfaction, particularly within the retail, service, and hospitality industries.

Kaplan and Kaplan
Preference Framework

Based on the idea that people prefer scenes that are engaging and involving rather than simple or boring, Stephen and Rachel Kaplan[42] devised a theoretical framework to organize environmental preferences according to four elements: coherence, legibility, complexity, and mystery.

- *Coherence* (making sense) refers to the way that objects in a scene come together to form some sort of understandable context. For example, a room with a fireplace, cushioned seating, a coffee table, and ambient lighting is immediately recognizable as a living room and is therefore a coherent space. A home office that doubles as a guest room but looks like a storage area, however, is an incoherent space.
- *Legibility* (the promise of making sense) refers to the level at which an individual is able to understand or categorize the scene and the objects within it. Legibility can be affected by items that serve dual or obscure purposes, such as a faux book hiding a treasured keepsake on a bookshelf.
- *Complexity* (involvement) relates to the number and variety of elements within the scene. The perception of complexity is highly variable; for example, minimalist design can provide the ideal level of complexity for some, yet appear sterile or stark to others.
- *Mystery* (the promise of involvement) is the degree to which a scene contains hidden information or begs exploration. Victorian architecture was bursting with features designed to pique a viewer's curiosity and invite investigation; most homes incorporated elaborate carvings and ironwork, built-in buffets, cabinets and closets situated in obscure places, and even hidden rooms or corridors.

Secret and special places beckon to the child in all of us; coves, nooks, and even intriguing sounds and smells all invite us to explore. However, Berlyne[43] suggested that as mystery and therefore uncertainty

Figure 2.9: In this hotel lobby, *coherence* in design styles is established through the minimal use of tall artifacts, which allows visitors distance views so they can identify points of interest or need. This environment has high *legibility*: A person can enter it and know immediately what it is. The variation in floor patterns and the sweeping staircase both add to the setting's *complexity*, and the hallways and staircase leading out of view provide *mystery*.

increase, cognition, which is initially arousing and pleasurable, will decrease (Figure 2.9).

Lynch's Elements of Legibility

Kevin Lynch, working with the city of Boston's planning department in the late 1950s, conceived of five predominating qualities or elements of a city that enhance its legibility to the average person: paths, edges, districts, nodes, and landmarks. As built environments become increasingly larger, many have become communities within communities (airports, malls, resort hotels, and cruise ships are all communities within communities, or microcommunities), and Lynch's elements of legibility can be applied to the built environment in general.

Microcommunities are discussed in greater detail in Chapter 14.

- *Paths* are channels people use as they travel from one area to another; examples include walkways, roads, and transit lines.

Table 2.3 Theories, Models, and Perspectives of Environmental Psychology

THEORY	MAJOR PREMISE	KEY CONCEPTS	RELEVANCE FOR DESIGN
Social learning theory	Determines that we learn by first observing others and eventually reproducing their actions	Reciprocal determinism, modeling	Encourages an understanding of established societal norms
Integration (integral) theory	Elements of the environment work in harmony to facilitate a particular behavior	Global environment, instigators, goal objects and noxients, supports and constraints, directors	Offers a holistic approach to design
Control theory	Group of theories that address behavioral constraints and a person's perceived control over his or her actions and behaviors	Psychological reactance	Suggests that design elements lead to perceptions of control
Behavior-setting theory	Public places or settings evoke particular patterns of behavior	Operant conditioning, interactional theory	Emphasizes that design is an important component of a setting, which contributes to certain behaviors
Stimulation theory	Environment is a source of sensory information (stimuli) that leads to arousal	Threshold, arousal, environmental load, overload, adaptation level	Holds that design styles can lead to over- or understimulation
Attention restoration theory	Mental fatigue is caused by excessive directed attention, and attentional capacity can be restored by engaging in effortless attention	Directed (i.e., voluntary) attention, attentional deficit, effortless (i.e., involuntary) attention, restorative experiences	Include views of green spaces for effortless attention within environments demanding much directed attention
Probabilistic lens model	Stimuli from the environment become focused through our perceptions	Distal and proximal cues leading to cue validity and cue utility	Emphasizes the perceptual relationship between design and the human observer
Affordances	The world is composed of substances, surfaces, and textures, the arrangement of which provides instantly recognizable function (i.e., affordance) of environmental features	Environmental layout, contextual cues, direct perception	Highlights perceptual influences of design styles and probable dual uses of designs
Collative properties	We respond to aesthetics based on their collative stimulus properties (i.e., properties that elicit comparative or investigative responses and cause perceptual conflict with other present or past stimuli	Novelty, incongruity, complexity, surprise, hedonic tone, uncertainty-arousal	Claims that the joint nature of design elements merge to develop one overall impression
Pleasure–arousal–dominance hypothesis	Three primary emotional responses are translated to positive feelings, excitement or challenge, and control over the setting or situation. Later modified to use a circumplex model, with pleasure and arousal as the two main axes	Pleasure, arousal	Offers a method to evaluate environmental designs
Preference model	People prefer engaging scenes to boring scenes	Coherence, legibility, complexity, mystery	Offers a method for designing engaging environments
Elements of legibility	Five predominating qualities (i.e., elements) enhance its legibility to the average person	Paths, edges, districts, nodes, landmarks	Offers a method to enhance an environment's legibility

Figure 2.10: In airports, digital screens that display flight information also serve as central landmarks.

- *Edges*, such as shorelines and fences, preclude travel and may appear to be boundaries.
- *Districts*, the largest elements, are regions having a particular character that people can readily identify: commercial, residential, artistic, and so on.
- *Nodes* are well-known points within the environment to and from which people travel; they are often places where paths converge, such as a bank of elevators or an airport.
- *Landmarks*, easily seen and singular components within an environment, are used for location orientation and are often found within districts and nodes.

In his classic book *The Image of the City*, Lynch stated, "Districts are structured with nodes, defined by edges, penetrated by paths, and sprinkled with landmarks. Elements regularly overlap and pierce one another."[44] Lynch coined his elements to describe cities, but they also apply to microcommunities such as malls, resorts, hospitals, airports, and even homes (Figure 2.10).

Theories, models, and perspectives offer ways in which to approach or evaluate the design process. The environment being designed often calls for the use of multiple theories, models, or perspectives. For example, if we were to design a hospital in the United States we would need to gain an understanding of established societal norms (social learning theory) such as expected privacy levels. We would also want to understand the interrelationship between the different areas within the hospital (integral theories), and the design elements that lead to perceptions of control (control theories). Table 2.3 shows the different theories, models, and perspectives. Review them and imagine the different and overlapping ways each can be used in the design of a mall, nursing home, school, hospital, and so on.

Summary Review

Excellent social science research has provided a much better understanding of how planners and designers can develop environments that are more supportive of human habitation. Research that addresses the human–environment relationship, environmental perception, and elements that enhance environmental legibility is particularly relevant to designers. When considered throughout the design process, this research can enhance the experiences of those who are intended to occupy the environment.

The predominating theories within the field of environmental psychology relate to learning, stimulation, control, behavior settings, and integration. Social learning theories maintain that we learn by first observing others and eventually reproducing their actions. Beginning as early as infancy, we learn socially acceptable behaviors and responses to certain stimuli. We know to lower our voices in places of worship, libraries, and museums. Likewise, we know that bars, nightclubs, and rock concerts are places where we can dress and act more provocatively. Because a host of environmental cues—including, but not limited to, the level of lighting, environmental volume, and behavior of others—are present in each of these environments, we can also say that these environments are behavior settings because each evokes its own typical patterns of behavior.

Integration (integral) theories are holistic approaches to environmental study that are used to understand the complexity of the person–environment relationship. Isidor Chein developed one such framework, consisting of instigators, goal objects and noxients, supports and constraints, directors, and global environments. By considering each of these elements within the framework, we can obtain a more comprehensive understanding of the relationship between the person and environment.

Control theories are a group of theories that address behavioral constraints and a person's perceived control over his or her actions and behaviors. We tend to have the most control in the privacy of our own homes and the least control in prisons. All other environments fall somewhere in between. Another group of theories, referred to as stimulation theories, regard the physical environment as sources of sensory information. Sight, sound, touch, smell, and, in some cases, taste stimulate the brain by providing sensations. As we move through environments, these sensations can be either over- or understimulating. In many situations either some sensations or all of them can be overloaded. Living next to a fish cannery, for example, may overstimulate a person's sense of smell, potentially provoking hostile behaviors or the desire to move.

How people perceive an environment will affect their overall appraisal and impression of the environment. Among the popular perceptual theories that guide the field of environmental psychology are Brunswik's probabilistic lens model, Gibson's affordances, and Berlyne's collative properties. Brunswik views the perceptual processes as similar to a lens; stimuli from the environment become focused through our perceptions. Gibson, in contrast, sees the environment as containing arrangements of substances and surfaces that afford detectable functions. A different approach is provided by Berlyne, who claims that we respond to aesthetics based on their collative stimulus properties (incongruity, complexity, surprise, hedonic tone, and uncertainty-arousal). These are properties that elicit comparative or investigative responses that cause perceptual conflict with other present or past stimuli.

Other theories discussed in this chapter include the pleasure–arousal–dominance hypothesis, the Kaplan and Kaplan preference model, and Lynch's elements of legibility. Pleasure, arousal, and dominance were the original responses identified by Mehrabian and Russell as being from an environment. They proposed that these three primary emotional responses were translated by the observer into positive feelings, excitement or challenge, and control over the setting or situation. Russell later dropped dominance from the model, developing a circumplex formed by two main axes: pleasure and arousal. Rachel and Stephen Kaplan took a different approach, devising a theoretical model to organize environmental preferences according to four elements: coherence, legibility, complexity, and mystery. Lynch proposed a theoretical model that organizes environmental features, especially in the city, according to five elements: paths, edges, districts, nodes, and landmarks. His model suggests that considering these elements within the design of an environment will positively contribute to its legibility.

Each of these theories, models, and perspectives offer ways in which to approach or evaluate the design process. Oftentimes the environment being designed calls upon the simultaneous use of multiple theories, models, or perspectives. These theories, models, and perspectives have relevance for the designer because they can provide the foundation or framework for the selection of materials and layout to be used in the design process. Therefore, the probability of satisfying a design objective for a particular environment becomes greatly enhanced.

Discussion Questions

1. Discuss a setting, other than a casino, that illustrates the principles of the integration theories: the global environment, instigators, goal objects, noxients, supports, constraints, and directors.

2. Discuss *architectural determinism* in terms of your own experience. Can you provide any true examples, or can all of your experiences be traced back to *operant conditioning*? How do your cognitive experiences affect your perception of this concept?

3. Discuss the room you are occupying in terms of the *Kaplan and Kaplan preference model*. How would it differ in terms of Berlyne's collative properties?

4. Using the *attention restoration theory*, how would you structure the class and recess time of a first-grade class? How would you structure the class time of a high-school student? Would you change the structure of your study and relaxation time? If so, how?

5. Consider the adage "Never judge a book by its cover." What does Brunswik's probabilistic lens model say about this? How might Brunswik rewrite this saying?

6. How would you describe your school's interior according to *Lynch's elements of legibility*?

Learning Activities

1. List five real-world examples of *synomorphy* and five that lack synomorphy. (These may be historical or current references.)

2. Rewrite "Goldilocks and the Three Bears" in terms of Gibson's affordances.

3. Team up with a classmate. Person A takes ten seconds to examine a room and closes his or her eyes. Next, Person B tells Person A to proceed to a specific destination in that room. How well Person A is able to reach that destination will indicate how well he or she was able to form a cognitive map. Some people do this very well, which is why they can follow visual directions easily.

Terminology

adaptation level theory   Premise that individuals adapt to certain levels of stimulation in certain contexts

architectural determinism   Theory that there is a direct relationship between the built environment and a particular behavior

arousal perspective   Theory that much of human behavior and experience is related to arousal levels

attention restoration theory (ART)   Premise that mental fatigue is caused by excessive *directed attention* and that attentional capacity and mental balance can be restored by engaging in *effortless attention*

attentional deficit   Inability to focus or concentrate; also, inadequate attentional capacity. Caused by mental fatigue due to excessive *directed attention*; can be ameliorated by *restorative experiences*.

behavioral controls   Physical or psychological elements that serve to restrict or encourage specific behaviors

behavior setting   Physical or psychological environment (i.e., place or occasion) that elicits or supports certain patterns of behavior that are based on the environmental design and learned as a result of *operant conditioning*

determinism   Theory that acts of will, occurrences in nature, or social or psychological phenomena are causally determined by preceding events or natural laws

directed attention   Intention- or goal-based attention; requires focused mental effort and can cause *attentional deficit*; also called voluntary attention

effortless attention   Interest-based attention that can serve to restore attentional capacity; also called automatic and involuntary attention

environmental load   State of excessive arousal; also called overstimulation

integration (integral) theories Theoretical models intended to encompass the complex range of human–environment relations

interactional theory Simplest form of *integration theory*; maintains that people and the environment are separate but interacting entities (i.e., all or most outcomes can be attributed to either the person or the environment)

operant conditioning Social process that teaches and reinforces acceptable/desirable behaviors; a form of behavior modification. Also called *stimulus-response learning.*

organismic theory Form of *integration theory* that focuses on the complex interaction of social, societal, and individual factors

pleasure–arousal–dominance hypothesis Premise that people have three primary emotional responses to an environment: positive feelings, excitement, and a sense of control

psychological reactance Attempt to regain one's freedom within or control over an environment stemming from feelings of lack or loss of control; also called *reactance*

restorative experience Episode that allows a person to function primarily in the effortless attention mode as a means of restoring attentional capacity and therefore relaxing

separatism Belief system that one entity must dominate the other in the human–environment relationship (*see interactional, transactional*)

social learning theory Construct that explains human behavior in terms of continuous reciprocal interaction among cognitive, behavioral, and environmental influences

stimulation theory Concept that explains the environment as a source of sensory information (stimuli) that leads to arousal

supports and constraints Environmental elements that facilitate and restrict human actions

synomorphy Principle that an environment's physical and social aspects should fit well together; also, congruity between the physical, psychological, and social aspects of an environment

threshold Point at which too much or too little stimulation has been received

transactional theory Belief that the human–environment relationship is mutually supportive (i.e., all or most outcomes can be attrib-

uted to both the person and the environment); *see interactional, separatism*

worldview Perspective or philosophy incorporating a general belief; may be held by an entire culture or generation

References

1. Rotter, J. B., Chance, J. E., and Phares, E. J. (1972). *Applications of a social learning theory of personality*. New York: Holt, Rinehart & Winston.
2. Rotter, J. B. (1982). *The development and application of social learning theory*. New York: Praeger.
3. Bandura, A. (1977). *Social learning theory*. New York: General Learning Press.
4. Bandura, A. (1986). *Social foundations of thought and action: A social cognitive theory*. Englewood Cliffs, NJ: Prentice-Hall.
5. Gifford, R. (2002). *Environmental psychology: Principles and practice* (3rd ed.), Canada: Optima Books.
6. Chein, I. (1954). The environment as a determinant of behavior. *Journal of Social Psychology, 29,* 115–127.
7. See note 5.
8. See note 5.
9. Wapner, S. (1981). Transactions of persons-in-environments: Some critical transitions. *Journal of Environmental Psychology, 18,* 102–112.
10. Weisz, J. R., Rothbaum, F. M., and Blackburn, T. C. (1984). Standing in and standing out: The psychology of control in America and Japan. *American Psychologist, 39,* 955–969.
11. Altman, I. (1975). *The environment and social behavior: Privacy, personal space, territoriality and crowding*. Monterey, CA: Brooks/Cole.
12. Brehm, J. W. (1966). A Theory of psychological resistance. New York: Academic Press.
13. Seligman, M. E. P. (1992). *Helplessness* (2nd ed.). New York: W. H. Freeman and Company.
14. Barker, R. G. (1968). *Ecological psychology: concepts and methods for studying the environment of human behavior*. Stanford, CA: Stanford University Press.
15. See note 5.
16. Wicker, A. W. (1987). Behavior settings reconsidered: Temporal stages, resources, internal

dynamics, context. In D. Stokols and I. Altman (Eds.), *Handbook of environmental psychology* (Vol. 2, pp. 612–652). New York: Wiley.

17. Bell, P. A., Greene, T. C., Fisher, J. D., and Baum, A. (2001). *Environmental psychology* (5th ed.). Orlando, FL: Harcourt College Publishers.

18. Bargh, J. A., Lombardi, W., and Higgins, E. T. (1988). Automaticity in Person Situation effects on person perception: It's just a matter of time. *Journal of Personality and Social Psychology, 55,* 599-605.

19. Wohlwill, J. F. (1966). The physical environment: A problem for a psychology of stimulation. *Journal of Social Issues, 22,* 4, 29–28.

20. Berlyne, D. E. (1960). *Conflict, arousal, and curiosity,* New York: McGraw-Hill.

21. Milgram, S. (1970). The experience of living in cities. *Science, 167,* 1461–1468.

22. Kaplan, S., and Kaplan, R. (1982). *Cognition and environment: Functioning in an uncertain world.* New York: Praeger.

23. Zubek, J. P. (Ed.) (1969). *Sensory deprivation: Fifteen years of research.* New York: Appleton-Century-Crofts.

24. Sapolsky, R. M. (1997). The importance of a well-groomed child. *Science, 277,* 1620–1621.

25. See note 15.

26. Ulrich, R. S. (1979). Visual landscapes and psychological well-being. *Landscape Research, 4,* 17–22.

27. Ulrich, R. S. (1984). View from a window may influence recovery from surgery. *Science, 224,* 420–421.

28. Ulrich, R. S. (1986). Human responses to vegetation and landscapes. *Landscape and Urban Planning, 12,* 29–44.

29. Ulrich, R. S. (1987). Improving medical outcomes with environmental design. *Journal of Healthcare Design, IX,* 2–7.

30. Ulrich, R. S., Simons, R. F., Losito, B. D., Fior-ito, E., Miles, M. A., and Zelson, M. (1991). Stress recovery during exposure to natural and urban environments. *Journal of Environmental Psychology, 11,* 201–220.

31. See note 18.

32. Brunswik, E. (1942). Organismic achievement and environmental probability. *Psychological Review, 50,* 255–272.

33. Brunswik, E. (1956). *Perception and the representative design of psychological experiments.* Berkeley: University of California Press.

34. Gosling, S. D., Ko, S. J., Mannarelli, T., and Morris, M. E. (2002). A room with a cue: Personality judgments based on offices and bedrooms. *Journal of Personality and Social Psychology, 82-2,* 279–298.

35. Gibson, J. J. (1976). The theory of affordances and the design of the environment. Paper presented at the annual meetings of the American Society for Aesthetics, Toronto.

36. Gibson, J. J. (1979). *An ecological approach to visual perception.* Boston: Houghton Mifflin.

37. See note 22.

38. Berlyne, D. E. (1971) *Aesthetics and psychobiology.* New York: Appleton-Century-Crofts.

39. Berlyne, D. E. (1974). *Studies in the new experimental aesthetics: Steps toward an objective psychology of aesthetic appreciation.* New York: Halsted Press.

40. Mehrabian, A., and Russell, J. A. (1974). *An approach to environmental psychology.* Cambridge, MA: MIT Press.

41. Russell, J. A., Ward, L. M., and Pratt, G. (1981). Affective quality attributed to environments: A factor analytic study. *Environment and behavior, 12,* 2, 259–288.

42. See note 22.

43. See note 20.

44. Lynch, K. (1960). *The Image of the city.* Cambridge, MA: MIT Press.

THREE

Human Factors Affecting Behavior

Environmental psychology is one of the few sciences recognized in the United States that exclusively examines the relationship between humans and their environments. Unfortunately, the environment itself is often neglected as a causal or supporting factor of human behaviors. Isidor Chein stated this most eloquently when he said, "Perhaps one of the most outstanding weaknesses of contemporary psychological theory is the relative neglect of the environment by many of the most influential theoretical viewpoints."[1] The environment as a causal factor is rarely considered when we seek to remedy physical and social issues, perhaps because humans have been able to dominate, or at least to drastically modify, their environments for centuries, whereas medicine and the human psych are still relative enigmas. Therefore, when we encounter socially deviant behaviors we tend to seek their source within those fields we have yet to conquer.

Comprehending the effects of the environment on humans requires that we first understand that people interact with the world around them on three different levels: physical, social, and biological. The physical environment consists of all of the physical elements found within an environment, including the atmosphere (temperature, humidity, and lighting). How we behave or react within the environment is often directly related to social factors stemming from our upbringing (family and educational and religious institutions). Biological responses include shivering in a cold room, allergic reactions to certain substances, and congenital defects caused by environmental pollutants.

Unfortunately, with the exception of researchers who purposely study the human–environment relationship, many researchers continue to look exclusively at social situations when investigating the effects of the environment on humans, even though the physical environment is often a contributing factor, as evidenced by the relationship between teen smoking and the proximity of cigarette advertising to schools. There is also a direct relation between the environment and asthma and allergies, but most medical professionals will treat the symptoms rather than modify the environment. Environmental psychologists consider the aggregate of the physical, social, and biological factors of the overall environmental experience.

This chapter briefly examines brain physiology and the neurochemicals responsible for many of our moods and behaviors; how personality type affects sensory intake; perception and cognition as fundamental to our understanding of our surroundings; memory as a form of cognition related to environmental recall; and, because environmental perception (as it relates to environmental psychology) draws heavily upon Gestalt psychology, how our brains interpret and organize the sensations around us.

Physiological Influences on Behavior

Environmental psychology, a collaborative field of study, draws upon much research generated from the social sciences and more limited research from the physical sciences. However, there has been some interest in furthering research into neurobiological reactions to various environments. Science may provide research data that could explain the neurochemical reactions to environmental combinations such as lighting, color, and odor. A better understanding of the environmental factors related

Parts of the Brain and What They Do

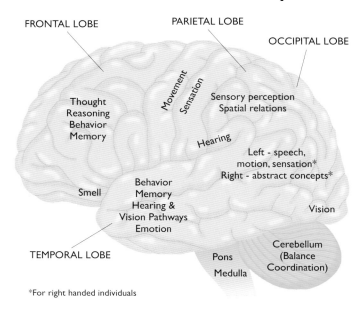

Figure 3.1: In this diagram of the frontal lobe of the cerebral cortex, both hemispheres of the hippocampus, amygdala, pineal gland, and medulla can be seen.

Chapter 6 discusses neuro-chemical responses in more detail.

to the secretion, absorption, and interaction of neurochemicals may enable us to predict more precisely human behavioral responses to certain environments. If we can comprehend our neurobiological responses to the environment, we can identify where "nature" begins and ends and where "nurture" begins, augments nature, or both. Our first step is to examine some of the more influential neurochemicals of the brain as well as the brain's basic physiology (Figure 3.1).

Brain Physiology and Behavior

All behavior is, presumably, in some way represented in brain physiology.[2] Studies have shown that certain parts of the brain, such as the frontal lobe of the cerebral cortex and both hemispheres of the hippocampus, are particularly active during memory recall. Two recognized types of long-term memory include procedural and declarative memory. **Procedural memory**, also called implicit memory, is based on the unconscious recall of information. This kind of memory is primarily used when learning motor skills such as riding a bicycle. **Declarative memory**, sometimes called explicit

memory, functions as the storage and retrieval of information that is available to the consciousness. It consists of factual information such as remembering a telephone number, a poem, or people.

Another important brain structure is the amygdala, a small subcortical structure that is part of the primitive limbic system of the brain. The amygdala plays key roles in both the stress response (also called *fight-or-flight response*, it is an automatic response to stress that is perceived to be a survival threat) and the conditioned fear response, influencing emotion and behavior in response to neurochemical triggers.

Neurochemicals and Hormones

The brain relies on several important chemicals to facilitate transmission of impulses among nerves. Among these chemicals are the neurotransmitters acetylcholine, dopamine, epinephrine, norepinephrine, and serotonin (Table 3.1). The hormones cortisol and melatonin are two other chemicals that affect our cognitive abilities. Hormones and neurotransmitters operate in a symbiotic manner. For example, in the body's stress response, cortisol is a measure of strain, whereas catecholamine is a measure of effort.

Acetylcholine is a chemical stimulant found in the brain and throughout the entire nervous system. In the brain, acetylcholine causes excitement and anticipatory actions; in the body, it causes muscle fibers to contract (tense up) in anticipation of an event. This is called the **fight–or–flight response**. Acetylcholine is quickly synthesized after fulfilling its intended function; if not, it can be destructive to nerve fibers throughout the system. Conversely, a shortage of acetylcholine can also negatively affect the body. For example, a shortage of acetylcholine in the brain has been associated with the onset of Alzheimer's disease; it is thought that sufferers may be experiencing a degeneration of cells that produce acetylcholine.

Catecholamines, a group of neurochemicals composed of naturally occurring compounds, serve as hormones, neurotransmitters, or both within the sympathetic nervous system, the branch of the autonomic nervous system that is responsible for breathing, circulation, and digestion. As with other neurotransmitters, catecholamines are released at nerve endings and facilitate signals from the nerve

Table 3.1 Neurotransmitters and Hormones Involved in Behavior

SUBSTANCE	FUNCTIONS
Acetylcholine (neurotransmitter)	• Concentrated in specific regions of the brain stem and thought to be involved in cognitive functions, especially memory • Causes excitatory actions in the brain and tensing of muscle fibers in the body associated with the fight-or-flight response • Deficiency may produce signs and symptoms of motor dysfunction • Severe shortage of acetylcholine may be associated with Alzheimer's disease
Cortisol (stress hormone)	• Secretion increases in response to physical or mental stress • Produces an increase in blood pressure and heart rate
Dopamine (catecholamine; neurotransmitter)	• Critical to brain control of physical movements and necessary for synthesis of epinephrine • Controls the flow of information within the brain and can cause a decline in neurocognitive function, particularly related to memory, attention, and problem solving • Associated with the pleasure system of the brain, related to feelings of enjoyment and reinforcement that motivate us to do, or continue doing, certain activities • Deficiency is a contributing factor in Parkinson's disease, and increased concentration has a role in the development of schizophrenia
Epinephrine (catecholamine; neurotransmitter)	• Produces a short-term stress reaction that increases heart rate and forcefulness of each contraction, dilates the pupils, and constricts small blood vessels in the skin • Elevates the blood sugar level by increasing the liver's conversion of glycogen (the stored form of sugar in the body) to glucose (a readily available form of sugar), while at the same time beginning the breakdown of lipids (fats) in fat cells • Sometimes called adrenaline
Glutamate (neurotransmitter)	• May be involved in cognitive functions such as learning and memory • Excessive amounts may cause neuronal damage associated in diseases like amyotrophic lateral sclerosis (Lou Gehrig's disease, which produces progressive loss of voluntary muscle contraction) and Alzheimer's disease
Melatonin (hormone)	• Production is regulated by light passing through the eye • Controls sleep patterns and is also involved in modulation of mood, sexual behavior, reproductive alterations, and immunological functions
Norepinephrine (catecholamine; neurotransmitter)	• Increases the level of excitatory activity within parts of the brain where attention, arousal, and impulsivity are controlled • Plays a role in the fight-or-flight response by activating the sympathetic nervous system and increasing heart rate in readiness for taking action • Sometimes called the stress hormone
Serotonin (neurotransmitter)	• Important for a range of brain functions, including mood control, regulation of sleep, pain • perception, body temperature, blood pressure, hormonal activity, appetite, and sexual desire Imbalances are associated with depression, bipolar disorder, and anxiety

cells to other cells within the sympathetic nervous system. Epinephrine (commonly referred to as adrenaline), norepinephrine (also called noradrenaline), and dopamine are all catecholamines. Norepinephrine, which is almost identical in structure to epinephrine, is released into the bloodstream from the adrenal gland under sympathetic activation and, along with acetylcholine, mobilizes the body's resources in response to a stressful event (the fight-or-flight response). The sympathetic nervous system functions in response to short-term stress, which is why norepinephrine and epinephrine are often referred to as stress hormones; they increase both heart rate and blood pressure. As mentioned, cortisol is also a stress hormone. These substances prepare the body to react to emergencies such as pain, fatigue, and shock.

Norepinephrine, dopamine, and serotonin are also associated with mood. Dopamine is necessary for the synthesis of epinephrine, which affects the activity of neural synapses. A deficiency of dopamine is thought to be responsible for the symptoms of Parkinson's disease, which is characterized by uncontrolled shaking.

Serotonin is a chemical that regulates appetite, mood, sexual desire, and sleep; in simple terms, low levels of serotonin are directly related to lower moods and depression. Inadequate serotonin levels compromise the signals between brain cells, and this often results in depression and anxiety. Sunlight plays a role in the reabsorption of serotonin, and other research suggests that tightly sealed office buildings, in conjunction with air-conditioning units, decrease levels of serotonin and norepinephrine, which leads to greater stress and depression.[3]

Cortisol is a stress hormone that, along with dehydroepiandrosterone (DHEA), rises in levels when the body experiences stress. Increased production of these hormones enables the body to better respond to stress. However, with chronic or prolonged stress, the body produces greater amounts of cortisol and lower levels of DHEA. These higher levels of cortisol interfere with brain function by impairing learning, memory, and mood. They can damage the hippocampus, which, as we have seen, plays an important role in memory. In fact, people with Alzheimer's disease have been found to have elevated cortisol levels. Elevated levels of cortisol during the night have been shown to interfere with REM (rapid eye movement) sleep, which is responsible for mental regeneration and energy restoration. Elevated cortisol also inhibits the production of growth hormones, which results in the impaired regeneration of physical structures throughout the body. The effect often manifests as depression and an acceleration of the aging process.

Melatonin is sometimes called the *Dracula of hormones*: Only when darkness occurs can the pineal gland (see Figure 3.1) produce melatonin and release it into the bloodstream. When melatonin blood levels rise sharply (usually around 9:00 p.m.) we begin to feel less alert as sleep beckons us. Melatonin levels normally stay elevated for about 13 hours before they return to barely detectable daytime lows (usually by around 9:00 a.m.). Bright light directly inhibits the release of melatonin, which the pineal gland cannot produce unless the person is in a dimly lit environment. Both sunlight and artificial indoor lighting can be bright enough to prevent the release of melatonin.

When a person first wakes up in the morning his production of melatonin during the night will cause him to be lethargic and cold. As light, both natural (the best) and artificial, passes through the person's retinas it triggers the reuptake of melatonin. As the person drives to work he is nearly in a car accident. This near accident triggers the secretion of acetylcholine and norepinephrine, which is responsible for self-preservation and is associated with the fight-or-flight response. Because norepinephrine and epinephrine are almost identical in structure, dopamine is released after the urgency of the event to synthesize the epinephrine, which brings blood pressure and heart rate down to normal. When the person finally arrives at work, he feels lethargic and moody. The reason that he feels lethargic is because he wakes up in the middle of the night and has difficulty falling back to sleep. This, along with the moodiness, can be a result of low serotonin levels, which can be caused by prolonged stress. The person then checks his voice mail only to find a harsh message left by his supervisor. In response to stress, the person's body releases cortisol. Because his supervisor routinely leaves such messages, the person experiences chronic stress. Therefore, the person's body routinely produces high levels of cortisol, which compromise his ability to learn and remember. The chronic stress will also cause the levels other neurotransmitters and hormones to be abnormal. The person's body has multiple responses that occur concurrently and a multitude of other physical, biological, and social variables affecting his physiological responses.

Understanding the effects of neurotransmitters and hormones on learning and behaviors is an important start to understanding personality. While it is true that neurochemical and hormonal imbalances will affect a person's disposition and capacity to function efficiently, people are more than the sum of chemical interactions. It is the aggregate of chemical, cultural, and social situations that determine our personalities.

Personality Traits

Personality traits are those unique attributes that generally define who we are. Scientists continue to debate the importance of nature versus nurture, and whether personality can be affected by environmental influences as a person develops into an adult. Whereas a study of twins found personality traits to be innate (exhibited throughout the life span),[4] other researchers contend that various environmental factors influence personality by shaping skills, values, attitudes, and identities and suggest that the opportunities afforded by different environments predict, to some degree, the manifestation of personality traits.[5] For example, if a person is born with an outgoing, social personality, it can be suppressed by long-term exposure to a crowded environment. How and why certain personality traits do or do not manifest is important insofar as certain traits may be supported or discouraged through environmental modification.

Personality traits are often expressed through the quantity and types of artifacts found within a built environment as well as the overall environmental style; the assumption is that individuals develop environments that reflect and reinforce who they perceive themselves to be.[6] Humans strive to create environments that best satisfy their personality needs, whether or not that environment is supportive of their offspring. Few of us realize that, through the creation of a particular environment—a casual one versus a highly structured one, for example—we shape our offspring's personalities and futures (Figure 3.2a and b).

Primary Components of Personality

Designers who strive to understand their clients' personalities are more likely to engage in more communication with their clients, which enables them to develop the most appropriate designs and thus better meet their clients' needs. There are many methods to determine personality traits. Two of the most well-known traits are the so-called Big Five Inventory and the Myers–Briggs Type Indicator.

The Big Five Inventory (BFI) was developed by Oliver John, who discovered, through statistical analyses, how different personality traits are correlated in humans. The Big Five were a result of analyses of traits that tend to co-occur in the general population.[7] For example, affectionate and kind are both traits associated with being agreeable, but a person can be kind without being affectionate.

Figure 3.2a and b: Analyze these two environments in an effort to understand the inhabitants' personalities and the likely personality traits of children reared in these environments. Client A's environment appears to be more casual; the design lends itself to more exploration, such as dropping balls from the second floor or hiding around the stairwell (a). Client B's environment seems more structured; as such, the children are likely to be raised with a high degree of order and discipline so that running and playing indoors would likely be stymied (b). We can therefore hypothesize that children growing up in Client A's environment would be more outgoing and inquisitive than those in Client B's environment.

Because each human is unique, variations occur; however, statistical studies show that most people who are kind are also affectionate, explaining the reason for the broader factor of "agreeable." The key to understanding the Big Five dimensions is to recognize that they are purposely broad and that each dimension consists of more specific traits.

Here are the BFI broad dimensions.[8]

- *Extraversion* (sometimes called *surgency*) encompasses such specific traits as talkativeness, energy, and assertiveness.
- *Agreeableness* includes traits such as sympathy, kindness, and affection.
- *Conscientiousness* includes being organized, thorough, and able to make plans.
- *Neuroticism* (sometimes reversed and called *emotional stability*) is characterized by traits such as tension, moodiness, and anxiety.
- *Openness* to new experiences (sometimes called *intellect* or *culture*) includes having wide interests and being imaginative and insightful.

Katharine Briggs and Isabel Briggs Myers developed the Myers-Briggs Type Indicator (MBTI) by expanding on personality types developed by Carl Jung (a pioneering psychologist) to include a judging–perceiving function. The resulting four primary personality dichotomies converge to create sixteen possible personality profiles. Each of the four dichotomies—introvert–extrovert, sensory–intuitive, judger–perceiver, and thinker–feeler—are identified, which is how they end up with personality profiles such as INTP, ENFJ, and so on. However, for our purposes, we can scale each of the categories according to extremes. Using a zero-to-ten scale for the introvert–extrovert component, clients are asked where they would rank themselves; a self-ranking of seven, for example, would indicate a person who is more extroverted than introverted (Figure 3.3).

Introvert–Extrovert

This personality component relates to a person being either outgoing or reserved. People with extroverted personalities tend to have high energy levels, prefer to multitask, and like to be around other people. They also tend to talk more than listen, act before thinking, and can be easily distracted. Those with introverted personalities tend to be quiet thinkers, prefer being in a supportive role where attention is not focused on them, and appear to be reserved. They enjoy time alone, prefer to focus on one task at a time, and possess great capacity for concentration.

People with extroverted personalities tend to prefer to be physically closer to others and therefore often use open furniture arrangements, whereas those with introverted personalities tend to use closed arrangements (and chairs as opposed to sofas) that establish distances appropriate to their comfort zones. Extroverts like to be near other people and do not allow furniture to separate them, whereas introverts prefer the safety of separation. In larger social gatherings, extroverts prefer group seating that facilitates greater contact and interaction, and introverts appreciate single seats and unobstructed paths that allow free mobility and easy escape (Figure 3.4).

Sensory–Intuitive

People who are sensors usually focus on details rather than the big picture. They embrace practicality, are aware of finer points and subtleties, remember significant attributes and comments, and view life as a step-by-step process; they are pragmatic, live in the here and now, and tend to trust actual experience. Intuitive people are more creative in their thought processes, prefer their environments to be more complicated, are inventive in their ideas, and consider future implications. They focus on big-picture potential, trust their gut instincts, and enjoy learning.

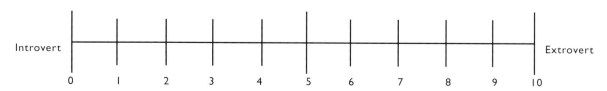

Introvert   Extrovert

0   1   2   3   4   5   6   7   8   9   10

Figure 3.3: People are rarely entirely introverted or extroverted. Instead, most individuals lay somewhere on a continuum.

Sensing clients will likely scrutinize the functional aspects of design, be more concerned with budget issues, and probably want a cost-benefit analysis of proposed designs. Intuitive clients will likely desire more complex designs, embrace the creative exploration of ideas and concepts, and view designs in their entirety as opposed to their individual components.

Thinker–Feeler

Thinkers tend to be reserved, draw their conclusions from objective facts, and respond best to rational nonarbitrary arguments; they are usually honest and direct, value honesty and fairness, and are motivated by end results. Thinkers are also inclined to be business oriented in that they view design in terms of cost-benefit ratios. They also see more flaws and often argue or debate issues. Feelers, on the contrary, often make decisions based on personal values and how they feel at the time; they appear to be warm and friendly and tend to be diplomatic and tactful. Feelers tend to value harmony, take issues personally, and avoid conflict.

Clients who rank high in either disposition can be somewhat challenging. Thinkers will demand extensive research and will question a designer's decisions whereas feelers will be less aggressive because they respect and value the professional and will seek to avoid friction. Feelers tend to make emotional rather than carefully considered decisions, and thus will rely heavily on a designer's ability to ask the right questions and read between the lines (Figure 3.5).

Judger–Perceiver

Judgers are inclined to be more serious and conventional in their preferred design styles. Such people tend not to mix work with social activities. They expect dedication and will not respond well to delays; they make decisions fairly easily but also value rules and order over creativity. Perceivers tend to be more playful and unconventional. They value the freedom of spontaneity and like to keep their options open; therefore, they usually have difficulty making and adhering to decisions. They can be oblivious to time and schedules and value creativity, especially when it goes against the norm (Figure 3.6).

Figure 3.4 (top): Notice the ample ingress and egress from either side allows easy withdrawal from conversations that become too intimate. The abundance of open space allows less intimate interaction and even privacy among others because people can move about without talking for too long with one person. This environment may appear best suited to extroverts, but closer inspection reveals that it is ideal for introverts who must engage in social activities but who want some distance between themselves and others.

Figure 3.5 (bottom): The inclusion of the pool with the rock waterfall may appeal to the thinker's business side as adding equity to the home. Conversely, the thinker may consider the extravagant waterfall as an unnecessary expense. The feeler will most likely view the pool and waterfall as being soothing and tranquil.

Judgers can pose a challenge for design professionals because not only do they tend to watch deadlines, hold designers to their projected schedules, and have little tolerance for delays, but also have a very traditional or conventional style from which they don't usually deviate (Figure 3.7). They often regard designers and planners as the hired help and will avoid casual social interaction. Perceivers, conversely, tend to embrace creativity and innovation in the design process and desire more social interaction; however, explicit communication is crucial, for if unchecked they can accumulate numerous change orders and will ultimately feel betrayed by the cost increases resulting from those orders. Table 3.2 summarizes design preferences according to the primary components of personality.

It is important to note that personality is not an all or nothing trait. As humans our personalities vary in degrees as well as evolve with age.

Figure 3.6 (top): Notice the whimsical style in the room's décor. These kinds of nontraditional designs tend to be attractive to perceivers because they not only go against the norm but also show a sense of creativity and uniqueness.

Figure 3.7 (bottom): Notice the dark leather sofa, the many books in the shelving, and the wood floors, all of which suggest that a person with traditional preferences occupies this space. Individuals having judgers' personality traits tend to prefer traditional furnishings and décor.

Table 3.2 Components of Personality and Associated Design Preferences

PERSONALITY TYPE	PERSONALITY TRAIT	DESIGN PREFERENCES
Introvert	Guarded	Desires safe haven or privacy. Prefers closed furniture arrangements.
Extrovert	Social	Desires interaction or stimulation. Prefers open furniture arrangements.
Sensory	Detail-oriented	Embraces practicality. Will scrutinize details and functionality of design.
Intuitive	Instinctual	Prefers complex creative environments. Is guided by gut feelings.
Thinker	Rational	Views design in terms of cost-benefit ratio and demands extensive research.
Feeler	Harmonious	Values harmony, respects professionals, but will rely heavily on designer's ability to ask the right questions and read between the lines.
Judger	Demanding	Has high expectations and conventional design preferences.
Perceiver	Unconventional	Values uniqueness and innovation but may have difficulty making and sticking with decisions.

Table 3.3 Locus of Control Characteristics

CHARACTERISTIC	EXTERNAL LOCUS OF CONTROL	INTERNAL LOCUS OF CONTROL
Overall view of life	External forces (fate, luck, chance, powerful others) control their destinies.	People's own actions, choices, and pursuits control their destinies.
Response to frustration and time orientation	Less able to tolerate delays in rewards or to plan for long-term goals. Decreases efforts in response to setbacks.	Works for achievements, tolerates delays in rewards, and plans for long-term goals. Increases efforts in response to setbacks.
Sources of support	Relies on religion and superstition	Internal, but able to utilize social supports
Space requirements	Prefers large interpersonal spaces	Tolerates higher-density situations

Other Influential Components of Personality

Two other personality components influence design choices and level of satisfaction: a person's locus of control orientation and the ability to screen or block out environmental stimuli.

Internal–External Locus of Control

Locus of control relates to how we view our opportunities and ourselves (Table 3.3). Individuals who have a strong **external locus of control (ELOC)**—or *externals*—tend to believe that they have no control over their lives because external forces (e.g., fate, luck, chance, or a higher being) control them. Conversely, those with a strong **internal locus of control (ILOC)**—or *internals*—believe that their own actions, choices, and pursuits control their lives.

The development of the locus of control depends greatly on our formative environments. For example, internals often grow up in families who emphasize effort, education, responsibility, and thinking, whereas externals tend to be of lower socioeconomic status and come from settings of financial instability. The key variable for externals is their perceived inability to influence future outcomes.

Externals tend to prefer larger interpersonal spaces,[9] whereas internals tend to tolerate higher-density situations.[10] Consider this from a control perspective: Internals believe that they can influence outcomes; thus, if their personal space is invaded they will not hesitate to attempt to regain control of that space or leave the situation. They are likely to be proactive throughout the design process and will try to influence future safety and resale

value. One study found that internals usually prefer the simplicity and orderliness of straight lines, whereas externals usually prefer more romantic-style buildings with rolling lines and greater detail.[11] Additionally, externals tend to be superstitious and gain support through external means, which is why they tend to have more artifacts.

Screener–Nonscreener

Our ability to screen out unwanted environmental stimuli (e.g., noise, glare, and odor) depends on how we respond to various distractions that arrive in different patterns. People who are less affected by a stimulus are considered to possess greater screening abilities, whereas those who are bothered or annoyed by a stimulus are thought to be nonscreeners. Nonscreeners are inclined to be much more sensitive to and affected by their environments than are screeners. The implications are clearly more profound with clients who are nonscreeners; however, just because screeners can filter out negative environmental factors does not mean that they are unaffected by them. Therefore, with both screeners and nonscreeners it is important for designers to consider the quantity of stimulation in the environment as well as the level or the degree of stimulation from each source. Because the nonscreener will be most affected by stimuli, understanding the different environmental uses and individual preferences will be important to the success of a design.

All life-forms are affected by numerous sources of stimulation within their environments. In humans, the five senses—taste, touch, sound, smell, and sight—transmit these stimuli to the brain. Negotiating among various and often competing stimuli is the brain's job. In this way, the brain functions as an information manager. However, when too much stimulation or information is provided, our brains cannot adequately filter and sort through everything. Designers, by analyzing the surrounding environments, can either increase or decrease levels of stimulation with their designs to meet their clients' needs and desires.

Information Management

Many humans see natural environments as stockpiles of raw material to fulfill their wants and needs.[12, 13] This statement can be considered not only physically, referring to natural resources such as water, wood, and oil, but also metaphorically because sights, sounds, smells, and tactile sensations are raw materials that the brain interprets and organizes according to preferences and desires. How we perceive, come to know, and remember a particular environment depends in part on the aggregation of the raw materials being filtered and processed by our brains. This section examines the roles of perception, cognition, and memory as they relate to our understanding and cataloging of the world around us. **Perception**, the first phase in our overall thought process, involves the interpretation of sensations. **Cognition**, the second phase, is the way that information and knowledge comes to be known, through the actions of perception, reasoning, or intuition.

Imagine several people shopping for a home and being shown an old, abandoned house. Each person's response to that property will be unique to some degree; some people may view it as being grotesque or even haunted, some may be excited by the challenge of renovation, and still others may disregard the structure completely and concentrate on the land. Such judgments are based on a person's perceptions of the available sensory information compared with a mental image of that person's ideal home.

Perception

One of the most influential psychological variables affecting design, perception can also be one of the most frustrating human attributes for designers because of its highly subjective nature and the numerous gray areas and myriad variables that affect interpretation. Most individuals will interpret an object or scene in the same manner, regardless of distance, angle, or brightness; however, **selective attention** allows them to focus on select stimuli and screen out others. Understanding how people perceive their environments is vital to the design process. Design professionals should strive to create as much perceptual consistency as possible because there are many ways in which people's perceptions differ. If the end product is not what the client had in mind, then the designer did not understand how the client sees the world.

Simply stated, perception is the interpretation of incoming sensory information, and is influenced by a variety of factors (e.g., the type and level of the stimulus as well as a person's past experiences, level of attention to detail, readiness to respond, level of motivation, and current emotional state). Once sensory organs gather stimuli, the brain interprets that information through the process we know as perception. As the brain continues to receive and organize the incoming information into patterns of understanding we move beyond perception to cognition. In this manner, perception consists of various elements of sensation organized into patterns that result in cognition. The functional perspective of standard perceptual theory claims that certain patterns of features or cues give us direct and immediate perceptions of an environment; however, some experts believe that we perceive individual features, and others believe that we perceive patterns.

Gibson provides a useful perspective: his holistic **ecological perception** theory states that instead of perceiving individual components of an environment, we organize all of those components into recognizable patterns. This suggests that much of our information is directly and immediately conveyed by perceptual patterns without higher-brain processing; that is, people notice and respond to meaning that already exists in an ecologically structured environment.[14] For example, through popular media we have come to regard the combination of graffiti, barred windows, and pawnbrokers' shops as being an unsafe environment. It is not the actual barred windows or graffiti in their singularity that convey the message that an environment is unsafe, but rather the aggregate of the scene compared with similar combinations that we have experienced in the past (Figure 3.8).

Figure 3.8: This scene contains specific elements to which people will respond, such as the fireplace, but the lack of other furnishings with descriptive characteristics means that the environment's overall purpose is unclear, It could be interpreted as a sitting room, home office, or library. This room therefore shows a limitation to Gibson's ecological perception theory.

Certain classifications of perception are germane to the design fields. For example, depth perception seems to rely almost exclusively on visual cues and can lead to perceptions of either real or illusionary depth. Many patterns and certain color combinations can either create or inhibit depth perception, as shown in Figure 3.9.

Our **attitude** or predisposition strongly influences our perception. Attitudes and beliefs tend to follow the values of the era and vice versa.[15] For example, during the late 1800s the general attitude toward design favored detail-oriented craftsmanship, whereas present-day attitudes tend to favor economical and easily assembled designs. Attitude is made up of a mental and neural state of readiness to respond, organized perspectives that have been established through experience, and feelings that exert a directive or dynamic influence on behavior.[16] Moreover, attitude resembles a behavioral disposition that is

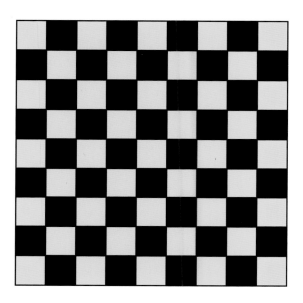

Figure 3.9: This illustration is two-dimensional, but the combination of black and yellow along with the checkerboard pattern create the illusion of depth for many people.

highly contingent on many external factors such as culture and tradition.

As a factor in the client–designer relationship, attitude consists of three psychological components: cognitive (thinking), affective (feeling), and behavioral (doing). These components are based on **cognitive truths**, beliefs held to be true about a particular instance, object, or situation. For example, if you know that ceramic tile floors feel cold to bare feet, this cognitive truth will generate an affective reaction to cold tile, which will lead to a behavioral response based on your cognitive truth. Therefore, a client to whom cold tile is unpleasant may forbid the use of tile anywhere in the home, whereas a client who finds it refreshing may insist on tiling an entire bathroom suite.

Cognition

Broadly defined, *cognition* is the process of thinking, knowing, or mentally processing information. **Environmental cognition** is a more specific concept that refers to how people understand, diagnose, and interact with the environment. Much of cognitive theory contends that solutions to problems are based on rules that either are not necessarily understood but promise a solution or are understood but do not guarantee a solution. Some researchers maintain that environmental cognition is simply the way in which we acquire, store, organize, and recall information about locations, distances, and arrangements.

Spatial cognition is a specialized thinking process that helps humans to navigate through their environments. Most people do this by forming **cognitive maps**, pictorial and semantic (language) mental images of how places are arranged. As we move through these spaces, items within the spaces themselves are often regarded as having volume and depth. Gibson argues that as the observer moves through space, there is a flow of stimulation on the retinas that leads to a better understanding of the three-dimensional nature of our world. In other words, Gibson believes that we do not really have depth perception in the strictest sense of the word. Instead, "when the observer moves[,] his or her optic array is stimulated by the motion"—this means that while we cannot see depth, we can un-

Cognitive maps and the process of wayfinding are discussed in detail in Chapter 5.

derstand the spatial relationships among things by the way they are arranged and how they change as we move through the environment.

It is debatable whether we see depth or simply understand the spatial relationship between our bodies and other bodies and objects, and the relationship between two or more bodies and multiple objects. However, as we proceed through environments, we do so by creating images in our minds. Some people find their way by identifying landmarks and others by using written directions, whereas those who are born sightless create cognitive maps based primarily on physical contact. Nonspatial environmental cognition is a mental model of how we conceptualize ideas and concepts (e.g., categorizing local restaurants according to food, price, location, and so on). This form of cognition is capitalized on by critics (whether food, fashion, film, literary, or design), who provide means to categorize information.

Memory

A form of cognition, memory is the process that enables us to store information and recall it at a later time. Some investigators have suggested that there are three distinct phases in the formation of memories.

1. Perception and recording of a stimulus
2. Temporary maintenance of a perception (short-term memory)
3. Encoding into long-term memory

As introduced on page 40, procedural memory and declarative memory are two recognized types of long-term memory. *Procedural memory* involves the recall of learned skills and actions, such as finding your way out of a building. This function involves a step-by-step process and includes landmarks. Procedural memory has relevance for design because the incorporation of landmarks assists with spatial cognition. *Declarative memory* recalls facts, rules, concepts, and events, as well as specific stimuli, such as a particular scent, sound, sight, taste, or texture. This function is associated with feelings; for example, the smell of roses may evoke in people strong memories of their mothers. Planners and designers can increase their clients' levels of satisfaction by creating environments that evoke positive memories simply by incorporating elements from their clients' declarative memory banks. However, without careful research the plan may backfire: Even the most exquisite rose garden would be traumatic for a client who has a strong negative association with roses.

Memory is linked to memory loss, and each of us seems to have a different capacity for storing and recalling information. Theories that help to explain why we forget things include the concept of disuse, which proposes that forgetting occurs because stored information is not used (and may explain why many of us lose our math skills once we leave school), and the concept of interference, which suggests that new information is forgotten when old information interferes with the new. In many cases, however, memory loss is related to a physiological process called *amnesia*, or occurs as a result of brain cell deterioration related to stroke, cardiovascular disease, or dementia such as Alzheimer's disease. Using design as a means of association can help users make appropriate neural connections. For example, placing the commode in the direct line of sight (with the bathroom door open) for a patient with Alzheimer's disease has been shown to reduce episodes of incontinence.[17]

Perception, cognition, and memory are important aspects of the human mind that are affected by design. Perhaps one of the most influential perceptual theories for the design fields is the Gestalt theory of perception. This method of viewing the organization of visual elements of form, in either simple or complex patterns, enables a designer to conceptualize visual forms at a broad, holistic level.

Gestalt Psychology

Gestalt psychologists study the ways in which people organize and select from the vast array of stimuli presented to them, focusing on visual stimuli. Because humans are primarily visual by nature,[18] perception is heavily influenced by what a person sees as well as by other cues originating from sound, smell, and touch. Therefore, perception as a whole is greater than the sum of its parts, which is the premise behind Gestalt psychology.

Gestalt psychology contends that we are innately driven to experience the world around us in a regular, orderly, simplified, and symmetrical manner.[19] Gestalt psychologists reject a reductionist approach to perception (which analyzes a person's perception part by part and aggregates that information to draw a conclusion) because they assert that it is the interplay between the parts that creates perception.[20] Therefore, to analyze how a subject perceives a bowl of fruit, a reductionist researcher would determine how the subject perceives each piece of fruit and the bowl separately, whereas a Gestalt researcher would analyze a subject's perception of the whole scene. Some researchers question Gestalt's role in perception research,[21] although it does explain why a scene is perceived differently by different people. For example, the average person tends to prefer symmetry because of the appearance of balance, whereas designers tend to prefer asymmetry because of the artistry. It also explains how design can be used as a means of creating illusions (e.g., making items look larger, more spacious, or more illuminated than they actually are).[22]

Environmental perception is the human awareness and understanding of the environment in a general sense.[23] It is based on our experiences and psychological variables that are not part of our simple sensations, such as prior experiences and enculturation. Because of overlapping ideologies related to prior experiences and enculturation, Gestalt ideas and concepts have had the greatest influence of any school of thought on current architectural design practices.[24]

Gestalt rules and principles help to explain the human–environment relationship by explaining how we organize our perceptions of the everyday world into a coherent whole. Gestalt psychology has several laws that explain how we perceive and remember the world around us; they are presented in Table 3.4.

Gestalt concepts are applicable not only to visual images but also to human cognition. If you experience an event that does not quite make sense, you will tend to remember it in a way that has meaning, regardless of the accuracy of that meaning. Likewise,

Table 3.4 Gestalt Laws Related to Perception

EXPLANATION AND EXAMPLE	DESIGN APPLICATION

Law of Closure: Our minds fill in missing areas in an incomplete figure.

Figure 3.10a: This letter D is written with a dotted, and therefore incomplete, line. But because the human mind will complete missing areas we have little difficulty seeing the letter D.

Figure 3.11a: Although we know that there are three seperate pictures on the wall, our minds allow us to fill in the blanks to see one image.

Law of Similarity: We group similar items together within a larger form to create some form of continuity.

OOOOOOOOO
XXXXXXXXX
OOOOXOOOO
OOOOXOOOO
OOOOXOOOO
OOOOXOOOO

Figure 3.10b: In this pattern of X's and O's, the human mind will naturally group similar items together to identify the letter T.

Figure 3.11b: Despite the difference in setbacks and height, the continued use of the arch helps the human mind to merge the two structures into one.

Law of Proximity: When items are close together, they are seen as belonging together regardless of actual connection.

Figure 3.10c: Most of us will interpret these three lines as horizontal rather than vertical.

Figure 3.11c: Most of us will attribute the three paintings on the left as being from the same artist regardless of whether this is true simply because of the three paintings' proximity to one another and similar styles.

Law of Symmetry: We are compelled to group dissimilar items together so as to create symmetry.

Figure 3.10d: In this example, most of us will see three equidistant, unfinished squares regardless of the closer proximity of the two inner brackets.

Figure 3.11d: Notice the end table and the potted tree. This is an example of dissimilar items being used to create symmetry in this scene.

Law of Continuity: We see things as a continuation or connection rather than as separate entities.

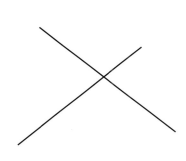

Figure 3.10e: In this image we are likely to see a cross or an X, but few people will interpret this image as two separate lines.

Figure 3.11e: Notice the door and windows. Most people will see these as an aggregate whole (door and windows), but few will see the individual panes of glass and the wood framing.

Law of Figure-Ground: We typically perceive only one aspect of an image when the image can be viewed in both positive–negative and foreground–background perspectives.

Figure 3.10f: In this example the positive image is darker in color; some may see it as an hourglass, some may see it as a goblet, and still others may see something completely different. However, not all people will be able to see a negative image of two faces, nose to nose, without having it pointed out to them.

Figure 3.11f: In this example the positive image can be either the grout lines or the tile squares. Likewise, the paintings to the right can capture the black lines, the white empty spaces, or the colored squares.

we usually recall a particular environment not in isolation, but rather in relation to its surroundings. For example, if I ask you to think of a red apple, you will probably conceive of the apple in a setting, such as on a tree, on a table, or in a bowl, but not in its singularity. However, there are limitations to Gestalt perceptions, and many now consider Gestalt theory to apply to only a limited number of situations and to provide only an understanding of visual forms at a broad and holistic level.

How much and to what we direct our attention is an important concept in understanding perception. Research suggests that we select a relatively small, manageable portion of the available information on which to focus our attention; that we either focus on specific details or vast expanses within an environment; and that we will more readily notice the comforts or discomforts within and any new feature or scene in an environment.[25] For example, in a waiting room we will either focus our attention on a painting or see the overall design without particularly noticing the artwork. Along the same lines, a simplified view of a classic psychophysics principle, the Weber-Fechner law, states that as we habituate (get used to) a particular stimulus, the level of intensity of a new stimulus must be greater or proportionate to the current stimulus for the new to be perceived as different.[26] Without any change in the environment, we run the risk of developing **environmental numbness** and not taking particular notice of an environment until some feature attracts our attention.[27]

Environmental numbness can cause us to overlook problems or hazards, but it can be prevented; we can consciously redirect our perceptions and cognitions within those environments we cannot alter, and we can periodically update or refresh our personal spaces.

Summary Review

Environmental psychology attempts to merge vital elements of biology, social science, and design practices as a means of supporting human occupation of the built environment. Our understanding of the neurobiological relationship between humans and their environments is still in its infancy and, due to lack of collaborative study among the social, biological, and neurological sciences and design,

the environment itself is often neglected as a behavioral factor. Only through continued scientific research and greater attention to the human experience in relation to design can we continue to learn about the effects of design on humans.

Our behaviors derive from a complicated mixture of social situation, developmental stage, personality, brain chemistry, and the physical environment. Neuroscience, for example, may provide research data to help explain the neurochemical reactions to environmental combinations such as lighting, color, and odor. As we gain more insights into the neurochemical reactions related to the secretion, absorption, and mixture of certain neurochemicals, we may be able to predict more precisely human behavioral responses to certain environments.

Contributing to the body's chemical reactions are each individual's personality, locus of control, and unique abilities to screen unwanted stimuli. A host of personality tests is currently available, including Oliver John's Big Five Inventory (BFI), developed through a statistical analysis of how different personality traits are correlated in humans, and the Myers-Briggs Type Indicator (MBTI), developed by Katharine Briggs and Isabel Briggs Myers by expanding on Carl Jung's personality types. In addition to these personality profiles, personal disposition, referred to in this chapter as internal locus of control (ILOC) and external locus of control (ELOC), has an important influence on how individuals view themselves in relation to the world (either through the belief that they can control their own lives or that their lives are controlled by fate); it also provides valuable insight into how they may react, and to some degree identify their design preferences.

The ability and level to screen out unwanted or undesirable stimuli is a unique trait of each person. Many of us cannot concentrate when music is playing in a room, while others have a hard time ignoring bright colors; both situations offer challenges that are routinely faced by designers. An understanding of the screening abilities and needs of the intended user of a designed environment will enable a designer to conceive and develop environments that are appropriate to the user.

Perception, cognition, and memory are at the foundation of all design projects. Designers hope their designs will be perceived favorably as a client or the general public interprets incoming sensory information and processes that information by reasoning, or intuition, to create knowledge or an opinion. This opinion becomes information stored to be recalled at a later time. Designers have often called upon the principles of Gestalt psychology to assist them in this challenge. By following these principles, designers can obtain a broad, holistic understanding of visual forms. However, when we view a scene, we must remember that we cannot do so without our values, opinions, attitudes, and emotions influencing our perceptions and subsequent cognitions.

Discussion Questions

1. Discuss the possible effects of a poorly designed apartment on the tenants' moods and identify which physiological responses they may have while coping with the design flaws. Consider flaws that tenants can manipulate as well as those they cannot (e.g., unattractive wall paint and kitchen cabinets that are too shallow to hold dinner plates).

2. Discuss the expected differences in preference for living space between an "adrenaline junkie" and a person who regularly practices deep meditation.

3. Discuss the effects of personality on career choices, and examine how a person's career choice affects his or her residential preferences. Compare and contrast different personality types.

4. Discuss the concept of *internal-external locus of control* in relation to the design process, as well as ways that you, as the designer, would be able to identify this characteristic in a client.

5. Discuss ways *perception* can be influenced, and consider them in relation to the design process, from site selection to trim selection. How may you prepare clients to consider a broader range of options?

6. This chapter refers to a study that demonstrated that Alzheimer's patients benefit by having commodes placed in their direct lines of sight. Discuss other ways that architecture and design can be used to improve the mental functions of students, children, employees, or patients.

Learning Activities

1. Design an experiment or a test that would help your clients identify their emotional and physiological responses to different styles of architecture.

2. Locate a website that offers personality tests (e.g., Myers-Briggs Type Indicator, Kiersey Temperament, or Jungian Tests). Team up with a classmate; after you both take the same test, swap results and, based on the information in this chapter (and without discussing the results), write a basic analysis of how you would work with a client of that personality type.

3. Based on the results of your personality test, design a room that would very clearly indicate your personality type. Using the descriptions in this chapter as a starting point, draw a section or sketch the room to illustrate your design plan. Write a brief response to your design as to whether this room would actually suit you, and discuss the effectiveness of personality profiling in design.

4. Design a classroom that would allow both *screeners* and *nonscreeners* to study and learn effectively, noting what allowances need to be made for both types. Keep in mind that even though screeners can block out external stimuli, each individual will have a maximum and minimum threshold.

5. Venture to a location you have never entered before (e.g., a restaurant, museum, or specialty store). Record your first impressions when you view the exterior of the building and again when you enter it. Spend time observing, smelling, touching, and listening in the interior space. After ten minutes, without consulting your previous notes, record your impressions on a fresh page. Continue observing, and discuss the location and the interior with someone and record your impressions. Upon leaving, reassess the exterior and record your thoughts. Review all of your notes, and compare the changes in your impressions based on increased environmental cognition.

6. Using the Gestalt rules and principles outlined in Table 3.4, create your own illustrations for each law.

Terminology

attitude   A belief that tends to follow the values of an era and vice versa; predisposition

cognition   Mental analysis; how information is interpreted, stored, and recalled; second phase in overall thought process

cognitive map   Pictorial and semantic (language) mental image of an environment or setting

cognitive truth   Belief that may not necessarily be factual but is held to be true

declarative memory   Recall that uses semantic representations as related to facts, rules, and concepts (see procedural memory)

ecological perception   Theory that much environmental information is conveyed by perceptual patterns that do not require higher-brain processing

environmental cognition   Analysis of how we understand, diagnose, and interact within the environment

environmental numbness   State of being unaware of one's environment until it or something in it changes

environmental perception   Our interpretation of the world around us as influenced by our experiences and sensations

external locus of control   Tendency to believe that our lives are controlled by external forces (e.g., fate, luck, chance, and higher powers) rather than ourselves

fight-or-flight response   An automatic response to stress that is perceived to be a survival threat

internal locus of control   Tendency to believe that personal actions, choices, and pursuits control our lives

perception   Initial gathering of information through the five senses and subsequent organization of that sensory input; first phase in the overall thought process

procedural memory   Recall based on performance, actions, and skills (see declarative memory)

selective attention   Ability to focus on select stimuli and screen out others

spatial cognition   Specialized thinking process used to navigate environments

References

1. Chein, I. (1954). The environment as a determinant of behavior. *Journal of Social Psychology, 39,* 115–137.

2. Gifford, R. (2003). *Environmental psychology: Practice and principles* (3rd ed.), Canada: Optimal Books.

3. Lambert, G.W., Reid, C., Kay, D. M., Jennings, G. L., and Esler, M.D. (2003). Effect of sunlight and season on serotonin turnover in the brain. *Lancet, 360,* 1840–43.

4. Harris, J. R. (1998). *The nurture assumption: Why children turn out the way they do.* New York: Free Press.

5. McCrae, R. R., and Costa, P. T. Jr. (1999). A five-factor theory of personality. In L. A. Pervin and O. P. John (Eds.), *Handbook of personality theory and research* (pp. 139–153). New York: Guilford Press.

6. Gosling, S. D., Ko, S. J., Mannarelli, T., and Morris, M. E. (2003). A room with a cue: Personality judgments based on offices and bedrooms. *Journal of Personality and Social Psychology, 83-3,* 379–398.

7. John, O. P., & Srivastava, S. (1999). The Big Five trait taxonomy: History, measurement, and theoretical perspectives. In L. A. Pervin and O. P. John (Eds.), *Handbook of personality: Theory and research* (2nd ed., pp. 102-138). New York: Guilford.

8. See note 7.

9. Heckel, R. V., and Hiers, J. M. (1977). Social distance and locus of control. *Journal of Clinical Psychology, 33,* 469–474.

10. Verbrugge, L. M., and Taylor, R. B. (1980). Consequences of population density and size. *Urban Affairs Quarterly, 16-3,* 135–160.

11. Juhasz, J. B., and Paxson, L. (1978). Personality and preference for architectural style. *Perceptual and Motor Skills, 47,* 341–343.

12. Merchant, C. (1993). *Radical ecology: The search for a livable world.* New York: Routledge.

13. Oelschlaeger, M. (1991). *The idea of wilderness: From prehistory to the age of ecology.* New Haven, CT: Yale University Press.

14. Gibson, J. J. (1979). *An ecological approach to visual perception.* Boston: Houghton Mifflin.

15. Bell, P. A., Greene, T. C., Fisher, J. D., and Baum, A. (2001). *Environmental psychology* (5th ed.). Orlando, FL: Harcourt College Publishers.

16. Allport, G. W. (1961). *Pattern and growth in personality*. New York: Holt, Rinehart and Winston.

17. Morgan, D. G., and Stewart, N. J. (1999). Multiple occupancy versus private rooms on dementia care units. *Environment and Behavior, 30-4*, 48–503.

18. Gifford, R., and Ng, C. F. (1983). The relative contribution of visual and auditory cues to environmental perception. *Journal of Environmental Psychology, 3*, 375–384.

19. Boeree, C. G. (1998–2004). *The history of psychology*. Retrieved 3 March 2004 from www.ship.edu/~cgboeree/historyofpsych.html.

20. See note 14.

21. Goldstein, E. B. (1999). *Sensation and perception* (5th ed.). Pacific Grove, CA: Brooks/Cole.

22. See note 14.

23. Whyte, A. V. T. (1977). *Field methods in guide lines for field studies in environmental perception*, MAB. Technical Notes. Paris, France: UNESCO.

24. Lang, J. (1987). *Creating architectural theory: The role of the behavioral sciences in environmental design*. New York: Van Nostrand Reinhold.

25. See note 2.

26. Sommer, R. (1973) *Design awareness*. New York: Holt, Rinehart and Winston.

27. Gifford, R. (1976). Environmental numbness in the classroom. *Journal of Experimental Education, 44-3*, 4–7.

FOUR

The Psychology of Behavior

When examining the human–environment relationship, we must consider the joint nature of utilitarian needs and aesthetic qualities. For example, furniture design can contribute positively to the overall décor of an environment as well as help to create the illusion of greater space. However, if the furnishings are not suitable for the intended users, then that environment has failed its primary purpose of supporting human habitation. Whereas many traditional design fields usually emphasize one over the other, research inspired by behavioral scientists has spawned a cooperative effort to develop designs that are both attractive and functional. Given the choice, however, the average person tends to prefer utilitarian over aesthetic qualities[1] for both practical and economic reasons. The designer's notion of good design may differ from that of the average person, due, in part, to the artistic nature that motivates most designers to pursue their chosen field. The average person, in contrast, is frequently motivated by convenience and functionality.

In general, people view an overall environment in one of two ways: according to personal preferences and desires (subjectively) or from a disinterested perspective (objectively). When viewing an environment in which they have no vested interest, such as an acquaintance's home, most people are customarily objective in their assessments. When viewing their own homes, however, their assessments are usually more subjective.

A person's vested interest will determine how and at what emotional level he or she will view an environment. Most individuals planning to occupy a particular environment will likely view it from more of a functionalist perspective; those who design an environment will probably have more of an aesthetic perspective. This incongruity can be a source of conflict if potential occupants who are viewing an environment for the first time prioritize incoming information according to utilitarian rather than aesthetic needs.

Consider the design of the sleeping quarters shown in Figure 4.1. Person A and Person B each view this hotel-room design and evaluate it according to their individual needs.

Person A
- Comfortable bed
- Nice dark room
- Quiet and peaceful

Person B
- Quiet and peaceful
- Nice dark room
- Comfortable bed

A hotel designed to accommodate Person A would benefit from having more of the budget assigned to the bed and bedding, whereas more funds for drapes, tapestries, and other sound-absorbing materials would be appropriate for Person B.

How we prioritize incoming stimuli influences our first impressions. Most people prioritize incoming environmental information according to their experiences. For example, if a person who is looking to purchase a house sees evidence of a wild party having occurred the night before at the house next door, there is a greater probability that he or she will be acutely aware of the potential for constant noise and be discouraged.

DESIGN APPLICATION. The process of having clients list and prioritize the attributes they find desirable in a home (or specific room) allows

Figure 4.1: This bed may not look soft and inviting, but to some people, it is more important that the room appears quiet and peaceful.

designers to see what bears the greatest importance for each client. Doing this greatly facilitates the creation of environmental designs that will more readily meet clients' individual needs. Designers should ask clients to list the features they believe influence their perceptions of an environment. Over the course of the week, designers should have their clients prioritize those features, so they can develop designs to accommodate those priorities.

The concepts discussed in this chapter are highly subjective and individualistic in nature and will therefore pose a challenge to design professionals. One person's interpretation of a particular environment may not be the same as another's, but designs that will appeal to most people can be developed more easily if planners and designers first identify common variables among the target occupants or users.

Psychological Health

Within the broad field of psychology is a subgroup of psychologists who seek to discover and promote the factors that allow individuals and communities to thrive. This approach differs from the traditional approach of the field, which has been to view people (and the world) from a medical perspective, as if they (and it) were ill and needed fixing. Instead, positive psychology attempts to look beyond the causes of disease and disorders to identify sources that bring about psychological health. This paradigm is well suited for the design fields because many designers already build on the positive by following trends and styles that please their clients.

When we consider psychological health in the context of design, we must include both the positive approach, identifying those design attributes that promote health and well-being, as well as the traditional approach, focusing on people's disorders to alleviate them. People who are in good psychological health are considered to have well developed ego strength, adjustment capabilities, and self-confidence; they seem better equipped to handle environmental stressors and, as such, are prone to making better choices regarding their environments. Those who are not can be compromised in their abilities to handle certain environmental stressors and may make poor environmental judgments. Clients who lack self-confidence may refrain from discussing what they consider to be a poor design concept for fear of looking foolish or making the designer unhappy. Poor psychological health seems to be perpetuated most by environments in which people are forced to surrender control, such as hospitals, prisons, workplaces, or schools. In these environments the person who is not in optimal psychological health often opts to be silent rather than be labeled a troublemaker.

Environmental attributes possess variables that help us make sense of our world. **Moderators** are variables that interact with another variable in a way that changes the effects of that variable.[2] **Mediators** are behavioral variables that work in a sequence between other variables. These variables mediate the relationship between the cause and action.[3] For example, a person who wants to work out in a gym will need artificial light to see because the gym has no windows. In this case the light is the moderator because whether the person works out is dependent upon the presence of light. Say the person gets to the gym and finds out that he is not allowed to work out because he has not paid his bill. Paying the bill is an example of a mediator because his behavior affects the relationship between the cause (going to the gym) and the action (working out).

Our environmental perceptions are also influenced by variables called *proceedings*, which in turn are affected by our psychological health. **Internal proceedings** are mental processes that help us to represent, explain, and predict the world around us; they are the thoughts and feelings that give order to our environments. These will influence our **external proceedings**, the way we interact with the physical environment and other individuals. For example, if we go to a neighborhood that seems run-down and we see graffiti, trash, and potentially hostile residents, our internal proceedings may lead us to conclude that we are not safe there. This belief will influence our external proceedings, and we will be less likely to engage in conversation or make eye contact with others and more likely to walk faster or to seek escape.

Listed below are five kinds of personal impressions that influence environmental perceptions.[4]

1. *Environmental descriptions* allow us to encapsulate certain aspects of an environment, namely the features or attributes (descriptors) that stand out in our minds after leaving it. Environmental descriptors—such as a church steeple—provide information about a place and therefore allow us to understand and respond to it.

2. *Judgment of beauty* is a notion that varies according to our culture and our individual preferences and experiences. For this evaluation, both the viewer and the scene must be considered by the designer who seeks to develop an aesthetically appropriate environment because an environment that may be beautiful to one person may be repugnant to another. However, two aspects of beauty seem to transcend time and culture: that of visual penetration, which is the ability to see for distances, and the amount of visual depth, which is the three-dimensional spatial relationship between objects in an environment.

3. *Emotional (affective) reactions* to an environment are typically less intense than other reactions, yet tend to be persistent and cumulative. Environmental factors, such as noise and pollution, combine with our individual sociability factors (whether introvert or extrovert) and our desires for arousal to influence our perceptions of environmental desirability. Once our threshold has been exceeded, we will likely react negatively to that environment. For example, if you work all day in a noisy, crowded factory and go to a noisy, crowded restaurant afterward, you are far more likely to perceive that restaurant negatively.

4. *Environmental meaning* develops as we gain greater familiarity with an environment over time. We first start to identify with certain environments and form attachments as a result; we then begin to **self-identify**, defining ourselves according to our own personal experiences and the tangible components that represent and symbolize our places in the world. For example, people from the Midwest and Northeast regions of the United States are used to having lush lawns and will prefer to have sod laid for aesthetic reasons even in desert regions. When individuals become attached to their residences, neighborhoods, workplaces, or recreational sites, those environments become more than mere places; they hold emotional meaning for the occupants and users. If a college that is located in a rough neighborhood is offered a new site overlooking a beautiful view, the alumni association will most likely oppose the move because the members' fond memories are tied to the original site.

5. *Risk of safety* simply refers to whether an individual perceives danger from crime, accidents, or physical hazards within an environment. Risk of safety is relative to a person's point of reference; for example, Chicago's South Side may seem risky to someone from a small town but perfectly safe to someone who grew up there.

Meanings of Place

The idea of place depends on how individuals conceptualize the world around them. In the field of environmental psychology, the word *place* encompasses more specific notions: place identity, sense of place, and place attachment. Each of these terms attempts to describe a host of emotions that define the meaning of place, which is, essentially, how we see ourselves in relation to others and a particular environment, and explains the emotional bond we may develop to that place over time. Some researchers feel that place identity, sense of place, and place attachment are becoming less clearly defined for people due to increased globalization and use of technology.[5]

Place identity refers to how people incorporate a place into the larger concept of their own identities or senses of self.[6,7] A place with which we identify generally provides a sense of continuity, helps to reinforce self-identity and self-esteem, enables us to get things done, and provides either a sense of individuality (distinctiveness from others) or a sense of belonging. Place identity cognitions have two basic functions: defining who people are and defending or protecting them from settings and properties that threaten who they are and what they want to be. For example, many Texans have incorporated their state's identity into their own, and this bond is manifested through displays of Lone Star pride; similarly, individuals who are satisfied with their workplace environments are more likely to incorporate them into their own identities; this translates to greater loyalty to the companies for which they work.

Sense of place develops when a level of comfort and feelings of safety are associated with a place, which for many people translates to a sense of belonging. On a cultural level, people may integrate a place into their cultural identity (e.g., most Muslims identify with the city of Mecca). On a personal level, a person's home often evokes a strong sense of place, as can a person's favorite hangout, store, or school. For people to develop a sense of place, they must feel as if they belong there and be able to make an emotional connection. For example, young people often form a sense of place with dance clubs, coffee shops, or other hangouts. However, a New England octogenarian is as likely to develop a sense of place for an alternative club in San Francisco's Haight-Ashbury district as a young punk rocker is to develop a sense of place for a bingo hall in rural America. In short, a person's personal history combines with a setting to form a sense of place.

Place attachment may be defined as a person's bond with the social and physical environments of a place.[8] These are settings that have deep meaning for people[9] because their identities are intricately woven into those places, which therefore serve as restorative environments.[10] Three broad elements serve to attach people to a place and affect their well-being: their personal characteristics and behaviors; the availability of facilities, opportunities, and resources; and a sense of belonging.[11] Simply put, we form attachments to places that not only define or express who we are (support our self-images) but also give us a sense of belonging, freedom, or both (provide psychological security).

People develop attachments to places after years of living and experiencing many emotions in one residence. Certain smells, artifacts, and sounds within an environment evoke memories and feelings. Place attachment is an important aspect of our lives, especially for the development of children.[12] We can positively influence the well-being of children and adolescents by establishing continuity and safety within their homes.[13–15] The development of place attachment can be compromised by circumstances, settings, or both; and our emotional bonds with our environments can change—for better or for worse—as a result of a significant event or the passage of time, as illustrated by the following examples.

> Example 1: A man from Illinois suffered incessant peer abuse throughout high school. As an adult, he suppresses his Midwestern upbringing and has globalized his emotions into abject disdain for the entire region.

> Example 2: On a ten-point scale, a person may have had an attachment level of ten to a tree house as a child but only a level of four as an adult.

Loss of place attachment can occur within any environment (personal, educational, professional, or recreational). Therefore, how we relate our experiences to our perceptions of a setting will affect our levels of attachment to it. Similarly, people who have developed strong bonds of place attachment often experience negative outcomes when those bonds are forcibly severed (e.g., an elderly person being relocated from a lifelong residence to a long-term-care facility).

Place attachment has six means of cultural transmission:[16]

1. *Genealogy*: People and places are linked through some sort of historical connection. For example, a family may have worked at the same local mill, or passed down the family homestead, for multiple generations.

2. *Loss and destruction*: When places are destroyed people often develop nostalgic feelings that lead to a form of attachment. Developers of urban spaces often utilize vacant spaces as building sites. If the empty space was once a community garden, long-time residents of the area may develop nostalgic feelings for the garden once the building takes over the space.

3. *Ownership*: When we own a place for a period of time it becomes part of us, and vice versa. For many, owning a home is a source of pride and sense of accomplishment. As such, ownership often translates into greater maintenance and custodianship. Many companies capitalize on this notion by providing profit-sharing programs to their employees. Designers can work with employees to develop unique designs for their work spaces as another way to facilitate feelings of ownership within the workplace.

4. *Cosmological*: A culture may have a religious or mythical connection to a certain place (Jerusalem, Mecca, and Bethlehem all have profound spiritual connections), and often-times groups of people see their sacred areas as the center of the universe. Designers can assure cosmological connections through the use of appropriate structures, artifacts, and images.

5. *Pilgrimage*: Usually a religious journey to a sacred site, a pilgrimage can also be secular. For example, an older woman who feels compelled to make a daily pilgrimage to her parents' burial site regardless of the weather, her state of health, and whether she has company is going on a secular pilgrimage, as is a married couple who returns each year to the place where they first met.

6. *Narrative*: People can become attached to a place through romantic or idealistic stories. During the early 20th century, thousands of Europeans immigrated to the United States because they believed stories that the "streets were paved with gold" (i.e., that wealth and opportunity were abundant), and many of their second- and third-generation offspring feel an attachment to the idea of "the old country" even though they never experienced life there.

Gifford described four processes relative to meanings of place that have the greatest applicability to the design field: attachment, ideological communication, personal communication, and architectural purpose[17] (Figure 4.2a–d). As noted earlier, *place attachment* is a profound personal connection to a site. *Ideological communication* is an abstract concept that a place or building signifies. *Personal communication* is what the site "says" about the occupants. *Architectural purpose* is the building's function relative to its form or appearance.

Territoriality

Although inherent in all animal species, territoriality is difficult to define. For our purposes, it can be explained according to the work of Julian Edney:[18] Territoriality involves the possession and defense of physical space, as well as the exclusiveness of use, marking, personalization, and identity (as a reflection of the self) of that space by the occupant or user. In most civilizations, territories serve to organize human behaviors so that acts of violence, aggression, and overt domination are reduced.

Territories provide individuals with reliable access to the social contacts they need; through the use of *organizers* (e.g., directional signs, fences, or edging), mutually acceptable ground rules are established and social behaviors can be transacted without confusion. When we are "on our own turf" we feel more secure and expect to be able to control or dominate an intruder. The level of dominance is closely associated with the amount and quality of a territory. For example, when a friend comes into your home it is expected that you will control the distribution of food and beverages. Social rules reinforce territorial boundaries, but as competition for resources increases so too will territorial behaviors by those with established territories, as well as territorial infringement by individuals who struggle to obtain resources. If food is a scarce commodity, you may be more reluctant to offer it to a guest, who may

Figure 4.2a–d: *Place attachment* refers to the attachment that many people develop to their homes over time. Despite how the surrounding environment has evolved and the size of the house, this property is clearly a castle in its owner's eyes (a). *Ideological communication* is exemplified with the University of Moscow in Russia, which illustrates former Soviet leader Joseph Stalin's preference for this distinctive shape, nicknamed "Stalin's Wedding Cake." For many people, this building is a symbolic representation of Stalin's rule (b). The *architectural purpose* of a home is usually that of a detached suburban home. However, many people have opted for homes that fulfill dual architectural purposes such as this, which serves as both a house and a boat (c). *Personal communication* refers to what a site "says" about the occupants. During the past few decades, people have opted to construct homes utilizing a host of nontraditional styles. Like most homes, these avant-garde styles represent some aspect of the inhabitant that he or she wishes to convey to the world (d).

b

a

c

d

be more likely to risk territorial infringement in search of it.

Most animals mark their territories (i.e., place an object or substance to indicate territorial intention or control); for example, a dog marks an object or area with urine, whereas a moviegoer marks a theater seat by placing a personal belonging on it. Most of us have been conditioned to recognize numerous signs and symbols indicating territoriality (Figure 4.3), but not all boundaries are clear to all parties. For example, not everyone is aware that many older people will prop a chair against a table to symbolize their claim to a particular seat. Humans often mark their territories through personalization in ways that represent some aspect of their identities (e.g., vanity license plates on cars or family photos in office cubicles).

Research indicates that "female" markers are much less effective than "male" markers (e.g., scarves versus sport coats) for territorial defense; therefore, a male's territory is less likely to be invaded than a female's.[19, 20] This may be due to primordial notions of dominance and submission. The concept of territorial marking can be integrated into the design of a built environment in overt or subtle ways. An overt example would be inscribing a person's name into a concrete walkway; a subtler example is shown in Figure 4.4.

Types of Territories

Different territories meet different needs. Territories as personal spaces can be thought of as being primary, secondary, or public. **Primary territories** are spaces that are generally owned by individuals or primary groups and are controlled on a relatively permanent basis. The psychological importance of a primary territory to its occupants is always high. **Secondary territories** are less important than primary spaces; they are usually not owned by the occupants, and possess only moderate significance to them. Psychological control of these territories is less essential to the current occupants and is likely to change, rotate, or be shared with others. **Public territories** are open to anyone in good standing within the community, and occupants cannot expect to have much control. A

Figure 4.3 (left): Territoriality involves the possession and defense (i.e., control) of physical space. This bedroom is a territory that is defended by *personalization* and *organizers*.

Figure 4.4 (below): Although the symbol on this fireplace mantel looks nondescript and may appear to be merely decorative, closer inspection reveals it is composed of two letter Ks back-to-back. The surnames of both homeowners begin with K; therefore, the symbol is actually a subtle territorial marker.

Newman's theory and others that relate to territorial control are discussed in detail in Chapter 6.

person's home is a primary territory, the workplace is a secondary territory, and a public park or beach is public territory. **Interactional territories** are temporarily controlled by a group of interacting individuals. There is usually little overt marking of these territories, yet entry into them is often perceived as interference. For example, groups of students often use library conference rooms as places to discuss group projects or for study groups; although no one student or group owns the room, should another student or group enter while the others occupy it, conflict may arise.

Territories can be permanent, temporary, or temporarily permanent. Whereas a home is a permanent territory, the guest room would be a temporary territory for out-of-town friends. Likewise, a rented apartment is a temporarily permanent territory for tenants (although the tenants don't own the building, no one can enter that territory without their permission as long as they pay their rent).

Territorial Infringement

Conflict and aggression can result when territories have high perceived value or when territorial boundaries are unclear (Box 4.1). **Territorial infringements** can be classified as invasion, violation, and contamination. **Territorial invasion** occurs when an outsider physically enters a territory with the intention of taking control of it. On a macro level, territorial invasion occurs when countries invade other countries; at a micro level, it occurs when gangs invade other gangs' turfs. Invasion need not be violent; members of blended families often feel invaded when forced to share their primary territories with new parents or siblings. **Territorial violation** is a temporary incursion into someone else's territory. The violator's goal is usually not ownership, but rather annoyance, harm, or power. For example, a territorial violation occurs when a child sneaks into and rummages through an older sibling's room. **Territorial contamination** is the intentional fouling of someone else's territory. Vandalism, graffiti, stink bombs, and excessive noise are only a few examples of territorial contamination.

Defensible Space

Territoriality is based on feelings of ownership. Defensible space is also related to control; we de-fend our control of a territory by anticipating infringement and acting to prevent invasion, violation, or contamination. Oscar Newman, the originator of defensible space theory, contended that the physical environment can create perceived territories and that certain physical features frequently encourage people to appropriate and exercise territorial control.[21]

Personal Space

Personal space is actually an *inter*personal phenomenon; it does not exist without interaction. Humans, like most animals, subconsciously use

---

Box 4.1 Problem Solving in the Real World

Rita and Mike had been dating for a little more than a year when he asked her to marry him. The two were wed six months later. Given that she lived in a three-bedroom house with her two daughters, ages 6 and 4, and he lived with his 13-year-old daughter in a two-bedroom apartment, it made sense for Mike to move in with Rita.

Rita decided to move her six-year-old into the four-year-old's bedroom so that Mike's daughter could have a room of her own. Over the next couple of months the six-year-old started acting out her emotions by deliberately scattering her belongings around the house and even started to write on the walls. I am not a licensed psychologist, but I knew from studies of territoriality that she probably felt invaded by Mike and even more so by his daughter; not only did she now have to share her mother and her home but also her bedroom. As a practicing designer, I suggested that we include the six-year-old in a brainstorming activity to determine how she could gain control over her new territory. The first thing we did was to hang drawstring draperies from ceiling to floor so she could enjoy privacy while sharing a room with her sister. Since each child was feeling somewhat disoriented by the merge, we decided that each child should select wall art for the dining room. The six-year-old, having lost the most, was allowed to select the piece that would serve as the room's focal point.

By understanding the role of territoriality, particularly in a primary territory setting, designers can assist in reinforcing a person's sense of belonging and ownership. In this case, we were able to help the child establish territorial boundaries and reassert her place in the family by allowing her to select a piece of art that represented her sense of identity, which then served as a focal point in the design.

consistent interorganism spacing to regulate basic biological processes such as mating and food gathering.[22] We tolerate less interpersonal distance when we feel strong, secure, or safe, and require more when we feel weak, insecure, or at risk. Personal space is a subjective experience. Although most of us are familiar with the concept of a fixed, invisible comfort zone or buffer that surrounds an individual, personal space is essentially a portable, flexible territory relative to other people and things. According to *social learning theories*, personal space is culturally acquired over time and results from a combination of a person's history and others' behavioral reinforcement; in other words, personal space is learned behavior for us.[23] For example, we tend to afford more personal space to those whom we perceive to be of greater or lesser status,[24] and the greater the difference in status or condition, the greater distance we create.[25] This attitude applies not only to social position but also to power, dominance, familiarity, and physical ability and appearance.

Personal space requirements—more precisely, interpersonal distance preferences—vary, depending on personality and stage of development, cultural and societal norms, and the physical environmental (e.g., social and spatial density, climate, and our level of familiarity with the environment). For instance, our personal space needs are likely to be much greater with a rude stranger in a public setting on a hot day than with an intimate partner in a personal setting on a cold night. Edward Hall defined four basic interpersonal distance zones: intimate (0 to 18 inches), personal (18 inches to 4 feet), social (4 to 12 feet), and public (12 to 25 feet).[26] These zones are illustrated in Table 4.1.

Robert Sommer's studies demonstrate the importance of both distance and angle of orientation in cooperative and competitive interactions: Individuals in competitive settings chose to sit farther apart using direct orientation (face-to-face seating), whereas those in cooperative settings sat closer together using indirect orientation (side-by-side seating).[27] However, in everyday situations, direct orientation usually leads to cooperation, whereas indirect orientation supports competition; for example, a couple will sit face-to-face over an intimate dinner, whereas same-sex friends will sit side by side as they compete for attention at a singles bar[28] (Figure 4.5a and b).

Michael Argyle and Janet Dean's *affiliative-conflict theory* suggests that we strive to balance our social needs because we simultaneously want to be closer to and farther from others and that we use interpersonal distance to balance these conflicting desires.[29] Eric Knowles clarified this *approach-avoidance concept*, noting that even our rewarding relationships involve avoidance tendencies, we do want to approach certain individuals, and interpersonal discomfort results when there is a discrepancy between our approach and avoidance tendencies.[30,31] During typical social interactions, we tend to believe that we are either closer to or farther from others than we actually are and that others occupy more of our personal space than we occupy of theirs.[32,33] We are less tolerant of closer distances in dimmer lighting,[34] seem to need more space in corners as compared with the centers of rooms,[35] and tend to prefer more personal space

Social learning theories are discussed in greater detail in Chapter 2.

Table 4.1 Hall's Interpersonal Distance Zones

PERSONAL SPACE ZONES	DESCRIPTIONS
Intimate (0–18")	Kept by two or more people who share a strong bond (e.g., lovers, close friends, and family members).
Personal (18"–4')	Used by casual friends or people with close social contacts (e.g., friendly acquaintances, same-department coworkers, and members of clubs or like organizations).
Social (4'–12')	Maintained by people who *know* of one another but do not really know one another and who come together for a common purpose (e.g., friends of friends, casual acquaintances, and fellow employees from other departments).
Public (12'–25')	Used by people whose only association is being in the same place at the same time. In public situations we usually prefer keeping as much space as possible between ourselves and the strangers around us, and when this distance is violated we often start to feel crowded (e.g., two people waiting for a train on the same platform).

when we are indoors than we do when we are outside.[36] In other words, we seem to require more personal space when there is or appears to be less physical space.

Intrusion of personal space by another person causes positive or negative arousal, which creates

Figure 4.5a and b: Traditional pubs, bars, and diners have been designed according to male personal space preferences. Stools line the length of counters and more often than not are occupied by men, perhaps because side-by-side seating limits self-disclosure and intimate conversations (a). Whereas restaurant seating is designed to support cooperative behaviors; tables that seat two or four people facilitate intimate conversations that a person can regulate by leaning forward or backward in his or her chair (b).

changes in the social relationship. When someone is slightly too close or too far away, we usually compensate for our discomfort by taking a step backward or forward. Several studies have shown that men become more uncomfortable as distances grow inappropriately close, whereas women become more uncomfortable as distances grow inappropriately far.[37–39] The effects of personal space violation can be profound. There are many ways to violate someone's personal space, including physical invasion, eavesdropping, staring or watching without permission, playing loud music, and reeking of perfume or body odor (Box 4.2).

As noted earlier, balance is important to social processes. Many people use environmental features to reinforce their boundaries; for example, a person with strong personal space needs may sit behind a desk during a meeting, whereas someone with a smaller comfort zone may prefer group seating (Figure 4.6).

DESIGN APPLICATION. Spacing mechanisms used in design serve to help maintain an individual's sense of personal space. In architecture, walls, windows, statuary, pillars, and varying floor elevations serve to assist in the management of personal space; in interior design, end tables, chairs with armrests, and potted plants can help to increase interpersonal distances. In interior design, furniture and layout often serve

Box 4.2 Characteristics of Personal Space

Personal space can best be described as an oval-shaped bubble that surrounds each of us as we move through the world around us. About three-quarters of the bubble extends ahead of us to ensure greater personal space before us and less behind us; however, our bubbles expand and contract based on the people and situations we encounter. We tend to require the least amount of personal space behind us. Sitting side by side causes personal space requirements to increase, and when one partner turns to face the other, the personal space continues to grow. Personal space is a highly subjective psychological phenomena. It is regulated by such factors as age (e.g., adults require more than children), gender (e.g., males require more than females), culture (e.g., Northern Europeans require more than Southern Europeans), and societal adaptation (e.g., most Asian cultures regulate personal space according to social rules of conduct, such as avoiding eye contact).

to establish appropriate interpersonal spacing. The size of tables can serve to regulate how close one chair is from another.

Privacy

Irwin Altman defined privacy as the selective control over another's access to our selves, our groups, or our environments.[40] Privacy involves more than just control of physical access; our visual, acoustical, olfactory, or informational privacy can also be infringed upon. There are many different interpretations of privacy because people's needs to regulate their access to others and their abilities to express those needs are influenced by their culture, personalities, stages of life, gender, and experiences. For example, young children need much less privacy than adolescents. Generally, our privacy needs vary according to the social situations in which we find ourselves.

Alan Westin[41] described four aspects of privacy: solitude, intimacy, anonymity, and reserve.

Figure 4.6: In an airport terminal, the width of the chairs in the seating area helps to support personal space zones, which are reinforced by the armrests. Most seating used for royalty, in high-end restaurants, and in first-class airline cabins are designed to accommodate personal space zones; maintaining our personal space is so important that we are willing to pay extra for it.

- *Solitude* refers to the state of being alone, free from physical invasion. Although most people associate privacy with solitude, solitude doesn't always equate with privacy; for example, many elderly people live alone not to ensure their privacy but because they are alone. Darhl Pedersen[42] distinguished solitude as the state of being alone among others (e.g., in the Swiss Family Robinson, the family members *are* alone on the island after their shipwreck) and *isolation* as the state of being alone with no others nearby (e.g., Robinson Crusoe, the early years, when he sets out alone, with no other company).
- *Intimacy* refers to group privacy and emotional bonds (e.g., lovers who want to be alone together). Whereas solitude refers to physical invasion, intimacy deals with visual and auditory invasion (e.g., a young couple showing their affection for each other in public may become annoyed with someone who stares at and makes comments about them). Pedersen[43] described two psychologically distinct forms: *intimacy with friends* and *intimacy with family*. The level and type of intimacy obtained from each form is highly contingent on a person's gen-

der, culture, and stage of life. For example, adolescents are more likely to share intimate thoughts with a friend and reveal intimate vulnerabilities to a family member.
- *Anonymity*, the desire to be invisible or unknown to others, is a form of privacy commonly lost by celebrities and others who want to be among others but do not want to personally interact with or be identified by them.
- *Reserve* refers to the distance people create between themselves and others by erecting psychological barriers to protect inner thoughts and feelings, in public or private. Most of us know people about whom we can say, "I've known them for years, but I really don't know anything *about* them."

Our notions of privacy depend greatly on our cultural backgrounds, socioeconomic levels, personalities, and the prevailing social norms and behaviors. To some, privacy is a behavioral expectation, while to others it is a personal value, preference, or need. Altman considered privacy to be central among human behavior processes related to space and noted four interpersonal control mechanisms by which people regulate their privacy: personal

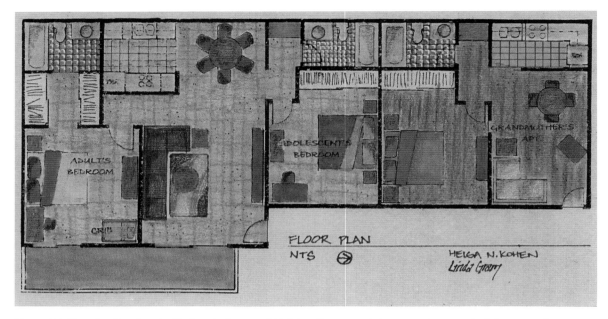

Figure 4.7: Many families faced with the challenges of high healthcare costs incorporate separate living areas (i.e., accessory dwellings) into their homes to accommodate elderly family members. However, elderly people must have a sense of control over both their privacy and independence. In this floor plan, the primary living centers for the main household and the accessory dwelling are located at opposite ends of the home, and each residence has its own entry.

space, territory, verbal behavior, and nonverbal behavior.[44] Westin described four essential functions of privacy: to regulate or protect communication, facilitate a sense of control, allow the integration of information about ourselves and our relationships, and allow emotional release.[45] Pedersen contended that privacy is a basic human need with six further functions: uninterrupted contemplation, rejuvenation, creative expression, recovery, concealment of self, and concealment of illicit activities.[46] Gifford and Price noted that privacy affects how we learn to adapt to space and is important during our development as children.[47] Drawing upon these ideas, we may deduce that people who are deprived of adequate privacy (e.g., institutionalized persons) can feel they lack control over their lives; this can lead to lack of autonomy, learned dependence upon others, and learned helplessness.

Privacy is controlled through verbal, nonverbal, cognitive, environmental, temporal, and cultural mechanisms;[48] also it is also controlled by economics. The wealthy can easily exclude others most of the time, and many middle-income families opt to live in gated communities that protect them at a minimum from door-to-door solicitors,

but lower-income and especially poor people must often struggle to maintain social and physical privacy.

Designers of the built environment are obliged not only to identify their clients' individual privacy needs, but also to design according to those needs. For example, designing a custom home involves identifying the owner's notions and expectations of privacy, whereas designing a workplace setting requires a broader approach to meet the needs of current and future employees (Figure 4.7).

DESIGN APPLICATION. Design professionals can ensure their clients' desired levels of privacy via city planning initiatives, such as transforming through streets into dead ends; landscape initiatives, such as the use of hedge lines and strategically placed bushes or trees; architectural initiatives, such as the incorporation of porches, photosensitive windows, and good insulation; and interior design initiatives, such the use of "occupied/vacant" signs on restroom doors, furniture arrangements that increase or decrease conversational privacy, and special wall textures (transparent, translucent, or opaque walls), as desired (Figure 4.8a and b).

Crowding and Density

Population density does not determine **crowding**, a subjective term that refers to people feeling physically constrained and that others interfere with them.[49] This happens to us when there are too many people, too little space, or both. Briefly, **density** is the ratio of individuals to an area. **Social density** is created by a varied number of individuals occupying a fixed amount of space, whereas **spatial density** is created by a fixed number of individuals occupying different size spaces. There is a link between density and crowding. However, density is objective; it is a mathematical formula used in building codes to calculate the maximum number of people who can safely occupy a space and exit it in an emergency. In contrast, crowding is psychological; it is individualistic and therefore highly subjective. For example, *social density* tends to be high in elevators, but because *crowding* is a psychological rather than a physical condition, most of the occupants may not feel crowded.

Planners and designers must be aware that perceptions and evaluations of crowding vary according to individual experiences, circumstances, belief systems, and personalities. Different cultures respond differently to high social density. Many Asian cultures, for example, tend to have smaller personal space zones due to centuries of high population density and have adopted social coping mechanisms such as avoiding eye contact and limiting expansive physical gestures. Whereas Asians prefer social barriers to crowding, people from the Mediterranean prefer physical barriers.[50] While these are only two examples, such cultural nuances can affect a person's idea of crowding. In most settings, density is relative to proximity (the number and nearness of others). Knowles proposed a proximity concept of social interaction: The effects of other people on an individual will increase with the square root of their number (crowding) and decrease with the square root of their distance (Figure 4.9).[51]

Three components of crowding are the situation, the emotion (affect), and the behavior produced by the emotion.[52, 53] The nature and organization of an environment make up the situation; this will evoke an emotional reaction, which, if unresolved, will result in a behavioral manifestation. Once we begin feeling the negative pressures of density, our predominating concerns are loss of

a

b

Figure 4.8a and b: In both of these instances, barriers create a sense of privacy: Trees shield the house from the street noise (a), while the Plexiglas barriers above the backs of the booth create a sense of personal privacy among the diners (b).

control, the inability to act toward a particular goal, having a limited number of options, or any combination of these. Imagine you are stuck in traffic and cannot determine the cause or the outcome. Your loss of cognitive control will likely cause you to experience more stress than another driver who can see that an accident down the road has just been cleared away; in this instance, knowledge is the mitigating factor between the situation and the affect

Figure 4.9: In the first frame of this comic strip, the woman notices the crowded conditions but is still fairly calm. In the second frame she starts to feel crowded; her senses become more acute and she feels anxious. In the third frame, she progresses to the fight-or-flight re-action as she pushes people out of her way.

(emotional reaction). The inability to act toward your goal is exemplified by being unable to arrive at work on time, which evokes feelings of frustration; here, the situation or environment is causing the af-fect. Your feeling that you lack control can be exac-erbated by your limited options; but whether you choose to breathe deeply and meditate until the traffic clears or drive along the sidewalk, your action is the behavioral response.

High density is a source of physiological arousal and stress, as demonstrated by numerous laboratory and field studies of its effects on skin conductance and perspiration; cardiac functions, including blood

pressure; and other stress indicators. High density is often, but not always, a precursor to feelings of crowding. However, a study of prisons found that crowding, but not density, was related to psycholog-ical stress.[54] This is supported by findings that crowding results in psychological stress when per-ceived control is lower.[55] Feelings of crowdedness are directly proportional to the level of stress a per-son feels; increased crowding equals increased stress and vice versa. Therefore, regardless of actual density levels, feeling crowded can negatively affect health.

Our experience of crowding within an environ-ment depends on our perceived levels of control over it, our purpose for being in it, our expecta-tions of it, and the others sharing it. For example, being in a police holding cell with two other occu-pants can evoke stronger feelings of crowding than being at an after-Christmas sale event with a mul-titude of shoppers. We expect airports and amuse-ment parks to be packed with people and do not usually experience much crowding in these envi-ronments; however, we also expect libraries and grocery stores to be relatively empty at certain times, and when they are not we tend to feel more crowded. Studies suggest that feelings of crowding are intensified when people are in an environment with others whom they perceive to be different from themselves.[56, 57] When dining out, a sophisti-cated urbanite will likely feel more crowded among working-class individuals at a greasy spoon than among the same number of peers at a chic café of equal size and space.

Feelings of crowding are highly contingent on individual personality factors. For example, people with a strong internal locus of control believe they can control many aspects of their lives and will at-tempt to control situations presented by crowded environments, which increases their odds of incur-ring greater levels of stress. In extreme situations, individuals subjected to crowding may engage in behaviors related to learned helplessness. Mood and timing are important factors (i.e., the less en-joyable a situation, the more crowded we feel).[58] High social density is a source of emotional arousal, and feelings of crowding are affected by a person's sense of control. Most of us would expect a popular club to be crowded, and when we choose to go dancing amid high social density we are unlikely to experience feelings of crowding.

Research has shown that people who prefer and expect high-density situations respond to them more favorably than people who have no preferences or expectations.[59]

Experience can help to alleviate some of the feelings associated with crowding. Consider the extremely dense populations of New York City, Hong Kong, and Mexico City; people who choose to live in such environments are better able to adapt to crowded conditions than those who are locked in by career or personal obligations. Experience may help us cope with crowding in secondary environments (e.g., grocery store or shopping mall), but not in primary ones (e.g., home or workplace).[60] Feelings of crowding can be minimized to some extent through the use of information. In a study resulting from the findings of a *postoccupancy evaluation*, visitors reported significantly reduced perceived crowding, discomfort, anger, and confusion when directional signs were added to a crowded lobby.[61] In short, the perceived, rather than actual, level of density determines our behavioral responses (Figure 4.10).[62]

DESIGN APPLICATION. Although designers have little control over occupancy loads, design can decrease perceptions of space confinement (e.g., by installing mirrors and increasing light levels), which will, in turn, decrease perceptions of crowding. Brightness (from wall or accent colors, natural or artificial light sources, or combinations of these) leads to less perceived crowding, and sunnier rooms are perceived to be less crowded than darker rooms.[63–65] Less crowding is elicited by rectangular rooms than square ones,[66] by rooms with well-defined corners as opposed to curved walls,[67] and by rooms with windows and doors (visual escapes). The presence of visual distractions—such as potted plants, wall art, and garden sculptures—leads to more perceived space.[68, 69] A room will be perceived to be more crowded if the furniture is arranged in the center rather than at the sides.[70] Sociofugal **(facing away) seating arrangements tend to elicit less crowding than those that are** sociopetal **(facing others).[71]**

Research has determined that people have spatial needs in both horizontal and vertical dimensions. If available space is limited in one, our spatial needs will increase in the other. The same study

Figure 4.10: Crowding is highly subjective and depends greatly on the person experiencing the effect, but there are mitigating factors. Just because a lot of people occupy a space does not mean that they feel crowded; for instance, if this environment is a local hangout where everyone knows everyone else, the likelihood of individuals feeling the effects of crowding will be low. However, if strangers were to walk in and realize that everyone already knows everyone else, they could feel insecure and therefore very crowded. Even the regulars may feel the effects of crowding if they are tired, not having fun, or made the object of derision or hostility.

also demonstrated that males associate greater ceiling height with less crowding.[72] According to another study, when temperatures rise, so do our perceptions of crowding; users of public transportation reported more crowding when the temperature was high although the number of passengers remained constant.[73]

Crowds are large, temporary groups of often emotional individuals. We tend to regard crowds in terms of negative consequences (consider the destructiveness of a lynch mob or riotous sports fans or concertgoers), but the excitement of a crowd can be infectious and help even the staunchest curmudgeon have fun and release tension. A crowd's key characteristics include the anonymity and suggestibility of its members, and the unpredictability of the group's behavior.[74] Emotions are intensified and amplified within crowds; as individual arousal increases, so does the group's, and people start to lose their individuality and engage in groupthink (the "mob mentality"). Emotional intensity can reach such a frenzied state that the emotions themselves become unstable. (Think of this in terms of being so happy or so angry that you burst into tears.) In a crowd of sports fans, for example, we see personal space boundaries shrink as the enthusiasm becomes contagious. In these situations the group is highly suggestible; people tend to behave not as individuals but rather as elements of the crowd. The crowd shares an emotion that can escalate to a state of frenzy that overwhelms the entire group—a condition that has resulted in the trampling deaths of individuals at contests, concerts, and political gatherings throughout human history.

Designers can incorporate safety features into buildings or facilities that will help law enforcement defuse mobs. Such examples include creating a stronger stimulus than that which caused the mob scene (e.g., very bright lights with a loud sound), but that doesn't cause a diversion that may feed the frenzy (e.g, a sprinkler system that may effectively break up a crowd but also create pandemonium and a stampede as people seek escape).

Summary Review

Our psychological health influences the way we perceive and make choices about our environments and cope with environmental stressors. Much study has been focused on the negative consequences of poor psychological health. However, other researchers are trying to understand the factors that lead to positive psychological health. We know that poor psychological health appears to be perpetuated by environments that preclude personal control. Conversely, good psychological health appears to be promoted through environments that satisfy our myriad needs.

When we stay within an environment for an extended period of time, we begin to assign meaning to it based on how we perceive it and the emotional bonds we develop to it over time. Place identity (how we incorporate a place into the larger concept of our identities), sense of place (sense of belonging with a particular environment), and place attachment (how we intertwine our experiences with a setting) are terms that describe the host of emotions that help define the meaning of place for an individual.

All residences, workplaces, and communities are territories and have territories within them, and territorial infringements can result from ignorance, competition for resources, or overt aggression fueled by a need to dominate. In Western culture, there are three main territories: primary, secondary, and public. Primary territories are generally owned and controlled on a permanent basis, while secondary territories possess moderate significance and are likely to change, rotate, or be shared. These differ from public territories, which are typically open to anyone in the community who is in good standing. Each of these territories can be invaded, violated, or contaminated. When this occurs, psychologists term the event a *territorial infringement*.

Personal space is a flexible, portable territory; it can stretch and shrink according to the environment, mood, time of day, and social relationship. It's an *inter*personal phenomenon, meaning that it does not exist without interaction and is contingent on factors such as hierarchical status, our orientations to one another, and our individual dispositions (happy, sad, healthy, ill, and so on) at a given time.

Privacy is a human need that must be considered in terms of both preventing invasions and providing or supporting essential functions. Physical, visual, acoustical, or olfactory privacy can be infringed upon through invasion, violation, or contamination. Our notions of privacy depend greatly on our cultural backgrounds, socioeconomic levels, personalities, and the prevailing social norms and behaviors. For many, privacy is a behavioral expectation, while to others it is a personal value, preference, or need. Whichever the case, we use many mechanisms to control our privacy, including verbal, nonverbal, cognitive, environmental, temporal, and cultural mechanisms,.

Although we can measure social density, crowding is a psychological construct that is highly individualistic. There are three components of crowding: the situation, emotion, and subsequent behavior. Feelings of crowding and the resultant behaviors depend greatly on personality and the particular situation. For many, reducing eye contact and restricting socialization can minimize feelings of crowding. Conversely, a person's perception of crowding can be enhanced by racial, ethnic, cultural, sexual, or social unfamiliarity. As we gain experience with a particular environment, the foresight we develop can help to alleviate some of the feelings associated with crowding.

space in nursery school children. *Canadian Journal of Behavioral Science, 11*, 318–326.

48. Harris, P. B., Brown, B. B., and Werner, C. M. (1996). Privacy regulation and place attachment: predicting attachments to a student family housing facility. *Journal of Environmental Psychology, 16–4*, 287–301

49. See note 2.

50. Nasar, J. L., and Min, M. S. (1984). Modifiers of perceived spaciousness and crowding: A cross-cultural study. Paper presented at the annual meeting of the American Psychological Association, Toronto, Ontario.

51. Knowles, E. S. (1983). Social physics and the effects of others: Tests of the effects of audience size and distance on social judgments and behavior. *Journal of Personality and Social Psychology, 45*, 1263–1279.

52. Montano, D., and Adamopoulos, J. (1984). The perception of crowding in interpersonal situations: Affective and behavioral responses. *Environment and Behavior, 16*, 643–666.

53. See note 4.

54. Schaeffer, M. A., Baum, A., Paulus, P. B., and Gaes, G. G. (1988). Architecturally mediated effects of social density in prison. *Environment and Behavior, 20*, 3–19.

55. Lepore, S. J., Evans, G. W., and Schneider, M. L. (1992). Role of control and social support in explaining the stress of hassles and crowding. *Environment and Behavior, 24*, 795–811.

56. Manning, R. E. (1985) Crowding norms in backcountry settings: A review and synthesis. *Journal of Leisure Research, 17*, 75–89.

57. Schaeffer, G. H., and Patterson, M. L. (1980). Intimacy, arousal and small group crowding. *Journal of Personal and Social Psychology, 38*, 283–290.

58. Mueller, C. W. (1984). The effects of mood and type and timing of influence on the perception of crowding. *Journal of Psychology, 116*, 155–158.

59. Womble, P., and Studebaker, S. (1981). Crowding in a national park campground: Katmai National Monument in Alaska. *Environment and Behavior, 13*, 557–573.

60. See note 4.

61. Wener, R., and Kaminoff, R. D. (1983). Improving environmental information: Effects of signs on perceived crowding and behavior. *Environment and Behavior, 15*, 3–20.

62. Rapoport, A. (1975). Toward a redefinition of density. *Environment and Behavior, 7*, 133–158.

63. Schiffenbauer, A. I. (1979). Designing for high-density living. In. J. R. Aiello and A. Baum (Eds.), *Residential crowding and design*. New York: Plenum Press.

64. Nasar, J. L., and Min, M. S. (1984). Modifiers of perceived spaciousness and crowding: A cross-cultural study. Paper presented at the annual meeting of the American Psychological Association, Toronto, Ontario.

65. Mandel, D. R., Baron, R. M., and Fisher, J. D. (1980). Room utilization and dimensions of density: Effects of height and view. *Environment and Behavior, 12*, 308–319.

66. Desor, J. A. (1972). Toward a psychological theory of crowding. *Journal of Personality and Social Psychology, 21*, 79–83.

67. Rotton, J. (1987). Hemmed in and hating it: Effects of shape of room on tolerance for crowding. *Perceptual and Motor Skills, 64*, 285–286.

68. Baum, A., and Davis, G. E. (1976). Spatial and social aspects of crowding perception. *Environment and Behavior, 8*, 527–545.

69. Worchel, S., and Teddlie, C. (1976). The experience of crowding: A two-factor theory. *Journal of Personality and Social Psychology, 34*, 36–40.

70. Sinha, S. P., Nayyar, P., and Mukherjee, N. (1995). Perception of crowding among children and adolescents. *Journal of Social Psychology, 135*, 263–268.

71. Wener, R. (1977). Non-density factors in the perception of crowding. *Dissertation Abstracts International, 37D*, 3560–3570.

72. Savinar, J. (1975). The effect of ceiling height on personal space. *Man-Environment Systems, 5-5*, 321–324.

73. Ruback, R. B., and Pandey, J. (1992). Very hot and really crowded: Quasi-experimental investigations of Indian "tempos." *Environment and Behavior, 24*, 527–554.

74. Weller, M. P. (1985). Crowds, mobs, and riots. *Medicine, Science, and the Law, 25*, 295–303.

Human Perception
and Environmental Design

The design of successful environments is dependent on factors that go beyond simple biology and are greatly influenced by the way in which we view the world. Over time, humans developed certain behavioral patterns that led to the survival of our species: Men were expected to provide and protect while women were expected to nurture and care. Throughout several millennia of established gender roles and expectations, men and women have evolved to experience their environments differently. Those experiences are often related to their respective roles in life. In the same sense, we have also come to regard aesthetics and color from different perspectives, including that of regional culture. Arctic cultures use dozens of specific terms to describe snow and those who live in xeric habitats (areas that require a minimum amount of moisture) similarly use numerous terms to describe sand. Just the same, people who are affected by and work with aesthetics are more sensitive to the nuances of color and design. For instance, the world of fashion and design uses many names to describe the color variations of pale red, but to most Western males, pink is pink.

Just as our genders contribute to our preferences and our perspectives of the world, so too do culture, tradition, and history. Consider the process of **wayfinding** (navigating to or from a particular destination). Finding our way involves various techniques and skills; some people use reference points such as landmarks, while others seem to have a built-in compass. However, an almost universal but incorrect assumption holds that men have a better sense of direction than women. Perhaps this is because men were the primary designers of our built environment and constructed it according to their wayfinding methods; had

women been the first builders, would we perceive their sense of direction as superior? Modern megastructures and concrete jungles have made wayfinding an issue of growing concern and a subject of intense study as scientists and design professionals strive to develop better means and methods that not only provide for ease of navigation but also blend into or even enhance overall designs.

Evolution and Gender

Men and women perceive, interpret, and describe their environments differently. This may be because the human psych has evolved more slowly than human technology; therefore, both sexes continue, at least to some extent, to behave and regard the environment according to primal instincts. Although current research is inconsistent with regard to gender differences in high-density conditions, traditional research suggests that males and females react as they do to these conditions because the socialization process teaches females to be relatively affiliative (i.e., able to connect or associate with others) and teaches males to be relatively competitive.[1,2] However, social gender roles are often based on the primary gender roles of early humans (primal gender roles).

Evolution of Gender Roles

In ancient hunter-gatherer societies, males hunted while females gathered edible vegetation. Men's primal gender role was to kill animals for food and protect the community. Hunting usually took place on open savannahs and plains with expansive views and few physical obstacles to navigate through or that would obstruct weapons in flight; males traveled wide ranges and dispersed to strategic positions

81

a

b

where they silently waited alone or in pairs for their prey. Individual males formed close groups only to conquer a potential meal or a group of invaders, after which they competed among themselves for the choicest cuts of meat, the enemies' weapons, or the most desirable females. Conversely, women in small groups foraged for vegetation within forests and jungles; these dense and complex environments limited peripheral and distance views, and hence promoted verbal communication (which additionally served to deter potential predators). Females were better at multitasking because they were responsible for childbearing and nurturing (offspring were usually either in, on, or near the mother's body), maintaining cooking fires, providing shelter, clothing, healthcare, and other domestic duties they shared with other females in the community.

The following research supports evolutionary theories of environmental behavior patterns:

- Numerous studies have shown that men consistently claim larger territories than women.
- Men prefer greater interpersonal distances than women, which explains why women may better cope with high density and feelings of crowding than men.[3]
- Women experience more negative moods in relatively low spatial density conditions, while the reverse is true for men.[4]
- Women are more helpful to others in need in complex settings; men are more helpful in simple ones.[5]
- Women are more apt to sit closer to people who look either happy or sad, whereas men tend to move closer only to those who look happy; however, both maintain greater distances from people who display fear.[6]
- Men require more personal space when ceilings are lower.[7]

Figure 5.1a and b: High-rise buildings often afford access to visual expanses. These city views provide a form of *prospect-refuge*, which means that occupants can survey their surroundings from the relative comfort and safety of their homes (a). The prospect-refuge theory holds that people prefer views of natural settings such as parks, canyons, and bodies of water. If such a view is afforded, it should be capitalized on and incorporated into the home's overall interior design (b).

• A study of pedestrians found that although both genders opted for the shortest route, the women chose more complex routes than men.[8]

An important evolutionary proposition, the **prospect-refuge theory**, suggests that humans prefer edge settings (environments at the edges between open and closed areas such as plains and forests, respectively) because open areas afford **prospect** (visual range for detecting food or danger at a distance) and closed areas afford **refuge** (safe haven or shelter).[9, 10] Other studies show that people prefer well-defined spaces that balance openness and enclosure to spaces that are extremely open or closed.[11] This preference for areas near safety and with visual access to open space helps to explain why properties near parks and beaches are highly valued, why some people find the Great Plains of rural North America somewhat forbidding, and why the ability to open and close

doors and windows is so important in primary and secondary spaces (Figure 5.1a and b).

The concept of involuntary or *effortless attention* makes a great deal of sense in an evolutionary context because it ensures that the cognitive apparatus focuses on urgent issues deriving from a dangerous and uncertain world.[12] For this reason, we are automatically fascinated by fires, loud sounds, and many other specific and important patterns of stimuli: "strange things, moving things, wild animals, bright things, pretty things, words, blows, blood, etc. . . . [13] Although such patterns of stimuli have held our attention since evolutionary times, the modern world presents myriad patterns that lack fascination but must be attended to anyway. When we cross a busy street, we must safely avoid the traffic although we don't need to notice each vehicle and driver. Today, some critics say that there are too many things competing for our attention and that there is no longer harmony between what is interesting and what is important (e.g., advertising is

> Effortless attention is discussed in more detail in Chapter 2.

Figure 5.2: In this environment, an individual is presented with a heavy load of visual stimulation. The person is subjected to the noise of people chattering, music overhead, and the clamoring of being jostled about. All of these concurrent stimuli can lead to *cognitive overload* resulting in confusion or triggering the fight-or-flight response.

difficult to ignore but is of little relevance). The discomfort and stress created by such situations is caused by exerting excessive *directed attention* toward numerous stimuli, which can lead to cognitive chaos or *overload*. The number of stimuli requires constant attention and discipline and makes it difficult for us to have a focus. Humans prefer to know what is going on and what needs to be done; lacking mental focus not only feels terrible but also makes it difficult for us to accomplish our purposes (Figure 5.2).

Gender Influences on Perception

Primitive men were aggressive, competitive hunter-warriors who spent much of their time in relative isolation amid open spaces. Because their primary role was to kill, they had to be able to screen out distracting stimuli—after all, when chasing down a meal or an enemy, they needed to be highly focused on the task at hand. This may explain the results of a study in which men outperformed women when doing mental arithmetic under noisy conditions.[14] Primitive women were affiliative breeder-nurturers who worked with and cared for others close to home. The **ethic of care theory** evolved from this role. It claims that it is in women's nature to focus on sustaining relationships and taking care of others' needs. Females had to be able to manage myriad tasks within limited areas, which may explain why modern females tend to approach high-density settings in a more cooperative way than males.[15, 16]

The degree to which instinct, genetic memory, or socialization is responsible for gender behaviors, especially at an early age, is open for debate. In a study of kindergartners and first graders, boys preferred simpler and larger settings more than girls.[17] As boys mature, their personal space requirements appear to increase more than girls' requirements until early adulthood, when their requirements stabilize.[18] A study of males and females, from ages 5 to 18 years, showed that older boys used larger interpersonal distances more than older girls, but among the younger children there were no personal space differences.[19] However, other researchers found that by the age of 4 years boys will keep greater distances from other boys than girls will keep from other girls.[20]

Numerous studies have shown that, generally, pairs of males typically maintain greater interpersonal distance than female pairs, and male-female pairs maintain the least distance, but this depends on both the social relationship and the culture (e.g., males in Latino cultures maintain much less interpersonal distance than Northern European males).[21] Primal gender roles may help to explain why men respond with more aggression than women in long-term high-density situations, such as incarceration. For example, when a Mississippi prison experienced a 30 percent reduction in the inmate population, inmate physical assaults decreased by about 60 percent; and later, when the population increased by 19 percent assaults increased by 36 percent.[22]

Interestingly, men respond more negatively to high density than women (i.e., men's moods, attitudes toward others, and social behaviors are more hostile) in laboratory settings; however, in field studies men often cope with high-density situations by leaving. It therefore appears that women handle the stress of high density better when there is no easy way out.[23, 24] Both genders are more tolerant of invasions of personal space by females than by males,[25, 26] but one study revealed that gender only influenced personal space when age, race, and the other person's gender came into play.[27]

DESIGN APPLICATION. Understanding the different ways in which males and females interpret and respond to high-density situations can help design professionals to better accommodate each gender's needs. However, with the exception of public restrooms, most environments are open to both males and females and should therefore be designed for the group that will be most affected. For example, to accommodate men's increased perception of high density and crowding, spaces that are intended for numerous people should have multiple entry and exit points along with oversize or double doors. Likewise, the space planning process should ensure that spacing between solid walls and furnishings is large enough to accommodate multiple *personal space* zones. Other methods of decreasing perceived *spatial density* include increasing the level of natural light and incorporating mirrors, higher ceilings, and large unobstructed windows.[28]

Aesthetics and Color

As with gender roles, aesthetics and color preferences evolve. However, they evolve according to fashion and trends, not out of necessity. Although men and women have evolved to excel at certain everyday chores, the role gender plays with regard to aesthetics and color seems to be more closely related to social norms. For the purposes of this text, aesthetics may be considered to be the values and expressions that the physical environment can embody and represent. The study of **aesthetics** in design is an attempt to identify, understand, and create environmental features that lead to positive (pleasurable) responses.[29] Color shapes the environment; it is integral to the design process because it strongly influences how we interpret and feel about our environments.[30] Our judgment of an environment's appeal or beauty is highly subjective because it is influenced by personal factors that include culture, age, gender, and experience; therefore, beauty truly is "in the eye of the beholder."

Aesthetics

Ideally, the purpose of design is to create attractive, pleasant environments that we enjoy. It is essential that planners and designers create environmental features that both elicit pleasurable responses and fulfill functional requirements. Evidence shows that aesthetics can be important in determining behavior;[31, 32] however, aesthetic design considerations may conflict with behavioral ones. *Pleasant* and *attractive* can be highly subjective terms, as can *function*; some beautiful structures do not function well.

There is a difference between the physical and psychological aspects of design aesthetics.[33, 34] Physical aspects are the focus of **formal aesthetics**, which looks at the following components of design:

1. *Dimensions*: shape, proportion, scale, novelty, illumination
2. *Enclosure*: spaciousness, density, mystery
3. *Complexity*: visual richness, diversity, information rate of environmental stimuli
4. *Order*: unity and clarity

Formal aesthetics has traditionally depended on the Gestalt theory of perception,[35] which hypothesizes that people's perceptions of stimuli affect their responses (see Chapter 3). **Symbolic aesthetics** complement formal aesthetics by moving beyond the physical world to the intangible world of meaning. Whether denotative (e.g., function or style) or connotative (e.g., implying an association, such as welcoming or forbidding), sources of symbolic aesthetic sources include the following:

1. *Naturalness*: the level in which natural elements were used in the design
2. *Upkeep*: the level in which designs can be easily maintained
3. *Intensity of use*: the intensity or presence of particular design features
4. *Style*: the overall design selection

Gestalt tradition dictates that if two individuals are exposed to an identical stimulus their reactions to it will be different, because their reactions are based on their separate past experiences. For example, the two people may have been raised in different size homes, one large and one small. When exposed to a midsize home later in life, the person who grew up in the large house will likely view the midsize home as being small, while the person who grew up in the small home will likely view the midsize home as being large.

Box 5.1 contains a survey form that can be used to evaluate the formal aesthetic qualities of any environment.

Color

Color speaks to each of us on an emotional level, but the manner in which color influences human behavior directly is still being investigated. The question of whether our reactions to color have a biological correlation or are merely a by-product of our socialization requires further exploration; for the purpose of design, there appears to be an association both ways because learned responses can cause biological manifestations. For example, imagine that you learned snakes were dangerous when you were a child, and you come face-to-face with one now that you are an adult. As you approach the reptile, your body will likely respond with a faster heart rate, higher blood pressure, and possibly even fear-induced paralysis. Your biological response was to an environmental element, but your psychological conditioning shaped that biological response.

Box 5.1 Formal Aesthetics Survey

To measure the beauty of the room shown in Figure 5.3 according to formal aesthetics, attribute a score of 1 to 5 (with 1 being the lowest and 5 being the highest) within each category, write your score in the last column, and total your scores. A total that is closer to 65 means the room is considered beautiful, a total closer to 39 means it is considered average, and a total lower than 39 means it is considered to be unattractive. Keep in mind that each individual's notion of beauty will differ based on past experiences; while one person may find this room very beautiful, another may not.

Figure 5.3: Upon entering this room, each individual will perceive each of the aesthetic categories below differently. The result will determine whether the environment is preferred.

DIMENSIONS		
Shape	Does this room have a shape that is appealing for its intended use?	1 2 3 4 5
Proportion	Are items in the room sized so that no single object dominates the scene?	1 2 3 4 5
Scale	Do furnishings and accessories fit the room without looking too large or too small?	1 2 3 4 5
Novelty	Are there elements or components of uniqueness or fascination?	1 2 3 4 5
Illumination	Is lighting sufficient and appropriate for the room?	1 2 3 4 5
ENCLOSURE		
Spaciousness	Does the room give the appearance of having space and not being cluttered?	1 2 3 4 5
Density	Is the floor space ratio ample in relation to objects occupying the room?	1 2 3 4 5
Mystery	Do elements within the room inspire or beg for exploration?	1 2 3 4 5
COMPLEXITY		
Visual richness	Are there interesting items to view while maintaining the room's unifying theme?	1 2 3 4 5
Diversity	Are a variety of objects or architectural features present within the room?	1 2 3 4 5
Information rate	Do all aspects of the room register with the viewer at an equal rate?	1 2 3 4 5
ORDER		
Unity	Is there a unified theme among all parts of the room?	1 2 3 4 5
Clarity	Is the purpose or function of the room and objects obvious?	1 2 3 4 5

TOTAL

Research has demonstrated that color is important to the perception of space, building form, wayfinding, ambiance, and image; its relationship to the practice of design can be understood within the four aspects that make up the following theoretical framework:[36]

1. Conceptions of designing (production, retail, experiential, and structural). Color is often used as a method of branding (i.e., identifying a product or service) and serves as a symbol that conveys a message. For example, the bright orange color vests worn by public workers and other construction crews has come to symbolize construction work in general, and a popular retailer of home-improvement products has capitalized on the color reference of "construction orange."

2. Place formation and the architectural experience (relationship of the person to the environment). Color coding enables us to use certain colors to facilitate wayfinding, and we also recognize universal uses of color as symbolic representations. For example, the color red means *stop* or *emergency*; in an emergency we can just search for the color red instead of having to depend upon our higher cognitive skills.

3. Understanding of the nature of the built environment (object, product, communication, and social domain). The interiors of most, if not all, antiseptic Western hospitals of the past were always white. Even today, just being inside a structure with white walls and floors can make us feel as if we were in a hospital.

4. Fashion and styles. Color is often associated with certain historical periods. For example, the popularity of avocado green, goldenrod, and burnt orange make us recall the early to mid-seventies; likewise, mauve and gray are representational of the early to mid-eighties.

Every color can be described according to three main attributes: hue, saturation, and brightness. It is important to note that objects are described in terms of hue, lightness, and saturation, whereas light sources are described in terms of hue, brightness, and saturation. Additionally, a color's *brilliance* is determined by its levels of lightness and saturation.

- **Hue** is the color family or name (such as red, green, or purple) that allows its identification; hue is directly linked to the color's wavelength.
- **Saturation** (also called chroma) is a measure of the purity of a color (how sharp or dull it appears) as well as a color's depth or intensity (i.e., its freedom from dilution with white).
- **Brightness** or **whiteness** (also called *luminance* or *value*) is the shade (darkness) or tint (lightness) of a color relative to its saturation (the degree to which a color reflects light).

Attributes of Color

Color is a property of light that depends on wavelength (Figure 5.4), and light is a function of energy. Warm colors (those having longer wavelengths along the electromagnetic spectrum) range from red to yellow; cool colors (those having shorter wavelengths) range from blue to violet. White sunlight contains the primary colors of light: red,

Figure 5.4: As light passes through a prism, the lightwaves disperse into bands of color.

green, and blue. A surface looks white when it reflects all of the light waves that strike it. Color, as we see it, is simply a portion of the spectrum of a light wave that is reflected by a surface.

The human eye has three different types of color-sensitive photoreceptors that are sensitive to the individual primary colors, which is why all other colors can be created from primary colors. We perceive color as light and as pigment (the substance that imparts color to another substance). The primary colors of light (red, green, and blue) are the *additive primaries*, used to create *transmissive color*. The primary colors of pigments (cyan, magenta, and yellow) are the *subtractive primaries* (so called because they absorb, or subtract, other colors), used to create *reflective color*. A room that has been painted blue reflects all wavelengths *except* blue, which is why the color can be perceived; other colors are not visible because their light energy has been absorbed by the blue surfaces and converted into heat energy. In other words, a room looks blue because it has reflected all of the light waves that are not blue, and there is nothing to manifest any other colors.

It is important to note that black is not a color, but rather a visual effect caused by the absence of light. Surfaces that absorb all light waves *appear* black and convert light waves into heat energy—an important consideration when designing outdoor settings.

Effects of Color

Many theorists and researchers claim that color acts on the body as well as the mind. Physiological changes occur when we are exposed to certain colors due to a phenomenon called *chromodynamics*. For example, one research team concluded that long wavelength hues are more arousing than short wavelength hues after determining that higher state–anxiety scores were associated with red and yellow than with blue and green. Because anxiety involves displeasure and high arousal, "these findings were consistent with results from studies of physiological reactions to color (demonstrating that red and yellow were more arousing than blue and green) and with studies of color preferences (showing that yellow and yellow-green were less pleasant than blue and green)."[37] However, another study conducted in a specially constructed learning setting found that higher level functioning such as math, reading, and motor task performances did not vary significantly in red, blue, or yellow rooms,[38] suggesting that color affects the involuntary biological systems more than the voluntary biological systems.

When we look at an object, our brain determines its color in the context of the surrounding colors. When two very similar colors meet, both appear to wash out and become indistinct because the borders between them are difficult to distinguish and the brain blurs them together. Similarly, bright complementary colors placed next to each other attract attention, but the effect is disconcerting. Looking at such combinations causes a vibrating or pulsing visual effect: the colors appear to pull away from each other, making our eyes feel like they are being shaken. This effect, called *color fatiguing*, occurs as the optic nerve sends confused signals to the brain (Figure 5.5).

DESIGN APPLICATION. Certain color effects, such as those of warm and cool colors, seem more universal than others. Warm colors appear to be closer to us than cool colors, but

Figure 5.5: Notice the bright complementary colors on the wallpaper. They attract attention, but their proximity to one another causes the optic nerve to send confusing signals to the brain. Outlining the complementary colors with a neutral color helps the brain keep the colors separated without causing discomfort.

vivid cool colors can overwhelm light, subtle warm colors. Using warm colors for foreground and cool colors for background enhances the perception of depth. Cool colors are frequently used for backgrounds to set off smaller areas of warm colors. Used together, cool colors can look clean and crisp, implying status and calm. However, bright cool colors are more stimulating than light, medium, or dark cool colors.

Factors Influencing Color Preference

Although red, yellow, and orange are generally considered high-arousal (warm) colors and blue, green, and most violets are considered low-arousal (cool) colors, a color's brilliance can alter its psychological message. Researchers have found that a significant variance in emotional response to color happens not because of the color's hue, but rather its levels of brightness and saturation.[39] One study demonstrated that different intensities of the same color affect people's responses: Subjects perceived light-green rooms as being less crowded than identical dark-green rooms.[40]

It should be noted, however, that the way in which we perceive color is regulated by our visual system. Our brains have the ability, termed *chromatic* or *color adaptation*, to adjust to varying colors in different illuminations. Color adaptation allows us to balance color signals detected by our eyes as we move through various environments. In this way, our brains are constantly working to process information retrieved by our eyes; without this ability, most light sources would probably make most of us ill. If you look at an object's color first under an artificial light source and second under natural daylight, like most people, you will not be able to observe a significant shift in color. However, if you were to photograph the same object under each lighting condition, the color of the object would look quite different.

Human perceptions of and reactions to color are, to some extent, also dependent on cultural belief systems. For example, in European cultures, brides wear white and mourners wear black, whereas in Chinese culture, brides wear red and mourners wear white. A study of color preference in Japan found that whereas *hue* relates more to perceived warmth, *saturation* (regardless of hue) relates most closely to preference (more saturated

a

b

Figure 5.6a and b: Notice the differences in the way these two offices look simply because of the colors used. Although the layout and furnishings are similar, the darker wall color in this room along with the dark wood trim and dark-colored upholstery make it appear more cozy and private (a). In this room, the bright-colored walls, lighter floors, and pale upholstery make the room appear larger and more active (b).

hues were evaluated as more elegant, more comfortable, and just better); moreover, the study found that *brightness* or *lightness* (regardless of hue) is related to perceptions of how active the room seemed (brighter colors were perceived as being fresher, lighter, and more cheerful than darker ones)[41] (Figure 5.6a and b).

The effects of color and color patterns on humans appear to be far-reaching. In one study, researchers demonstrated that rooms designed with lighter colors are perceived as more open and spacious.[42] Another study identified more cooperative behaviors among children in day-care centers where rooms had varied wall color as opposed to uniformity.[43] Research has also shown a correlation between our perceptions of ambient temperature and the color of our surroundings. For example, a room designed with "cool" accessories (e.g., tile, stainless steel, glass, and the color blue) can reduce an observer's perception of the ambient temperature by a few degrees. From the vast and diversified research in this area, we can see that color can be used to create illusions of spaciousness, as an adjunct for the facilitation of certain behaviors, and, through perception, as a mild method of temperature regulation.

Whether our reaction to color is the result of selected combinations of light waves hitting our retinas and subsequently causing the secretion or reuptake of neurochemicals, a learned response passed from generation to generation, or a combination of these processes remains to be determined by empirical research. Our experience of color is affected by a combination of biological, physiological, psychological, social, and cultural factors; in fact, the manner in which people associate colors is often the most meaningful aspect of visual experience.

Wayfinding

In modern society, our abilities to find our way within an environment, or wayfinding, often makes use of color. We depend on the technique of color-coding and symbolic representations that rely on color (red = stop and green = go) to navigate within the built environment. Although wayfinding may seem like a relatively new phenomenon, it has been a necessary function of humanity since our earliest beginnings. Whether hunting on an open plain or gathering in the dense bush, humans have had to travel away from their homes in search of food and water and therefore had to devise ways to find their way back. The methods that humans used might have included the formation of paths, breaking branches, retracing their tracks, or maybe even using their cardinal senses. Because historically men and women had different roles and were subjected to different environments, their methods of wayfinding inevitably evolved differently.

How we find our way in the world is a psychological process that can be highly subjective and individual. To successfully navigate an environment—which changes as we move through it—we must continually acquire, process, reassess, recall, and respond to different stimuli and objects.[44] Wayfinding consists of three major actions that are generally performed sequentially: [45, 46]

1. Deciding what to do and how to do it.
2. Moving from decision to action.
3. Applying information obtained through sensory input and cognitive processes; in other words, environmental problem solving.

How these decisions and processes are categorized in our brains depends on our cognitive information retrieval methods, which the built environment can support or constrain. For example, hallways that cannot accommodate traffic flow, lack visual access, and lack reference points all contribute to poor wayfinding ability.

Scenographic (or picture-based) **representations** and **abstract** (or data-based) **representations** are the two most common ways in which people perceive, comprehend, and store information.[47] Some people map out a route in their heads using visual images or landmarks to orient themselves. Others use such information as actual mileage, the cardinal directions, and street signs. And a third group of people uses a combination of both picture- and data-based representation.

Cognitive Maps

Understanding how people perceive and conceptualize space is key to helping them interact effectively with an environment. We can measure geometric space, but we must construct a **cognitive map**, or mental image, of **navigational space**, the space we move through and explore, which usually cannot be seen all at once. Cognitive maps are based on sensory information, imagination, and language. In short, our understanding of a space is based on objects within it and their meaning and relationship to us.[48] We understand the space around us three-dimensionally (based on head–feet, front–back, and left–right axes) and use these directional cues to learn about an environment's spatial arrangement, but our understanding of navigational space is generally two-dimensional and therefore subject to conceptual errors.[49] This dichotomy occurs because we learn about spaces three-dimensionally, but we recall or imagine space two-dimensionally, which helps to explain why design clients strongly prefer models over renderings.

We use cognitive maps as well as the physical objects and elements within a space to locate and reach our destinations (goals) as efficiently as possible. As mentioned, some people rely heavily on mental floor plans, while others rely on orientation or reference points such as landmarks. Research indicates that the number one method of wayfinding by humans is through the use of landmarks. However, wayfinding techniques and abilities appear to differ between men and women. Men rely more on reference points, distance estimates, and **cardinal directions** (the compass directions of north, south, east, and west) than women, and they exhibit greater confidence in their wayfinding skills.[50, 51] This gender difference may be related to levels of anxiety rather than ability.[52, 53] During childhood, boys are usually allowed to roam farther from home than girls, and experience engenders both ability and confidence.[54, 55] People who question their directional abilities are more likely to experience spatial anxiety (i.e., fear of becoming lost) in a new setting,[56, 57] and over time may come to limit their interactions with the physical environment.[58]

Wayfinding Mechanisms

The ability to navigate through an environment easily influences our overall perception of it.[59] Greater environmental legibility facilitates greater exploration, which leads to greater understanding or at least to a sense of familiarity, all of which promotes greater overall satisfaction with an environment. Wayfinding is made easier through spatial organization (ordering functions and facilities to create an effective circulation system) and environmental communication (architectural and graphic information). Therefore, circulation should be clearly articulated in the spatial organization of a structure so that signage is a secondary means of communication.[60] Without good wayfinding measures built into the design, people will experience difficulties reaching various destinations quickly and efficiently.

Wayfinding measures that can be built into the design include visual access, architectural delineation, signage, and building layout:[61]

- **Visual access** refers to *prospect* or visibility (e.g., clear lines of sight that serve to increase visual access to a destination or reference point).
- **Architectural delineation** refers to the separation of one area from another via architectural elements or features (e.g., thresholds, walls, or variations in ceiling height and floor depth).
- **Signage and numbering systems** enable us to match displayed codes with the messages or symbolic meanings that we either bring with us (e.g., when we know that a friend occupies a certain hospital room) or obtain from on-site sources (e.g., what we learn from information centers, "you-are-here" maps, or by asking directions).
- **Building layout** relates to logical spatial progression and organization (e.g., in a department store, we expect to find women's shoes near women's apparel, not home appliances).

These mechanisms can be applied to a microenvironment such as a café, but are equally efficient in larger settings such as hospitals, campuses, malls, offices, airports, and so on. Figure 5.7 illustrates how such wayfinding mechanisms can be incorporated into the design of a built environment.

People use the psychological construct of **segmentation bias** to cope with long distances. It is estimated that we will walk for only about 100 yards and drive for about 60 minutes before the effort becomes intolerable. When we have to travel greater distances, we mentally segment or divide the path into smaller, more manageable sections. For example, when driving long distances we segment our route according to the highways (90E for about 35 minutes to the 290N for about 25 minutes to the 190N for about 20 minutes). In large facilities, design can support segmentation biases through the incorporation of sitting areas, changes

Figure 5.7: Various components of this café serve to illustrate *wayfinding mechanisms*. When people who enter the environment have an unobstructed view of their target destination, the service counter, they have *visual access*. *Architectural delineation* is established by the three architectural features that help direct customers to the service area: the ceiling accent, the two freestanding walls astride the service area, and the countertop above the display of merchandise. *Signage and numbering* is illustrated in the menu in the service area. *Building layout* is exemplified by the service counter that is directly opposite the entryway, seating that is available on both sides of the service area, and the freestanding walls that delineate different types of seating arrangements (bar, standing bar, and tables).

Figure 5.8: Segmentation bias is any route that the mind can break up into smaller, more manageable pieces. A sitting area creates a natural resting place along a long busy pathway.

in flooring material and lighting, and the number and placement of windows.

DESIGN APPLICATION. In design, elaborate wayfinding mechanisms indicate that a structure or environment is not legible enough on its own.[62] The more intricate the floor plan, the more problems people will have with wayfinding.[63–65] One way to mitigate such problems is by increasing visual access to the environment;[66] many large offices with open floor plans delineate work spaces by dividing space with partitions that employees can see over. Many people use reference points for orientation purposes;[67] in a resort, for example, the lobby, a landmark, or a particular amenity are all reference points. One study recommends the use of floor plans with greater symmetry as well as multiple architectural elements that interact so as to facilitate wayfinding, noting

that such measures are more effective than the use of signage.[68]

Multistoried structures with long corridors (e.g., large hotels, cruise ships, hospitals, and office and apartment buildings) can seldom use ceiling height to facilitate the wayfinding process. However, we can tell when we have entered an auditorium or ballroom simply because the ceiling has risen. Long corridors and other monotonous paths can appear endless and often lead to confusion in wayfinding, as well as to increased perceived crowding. Design can introduce segmentation bias by incorporating intersections or objects that help people to mentally break a route into separate, more manageable segments (Figure 5.8).[69]

"You-Are-Here" Maps

A "you-are-here" map is most effective when it matches both the structure and the orientation of the environment: The "you-are-here" symbol should be accurately placed on the map, which itself should be positioned so that users can easily correlate their locations within the environment to that shown. The map should depict actual sites and landmarks within the setting, and the map's alignment should be the same as the actual setting (e.g., north is north), with the top of the map representing "straight ahead" (Figure 5.9)[73] However, good signs require considerably less cognitive effort than such maps, even good ones.[74]

a

b

c

Figure 5.9: The primary purpose of "you-are-here" maps is to locate yourself at a given point,[70 71] and to find the destination on the map; however, such maps are generally used more for conceptual orientation rather than for actual wayfinding.[72] Whereas a good map serves to improve the legibility of an environment, trying to make sense of a poor map can be more frustrating than having none at all.

Figure 5.10a–c: No words are used to convey messages in these *pictographic* signs, which is one reason they can be imprecise: They rely on the observer's ability to understand the symbols.

Signage

Research findings concerning the influence of signage on wayfinding are contradictory and inconclusive,[75] perhaps because signs themselves can be illegible due to imprecise wording and lack of detail. Such lack of detail may result from the size constraints of signs, which limits the number of words that can be listed on a sign as well as the illustration detail. Signage is an important form of environmental communication that enhances environmental legibility when properly executed and installed. Words, pictographs (symbols, logos, and images), directional arrows, and numbering systems serve to identify objects and locations and to direct and regulate human activities. Typeface, color(s) and color-coding, size, shape, specificity, accuracy, consistency, and visibility all contribute to overall signage legibility. A sign is useful only if it can be clearly seen and understood; for example, displaying the international "No Smoking" symbol in a restaurant will not prevent patrons from lighting up if the sign itself is not well lit. Figure 5.10a–c shows more examples of pictographic signage.

Summary Review

Our species is still evolving in a dangerous and uncertain world, and the primal gender roles that were fundamental to our early survival led men and women to perceive, interpret, describe, and navigate within the environment differently. Because the human psych has evolved much more slowly than human technology, both sexes continue, at least to some extent, to behave and regard the environment according to primitive instincts. In ancient hunter-gatherer societies, males hunted while females gathered edible vegetation. Men's primal gender role was to kill animals for food and protect the community. Hunting usually took place on open savannahs and plains with expansive views and few physical obstacles to navigate through or that would obstruct weapons in flight. Conversely, women in small groups foraged for vegetation within forests and jungles; these dense and complex environments limited peripheral and distance views and therefore promoted verbal communication (which additionally served to deter potential predators). An important evolutionary proposition, the prospect-refuge theory, suggests that humans prefer edge settings (environments at the edges, between open and closed areas such as plains and forests, respectively) because open areas afford prospect (visual range for detecting food or danger at a distance) and closed areas afford refuge (safe haven or shelter).

Color and aesthetics are primal elements that continue to shape the environment, and both are integral to the design process. Color and level of perceived beauty (e.g., perceptions of spaciousness, cheerfulness, and warmth) are among the strongest factors that influence how we interpret and feel about our environments. Our judgment of an environment's appeal or beauty is highly subjective because it is affected by personal factors that include age, gender, culture, and experience. The study of aesthetics differentiates between the formal aspects of a design, which consist of dimension, enclosure, complexity, and order, and the symbolic aspects, which move beyond the physical world to the world of meaning. Both formal and symbolic aesthetics are strongly influenced by color because color affects the perception of space, building form, wayfinding, ambiance, and image.

Every color can be described according to three main attributes: hue, saturation, and brightness. Color is a property of light that depends on wavelength, and light is a form of energy. Warm colors have longer wavelengths along the electromagnetic spectrum and range from red to yellow. Cool colors have shorter wavelengths and range from blue to violet. Many theorists and researchers claim that color acts on the body as well as the mind. Physiological changes occur when we are exposed to certain colors due to the phenomenon of chromodynamics. Human perceptions of and reactions to color are, to some extent, also dependent on cultural belief systems. Understanding the relationships of such subjective attributes as beauty and color in the built environment helps designers to better perceive and conceptualize space, which in turn enables the users of that space to interact more effectively in that environment.

Both color and aesthetics can be powerful tools in the process of wayfinding, which is our ability to find our way within environments. To successfully navigate through an environment—which changes as we move through it—we must continually ac-

ing Home for Advanced Dementia of the Alzheimer's Type. *Environment and Behavior, 32-5,* 684–710.

47. Abu-Obeid, N. (1998). Abstract and scenographic imagery: The effect of environmental form on wayfinding. *Journal of Environmental Psychology, 18-2,* 159–173.

48. Tversky, B. (2003). Structures of mental spaces: How people think about space. *Environment and Behavior, 35-1,* 66–80.

49. See note 48.

50. Lawton, C. A., (1996). Strategies for indoor wayfinding: The role of orientation. *Journal of Environmental Psychology, 16,* 137–145.

51. Lawton, C. A., Charleston, S. I., and Zieles, A. S., (1996). Individual- and gender-related differences in indoor wayfinding. *Environment and Behavior, 28-2,* 204–219.

52. Burns, P. C. (1998). Wayfinding errors while driving. *Journal of Environmental Psychology, 18,* 209–217.

53. Sholl, M. J., Acacio, J. C., Makar, R. O., and Leon, C. (2000). The relation of sex and sense of direction to spatial orientation in an unfamiliar environment. *Journal of Environmental Psychology, 20-1,* 17–28.

54. Matthews, M. H. (1986a). Gender, graphicacy and geography. *Educational Review, 38,* 259–271.

55. Matthews, M. H. (1986b). The influence of gender on the environmental cognition of young boys and girls. *Journal of Genetic Psychology, 14-7,* 295–302.

56. See note 51.

57. See note 53.

58. See note 53.

59. See note 51.

60. Passini, R., Rainville, C., Marchand, N., and Joanette, Y. (1998). Wayfinding and dementia: Some research findings and a new look at design. *Journal of Architectural and Planning Research, 15-2,* 133–151.

61. Weisman, J. (1981). Evaluating architectural legibility: Way-finding in the built environment. *Environment and Behavior, 13-2,* 189–204.

62. See note 21.

63. See note 61.

64. Moeser, S. D. (1988). Cognitive mapping in a complex building. *Environment and Behavior, 20,* 21–49.

65. O'Neil, M. J., (1991). Effects of signage and floor plan configuration on wayfinding accuracy. *Environment and Behavior, 23-5,* 553–574.

66. Gärling, T., Lindberg, E., and Mantyla, T. (1983). Orientation in buildings: Effects of familiarity, visual access, and orientation aids. *Journal of Applied Psychology, 68,* 177–186.

67. See note 51.

68. See note 65.

69. Allen, G. L., and Kirasic, K. C. (1985). Effects of the cognitive organization of route knowledge on judgments of macrospatial distance. *Memory and Cognition, 13,* 218–227.

70. Levine, M., (1982). You-are-here maps: Psychological considerations. *Environment and Behavior, 14-2,* 221–237.

71. Talbot, J., Kaplan, R., Kuo, F. E., and Kaplan, S. (1993). Factors that enhance effectiveness of visitor maps. *Environment and Behavior, 25-6,* 743–760.

72. Cohen, M., Winkel, G., Olsen, R., and Wheeler, F., (1977). Orientation in a museum: An experimental visitor study. *Curator, 20-2,* 85–97.

73. See note 70.

74. See note 21.

75. See note 65.

SIX

Environmental Risk Assessment

We often think of environmental risk factors as those that lead to physical injuries or cause long-term health issues. However, environmental conditions can affect our psychological health negatively as well, either directly (e.g., a fight between neighbors over excessive noise) or indirectly (e.g., depression resulting from a chronic disability caused by exposure to a toxic agent). Other negative effects of environmental stress include learned helplessness, abusive behaviors, and—in extreme cases—paranoid delusions.

Many aspects of pollution—air quality, dust levels, odor, and noise—can affect human stress levels directly. Pollutants both derive from and infiltrate built environments, which is why both exterior and interior sources must be mitigated. Exterior pollution can be minimized through the use of architectural and landscaping strategies, and interior pollution can be minimized with a combination of architectural and interior designs. Men tend to report less concern for and negative effect from environmental issues than women;[1] however, stress is a physiological response to stimuli that occurs regardless of verbal acknowledgment.

Fear of invasion is a common source of stress that triggers biological self-preservation reactions. When an intruder enters someone's home, the startled occupant instantly and automatically enters a fight-or-flight state in which all of the body's resources are dedicated to survival. To thwart criminal intentions and thereby reduce occupant fears, designers can implement into the design process defensible space measures.

Stress and Behavior

The World Health Organization defines health not only as the absence of disease and infirmity but also as a state of optimal physical, mental, and social well-being. Designers must assume the responsibility of ensuring that the occupants for whom they create environments can maintain optimum health. Incidents of injury and illness often result from the human–environment relationship simply because the environment is a causal factor. This fact emphasizes the interrelationship between the design fields and human health. Fear of injury or victimization related to the environment typically result from a combination of personal experiences, peer influences, and media messages and can be either real or imagined. For example, the exposed corners of walls that meet at right angles present a real risk for broken toes, facial injuries, and minor concussions, but riding in a glass elevator along the exterior of a high-rise could stimulate an irrational fear of falling. Imagined threats are often, but not always, a result of irrational fears that are very real to the individual but highly unlikely in normal circumstances (**phobias**).

Because many older designs focused almost exclusively on artistic and aesthetic qualities, older buildings often fail to protect their occupants from exposure to risk factors or disease-causing organisms. For example, poorly ventilated high-density housing increases the rate of communicable diseases and facilitates the degeneration of mental health.[2] Numerous studies indicate that the leading causes of death for children in developed countries are injuries sustained from biological and environmental sources and psychological and physical reactions to stress. Clearly, both physical and psychological health are affected by implemented design (Figure 6.1).

Stress and Stressors

Stress is a psychological or physiological response to a stimulus or *stressor*. Our daily stress levels derive

Figure 6.1 (top): Childproofing mechanisms in the home can easily prevent infants and small children from injuring themselves or suffering fatal accidents. Considerations include installing safety locks on kitchen and bathroom cabinets, placing plug covers into electrical outlets, removing low-hanging cords from draperies and blinds, and incorporating various window safeguards (such as safety screens that can be unlatched in an emergency, devices that limit windows from opening all the way, and installing windows upside down so that they only open from the top).

Figure 6.2 (bottom): The smoke in this illustration is an external *chronic stressor*. When nearby residents simply live with the nuisance rather than complain or organize a protest, the smoke becomes an *internal stressor* as well.

from a variety of situations, whether social (e.g., an employer's unrealistic demands), physical (e.g., trying to concentrate in an open office setting), or bio-

logical and chemical (e.g., carpet fumes that cause nausea, headaches, and fatigue), all of which affect our responses. Human stress can be caused by internal or external sources.[3] **External stressors** include variables from the physical environment, such as noise, temperature, crowding, and over- or under-stimulation; **internal stressors** include interpersonal conflict or violence, disorganized daily life, or a combination of these. However, both types of stress can build over time and manifest as physical ailments. For example, traditional gender roles for men encourage stoic responses to physical and emotional pain. However, just because a man does not complain doesn't mean that he doesn't experience stress. Instead, the likely reaction will be an ulcer, a heart attack, or a stroke. The stressor itself must be examined to determine if the stressful episode is acute or chronic. An **acute stressor** is sudden, intense, and short-lived; a **chronic stressor** is ongoing or recurring and has the most significant and detrimental effects, such as having a home located near smokestacks (Figure 6.2).[4,5]

DESIGN APPLICATION. Designers can minimize external stressors dramatically by using sound-dampening materials to reduce noise; employing varying ceiling heights to control heat; and incorporating large windows, mirrors, or paintings for visual escape. Designers can also help to minimize some internal stressors by incorporating ample storage areas and providing adequate spacing between workstations, customer service counters, and seating.

Stress itself does not cause injury or illness, but how we respond to it can, especially over time. Bioemotional reactions to stressful environments can result in a wide range of physiological responses (including increased activity in the heart, stomach, intestines, and endocrine glands), which can result in stress-related illnesses such as increased heart rate, high blood pressure, ulcers, and migraine headaches. Behavioral responses to stress include aggression, withdrawal, and compulsion, and in extreme cases lead to violence, delusions, or psychosis. The effects of stress "outlive" the stressor: Our physical and psychological responses continue even after the stressful event or experience has ended.[6] Medical experts declare that if the body must continually cope with particular stressors over a long period of time, the circulatory, cardiovascular, gastrointestinal, and hormonal (glandular) systems may suffer permanent damage.

Environmental sources of psychological distress include air, odor, and noise pollution as well as the perception of being at risk. Stressors such as odors, heat, noise, and crowding are often referred to as **ambient stressors**[7] because they are chronic, nonurgent, physically perceptible, and limited to a particular environment. Chronic environmental stressors (e.g., feeling unsafe in our homes or neighborhoods) slowly wear away our abilities to cope. A stressor's ambience or chronicity is determined by its frequency and its impact on a person's level of stress. For example, one person may find the scent of a candle factory to be a perpetual annoyance (chronic stressor), while another may enjoy all but one or two distinct fragrances (ambient stressors).

Physiological Stress Response

During times of stress, the body releases catecholamines (dopamine, norepinephrine, and epinephrine) into the peripheral and central nervous systems.[8] Catecholamines stimulate essential body systems (e.g., the heart and muscles) and divert energy from nonessential ones (e.g., digestion) in preparation for basic survival behaviors (e.g., the fight-or-flight response). When released, catecholamines activate the amygdala, a primitive subcortical structure that promotes arousal and expression of negative emotions and responds to nonverbal signs of anger, avoidance, defensiveness, and fear. The amygdala initiates such physiological reactions as sweaty palms, clenched jaws, and fear-based paralysis. With the activation of the amygdala our memories begin to consolidate; however, our prefrontal cortex, which controls higher brain functions such as rational thought, is suppressed. Therefore, we are more apt to experience cognitive dysfunction[9] and to respond in a primitive manner (e.g., striking someone, throwing an object, or making inappropriate remarks). Exposure to mild or moderate uncontrollable stress (e.g., loud noises) impairs prefrontal cortical processes (e.g., spatial working memory).[10] This basically means that memory of where items are located is impaired. In short, stressful conditions enhance primal survival instincts and suppress rational thinking processes. Exposure to acute uncontrollable stress causes us to become distracted and confused and our habitual and primal responses to control our behaviors.[11]

The amygdala also controls the conditioned fear response, in which a neutral stimulus becomes aversive by association with a stressful stimulus.[12, 13] When an object, circumstance, or environment (stimulus) is encountered that caused great stress or fear in the past, the mere memory of it (**stimulus association**) in a new but similar situation will cause the body to reproduce its initial response. The sounds of screeching tires, crunching metal, and breaking glass can be traumatic to a person who was once severely injured in a traffic accident. This primal survival response may explain why children in stressful home environments can exhibit behaviors resembling those caused by disorders of the prefrontal cortex, such as attention-deficit/hyperactivity disorder (ADHD).

Cortisol (hydrocortisone) is often called the *stress hormone* because its secretion increases as part of the body's reaction to any type of physical or mental stress. This steroid hormone, which is produced by the adrenal glands, has among its important functions the regulation of blood pressure and cardiovascular function. Cortisol secretion increases in response to stress in the body, whether physical (illness, trauma, or temperature extremes) or psychological (crowding, deadlines, or interpersonal conflict). Everyone can be affected by environmental stressors: One study determined that cortisol secretions begin to occur every 24 hours at just three months of age, thereby rendering even infants susceptible to stress-related illnesses.[14]

Environmental Pollution

Designs that affect human health address three primary sources of environmental pollution: air, noise, and organic matter. Both air and noise pollution are present inside and outside the built environment. One source of these pollutants is jet planes; the noise from their engines permeates building walls, and the particle emissions created from burning fuel are easily tracked indoors as people enter a building. Organic pollutants derive from living organisms (e.g., humans, animals, mildew, and mold). This chapter surveys each of these sources of pollution and their detrimental effects on human physiological and psychological health.

The body's response to stress is discussed in more detail in Chapter 3.

Exterior Air Pollution

Sources of exterior air pollution are predominantly associated with emissions from internal combustion engines. Although most people associate this type of pollution with motor vehicles, small combustion engines such as those in snow and leaf blowers and lawn mowers are significant sources of these emissions (Figure 6.3). The pollutants emitted, which include benzene; 1, 3-butadiene; diesel; particulate matter; carbon monoxide; reactive organic gases; and oxides of nitrogen,[15] are associated with respiratory illnesses such as asthma and immune system deficiencies, thus increasing our susceptibility to common colds and influenza.

Engine exhaust also produces lead dust, which often becomes airborne and infiltrates buildings that are not airtight, especially along or near busy streets and intersections.[16, 17] These types of pollutants are particularly problematic for older residential properties or businesses such as restaurants and specialty stores that operate out of former residences since they are not airtight and often situated near freeways, highways, and major roadways.

Persistent organic pollutants (POPs) are chemical substances that persist in the environment as a result of the breakdown of chemicals such as DDT and chlordane, which were once commonly used in building materials and to control pests. The primary sources of POPs in modernized Western countries derive from dioxins and furans, which are produced from most forms of combustion, including municipal and medical waste incinerators, open burning of trash, and industrial processes. The predominating issue of concern regarding POPs is that they bioaccumulate through the food chain. This means that if a fish is contaminated with POPs and you consume that fish, then you will have POPs in your system. Because the human body does not metabolize or excrete POPs, but instead stores these contaminants in fat cells, you may eventually develop very high levels of these substances. Another issue of concern regarding POPs is that they circulate globally via the atmosphere, oceans, and other pathways. This means that if POPs are released in one part of the world, they can travel far from that source. Currently POPs have been linked to cancer, damage to the nervous system, reproductive disorders, and disruption of the immune system.

Figure 6.3 (left): Most small combustion engines lack environmental controls and, as such, negatively contribute to environmental noise and air pollution. The pollutants being emitted by this leaf blower taint the air we breathe as well as our homes; they not only waft in through windows and doors, but also are carried in whenever we enter the space.

Figure 6.4 (right): Both air and noise pollution increases when developments lack sufficient landscaping. Green leafy trees absorb and trap many harmful pollutants that would otherwise be inhaled.

DESIGN APPLICATION. Inner-city communities are most affected by exterior pollution, largely because they often lack adequate landscaping. Plants not only absorb certain pollutants but also trap pollutants that cling to their surfaces and sap. Plants release oxygen and moisture into the air, which helps to improve the overall air quality and to weigh down particulate matter (e.g., lead dust), respectively. For these reasons, consider placing a low-level hedge line along roadways where vehicular particle emissions are at their greatest concentrations and incorporating leafy trees into exterior designs and landscapes (Figure 6.4).

Cracked windows or doors and weather-damaged seals are obvious points of access for exterior pollution. Simple measures to help prevent infiltration include tight window and door seals and the use of double- or triple-paned windows and glass doors. The interior spaces of large office buildings can be pressurized so that when a door is opened air will blow out, precluding exterior pollutants from blowing in. If the windows, doors, and their seals are routinely monitored and maintained to ensure their integrity, the success of these measures will extend to improving energy efficiency and helping to dampen exterior sources of noise.

Health-related complaints from exterior pollutants include headaches, dizziness, nausea, and shortness of breath. People who experience any of these symptoms are more likely to have shorter tempers, be easily frustrated, and associate negative feelings with those environments.

Interior Air Pollution

Unfortunately, buildings that are designed to be airtight to prevent exterior pollutants from entering also prevent interior pollutants from escaping. Low levels of outdoor air combined with indoor humidity reduce overall indoor air quality.[18] Table 6.1 lists common sources of indoor air pollution. These include volatile organic compounds (VOCs)—chemicals that easily evaporate at room temperature, such as benzene, formaldehyde, and ethylene glycol—and polycyclic aromatic hydrocarbons (PAHs)—cancer-causing agents generated by combustion, such as carbon monoxide and nitrogen dioxide.

Interior pollutants also include particulate emissions from things such as fibers, soil, dust mites, bacteria, and human (and pet) skin cells and hairs. Particulate emission levels consist of both newly generated and existing particles, and the level of air pollution within a structure depends on factors such as vibration, humidity, temperature, particle accumulation, and air velocity.[19]

Table 6.1 Sources of Indoor Air Pollution

POLLUTANTS	SOURCES
Airborne particles, including lead, asbestos, carbon monoxide, and nitrogen dioxide	Fireplaces, wood stoves, kerosene heaters, gas stoves, leaking chimneys, furnaces, vehicular exhaust, sanding or burning lead-based paint, and deteriorating insulation and fireproofing
Chemical compounds, including formaldehyde, pesticides, insecticides, and other organic pollutants	Hardwood flooring, plywood wall paneling, particleboard, fiberboard, permanent-press drapes and other textiles, glues, paints and paint strippers, wood preservatives, aerosol sprays, cleansers, disinfectants, mothballs, termite treatments, and lawn and garden products
Mold, mildew, and fungus	Wet or moist walls, ceilings, and carpets; poorly maintained humidifiers, dehumidifiers, and air conditioners
Naturally occurring pollutants, such as radon and uranium	Underlying earth and rock strata, well water, and building materials

Source: Modified from American Lung Association (2004). Health House 2004 brochure 9.04. www.HealthHouse.org.

As materials such as carpeting are damaged or deteriorate, they release dust and fibers; occupants interacting with the environment release skin cells, hairs, and so on. Inhaling this combined particulate matter "cocktail" can cause potential damage to the immune system. These effects are increased in people who have preexisting sensitivities. For example, when an asthmatic child roughhouses indoors on the living room carpet with the family dog, particulate matter as well as human and animal dander become airborne. Inhaling these particles may then trigger an asthma attack. If the level of air pollution does not decrease, the child will probably experience asthma attacks more frequently and may subsequently adopt behaviors of learned helplessness. (Part of the problem could be eliminated by installing natural-fiber carpeting, which would produce significantly lower levels of pollutants than synthetic carpeting.)

Another common source of interior pollution comes from polyvinyl chloride (PVC). Used in a wide range of products, including piping and wall and floor coverings, PVC can make up most of a structure's interior surfaces as well as its water delivery and plumbing systems—much to the detriment of its occupants. PVC products have been shown to release phthalic acid esters, an environmental pollutant found in indoor air and house dust that has been linked to respiratory cancers and sexual dysfunction.[20]

A recent study of urban homes found that exterior pollution was the main source of indoor particulate matter and that the concentration of household pollutants increased dramatically in air-conditioned homes.[21] (Air conditioners usually recycle existing air and use very little fresh air.) The researchers noted that emissions and concentrations of indoor VOCs and PAHs resulted mostly from the occupants' lifestyles (e.g., occupants who smoke, fry foods, and don't keep their homes clean) and the home products they used (e.g., air fresheners, mothballs, and many cleaning supplies). VOC particulate emissions were highest when hazardous chemicals, such as paints, solvents, and the like, were stored within the home. Exposure to VOCs can cause eye, nose, and throat irritation, as well as headaches, loss of coordination, and nausea. Prolonged exposure, through inhalation, to cleaning agents has been shown to permanently damage the central nervous system, liver, and kidneys, and some VOCs have been linked to certain cancers (e.g., leukemia and breast cancer).

Sources of exterior PAHs include hazardous waste sites and sites where coal, wood, gasoline, or other flammable products are burned. Exterior PAH levels are often ten times greater in urban environments than in rural environments. Many U.S. water supplies have low levels of PAHs as a result of contamination with burned matter. Interior PAHs typically derive from tobacco smoke, wood-burning stoves and fireplaces (especially when creosote-treated wood products are burned), cooking, candles, and incense. A residential study demonstrated that area vehicular traffic is the primary source of indoor air contamination, and that, in nonsmoking households, the highest average PAH emissions are caused by frying or sautéing, followed by candle burning, baking, boiling, and broiling.[22] Burning incense sticks, an ancient Asian worship practice, creates smoke that has been found to contain cancer-causing PAHs.[23] It has been suggested that possible long-term health effects of PAHs include cataracts and kidney and liver damage.

Sick Building Syndrome

Poor air quality resulting from PVC emissions and other indoor contaminants often leads to **sick building syndrome (SBS)**. According to the U.S. Environmental Protection Agency (EPA), this term describes situations in which occupants experience acute health and comfort problems that seem linked to the time they spend inside a building but for which no specific illness or cause can be identified.[24] Sick buildings contain airborne substances (contaminants) that are health threatening.[25] Researchers have determined that two different sick building syndromes exist.[26] The term **building-related illness** describes symptoms of diagnosable illnesses that are found to some degree in occupants of all office buildings; the term **building-specific illness** refers to symptoms that occur only in air-conditioned buildings. SBS symptoms include headaches; fatigue; dry or itchy eyes; sore or dry throats; coughs; cold and flu symptoms; irritability; skin rashes; and neck, shoulder, and back pain. These physical afflictions often lead to the manifestation of stress and other psychological ailments. The EPA cites inadequate ventilation, chemical contaminants from indoor and outdoor sources, and biological contaminants (organic pollutants) as causes of, or contributing factors to, SBS.

Organic Pollutants

Living organisms create organic pollutants, which act as **allergens** that commonly wreak havoc on the human immune system. For example, *hay fever* is an allergic reaction to airborne pollen from flowering trees and plants. Humans, family pets, and vermin release **bioeffluents** such as carbon dioxide, skin cells, hairs (or scales or feathers), and microbes (bacteria, germs, and viruses) in the course of normal activity; vermin include rodents (rats and mice), insects (flies, fleas, cockroaches, and the like), and arachnids (dust mites and spiders). The carcasses and fecal matter of vermin, as well as those of other animals and birds, become greater human health risks as they decompose. Vermin can be especially problematic in interconnected buildings—where they can travel freely from unit to unit through interconnecting walls—and in rural environments. Adjoining or abutting structures have a unique problem: When one building is fumigated, the vermin simply travel through the walls to the neighboring building and eventually work their way back.

Fungus, mildew, and mold are all hazardous to humans. Mold has been identified as a primary source of many health-related problems. Many respiratory illnesses have been linked to excess moisture and the growth of mold and mildew.[27] Different types of microbial growth cause different health problems (e.g., *Actinobacteria*, *Stachybotrys*, *Trichoderma*, and *Aspergillus versicolor* indicate moisture damage; *Penicillium*, yeasts, *Cladosporium*, and *Aspergillus* indicate background fungal concentrations).[28] Sources for mold growth include wood with a moisture content greater than 30 percent and the presence of damp items, such as wet hanging clothing, leaking water connections, and humidifiers indoors.[29]

Masonry (brick and concrete) construction is more often associated with moisture damage and increased respiratory problems than wood-frame construction.[30] Porous masonry is often less dense than wood and can facilitate the passage of moisture through the process of osmosis. Moisture can also leak or seep into inner walls via window and door frames, poorly sealed construction materials (e.g., roofing materials, piping, and foundation), or inadequate drainage systems (e.g., rain gutters, downspouts, and landscaping gradient). Older brick buildings are especially susceptible to moisture damage, whereas modern construction methods incorporate water exit points and waterproof membranes between outer and inner walls to prevent moisture from permeating. Moisture can also seep in from the ground via the process of diffusion. This moisture not only provides a medium for mold, but also reacts with proteins within the foundation's mortar, causing VOCs or other hazardous substances to be released into the air.[31]

DESIGN APPLICATION. Designers must be cognizant not only of myriad organic pollutants and their sources but also of certain design features that facilitate their transmission. Consider the role of allergens and other interior pollutants when determining how much soft fiber (carpeting, cloth furnishings, and drapery) to use within the environment, especially since these items tend to contribute the most to interior pollution. To reduce interior moisture levels, consider using dehumidifiers, ventilation systems, and ceiling fans to help circulate fresh air.

Odor Pollution

European studies have found that offensive odors yield numerous unpleasant psychological reactions, including frustration, annoyance, and a desire to flee the environment.[32, 33] Exposure to certain odors serves as an ambient stressor for which individuals must develop coping mechanisms.[34] Other environmental pollutants, such as rubbish, petroleum products, and burning materials, are also sources of undesirable odors, which can lead to unsatisfactory or intolerable living conditions. In a study of a community landfill, residents who lived near it reported experiencing increased respiratory-related symptoms (asthma, difficulty breathing, and so on), as well as eye, ear, and nose irritation caused by everyday exposure to the strong pollutant odors.[35]

Other forms of odor pollution occur indoors in settings such as malls, hospitals, and office buildings. Perhaps the most notable odor pollution occurs in malls during the holiday season, when

Methods to reduce concentrations of indoor contaminants through office design and décor are discussed in Chapter 12.

perfume salespeople arbitrarily spray scents with the hope of enticing people to purchase the fragrances. Antiseptics, which are commonly used throughout hospitals, are often sources of odor pollution because of their overpowering smell. Carpeting is a common source of odor pollution that predominantly affects those who spend extended periods of time in office buildings and other sealed environments. The potential for odor pollution must be considered during the design phases of both residential and nonresidential settings.

Noise Pollution

The word *noise* is a subjective term. We interpret *sounds* as being either pleasant (*euphony*) or unpleasant (*cacophony*) according to our preferences; however, *noises* may always be defined as unwanted, uncontrollable, and unpredictable sounds.[36] The damaging effect of chronic noise exposure is an increasing problem worldwide;[37] therefore, understanding the differences between noise and noise sources, as well as the effects of noise on the human psych, is a vital part of a designer's scope of practice.

Research conducted on working conditions found that **ambient noise** (irrelevant sounds related mostly to exterior sources) can negatively impact physiological health and well-being by affecting the immune system, which is partially regulated by the sympathetic nervous system.[38] The top two emotional responses to noise are annoyance and anger, which people express either externally (by showing irritability or aggression) or internally (by feeling increased levels of stress).[39]

Noise-induced stress causes the human survival system to pump adrenaline (epinephrine) into the bloodstream when the body perceives a danger signaled by noise. This worked well for early humans, but the constant internal alarms signaled by modern (especially urban) noise levels is destructive to the human body; noise can lead to numerous health problems, including tinnitus (ringing in the ears), fatigue, headaches, and stress-related illnesses such as increased heart rate, high blood pressure, ulcers, and migraine headaches.[40] If the noise is both loud and sustained, hearing can be impaired or lost. Infants exposed to continuous noises in neonatal intensive care units are at risk for either hearing loss or slow growth and development;[41] almost 12.5 percent of U.S. children from ages 6 to 19 years already have noise-related hearing problems.[42]

Obvious sources of noise pollution include internal combustion engines; construction and demolition operations; and horns, sirens, and alarms (Figure 6.5). Studies have listed highway vehicles, aircraft, and urban traffic as the most bothersome sources of noise, followed by loud music and movies, restaurants, garden and lawn equipment, recreational vehicles, bars and nightclubs, and neighbors.[43, 44] In addition, complaints of neighbors making too much noise have increased sharply in recent years,[45] but noise pollution is not limited to exterior environments or sources; televisions, sound systems, video games, and cellular phones generate a great deal of interior noise—as do children in day care, preschool, and classroom settings.

Research has defined two basic types of noise: **irrelevant sound** (related mostly to exterior sources) and **extraneous noise** (related to speech or vocal tones). It links impaired cognitive performance to irrelevant sounds and negative mood changes to extraneous noise.[46] Another study refers to irrelevant sound as being ambient and suggests that children exposed to excessive ambient sounds

Figure 6.5: Combustion engines, found predominantly in motor vehicles, cause a great deal of city noise. Construction work is another significant source of noise, as are emergency sirens and vehicle horns. Such city noises are amplified when they echo or bounce off tall buildings.

may experience greater problems with learning.[47] Other research teams found that children who have trouble reading also experience delayed development in their language skills and claimed that since ambient noise negatively affects reading comprehension, it is also indirectly responsible for causing delays in language skills.[48, 49] Another team found that consistent exposure to high levels of noise adversely affects preschool children's language and pre-reading skills.[50]

Research shows that quiet environments contribute to creative performance,[51] whereas noisy ones impair cognitive and language development in children.[52, 53] Poor reading skills have been associated with chronic noise exposure in the classroom setting,[54] whereas improved reading scores have been directly linked to quieter school environments.[55] A survey of Phi Beta Kappa graduates found that the students' parents had provided quiet places and times for them to read, think, and do homework.[56]

Nearly everyone is adversely affected by noise. The process of placing items in order in our short-term memories (called *seriation*) is easily disrupted by noise, especially during cognitive tasks.[57] Research indicates that personality traits, combined with the type of noise and task at hand, influence mental performance.[58] One team found that adult introverts seem to experience less annoyance and fatigue and perform cognitive tasks better in quieter conditions than when subjected to noise;[59] these researchers referred to other studies that suggest introverts experience stronger responses to noise while performing mental tasks.[60, 61] This may be because socially withdrawn introverts have less experience coping with noise (and are less able to screen it out than socially active extroverts) or because extroverts prefer more stimuli. In the same vein, people are less likely to help someone in need in a noisy environment, presumably because people will be more concerned with escaping the noise than taking the time to help someone else.[62] Several studies from the late 1960s and early 1970s reported higher admission rates to mental hospitals for those who lived near airports, and a more recent study found that greater mental instability, depression, and overall nervousness were found in people who were exposed to intense noise from an air base near their homes.[63]

Although noise is generally problematic, it may actually improve performance if a task is repetitive, boring, and requires little concentration (e.g., assembly line work).[64] Guidelines for acceptable noise levels indicate that noise above 90 decibels (dB) will markedly decrease performance.[65] For activities requiring creative thinking, concentration, or decision making, noise levels in the workplace should not go above 55 dB; for simple or partially mechanized activities, levels should not go above 70 dB; and for all other activities, levels should not go above 85 dB. For comparison, typical sound levels are about 50 dB in a quiet office, and 80 to 90 dB in a photocopy room with several machines running in it[66] (Table 6.2).

Table 6.2 Decibel Rating Chart

SOURCE	DECIBEL RATING
Normal breathing	10
People whispering five feet apart from each other	20
Quiet office or library	40
Large office	50
Rainfall	50
Refrigerator	50
Washing machine	50–75
Air conditioner	50–75
Dishwasher	55–70
Normal conversation	60
Vacuum cleaner	60–85
Power lawn mower	65–95
Freeway traffic	70
TV/radio	70
Garbage disposal	70–95
Toilet flushing	75–85
Doorbell	80
Blender	80–90
Heavy traffic or noisy restaurant	85
Factory machinery	100
Snow blower	105
Shouting in ear	110
Leaf blower	110
Car horn	110
Nightclub	110
Ambulance siren	120
Heavy machinery	120
Jet plane at ramp	120
Jet engine at takeoff	150

Source: League for the Hard of Hearing (2003). "Noise Levels in Our Environment" fact sheet. www.lhh.org/noise/decibel.htm.

DESIGN APPLICATION. Sound levels in interior environments can be decreased via architectural variations and the strategic use of interior materials. Research indicates that noise can be controlled by a combination of floor plan layout, interior finishes, and equipment selection and placement.[67] Ceiling angles and materials have the most potential for acoustical control and designers can use suspended ceilings, partitions, and specific insulation materials to reduce noise.[68] Extraneous noise can be inexpensively masked in work spaces simply by providing a continuous noise stream of music at about 45 to 50 dB; this increases the pitch baseline, which decreases the perceived impact of the original source of noise. To reduce noise in preschool classrooms, consider focusing on the shape of the room, varying ceiling heights, and limiting the amount of hard and smooth surfaces,[69] as noted earlier.

Each design field has different tools, methods, and strategies that can be applied to mask, diffuse, or dampen noise. Landscape designers can create green spaces to help absorb noise, incorporate water features to help mask noise, and vary a property's elevation because noise travels downhill. Architects can use construction materials and architectural designs to help reduce the negative effects of noise; for example, they can incorporate non–right angles, which help to reduce noise by reflecting sound more randomly.[70] Interior designers can reduce noise by incorporating tapestries, fabric-covered soft furnishings, and other decorative pieces and by utilizing circular, octagonal, and trapezoidal furnishings. Noise abatement is a crucial component of successful design, especially in built environments such as schools and workplaces that are intended to promote retention and cognition (Figure 6.6). Collaboration among the various design fields will enable clients to benefit fully from the respective design options available.

Crime Prevention

The mitigation of pollution often involves using green spaces. Greenery not only filters noise and carbon dioxide but also reduces the amount of airborne particulate matter by providing a multitude of surface areas to which the particulate matter may adhere. Likewise, people tend to judge environments by the presence or absence of maintained green spaces. Places without maintained green spaces often signify a lack of community control and involvement, which then translates to an overall apathetic view of crime within a given community or neighborhood.

Numerous studies have linked property crime with neighborhood layout (the way streets and buildings are designed). However, social, cultural, and economic factors almost always affect local crime rates far more than design features.[71, 72] Much of this research omits the physical environment as a causal factor. Crime rate determinants include what would-be criminals can deduce about a target's value prior to committing any offense; how long it takes to get to and away from the target or victim; and the probability of being seen, recognized, or caught before, during, or after the offense. Communities with narrower streets,

Figure 6.6: Notice the variation in ceiling height in this workplace design that will help to reduce noise via the different trajectories from which it can bounce, and the Plexiglas barriers rising above the cubicles that allow visual access and also increase acoustical privacy. The fish tank serves as a source of white noise, and the leafy plants absorb both noise and other environmental pollutants. The rubber flooring not only helps to reduce noise and bad odors associated with carpeting, but is also easy to clean.

more one-way streets, fewer entrance and exit streets, or more turns to navigate through the neighborhood tend to have lower property crime rates.[73] Therefore, the more permeable by outsiders an environment is, the greater the probability of criminal activity.

Condition and reputation also contribute to an environment's vulnerability. Physical deterioration and associated disorderly behaviors often lead to further decay, more crime, or both. The notion that "grime causes crime" is supported by the **broken windows theory** developed by James Wilson and George Kelling.[74] They demonstrated that increased evidence of decay over time in an area (e.g., broken windows, trash heaps, run-down buildings, abandoned vehicles, and gang graffiti) causes the people who live and work there to become fearful, withdrawn, and unwilling to intervene to maintain social order or to amend physical degradation. These researchers found that as residents continue to withdraw, harassment, vandalism, and other crimes escalate; they also found that offenders from outside the area are then attracted to what has become a "safe" site for criminal behaviors. In other words, a single broken window can lead to the decline and fall of an entire community. This correlates to the psychological concepts of **implicit behavioral cues** and **virtual modeling**: We leave behind cues that indicate our behavior in that environment and imply its acceptability to those who follow, who may then more readily model their behavior after ours. For example, if someone breaks a window and ignores the debris, the implicit cue (the shattered glass) will not only inform others that a window has been broken but also imply that another can be broken without consequences; this understanding will lead to further destruction. Wilson and Kelling noted that people fear being bothered not only by criminals but also by disreputable or unpredictable individuals (e.g., loiterers, panhandlers, rowdy teenagers, drunks or addicts, prostitutes, and mentally disturbed persons).

People create mental images of an environment over time that help them make judgments about safety.[75] They use environmental cues, such as the potential for concealment and entrapment, to assess a setting's safety. One research team found that physical factors associated with concealment (e.g., dense shrubbery, opaque fencing, or poor lighting)

frequently evoked fear in subjects. These researchers recommend both illuminating potential areas of concealment with uniform and diffuse lighting to increase perceptions of safety and using outdoor public space for group activities to increase the presence of community members and to help them identify strangers and notice problems.[76] People need to feel safe within their environments, especially their **primary territories**, and social interaction is a primary source of crime deterrence.

Defensible Space Theory

The **defensible space theory (DST)** evolved as a means of empowering residents of urban public housing complexes, but it can be effective in all built environments. DST contends that the degree to which crimes occur in a given environment correlates directly with the level of the occupants' defense of that space. According to its originator, Oscar Newman, the physical environment can create perceived territories, and certain physical features tend to encourage people to appropriate and exercise **territorial control**—which reduces both the opportunity for and the fear of crime.[77] In other words, the more a person claims and defends a territory (i.e., signals ownership of, watches out for, and takes care of it), the less likely that space is to be violated.

Territoriality

Territoriality is rooted in the notion of proprietorship and is indicated by physical or symbolic markers. One example of the latter is graffiti, which usually indicates that the general population has little control over certain human elements of the community (Figure 6.7).

A study of Philadelphia street gangs demonstrated that wall graffiti is often an accurate indicator of gang territorial ownership and that there is more intergang violence when territorial boundaries are disputed or unclear than when they are well established.[78] However, the more complex and anonymous an environment, such as a territory, the more difficult it is for occupants to establish and enforce codes of acceptable behavior.[79] Likewise, the larger the number of people who share a given territory, the less likely it is that they will identify it as their own or feel they have a right to control or determine the activity within it.[80] The breakdown

Figure 6.7 (left): True urban street art has aesthetic value, but most of the graffiti in disorganized communities relates to territorial control by gangs and to nuisance violation by young kids. Because gang and nuisance graffiti are often indistinguishable to most people, the average person has no way of knowing if this is a childish prank or a turf marker.

Figure 6.8 (below): Gated communities have proliferated over the past few decades. The principal benefit of this type of community is the ability to control access to an area by uninvited guests, unwanted solicitors, and would-be criminals. But there are drawbacks as well because the barriers cut the gated community off from the diversity and stimulation of the world outside.

of territorial boundaries and social organization then results in the need for a community to create barriers.[81]

Defensible Space Markers

Defensible space markers establish territorial boundaries by denoting an occupant's physical presence in a space. Newman cited two types, as shown in Figure 6.8: **physical barriers** (e.g., locks, fences, high walls, road closures, and other barricades) and **symbolic barriers** (e.g., signs, gardens, hedges, borders, low railings, landscaping, and changes in construction materials).[82]

When the physical layout of a built environment allows occupants to control the areas in and around their primary territories, neighbors can relax in those areas and enjoy themselves according to their commonly held values and lifestyles.

Strategies to Enhance Crime Prevention

Physical appropriation of the space surrounding a territory relates both to **social appropriation** (greeting, talking, or spending time with others in the space) and **territorial appropriation** (feelings of ownership, taking care of and monitoring the space, or noticing and intervening if destructive or illegal activities occur there).[83] Research suggests that it is ideal for planners and designers of public housing to provide playground equipment within suitable distances, benches and shaded areas to accommodate adult supervisors, and gardening or other areas near the home that residents are encouraged to decorate (Figure 6.9).[84] Well planned circulation can increase user traffic; therefore, consider the physical and visual connections among spaces, as well as how those spaces will be used and perceived during different times and seasons.[85]

Figure 6.9: The playground serves to develop children's gross motor skills, the benches and greenery provide for attention restoration, the shade trees offer protection from excess heat and direct exposure to sunlight, and increased user traffic results in increased area surveillance.

The significance of DST programs over the past 30 years spawned the criminological subdiscipline known as crime prevention through environmental design (CPTED). This idea is based on the notion that design and effective planning of the physical environment can reduce the fear of crime.[86] The premise behind the concept is that since the physical environment can influence the probability of a crime occurring, designers should focus on the settings where crimes occur and employ techniques for reducing criminal susceptibility in these settings. See Box 6.1 for more specific information on CPTED. Newman found that public areas with well-defined boundaries are less likely to be vandalized than those without clear indications of ownership.[87] Although one study supports the DST—it found that burglarized homes had more signs of public use (e.g., people cutting through yards and

---

Box 6.1 Crime Prevention Through Environmental Design

Potential criminals decide whether to engage in criminal activity based on the following information:
- How difficult does entry appear on a potential target?
- How enticing, visible, or vulnerable does the potential target appear?
- What is the likelihood of a criminal being seen while committing a crime?
- If detected, what is the likelihood that a witness will be able to do something to halt the crime?
- Is there a quick, direct route for leaving the location after the crime is committed?

Four approaches to making a location more resistant to crime or crime-related problems include the following:
1. **Housing design or block layout.** Making it more difficult to commit crimes by reducing the availability of crime targets, removing barriers that prevent easy detection of potential offenders or of an offense in progress, and increasing physical obstacles to prevent crime.
2. **Land use and circulation patterns.** Creating safer use of neighborhood space by reducing routine exposure of potential offenders to crime targets. This can be accomplished by paying careful attention to walkways, paths, streets, traffic patterns, and locations and hours of operation of public spaces and facilities. These strategies may produce broader changes that increase the viability of territorial behaviors and signage on a smaller scale. For example, street closings or revised traffic patterns that decrease vehicular volume may, under some conditions, encourage residents to keep the sidewalks and streets in front of their houses in better condition.
3. **Territorial features.** Encouraging the use of territorial markers or fostering conditions that will lead to more extensive markings indicating that vigilant residents occupy the block or site.
4. **Physical deterioration.** Controlling physical deterioration to reduce perceptions that areas are vulnerable to crime and that residents are so fearful or apathetic they would do nothing to stop a crime. Physical improvements may reduce the signals of vulnerability and increase commitment to joint protective activities. Physical deterioration, in all probability, not only influences cognition and behavior of potential offenders but also shapes how residents behave and what they think about other residents.

Figure 6.10a and b: According to the defensible space theory (DST), the home with tall opaque fencing is a likely target for crime because once the fence has been penetrated, the perpetrators cannot be seen from outside and can therefore take their time (a). DST asserts that the home with the low-level fence is less likely to be violated because its windows, front door, and walkway are clearly visible from the street. Should someone attempt to break in, or succeed, there is a higher probability of a passerby or neighbor noticing and calling the police (b).

fewer signs of occupancy), as well as fewer physical and symbolic barriers[88]—another study contradicted the DST and found that burglars do not necessarily avoid residences that seemed well cared for because they assume such homes contain more valuable objects.[89] A study in which police officers assessed homes for their likelihood of being bur-

glarized showed that the less visible a home is from the road (i.e., set back from the road, secluded, or protected by tall fences, shrubs, and other barriers), the more vulnerable it is to burglary; it also demonstrated that as home value increases, so does the interest of prospective burglars (Figure 6.10a).[90] Newman recommended placing plantings so as not to shield doors and windows from the street or walkways leading from them (Figure 6.10b).[91]

There is a direct correlation between occupant or community involvement and the likelihood of crime. Feeling safe results in greater community cohesiveness, which, in turn, affects people's feelings of safety.[92] An understanding of how architectural and landscape design affects people's fear of crime can help designers to create more comfortable spaces that may also be less prone to crime.[93] DST is a powerful self-help tool: It depends on occupant involvement to reduce crime and remove the presence of criminals and serves to bring people together for their mutual benefit.[94]

DESIGN APPLICATION. Consider internal and external visibility when designing a home, as both tend to deter burglars. Occupants who appropriate the spaces surrounding their territories can help to create environments that are safer, more cohesive, and more supportive. Designers can help promote such social appropriation by incorporating front porches, ensuring ample greenery (lining sidewalks and streets with trees), and reducing noise via traffic calming and control of air traffic. Architectural and other environmental design practices can also be used to reduce criminality: Layout, lighting, fencing, and landscaping all help to define spaces and maximize an occupant's field of observation and sense of ownership and therefore promote greater community safety. Conversely, avoid hedge lines and fences that are more than four feet tall and large leafy trees that obscure doors and windows; if possible, do not place homes too far back from the street.

Summary Review

Since the dawn of time humans have struggled with environmental threats, and our biological and psychological coping mechanisms have aided in our survival. Ironically, modern civilization has created and perpetuated many of those threats; pollution, overpopulation, diseases, and technological hazards are only a few examples. Today, we are exposed to a host of environmental risks related to air, odor, and noise; a plethora of synthetic and sometimes toxic construction and furnishing materials; and increasing numbers of people and other living organisms, all of which often lead to negative physical and behavioral outcomes. Design is key to ensuring the physical and psychological safety of the occupants of built environments; it has been proven to influence neurochemical responses within the brain and, subsequently, cognitive perception. The design industry, with its myriad tools, is ready to take a proactive role in the mitigation of many environmental risks.

Stress has become a part of many people's lives. It is a psychological or physiological response to a stimulus, whether social, physical, or biological. The World Health Organization defines health not merely as the absence of disease and infirmity, but rather as a state of optimal physical, mental, and social well-being. Stress is known to affect physical, mental, and social well-being, and it derives from many environmental sources. Designers have the ability to reduce levels of stress by developing designs that consider the needs and desires, as well as the risks and fears, of the intended occupants.

In addition to being a source of stress, there are many other ways in which the environment affects humans. Air, noise, and organic matter can harm humans and cause health problems. The principal source of exterior air pollution is emissions from internal combustion engines, which release benzene; 1, 3-butadiene; diesel particulate matter; carbon monoxide; reactive organic gases; and oxides of nitrogen into the environment. Many of these pollutants are linked to respiratory illnesses such as asthma and immune system deficiencies. Other sources of pollution derive from indoor environments. These include benzene, formaldehyde, and ethylene glycol, which are classified as volatile organic compounds (VOCs), and carbon monoxide and nitrogen dioxide, which are compounds known as polycyclic aromatic hydrocarbons (PAHs). Chronic exposure to these indoor pollutants can cause headaches, scratchy throats, and dry eyes.

Offensive odors are another form of pollution, a form that is sometimes overlooked. Some European studies have found that foul odors lead to unpleasant psychological reactions, which include frustration, annoyance, and a desire to flee the environment. Offensive odors are also ambient stressors. Sources of bad smells within indoor environments commonly come from chemicals used to treat fabrics such as carpeting, drapery, or clothing. These smells are usually a combination of formaldehyde and dyes. Other sources of bad smells within the indoor environment include strong perfumes and cleaning supplies.

Noise is another pollutant that has been shown to negatively affect people's health. Noise can be classified as *euphony*, pleasant sounds, or *cacophony*, unpleasant sounds. Typically, it is the unpleasant sounds that we regard as being ugly or disturbing, and therefore, as being noise. The two most notable responses to noise are annoyance and anger. These responses may then be expressed externally (by showing irritability or aggression) or internally (by feeling increased levels of stress).

All designers must have a working knowledge of pollutants so they can implement appropriate measures to ensure optimum health, safety, and well-being for users; therefore, risk assessment is an important aspect of, and must take place early in, every design process. City planners can use this knowledge to help determine the placement of new roads and landfills and the termination of through streets in residential communities. Landscape designers can use it to strategically place appropriate plant material (e.g., tree-lined roads, vegetated medians, and greenbelts) to reduce environmental pollution. Architects and contractors can apply it to determine how far ventilation systems should be placed from sources of pollution and to select appropriate construction materials and designs that will both keep exterior pollution out and dampen noise levels (e.g., placing and constructing a garage so that neither exhaust nor noise will affect a home's occupants). Interior designers can use it to break away from mass-production and traditional furniture designs and layouts and use creative layouts and natural materials to reduce interior pollution.

Although much of the research in crime prevention excludes the physical environment as a causal factor for crime, ideas proposed in the broken windows theory (e.g., implicit behavior cues and virtual modeling), defensible space theory (e.g., maximized visual penetration), and crime prevention through environmental design practices emphasize the importance of environmental design as a variable in crime prevention. Therefore, designers need to have a thorough understanding of how architectural and landscape design affect people's perceptions of the environment as fearful places, safe places, or targets for criminals.

Discussion Questions

1. Discuss ways in which physical and psychological health are affected by implemented design.
2. Discuss the *chronic*, *acute*, and *ambient stressors* in your work or study environment. What effect do these stressors have on you (e.g., you lose focus or sneeze a great deal)? What techniques or mechanisms can you use to control or nullify these stressors?
3. Discuss the effects of air, noise, and organic pollution and stress on a child being reared in an inner-city neighborhood. Assuming that this child has two parents and a loving home, what challenges does he or she have to overcome that a child from a suburban area does not?
4. Research has shown a dramatic increase in childhood asthma over the last several decades. Discuss the positive and negative effects of our increased ability to control our internal spaces.
5. Discuss techniques for preventing the buildup of indoor air, odor, and organic pollution.
6. Discuss the possibility that landscaping not only dampens sound but also is soothing enough to cause people to be less aware of *extraneous noise*. How might you investigate this quantitatively?
7. Discuss the viability of homeowners' associations relative to crime prevention, as well as possible outcomes resulting from organizing neighborhood groups in low-rent areas and encouraging the community to participate proactively in neighborhood watch programs.

Learning Activities

1. Draw a sketch of your living space and label the items and design characteristics that pose a risk for injury or illness.
2. Create a flowchart of brain activities related to stress. Devise an *external stressor* (e.g., a train passing near your studio while you are working) and show the effect it has on the brain and body via the flowchart.
3. Find a map of the city or town where you live, make a black-and-white copy of it, and use colored pencils or highlighters to define neighborhoods or regions (e.g., residential, business, high-density/high-rent, or high-density/low-rent). Compare highly sought after regions with less desirable areas to determine what makes the former so valuable. List the regions by category, and describe the qualities of each category in terms of the theories and concepts discussed in this and earlier chapters (e.g., a location next to a public park is desirable according to the prospect-refuge theory).
4. Contact the management office of a large local building (e.g., office tower, hospital, or school) and arrange to interview someone about what, if any, measures are taken to avoid indoor pollution and *sick building syndrome*. Without criticism, discuss the reasons behind the incorporation or exclusion of such measures. Summarize your findings by drawing a sketch of the interior spaces showing what measures are present or missing.
5. Focusing on noise pollution, design a space that will be used not only for creative problem solving and design, but also for repetitive tasks (e.g., a small business that designs and makes greeting cards). How should the space be divided up, and what architectural features can be used to maximize productivity for both types of work?
6. Visit a local park and sketch its layout; then, according to your perception of *noise*, illustrate what effectively dampens noise in that park.
7. Design *defensible space measures* for a person's work cubicle and home.

Residential Environments

Shelter, or the home, has taken many forms throughout human existence. Early forms included caves, huts, tepees, and yurts, but as human societies evolved, their housing demands did as well. Wooden, earthen, or stone structures with only one room were slowly replaced by more complicated structures. The level of complexity or **segmentation** (separation or partitioning) of indoor space was often related to the sociopolitical complexity of the culture. The segmentation within the home, specialized use of each room, and hierarchical ordering of the rooms also reflected the culture. The more complicated the society, the more complicated its structures. For example, homes were quite segmented in Victorian times when society strictly enforced elaborate codes of conduct, whereas modern buildings tend to have open floor plans that better suit a society with far fewer social restrictions (Figure 7.1a–c). Throughout history and around the globe, our dwellings have always mirrored the complexity of our societies.

Notions of what constitutes the physical aspect of a home vary by culture, but the psychological components are fairly static: emotional attachment to place and perceived safety and security. Nomadic tribes in Tibet, Mongolia, and other parts of the world wander over vast expanses of land, setting up their villages for periods of time only to disassemble and set them up someplace else. For these people the notion of home is much larger than their immediate sleeping quarters; it consists of the vast plains they roam. Similarly, Romany (Gypsy) clans travel the European countryside in colorful caravans, RV dwellers roam throughout North America, and many military families relocate frequently. However, in Western culture home is usually interpreted as the built environments where we reside and from which we travel with the intention of returning. As we travel away from home, greater distance is analogous to greater abstraction of the notion of home. If an American man from Amherst, Massachusetts, while visiting another country, were to be asked where his home is, he would probably say the United States. However, if he were in another state, he would probably say Massachusetts. If he were in another town in Massachusetts, he would probably say Amherst and so on.

When inquiries zero in on our home's location, we tend to feel more invaded at how personal the questions are becoming. For example, if a complete stranger were to ask you for your street address, would you reply? When we do allow someone into our homes, we open up our lives and reveal a great deal about us; this may explain, in part, why some of us implement controls over who may enter. As designers, it is important to know our clients' personal interests and preferences so that we can develop a design they can identify with, although we can obtain much of that information by simply analyzing their surroundings. For example, a client may have a strong religious orientation and desire statues of deities or enjoy recreational adult entertainment and request unique features in a bedroom or basement. As a designer, it is your choice to accept or reject the job, but as a professional it is your ethical responsibility to not make value-based judgments regarding design preferences or desires.

In the past, many people remained in one home or geographic area their entire lives. This trend is changing rapidly: Approximately 43 million Americans relocated between March 1997

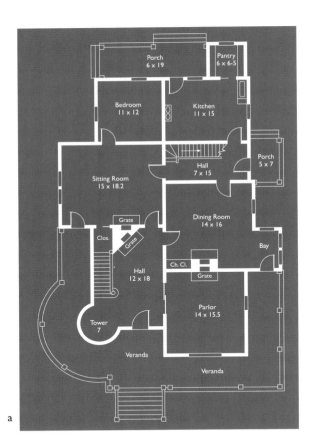

Figure 7.1a–c: Notice how typical U.S. homes have progressed from being more ornate and highly segmented to having fewer walls and large areas encompassing many rooms. (a) Floor plan of a typical home from the late 1800s; (b) Floor plan of a typical home from the 1950s; (c) Floor plan of a typical home from the 1990s.

a

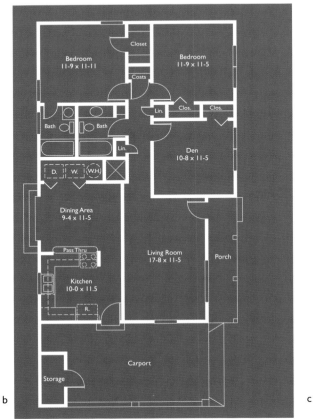

b

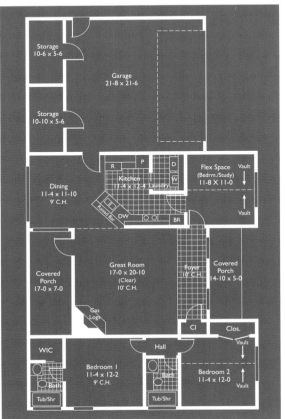

c

and March 1998, with only 27.1 million moving within the same county.[1] This means that a growing number of Americans are moving away from their historical roots—to other counties, states, and even countries—often taking with them their ideas of beauty and design preferences. Therefore, a successful designer's notion of design must expand beyond regional ideas and styles to include more cosmopolitan designs. It would behoove the person commissioned to design the home of the Southern Californian client who relocated to New England, mentioned in Chapter 1, to integrate meaningful artifacts and objects supporting the regional designs of Southern California with new items that reflect the regional designs of New England. A sensitive designer should be able to perform this integration as a means of retaining the client's emotional connection to his or her past in a way that supports adaptation to the new environment.

Concepts of Home

The concept of *home* is an evolving psychological notion based on people's cultures, traditions, and personality traits. Home falls somewhere along each of five different continuums:[2]

1. Permanent versus temporary
2. Homogeneous versus differentiated
3. Communal versus noncommunal
4. Identity versus commonality
5. Openness versus closedness

People who have extroverted personalities tend to view their homes as being more temporary. Extroverts prefer a more homogeneous floor plan, have guests and visitors often, possess more mainstream objects, and consider their homes to be very open both physically and socially. Conversely, people who have introverted personalities tend to view their homes as safe havens and as being more permanent. Introverts prefer a more differentiated floor plan that allows them to spend time in different environments, have few guests, and control who may visit or stay. Their homes will probably contain many artifacts that have strong personal meaning and reflect their individuality.

Although these two examples illustrate extremes within the five continuums, each person's perception of home will vary, and each person will view his or her position on each continuum differently. Some people may be at one extreme on one point, in the middle on another, and at the other extreme on a third. To get a better idea of these continuums, let's examine each of the categories in greater detail.

Permanent versus Temporary

In older communities, residents typically occupy permanent dwellings that have been in their families for generations. These tend to be permanent standing structures that are occupied for the duration of a person's adult life, as opposed to residential structures that can be disassembled and transported elsewhere at any time such as tents, mobile homes, or recreational vehicles. As a **psychological construct** (e.g., conceptual representation), *home* can be defined by a person's intentions. Young adults, for example, often live in temporary homes (e.g., college dorms, military barracks, or small apartments) with the intention of moving to more permanent dwellings. It is important to note that many people regard their current homes as being temporary and that this feeling can last for several years: think of an apartment dweller who, in every conversation, talks about moving. Conversely, people who move from home to home, each time swearing it will be the last move, view their homes as permanent regardless of the number of times they relocate. Affluent people who find that their permanent residences don't meet all of their needs may augment their primary residence with a secondary or vacation home.

What is important in understanding this continuum from a design perspective are the expectations of and willingness for alterations. A person who intends to reside in a home on a permanent basis will have higher expectations of the structure's quality and function and will be more apt to use greater financial resources in the overall design and decorating of the landscaping and the interior. People who regard their homes as being temporary will not be worried about a structure's quality and function, will desire items that are easy to move new homes, and will often view the landscape and interior design as being none of their concern—especially if they are renting.

Homogeneous versus Differentiated

Many of our ancestors occupied single-room dwellings (homogeneous homes). In modern-day cultures, as with early cultures, a single room serves multiple uses: cooking, eating, sleeping, socializing, working, and recreating. When society and social rules became more complex our homes did as well. We started to develop structures with multiple rooms (differentiated homes) that each served a specific purpose (see Figure 7.1a–c on page 124). Many European buildings from the Victorian and Edwardian eras are highly segmented. This type of layout was preferred both because it is easier and cheaper to keep small rooms warmer than large ones and because in these socially complex eras the predominantly wealthy owners of the period had the services of many servants but found it undesirable to see their work in progress. This is also why many older homes have a door between the kitchen and dining area.

There is often a positive correlation between the level of differentiation and wealth of the occupant; for example, a sharecropper's cabin is a homogeneous home, and Hearst Castle is a differentiated home. The manner in which occupants spend their leisure time within their homes is strongly affected by size and differentiation. Occupants of homogenous homes (e.g., studio apartments) may spend less time at home than occupants of differentiated homes (e.g., mansions) who have many rooms in which to wander. Although homogeneous homes are often associated with lower levels of wealth, an interesting trend seems to be challenging this concept. Many upper-middle-class people have opted for homogenous loft spaces in urban areas instead of the differentiated home in the suburbs. However, even in the suburban home social interaction areas are becoming more homogeneous while private spaces are becoming more differentiated. The great room

Figure 7.2: This home has an open floor plan with only two separate areas, a trend that is becoming increasingly popular for two reasons. The first relates to space: High-density residential communities (e.g., apartments, condominiums, and town houses) have relatively small floor plans, and open spaces enable occupants to perceive the space as being larger. The second reason reflects our society's growing trend toward multitasking: We now often try to cook, clean, help with homework, and monitor our environment for accidents and intrusions; homogeneous spaces in the social interaction areas not only provide optimum visual access but also are ideal for accomplishing all of these tasks concurrently.

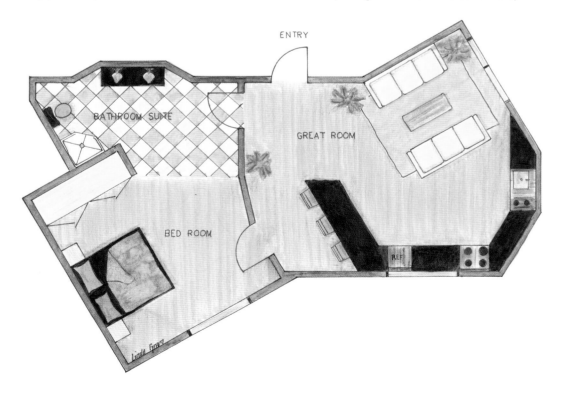

(which usually encompasses the kitchen, dining, and living room areas) is becoming a popular trend as evidenced in homes built during the late 1990s and early 2000s (Figure 7.2). Private areas in some larger homes, such as master bedroom suites, appear to be more differentiated with large walk-in closets, large bathrooms equipped with spas, reading areas, and even small kitchenettes sometimes. Some researchers contend that privacy, territoriality, and crowding are strongly affected by a home's degree of differentiation.[3]

DESIGN APPLICATION. It is essential for designers to both understand and design appropriately for spaces that serve multiple purposes. For example, in homogeneous spaces such as studio apartments, consider incorporating dual-purpose items, such as sofa beds, as well as furnishings that help delineate spaces in large homes with great rooms. Recreational vehicles make excellent use of dual-use furnishings, for example, in dining areas and quasi–living rooms that convert into sleeping spaces (Figure 7.3).

Figure 7.3: In Western societies, temporary homes include college dormitories, apartments, assisted-living units, and even recreational vehicles. Many older people opt to exchange their permanent dwellings for the freedom offered by a home on wheels, thus adopting nomadic lifestyles similar to, but with more resources than, those of the native inhabitants of Mongolia and the Tibetan plateau.

Communal versus Noncommunal

Communal homes are shared by entire families or even communities; noncommunal homes are limited to the nuclear family. Communal spaces include religious monasteries, college dormitories, the kibbutzim of Israel, and the tenements of the former Soviet Union, where several families lived on one floor, sharing a common kitchen, bathroom, and living space.

For centuries, Western societies engaged in communal living: Commonly, residences were shared by large extended families and often their hired help as well. With mid–20th century affluence came the splitting up of the extended family: Most individual families were able to afford—and were therefore expected to have—their own homes, and communal living arrangements were limited to school and military dormitory settings or to groups of young people cohabiting to split costs. Today's economy has sparked a resurgence in communal living; it is no longer uncommon to find families pooling their resources to acquire a first property, hold it for five years, and use their equity to purchase separate homes.

The fundamental concept behind communal living is that each individual brings with him or her a particular talent or skill and utilizes it for the betterment of everyone in the community. Although the realities bring many challenges, the idea of communal living as a means of attaining a sense of belonging and happiness has periodically flourished in the United States. More than 600 "intentional communities," such as the Utopian Socialist Societies, arose and dissolved in the 1800s alone.[4] The latest U.S. communal living trend, however, takes a financially proactive stance in a market where the cost of living has increased faster than the average annual wage by almost 100 percent. Some families embrace the notion of developing compounds where several homes share one piece of property; others merge their resources to purchase smaller multifamily residences or very large homes for cohabitation. For example, many members of the Filipino community of National City, California, purchase properties with more than one residence. The parents typically reside in the main home and their adult children in one of the secondary dwellings; one family might have a house, a duplex in the back yard, and another unit over the garage.

DESIGN APPLICATION. Although designers probably will not be commissioned to design communal habitats in the strictest sense, they

can contribute much to homeowners' association projects (planned communities, condominiums, and retirement villages), all of which entail negotiating among public forums and boards of directors, particularly when developing the budget. Designers working at this level must have strong presentation, communication, and facilitation skills. They must also have patience, well developed listening skills, the ability to understand multiple points of view, and knowledge of the various issues, which are all key when working with community members who may tend to focus on issues directly affecting them rather than on the project as a whole. For example, an adjacent property owner to a new development may be concerned only with his or her parking situation rather than considering the value that a new development may bring to a community. Hence, designers must be patient when vocal residents push their personal agendas. They must possess excellent listening skills to discern important concepts, exhibit the capacity to understand each person's point of view, and be able to educate people about alternatives that best fulfill their needs. Designers who lack these skills should hire a consultant who specializes in them.

Identity versus Commonality

In this and subsequent discussions, a sense of individuality as opposed to commonality will be an issue of concern because a home's identity is partially formed when the physical construct depicts

an occupant's specific interests and needs. For example, the exterior fencing at Graceland has musical notes and guitars incorporated into the design, and the palaces of European nobility are rich in architectural detail; the former home denotes an obvious interest in music, whereas the latter is obviously one of social prominence and wealth. An example of commonality is a community of mass-developed homes that look alike, where residential associations keep tight controls over what can be displayed in the front yard. In this community people cannot deduce any particular attributes or characteristics of the inhabitant from the exterior architecture (Figure 7.4). Both identity and commonality can be examined on three different levels: physical, psychological, and individual.

Architecture, landscaping, and interior décor reveal a home's physical identity. In the past, a home's physical identity was highly valued, as were the creator's skills, craftsmanship, and painstaking attention to detail. In the United States, owners often sought to imitate the ornately detailed homes of the European aristocracy, and their basic social status could be deduced simply by the level of detail in their homes. Today, economic efficiency often overshadows detail and innovation, in effect shifting design from physical identity to physical commonality.

In the 1980s, large-scale developers began to attribute names and logos to developments (psychological notions of identity rather than physical identity) to create a sense of pride for the occupants. For example, Leisure World develops retirement communities internationally, and its logo is a giant globe. Such names and logos also serve to **commodify** developments. The U.S. communities of Palm Springs, California; Palm Beach, Florida; and Newport, Rhode Island; all have brand-name recognition associated with wealth (a home in these areas can cost four or five times more than an identical home in York, Pennsylvania). Developers strive to elicit this kind of positive

Figure 7.4: Many U.S. development firms find it more economical to purchase only one or two architectural renderings and make subtle changes to the floor plans and exterior details. Limiting the architectural style of homes saves design costs, allows the developer to purchase materials in bulk, and results in megacommunities with very little distinctive design identity.

identification. Ideally, identity is expressed through design choices (physical identity), but it can be established, reinforced, or even made memorable simply by naming a property (psychological notions of identity). For example, Cornelius Vanderbilt II built his Newport mansion where he could watch the waves break on the shore; therefore, the mansion, referred to as the Breakers, is given identity with that name, which suggests an important attribute of the home. Likewise, William Randolph Hearst constructed and decorated his estate to resemble a European castle; his mansion is referred to as Hearst Castle, and that name clearly reflects the main attribute of the home. Psychological notions of identity are not reserved exclusively for the rich; it works the other way as well. For example, the general public often associates Watts in Los Angeles, Harlem in New York, and the South Side in Chicago with crime and violence. Negative identification is very difficult to change; cities will often rename these areas in the hopes of building positive identification associations from scratch. However, it should be noted that many residents of these neighborhoods often have just as much pride in and affiliation with their homes—especially in places with historic or cultural significance, such as Harlem—as do residents of Palm Springs, Palm Beach, and Newport.[5]

The idea of identity–commonality can also relate to how individuals choose to design their spaces. People who regard their homes as safe havens tend to adorn them with personal artifacts (objects that express their identities); their décor can range from traditional to eclectic, but the design style has a specific and satisfying personal meaning to them. For example, a person may choose to display a collection of ancient weaponry, which an outsider may perceive as a messy, mismatched array and a design faux pas. Another person may choose to display only items that complement a particular design theme and invest very little emotionally. The former ranks high on identity because we can gain insight into the weapons collector's personality; the latter ranks high on commonality because the style is too generic and makes it nearly impossible for anyone to learn anything about the occupant's individuality.

Although most people perceive their homes as extensions of themselves, self-expression through home identity is often limited to a home's interior

Figure 7.5a and b: Buildings such as the Transamerica Tower in San Francisco (a) and the Leaning Tower of Pisa (b) are instantly recognizable landmarks associated with specific locales and are high in architectural identity. Many cities incorporate such landmarks to give their communities unique identities.

in relation to strict association rules and codes of décor. Large-scale developers capitalize on the human need for positive identification through name recognition, place commodification, or both. In effect, residents pay for the psychological idea of what it means to live in a particular development. Self-expression through architectural identity has all but vanished in modern home development and seems to be limited to structures such as the Transamerica Tower and the Leaning Tower of Pisa (Figure 7.5a and b). Architecturally, homes have shifted along the continuum from high identity to high commonality.

Openness versus Closedness

Both openness and enclosure can be perceived psychologically as well as physically. Many modern homes have open interiors; pillars, archways, and service bars are used to separate floor space between rooms rather than floor-to-ceiling walls that conceal one room from another. These types of physically open homes rely on social and psychological rules to prevent intrusion, such as keeping down noise levels so as not to disturb others. In Indonesia, where most homes are open to the natural elements, the culture enforces strict rules regarding access to private spaces.

Closed environments have physical or symbolic barriers that keep out the natural environment or other people and thus signal an occupant's desire for privacy. Concomitant with physical enclosure is the psychological perception that a place is uninviting or closed. Moats, drawbridges, and enclosing walls ensured the protective privacy of ancient castles, whereas today's barrier designs range from locked doors and vegetation to security cameras and electrified fences.

Whether a residence is opened or closed depends on the degree to which the occupants are willing to interact with their neighbors or other visitors. There are still many small towns across North America where people leave their doors unlocked; however, many residents of New York City have multiple dead bolts on their front doors and Hollywood celebrities barricade their homes with a series of defensive devices. Understanding the occupants' desired levels of openness will assist in developing designs that complement their needs.

Meaning of Home

Homes are not merely physical places where people live. Homes are created by how people think about and interact within them. A home plays a significant role in shaping a person's life and identity.[6] A good way to define a home is that through self-expression and personalization, it comes to resemble or represent who we are; provides a sense of connection to other people, our pasts, and our futures; provides both physical and symbolic warmth and safety; and is physically suitable for our physical and psychological health.

To most of us the ideal home symbolizes stability, security, and safety. Popular films and books have long capitalized on these romanticized ideas of home by depicting characters who return to former homes and relive events ranging from heinous acts of violence to precious moments with family members. This theme illustrates how intense emotion can be woven into a physical place inextricably, thereby forming place identity. This is why places are so important to people: They provide paths to self-identity by way of memories and emotions. The home environment can be considered in terms of its capacity to nurture and sustain psychological and social processes.[7]

Some notions of home correspond to basic human needs, as outlined by Maslow (see Chapter 1). For example, individuals who have limited economic means rank their residential concerns in order of priority: safety, health, familial needs, and aesthetics; wealthier individuals are more sensitive to their homes' aesthetic qualities (presumably because their more basic needs are not at risk).[8] In lower-income communities, design is often less of a concern than safety and finances. If we subscribe to Maslow's model of a hierarchy of needs, we may conclude that as people become wealthier and reach higher levels of the pyramid, they become more concerned with abstract concepts such as aesthetics and even self-actualization.

Place Meanings

Concepts of *home* are often tied to *place meanings*; both terms identify a state of mind rather than a physical place. What a place means to someone (i.e., the feelings a person associates with a physical place) is an important concept related to the self, others, and environments. Some researchers feel that people's distinctions of place, *sense of place*, and *place identity* are becoming less clear due to increases in technology and globalization.[9]

Place meanings change over time. Aspects of our experiences and personalities, as well as our relationships with others and the physical environment, interact to create and define the meanings that we attribute to places. Suppose that every time two friends visit the city of Tempe, they also visit the Arizona State University (ASU) campus and drive past certain places because one of the two friends was a student there. The university and surrounding area has meaning for him or her and it has become so strong that it has been incorporated into his or her identity. Conversely, a person who grew up feeling like an outsider and harassed by peers may deny any affiliation with the place where these events occurred once he or she has moved away. In the first example, the person exhibits a strong place attachment to ASU; in the second example, the individual has no attachment to the place. However, both examples illustrate how meaning can become attributed to a place, whether positive or negative.

One task of environmental psychologists is to help create a sense of place for people. An environment's distinct spatial features, how it compares with others, its connections to personal life paths, and its potential for change combine to affect the meanings places have for people. The person who developed place attachment to the ASU campus holds positive memories of past experiences; however, if this person were to move back to Tempe, the incongruity between past and present experiences could destroy the place meaning. Similarly, if a person were to move to a new place and experience elation and success, those feelings would be based on the experiences that led up to that moment; however, if this person were to have moved just a few years earlier, the experience could have been different. Place meaning should precede place attachment. However, just because a place means something to us does not guarantee that we will form an attachment to it—because it can mean something negative. For example, a person who experiences physical and emotional pain may develop strong negative feelings for the place; therefore, this person will not develop place attachment.

Place Attachment

Place identity cognitions have two basic functions: They define who people are, and they defend or protect people from settings and properties that threaten who they are and what they want to be.[10] Three broad elements influence people to become attached to places and affect people's well-being: personal characteristics and behaviors; the availability of facilities, opportunities, and resources; and a sense of belonging.[11] Place attachment refers to a person's bond with a place's social and physical environments.[12] We form attachments to places that not only define or express who we are (i.e., support our self-images) but also give us a sense of belonging, freedom, or both (i.e., provide psychological security). Consider the case of a design team who, through blood, sweat, tears, fun, and laughter, turned a condemned building into a stunning home, which they then refused to sell. It could be that through the process of rehabilitation, the team developed an attachment to the structure because of the memories they took with them from the experience. Clearly, a person who is very attached to a home is less likely to move.

Place attachment is an affiliation between a person and a place; it is a personal sense of connection that elicits feelings of comfort and security. It can be facilitated or destroyed by a person's level of control over household members, neighbors, or both—an important concept for both developers and designers, as many problems stemming from the lack of control can be mitigated by design. One study shows that greater place attachment is linked with greater ease in regulating privacy, an important part of identity (sense of self).[13] For instance, older teens are more likely to leave home if they have too little privacy, and tenants are more apt to leave apartments where they feel their personal freedoms are infringed upon (e.g., being blamed for or subjected to excessive noise). In such circumstances, doors, windows, and landscaping can be positioned to decrease visual exposure to other occupants, and shared walls can be constructed to dampen sound and augmented with design elements such as carpeting, tapestries, or both.

Memories are fundamental to attachment and may be evolved through meaningful objects or artifacts. Many clients demonstrate this by walking designers through their homes and recounting

Place meanings are discussed in greater detail in Chapter 4.

Figure 7.6: This environment reflects a fondness for, or an affiliation with, the Southwestern region of the United States.

when and where every artifact was obtained. For designers, the development of place attachment should precede discussions of aesthetics. A key question to ask clients before deciding on an architectural style, design scheme, or individual piece is, "What does this mean to you?" Because the person in the ASU example developed place attachment to the university and still identifies with it, inclusion of a modest ASU artifact would help to extend this past emotional connection to his or her present-day surroundings (Figure 7.6).

Personalization often reflects self-identity; the manner in which people decorate their homes reflects their realistic or idealized self-images. The complexity of a residence's interior is analogous with the owner's materialistic values.[14] In other words, greater interior complexity is directly associated with greater materialism, while less complexity is directly associated with lower material values. Place attachment may be increased by the comfortable, "homey" feelings instilled by personalization;[15]

since women tend to engage in more personalization, it comes as little surprise that they develop greater feelings of attachment to their homes than men.[16, 17] Conversely, place attachment and identity may be stifled in environments where personalization of a home or work space is restricted. In many housing developments, for example, the homeowner associations restrict the level of personalization that residents may display through landscape and architectural design. Residents in these developments are far more likely to develop weaker (if any) place attachment to such homes than people who own homes that they may personalize freely—and therefore they are more likely to move. The degree to which the neighborhood, exterior design, and interior décor reflect an occupant's sense of self (self-identity) is directly associated with the occupant's level of meaning and attachment.

We can use four perspectives to measure place attachment. The first relates to *fulfilling psychological needs* because the manner in which a person perceives and plans to use a home (as a means to escape stress, enhance social relations, or maintain identity) is key to developing attachment. The second perspective relates to *monetary value* (i.e., the structure for the occupant is primarily a means to acquire wealth). For example, some people opt to purchase homes in foreclosure during periods of economic strife and sell them when real estate prices increase. The third perspective focuses on *amenities* or *attributes* (e.g., appliances, storage space, and views). This third evaluation has been made traditionally by women as the primary occupants, but as homes become more digital and as more men either assume domestic roles or work from home, men are evaluating amenities as much as, if not more than, women. The fourth perspective relates to *specific functionality* (i.e., how well each room allows for its desired functions); for example, having the kitchen and dining room on opposite sides of the home would be problematic for occupants who enjoy cooking for and entertaining guests. The current cultural phenomenon of both parents having to work outside the home means that designers must ensure that kitchens and living rooms are large enough to accommodate the family as they prepare meals and share activities.

These four perspectives are not exclusive of one another but rather ranked according to relative importance. Therefore, a career woman may value her home for its ability to satisfy her psychological need for stress relief, a businessman may view his home only in terms of the equity it can produce, and a stay-at-home mom or dad may measure her or his home in terms of its amenities and its ability to fulfill various necessary functions. As mentioned, evaluations can also change over time. Thus, one person may measure his or her home in this sequence: monetary value, amenities, functionality, and psychological fulfillment. For this person, home is a means to increase wealth, which is why amenities (upgrades that tend to increase property value) are ranked second. Another person may view his or her home in the same way, but over time these priorities could change to the following: amenities, functionality, psychological fulfillment, and monetary value. The difference between these two people is that the former is younger and eager to acquire wealth; the latter is older and has no desire to leave the home where he or she intends to spend his or her retirement. Understanding how a client perceives his or her home will allow a designer to create the most appropriate design. The older person in the example will want creature comforts that increase the home's functionality and ability to satisfy needs; however, designers should keep in mind that people who want nice things to portray current status and that serve as reminders of former accomplishments may not want to spend excessive amounts on them.

Functionality

For most people, the meaning of home is analogous with its ability to satisfy their needs at a functional level. There are three classifications of functional space in a residence: primary, secondary, and tertiary (i.e., first, second, and third environments situated within larger territories). **Primary spaces** are communal or common areas where most of a resident's communication and social interaction take place (e.g., living and dining rooms). **Secondary spaces**, also communal, are where communication and social interaction migrate to and from (e.g., kitchens and porches). **Tertiary spaces** are private or personal areas (e.g., bathrooms and bedrooms) where a resident goes to be alone.

Five themes related to a pleasant atmosphere are also crucial to the functionality of successful design:[18] communication, accessibility, freedom to do any desired activity, occupation, and relaxation.

Communication

Designers must first determine where and when most communication occurs within a residence, as this varies among different families. Primary communal spaces tend to be in or around the kitchen during food preparation times and eventually shift to the dining and living rooms. Communication between primary, secondary, and tertiary spaces can be compromised by distance, closed doors, sleep schedules, and so on.

DESIGN APPLICATION. The structural design should allow for comfortable dialogue between secondary and primary spaces (kitchen and adjacent rooms or areas). This can be accomplished with openings, partial walls, service bars, or islands along shared walls or dividing points and by adding features that will accommodate other common activities (e.g., a place

Figure 7.7: This small alcove placed just outside the parents' bedroom can serve as a convenient bedroom for very young children yet allows for ample privacy. Later on, the alcove can be converted into a home office, large closet, or small sitting or reading room.

to do homework or crafts, a small television, or a comfortable seating area for reading) in the secondary space.

An intercom system can facilitate communication among primary, secondary, and tertiary spaces, allowing for the delivery of brief messages or for a parent to listen in on a sleeping infant. However, there are many who do not trust the reliability of an intercom system and would rather have their infant or toddler closer to them. Figure 7.7 illustrates this design solution to facilitate communication between different functional spaces.

Accessibility

Accessibility means having space for group interaction and sharing and for ensuring adequate privacy. For designers this means not only developing primary communal spaces (e.g., great rooms), but also distancing them from secondary and tertiary spaces (e.g., home offices, gyms, bedrooms, and bathrooms). Many features that enhance communication can also enhance access, and visual and acoustical privacy must be considered both visually and acoustically.

DESIGN APPLICATION. For visual privacy, place bedrooms away from primary areas and use solid doors. For acoustical privacy, use interior features to dampen sound. Hard rooms (with bare floors, minimal decoration, and modern or industrial furnishings) can act like echo chambers, whereas soft rooms (with carpeting, canvasbased artwork, or overstuffed furnishings) absorb sound. Low ceilings in hallways, carpet runners, and other creative sound-dampening items should be used between communal and private spaces. Architects should consider designing larger, better-spaced units to accommodate children for people who live in multifamily dwellings.[19]

according to another, increased time spent in green outdoor settings can reduce overall symptoms related to attention deficit/hyperactivity disorder (ADHD) in children.[44] Views of nature are fundamental to satisfaction and well-being, and windows provide opportunities for both *prospect-refuge* and *restorative experiences*.[45] Voluminous research demonstrates that people prefer rooms with windows.[46, 47] Likewise, exterior landscaping not only helps to produce natural scenes, but also helps to reduce the amount of atmospheric pollutants that can infiltrate a home and build up on exterior surfaces.[48] Leafy vegetation absorbs pollution by way of its natural cycle and provides additional surface area to which particulates will cling instead of the home, thereby not only providing the opportunity for prospect-refuge and attention restoration, but also enhancing the overall view.

DESIGN APPLICATION. Understanding that natural elements attract people to outdoor spaces can help designers create environments that promote well-being and social interaction. Developers and city planners should take active measures to maintain and preserve existing natural features in and around urban locations, and designers should create attractive landscapes by utilizing natural elements such as water, rocks, and trees in interior and exterior designs. Although not all homes can offer breathtaking vistas, measures can be implemented to ensure attractive and natural views for most residential properties.

Figure 7.10: Views of nature, including greenscapes and waterscapes, afford both physical and mental restorative value. As discussed in subsequent chapters, research has demonstrated that patients in hospital rooms with a view recover quicker and children who are exposed to green spaces have better cognitive abilities.

Summary Review

The idea of *home* has taken many forms throughout human existence. Caves, huts, tepees, and yurts provided basic shelter, but as societies evolved so too did housing demands, from relatively permanent, homogeneous structures open to the community to more permanent, differentiated, private homes. As societies continued to evolve, residences of varying sizes and levels of detail, as well as a multitude of adornment and furnishing styles, became a form of personal expression (self-identity) that indicated an occupant wealth and status (societal role). The modern concept of home has different meanings for different people. For some, home is a safe haven that provides privacy, security, and refuge

from the outside world; all of these dimensions of home provide identity and continuity, shape life experiences, and support patterns of daily life.

The meaning of home is highly subjective and contingent on a person's personality, age and stage of life, gender and social role, culture, and physical influences (including green spaces). For example, a 35-year-old businessman with a type C disposition will desire a large home with vaulted ceilings, expensive pieces of art, and an open floor plan that facilitates movement and large social gatherings. For this client, the primary interior spaces should be rectangular, not only to encourage social interaction but also to create the illusion of greater space; the exterior space should include a patio area large enough for gatherings, especially if the climate encourages outdoor activities.

Green spaces and access to nature enhance learning, concentration, and well-being by providing restorative physical and psychological benefits for people of all ages. They also increase a property's monetary value: Homes with natural vistas command the highest prices. Collaboration among design fields will ensure that residents be able to take full advantage of nature's benefits. City planners can ensure green street views by lining roads with trees and other vegetation. Architects can plan homes wherein oversize windows will capture the best daylight and views. Landscape designers can create natural tableaux or scenes that may be viewed from windows or traveled through as a person enters or exits the property. Interior designers can accentuate windows and incorporate natural features into the interior space.

In sum, people prefer residences that have attributes allowing them to fulfill their values.[49] Where we are in our lives (career, relationship, and family ties), the manner in which we portray ourselves to society (lineage, accomplishments, status, and wealth), and what we prize are all evident in our homes. Designers in every discipline who identify and understand their clients' needs, wants, desires, and values are far better equipped to develop designs that meet their clients' expectations and increase feelings of residential satisfaction.

Discussion Questions

1. How do you define your home? Is it your childhood home? Is it wherever you are at the moment? Is it permanent or temporary? What types of objects make a location feel like home?

2. Using the five dimensions of home to define your space preferences, give examples from your life that support each choice.

3. Discuss the effect of a highly segmented residence on family dynamics. Assume that a family of four (mother, father, son, and daughter) and the family pet live in a Victorian-style home. What *constraints* or *supports* does the home's layout provide?

4. Discuss U.S. culture in terms of living envi-

ronments. Imagine having no knowledge of U.S. history, tradition, culture, beliefs, morals, or language. What would you infer about U.S. lifestyles based solely on residences?

5. Discuss differences in how people navigate through a homogenous neighborhood versus an eclectic one. For example, Amsterdam is famous for the intricately detailed homes along its canals, many of which predate the use of house numbers (e.g., 123 Canal Street) and had "addresses" such as "the blue and yellow house with the sculpture of Neptune over the door."

6. Discuss places to which you are attached. What characteristics evoke the emotional responses that lead to your *place attachment*? How would you design a bedroom to ensure calm and peace, relative to place attachment?

7. Discuss how you would determine the design needs of a family of four plus a set of grandparents. What questions would you need to ask to design effectively?

8. Discuss ways to advertise or market downtown condominiums or town houses to both men and women. What design aspects or *attributes* would you need to incorporate to increase the value. How would you highlight them differently?

9. Based on information in this chapter, discuss possible reasons for the current popularity of Asian-inspired architecture and design.

Learning Activities

1. Poll 20 people outside of this class. Ask where they are from and record their answers, graphing the data according to category (e.g., city, state, region, and country). Then ask the same subjects to list where they have lived, and graph the number of locations (e.g., bar graph: x-axis = locations, y-axis = individuals).

2. Draw a humorous sketch or write a story illustrating the imaginary encounter of a historical figure in a modern architectural structure (e.g., Marie Antoinette in the Guggenheim Bilbao).

3. Draw two sketches: one depicting an environment suited to a person who considers his or her home to be permanent and the other de-

picting an environment for someone who considers his or her home to be temporary.

4. Conduct research at the library or on the Internet to find a floor plan for a highly *segmented* home, and draw it using ¼" = 1' to 0" scale. Overlay a *homogenous* floor plan on the same blueprint, then compare and contrast the similarities and differences between the spaces.

5. Design a home for you and four other students to share, showing floor plans as well as circulation. What features are essential for communal living? What typical residential features can easily be excluded from your design?

6. Photograph two local neighborhoods and use the photos to create a poster that illustrates *identity* versus *commonality*. Look for clues that identify the community as being close-knit or casual, using this chapter as a guide to identifying specific characteristics of each neighborhood. Your poster should identify what inferences and conclusions you have drawn, and why, from each neighborhood.

7. Draw a sketch of your residence, focusing on *personalization*. Highlight areas that are highly personalized (e.g., a bookcase with a collection of photos) and those that are not (e.g., a bathroom). Repeat this exercise in a friend's residence; then compare and contrast the level of personalization with your personalities. How could this information aid your design process? What attributes about your residences would you consider when designing a new home?

8. Contact a realtor and ask if you can work together to poll prospective home buyers. Create a short survey that gathers nonspecific background information: age range, occupation, number of residents, expected period of residence, and so on. Ask home buyers to rank their prospective or ideal home according to amenities, functionality, monetary value, and psychological fulfillment. Share all data if the realtor desires, and ask if she or he already collects similar information or uses a similar technique for establishing clients' residential preferences.

9. Sketch examples of living rooms for each of the five personality types (A through E), mak-ing sure to label significant objects.

10. Draw a timeline of housing in North America, from cave dwellings through modern trends.

Terminology

commodify   To commercialize; to turn an intrinsic value into a commodity (i.e., a recognizable unit of economic production)

hard room   Room decorated with bare floors, minimal wall and standing artwork, and modern or industrial furnishings

primary spaces   Common areas in territories such as residences and workplaces where communication and social interaction take place (e.g., living rooms and conference rooms)

psychological construct   Conceptual representation of an environment or idea; a way of thinking about or conceiving of a place or idea

secondary spaces   Common areas in territories such as residences and workplaces to and from which communication and social interaction migrate (e.g., kitchens and reception desks)

segmentation   Division of a whole space or structure by separation or partition into smaller areas/sections

soft room   Room decorated with carpeting, canvas-based artwork, and overstuffed furnishings

tertiary spaces   Private or personal spaces or areas where people go to be alone

References

1. U.S. Census Bureau (as reported in the online publication *Relocation Journal & Real Estate News*, January 24, 2000). *Newsbreak 6–4*: Moving from here to there. www.relojournal.com /nbarchive/nbn216.htm.

2. Altman, I., and Chemers, M. (1980). *Culture and Environment*. Monterey, CA: Brooks/Cole.

3. Gifford, R. (2002). *Environmental psychology: Practice and principles* (3rd ed.). Canada: Optimal Books.

4. Bedford, G. (2003). *Women's Roles and the Presence of Gender Equity in Utopian Societies*. http://athena.louisville.edu/a-s/english /subcultures/colors/red/g0bedf01.

5. McAuley, W. J. (1998). History, race, and at-

tachment to place among elders in the rural all-black towns of Oklahoma. *Journal of Gerontology: Social Sciences, 53B-1*, S35–S45.

6. Popay, J., Thomas, C., Williams, G., Bennett, S., Gatrell, A., and Bostock, L. (2003). A proper place to live: Health inequalities, agency and the normative dimensions of space. *Social Science & Medicine, 57*, 55–69.

7. Lawrence, R. (1987). *Housing, dwellings, and homes: Design theory, research, and practice.* Chichester, England: Wiley.

8. Salling, M., and Harvey, M. E. (1981). Poverty, personality, and sensitivity to residential stressors. *Environment and Behavior, 13-2*, 131–163.

9. Gustafson, P. (2001). Meanings of place: Everyday experience and theoretical conceptualizations. *Journal of Environmental Psychology, 21*, 5–16.

10. Proshansky, H. M., Fabian, A. K., and Kaminoff, R. (1983). Place-identity: Physical world socialization of the self. *Journal of Environmental Psychology, 3*, 57–83.

11. See note 6.

12. Brown, B. B., and Perkins, D. D. (1992). Disruptions in place attachment. In I. Altman and S.M. Low (Eds.), *Place attachment: Human behavior and the environment* (Vol. 12, pp. 279–304). New York: Plenum Press.

13. Harris, P. B., Brown, B. B., and Werner, C. M. (1996). Privacy regulation and place attachment: predicting attachments to a student family housing facility. *Journal of Environmental Psychology, 16–4*, 287–301.

14. Weisner, T. S., and Weibel, J. C. (1981). Home environments and family lifestyles in California. *Environment and Behavior, 13–4*, 417–460.

15. Becker, F. D., and Coniglio, C. (1975). Environmental messages: Personalization and territory. *Humanities, 11*, 55–74.

16. Sebba, R., and Churchman, A. (1983). Territories and territoriality in the home. *Environment and Behavior, 15–2*, 191–210.

17. Tognoli, J. (1980). Differences in women's and men's responses to domestic space. *Sex Roles, 6–6*, 833–842.

18. Pennartz, P. J. J. (1986). Atmosphere at home: A qualitative approach. *Journal of Environmental Psychology, 6*, 135–153.

19. Evans, G. W., Lercher, P., and Kofler, W. W. (2002). Crowding and children's mental health: The role of house type. *Journal of Environmental Psychology, 22–3*, 221–231.

20. Michelson, W. (1977). *Environmental choice, human behavior and residential satisfaction.* New York: Oxford University Press.

21. Lindberg, E., Gärling, T., and Montgomery, H. (1986). Beliefs and values as determinants of residential preferences and choices. *Umea Psychological Reports*, Number 194.

22. Lindberg, E., Gärling, T., and Montgomery, H. (1989). Preferences for and choices between verbally and numerically described housing alternatives. *Umea Psychological Reports*, Number 189.

23. Tognoli, J. (1987). Residential environments. In I. Altman and D. Stokols (Eds.), *Handbook of environmental psychology*. New York: J. Wiley & Sons.

24. Canter, D. (1983). The purposive evaluation of places: A facet approach. *Environment and Behavior, 15*, 659–698.

25. Amaturo, E., Costagliola, S., and Ragone, G. (1987). Furnishing and status attributes: A sociological study of the living room. *Environment and Behavior, 19–2*, 228–249.

26. See note 3.

27. Nasar, J. L. (1981b). Visual preferences of elderly public housing residents: Residential street scenes. *Journal of Environmental Psychology, 1*, 303–313.

28. Nasar, J. L. (1983). Adult viewers' preferences in residential scenes: A study of the relationship of environmental attributes to preference. *Environment and Behavior, 15*, 589–614.

29. See note 3.

30. See note 20.

31. Franck, K. A. (2002). Women and environment. In R. B. Bechtel and A. Churchman (Eds.), *Handbook of environmental psychology* (p. 349). New York: John Wiley & Sons, Inc.

32. Peterson, R. (1987). Gender issues in the home and urban environment. In E. H. Zube and G. T. Moore (Eds.), *Advances in environment, behavior and design* (Vol. 1, pp. 187–220). New York: Plenum.

33. Keeley, R. M., and Edney, J. J. (1983). Model house designs for privacy, security, and social

interaction. *Journal of Social Psychology, 119,* 219–228.

34. Csikszentmihalyi, M., and Rochberg-Halton, E. (1981). *The meaning of things.* Cambridge: Cambridge University Press.

35. Hasell, M. J., Peatross, F. D., and Bono, C. A. (1993). Gender choice and domestic space: Preferences for kitchens in married households. *Journal of Architectural and Planning Research, 10,* 1–22.

36. See note 3.

37. Rothblatt, D. N., Garr, D. J., and Sprague, J. (1979). *The suburban environment and women.* New York: Praeger.

38. Widmar, R. (1984). Preferences for multifamily housing: Some implications for public participation. *Journal of Architectural and Planning Research, 1,* 245–260.

39. Baird, J. C., Cassidy, B., and Kurr, J. (1978). Room preference as a function of architectural features and user activities. *Journal of Applied Psychology, 63,* 719–727.

40. Gifford, R. (1999). The Adjustment of the elderly to congregate care housing. Report to the Canada Mortgage and Housing Corporation.

41. Levine-Coley, R., Kuo, F. E., and Sullivan, W.C. (1997). Where does community grow? The social context created by nature in urban public housing. *Environment and Behavior, 29–4,* 468–494.

42. Ham-Rowbottom, K. A., Gifford, R., and Shaw, K. T. (1999). Defensible space theory and the police: Assessing the vulnerability of residences to burglary. *Journal of Environmental Psychology, 19–2,* 117–129.

43. Gottfried, A. W., and Gottfried, A. E. (1984). Home environment and cognitive development in young children of middle-socioeconomic-status families. In A.W. Gottfried (Ed.), *Home environment and early cognitive development.* Orlando: Academic Press.

44. Taylor, A. F., Kuo, F. E., and Sullivan, W. C. (2001). Coping with ADD: The surprising connection to green play settings. *Environment and Behavior, 33-1,* 54–77.

45. Kaplan, R., and Dana, S. T. (2001). The nature of the view from home: Psychological benefits. *Environment and Behavior, 33–4,* 507–542.

46. Ne'eman, E., and Hopkinson, R. G. (1970). Critical minimum acceptable window size: A study of window design and provision of a view. *Lighting Research and Technology, 2–1,* 17–27.

47. Verderber, S. F. (1986). Dimensions of person-window transactions in the hospital environment. *Environment and Behavior, 18–4,* 450–466.

48. Ullah, M. B., Kurniawan, J. T., Pho, L. K., Wai, T. K., and Tregenza, P. R. (2003). Attenuation of diffuse daylight due to dust deposition on glazing in a tropical urban environment. *Lighting Research and Technology, 35–1,* 19–29.

49. Lindberg, E., Hartig, T., Garvill, J., and Gärling, T. (1992). Residential-location preferences across the life span. *Journal of Environmental Psychology, 12,* 187–198.

EIGHT

Environments for Youth

Although the physical environment affects the behaviors of all people, the effects can differ among groups. Children especially stand out as users of environments because they develop from completely helpless beings into young adults who have learned how to live within those environments. The manner in which the environment affects young people varies by circumstance and is highly contingent on their stage of development. Young people mature in stages, distinguished in this chapter as fetal or prenatal, infant, toddler and preschool, child, preadolescent, and adolescent. The fetal or prenatal period spans the eighth week after conception to birth, and its environment is made up of the mother's womb and all that she is exposed to. Infancy is the stage from birth to about one year. Toddlers and preschoolers range in age from one to five years. The school-age child stage is from 5 to 8 years, while the preadolescent stage ranges from ages 9 to 11. The adolescent stage is from about 12 to 19 years. Although these age delineations vary among young people, they help designers develop age-appropriate environments.

Considerations in Environmental Design for Youth

Designers must consider several important issues when creating environments for children of each developmental stage: stress (internal and external); injury and illness; issues of space, place, and privacy; the importance of play; and housing and green spaces. A brief discussion of each issue follows.

Stress

The result of stress on people can range from shortened gestation periods to alterations in the brain's chemistry and function, which contributes to lower disease resistance.[1,2] The negative impact of stress on a fetus can lead to premature birth, malformation of fetal brain function, or both.[3] The effects of stress seem to be more profound in children who are younger than ten years of age, are male, or who experienced prenatal stress. Children who live in poverty or in violent communities or are bullied in school settings are also subject to more external stress than other children.[4] Children who have lower thresholds for external and internal stimuli find a wider variety of social events and conditions to be negatively stressful as measured by cortisol levels.[5]

A child's physical response to stress is usually much more intense than an adult's and involves the entire body. Stress in children often manifests as overt physical reactions, such as crying, sweating palms, running away, aggressive or defensive outbursts, rocking and other self-comforting behaviors, headaches and stomachaches, twirling or pulling the hair, chewing and sucking of thumbs or fingers, biting of skin and fingernails, bed-wetting, and sleep disturbances.[6–8] Other signs of stress include depression and avoidance; excessive shyness; hypervigilance; excessive worrying; obsessive interest in objects, routines, and food; persistent, strong concerns about "what comes next;" and excessive clinging.[9]

Stress has greater effects on children, particularly those younger than six years, because children are developmentally less capable of thinking about a stressful event in its entirety. They don't have the experience to discern between possible behaviors to respond to a stressful event. They don't understand that an event is separate from them and their feelings and that they can change their reactions in response to a change in stimuli.[10]

One factor in the breaking point of stress for children is that of *threshold*, the point at which a person can no longer psychologically handle additional stress. Once a threshold is exceeded, the resulting manifestation is either internal (e.g., learned helplessness, eating disorders, suicide attempts, or reclusion) or external (e.g., firing a gun into crowded areas, open hostility to others, or random acts of violence). Sources of stress can derive from multiple venues and accumulate in a person's psych. As stress levels increase during the day, people must spend equal or more time in a stress-free environment to allow those levels to decrease. What goes up must come down; if a person has no stress-free environment or his or her exposure to it is minimal, the stress level will eventually reach the breaking point.

Prolonged exposure to a single stressor can lead to the continued use of coping strategies that may result in entrenched behavior patterns, especially if children perceive their strategies as effective.[11, 12] Stressors often converge, causing a seemingly low-stress event to be perceived very differently by children; the interaction of these stressors can have cumulative and long-lasting effects on children.[13] Examining the causes and manifestations of stress in children helps to illustrate the importance of designing stress-free environments and of redesigning environments that cause stress (Table 8.1).

Table 8.1 Sources of Stress in Children[14]

INTERNAL SOURCES	EXTERNAL SOURCES
Hunger	Separation from family
Pain	Change in family composition
Sensitivity to noise	Exposure to arguing and interpersonal conflict
Sensitivity to temperature changes	Exposure to violence
Sensitivity to high social densities	Aggression from others (e.g., bullying)
Fatigue	Loss of something cherished, such as a pet
Environmental over- or understimulation	Excessive expectations for accomplishment

Injury and Illness

Incidents of injury and illness are good examples of the human–environment relationship because the environment is often a causal factor. The probability of accidental injury and victimization can be real (physical threats to safety) or perceived (fearful expectations instilled by a blend of personal experience, peer influences, and media messages). Injury is the number one health risk for children younger than 15 years. According to statistics compiled for children ages 14 and younger, each year more than 14 million—1 out of 4—are injured seriously enough to require medical attention, and nearly 92,000 children become permanently disabled.[15] Falls are the leading cause of unintentional injuries. In 2002 92,500 children under the age of 14 were treated in emergency rooms for burn injuries. Additionally, in 2002 about 115 youngsters drowned in or around the home;[16] and 206,000 children, mostly boys, were treated in U.S. hospital emergency rooms for toy-related injuries.[17] The desire to prevent accidents and victimization is a basic parental instinct, yet injury is the leading cause of death for children in developed countries, more so for boys than for girls.[18]

Allergies and disease prevention are other important considerations for designers. In the United States, allergic asthma affects about 3 million children (8 to 12 percent of all children) and 7 million adults at an estimated cost of $6.2 billion a year. Researchers implicate the increased time youngsters spend indoors and the resulting exposure to carpeting and other materials that hold allergens with which people in developed nations surround themselves.[19] Scientists recommend not only preventing the growth of mildew and mold in homes by eliminating sources of indoor moisture (e.g., leaky roofs and plumbing), but also encouraging caregivers to increase their awareness of environmental triggers to reduce school absenteeism associated with asthma. For example, homes where pets have access to the entire house are associated with more cases of asthma among children than homes in which pets are denied access to children's bedrooms.[20] A child's exposure to allergens can be reduced by limiting pet access to certain rooms and removing stuffed animals, rugs, curtains, and lamp shades from an asthmatic child's bedroom.[21]

DESIGN APPLICATION. Designers must acknowledge the basic law of physics: For every action, there is an equal and opposite reaction. Designers of the built environment have the goal or obligation to alleviate as many safety threats as possible through their design initiatives. Additionally, designers must beware of risk factors that their designs may create. When designing homes, one of the first steps for designers is to understand their clients and their clients' particular needs from an environment. Clients who have young children or who are planning to have a family in the near future will have a significant impact on the overall design not only in the selection of materials to be used but also in the actual space planning. If a design element is labeled a risk by the media or through personal experience, then that element will affect a client's perception of the overall design. For example, parents may insist on getting plantation shutters if a neighbor's child suffered a fatal accident with a curtain string. When developing an environment for a child, every designer must be acutely aware of multiple factors that may lead to injury, illness, or both.

Space, Place, and Privacy

Residential space, place, and privacy preferences and evaluations are important considerations to environmental psychologists, and outdoor spaces are just as valuable as those indoors. Developers often build megahousing complexes made up of fairly large houses on small parcels of land or high-density housing such as condominiums with reduced floor space in their efforts to maximize land use and increase profits. Ideally, such projects should at least incorporate recreation areas containing facilities such as basketball courts, soccer fields, and playgrounds, and at most they should include swimming pools, whirlpool baths, and clubhouses. Such amenities, while not feasible on most single parcels, are an important factor in the development of children's gross motor and social skills. Because the physical environment can promote or hinder social relationships that are crucial to personal and community well-being,[22] outdoor spaces with natural landscaping can build a sense of community and facilitate the development of social skills.

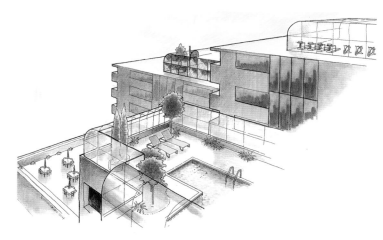

Figure 8.1: In high-density urban areas where space is at a premium, many developers find it difficult to provide separate recreational areas. One option is to utilize rooftops. In this illustration, four recreational zones are separated by height rather than by physical proximity. There is a fitness center on the uppermost deck. There is a basketball court on the next level; the height of the curved fencing prevents the ball from leaving the area. Below the basketball court is a swimming pool, and on the lowest level there is an outdoor entertainment center for barbecues and other social gatherings. The tall Plexiglas encases everything and serves a dual function: It prevents people from falling over or throwing anything over the edge of the building and allows for attractive views from both roof and ground levels.

Although young people often identify natural settings as their favorite places, those with high fear-expectancies; disgust sensitivities toward insects, dirt, or dampness; or desires for modern comforts are more likely to prefer manicured outdoor settings to wild land environments.[23] Although older adolescents seek affiliation with their peers, they often seek solitary places to relax and gain perspective on events that threaten their self-esteem and sense of place in the world.[24] It is therefore important for developers and landscape architects to understand the cultural and developmental norms of the population that intends to inhabit or use a particular development, such as this rooftop recreation area (Figure 8.1).

Crowding

Residential crowding can negatively affect children's psychological health[25] and increase both undesirable classroom behaviors and parent–child conflict. Children who experience high residential crowding tend to use less sophisticated speech and be less verbally responsive. Researchers speculate that this may be one reason why children in crowded homes have delays in cognitive development.[26] One study found that incidents of child abuse increased significantly when residential density exceeded 1.5 persons per room.[27] The violation of a child's need for privacy results in either physical aggression or psychological withdrawal, depending on the child's personality and the length of crowding; children are more susceptible to behavioral disturbances (e.g., aggression, anxiety, depression, or hyperactivity) when chronically exposed to excessive high density in the home, in child-care settings, or both.[28] In sum, children's growth, development, and behavior all suffer in high-density households.

DESIGN APPLICATION. In homes where population density is high it is especially important to provide safe spaces where children can obtain a degree of privacy. A small clubhouse can provide a space in which children can engage in pretend play, contemplate stressful events, or seek temporary refuge. In the future, the clubhouse could be converted to a home gym or home office.

See Chapter 3 for more information regarding the integration theories.

Place

Place identity is fundamentally formed by our experiences and plays a role in our emotions and **self-regulation** (expression of pleasure and pain and the experience of the self).[29] For example, when a person visits a family home after being away for many years, old memories will likely surface and may even bring about old behavior patterns. Although places can provide feelings of privacy, control, and security, children can also identify places of fear and danger and develop negative feelings toward their environments.[30] To a child who associates positive feelings with Grandma's house, the mere mention of going there evokes happy feelings and behaviors; conversely, to a child who associates negative feelings with school, the mere mention of going to school will evoke fearful and anxious feelings and behaviors. Other research findings show that people form *place attachments* to specific places that allow them to fulfill emotional needs.[31] From the first perspective, the human–environment relationship is *transactional*; from the second, it is *interactional*.

For more on place identity see Chapter 4.

People influence environments and vice versa: Imagine yourself as a small child at a doctor's office. In the waiting room, you become upset because other children are crying. Later, when the doctor gives you a shot, it hurts. When you are back in the waiting room, you upset another child because now you are crying. These concepts of interaction and transaction are components of the *integration theories*, which describe the way people see themselves in relation to their environments. A third component, the *organismic* perspective, combines multiple contributing factors (e.g., the child's experiences that day, the child's health, and the parent's mood) with the memory of pain and other children crying in the waiting room.

Children select and compete with other children for places within their territorial ranges; however, social restrictions such as parental or physical restrictions such as traffic can limit the range of environments from which they can choose. Young people's evaluations and choices of places are affected by variables, including their prior exposure, their upbringing (whether urban or rural), exploration restraints, the selective portrayal of environments by the media, and their peers' preferences.[32] Age, gender, and the effects of specific environments determine a child's environmental behavior and opinions.[33] Young boys prefer places where gratification and protection are readily available, whereas older children and adolescents of both genders tend to favor places that are comfortable, calm, relaxed, and beautiful.[34]

Privacy

Bedrooms are personal territories. Children need and desire their own territories not only for self-expression and identification, but also as private places for contemplation and relaxation. The desire for privacy is contingent on developmental stage and concepts of self-identity and self-esteem.[35–37] *Personalizing* their private spaces gives young people tangible ways to express their individuality;[38, 39] children as young as age three prize a room they can personalize and to which they can retreat when they are upset or wish to be alone.[40] However, children have fickle desires that change fairly rapidly, and designs should be inexpensive and easily modified.

Adolescents value the freedom and control they

feel in their solitary places, yet also value places where they can interact socially.[41, 42] A study of Swedish children ages 13 to 17 found that girls preferred private places, whereas boys' preferred public ones.[43] Girls tend to be more affiliative and as such prefer private environments where they can discuss personal thoughts and feelings with other girls their age. It is through these personal revelations to others that they solidify social bonds and friendships. Boys tend to prefer environments that are more public and allow them to see and be seen. It is through this sense of belonging to something larger than them (the group) that they gain confidence and forge a support system of lasting friendships.

Housing and Green Spaces

In the United States, understanding the human–environment relationship has been commonly regarded as unnecessary until recently. However, valuable research is coming from European, Mediterranean, and Asian countries. A study conducted on the island of Cyprus found that the concept of home differed between children and adults; the children's wants and needs for their homes matched or exceeded the general standards common to U.S. suburbs and included the desire for a grass lawn.[44] This study, while not necessarily generalizable to other cultures, is evidence that children are conscious of their housing conditions and society's housing norms.

More U.S. research is accumulating on the human–environment experience, providing a better understanding of how the environment affects our behaviors. For example, according to one study:[45]

- Children, especially when young, spend a majority of their time at home, and housing quality has been shown to affect children's general psychological health and task persistence.

- As with noise and crowding, chronic exposure to poor-quality housing can decrease children's sense of control over their environments and contribute to their sense of helplessness.
- Children living in higher-quality housing not only have fewer behavioral problems and lower incidences of anxiety, depression, misconduct, or deviant acts, but also score higher on tests designed to measure personal motivation.

Natural environments provide mental and physical restorative benefits. This seems especially true for young people: Children run, jump, and tumble in open spaces, which allows them to develop their gross motor skills. Children also develop their imaginations (e.g., pretending to be superheroes and inventing new games) and social skills (e.g., playing team sports). Studies on how children behave in outdoor spaces of public housing show that they engage in significantly more play—and more creative play—in high-vegetation areas than in barren spaces[46] and both teacher-led activities and pretend play in school yards concentrate in natural places.[47] Research has also determined that children who relocate to homes with improved natural views tend to have more attentional capacity,[48] that children with attention deficit/hyperactivity disor-

Figure 8.2: Children who live in homes that have natural views tend to have greater attention capacity. The desk in this image is positioned so that a child can enjoy the view during a moment of rest, not so that the child is continuously looking out the window. From this vantage point, the child also can easily see who enters or leaves the room, which affords the child a sense of mastery over the environment.

Figure 8.3: This floor plan allows parents to prepare dinner while supervising their children as they watch television or do homework.

der (ADHD) function better than usual following activities in green settings, and that the symptoms of ADHD are less severe in children who have access to greener play areas.[49] For these reasons, both indoor and outdoor natural spaces must be considered in the overall design process (Figure 8.2).

The following design features have been reported as some of the most important components, in addition to overall quality, of a good housing project, for single-parent families:[50]

See Chapter 3 for more on the mental and physical restorative benefits of natural environments.

- On-site or nearby child-care facilities
- An open kitchen–living room area for simultaneous functions (Figure 8.3)
- Separate common areas for children and parents
- Close proximity to public transportation
- Classroom space for doing homework or homeschooling
- Indoor and outdoor play spaces

Parks, Playgrounds, and School Yards

Playing allows children to learn, discover, create, and interact with their environments. However,

children's contact with the natural environment, particularly within schools and playgrounds, is declining in part because of safety concerns, time constraints on parents, and the loss of natural spaces brought about by increased urban and suburban development.[51] Today's children are increasingly regimented in their daily activities as they are shuttled between child-care centers, schools, after-school programs, and organized sports activities. Currently, more than 5 million U.S. children younger than three years of age are cared for by adults other than their parents during the workday. These are typically facilities outside the home, usually day-care centers and preschools for very young children and public and private schools for older children and teens. Often the care of these children is substandard,[52] and there is little time for unstructured play. When there is time, the only areas available for unstructured play may be construction sites, alleys, washes (dry river beds), or vacant lots.

Inactivity among children can adversely affect their health, well-being,[53] and social and emotional competence.[54] Likewise, research shows that increasing a child's physical activity can reduce risk factors for diseases such as osteoporosis and heart disease and that children should engage in moderate to vigorous exercise daily.[55]

Unstructured playtime is valuable for the development of children in the first seven or eight years of life. Areas devoted to unstructured play must not only include space for physical activities such as running, jumping, climbing, and swinging, but also allow for, and stimulate, fantasy play, social dramatic play, sensory and exploratory play, and construction play (building things with material such as sand, gravel, water, or dirt).[56] These outdoor spaces must suit children's developmental needs related to both diverse play and learning opportunities.[57] Green school yards and playgrounds, for example, promote physical activity, more creative play,[58] and social interaction.[59]

Despite research that shows the positive benefits of vegetation on attitude formation,[60, 61] many school yards and playgrounds remain bleak and monotonous. Researchers suggest that the reason why school yards and playgrounds across the United States have been neglected is a result of increased school enrollment, crowded school grounds, shortening of recess, removal of play equipment, and increased cases of bullying.[62] The extent to which these issues affect the presence and maintenance of school yards and playgrounds is unknown. What is known, however, is that a large part of a child's development depends on his or her environment.[63]

In many Western societies, schools are an environment wherein physical and cognitive skills can be both fostered and encouraged. However, traditional school yards and playgrounds are often limited to physical development. This is because typical school yards and playgrounds contain only fixed play structures (e.g., swings, jungle gyms, and slides) and green areas. Research on these types of playgrounds has shown that children are more likely to establish social hierarchies based on physical prowess.[64] In contrast, school yards and playgrounds with natural features and vegetation encourage children to develop social hierarchies based on communication skills and creativity, which leads to greater academic performance.[65] This is not to say that fixed playground equipment should be eliminated; on the contrary, it should be augmented so that school yards or playgrounds facilitate both physical and cognitive development.

Researchers stress the importance of creating environments that minimize the potential for children falling or running into things.[66] A child who falls just 3 to 5 inches onto concrete or asphalt can sustain a 210 g-force impact, which is enough to cause a fatal injury.[67] Surfacing mats made of safety-tested rubber or rubberlike materials may be utilized as long as use is kept to a minimum. Such mats usually come in dark colors, and dark surfaces absorb the sun's ultraviolet (UV) rays, thereby increasing the ambient temperature, potential for heat-related illnesses, and probability of sunburn. These dark mats produce the same effects as asphalt, which often covers large areas. Asphalt also reflects glare, as do mirrors, metals, glass, and white- or light-colored surfaces. Careful consideration must be given to their placement in outdoor play spaces. Premature aging, skin cancer, and eye damage are linked to high UV radiation levels, and children are most vulnerable to the negative effects of UV rays.[68] Younger children's skin and eyes are most sensitive.

The complexity of the school yard and playground environment should reflect the developmental abilities of the children using it[69] and should foster and promote physical, cognitive, and social skills.[70] Improving school yards and playgrounds to better suit the needs of children can help their physical and social development while promoting diverse, safe outdoor play and teaching activities. Included in these areas should be components that foster cognitive activities, such as bushes, gardens, and sandpits, along with components that support physical and motor skills, such as fixed play structures and paved areas.[71] Elements of a park, playground, or school yard that promote necessary developmental skills in children include:

- Multiple spaces for diverse activities such as team sports, solitary play, and play with natural elements or loose parts.[72] Consider, however, that today's children are growing up faster, but also staying young longer.[73] This means that the play structures used to attract children whose ages range from five to their preteens in the 1970s now are used predominately by eight-year-old children.[74] Likewise, modern-day 10-year-olds often prefer to engage in more sophisticated activities alongside 18- to 20-year-olds and therefore require parks and playgrounds that contain bike trails, skateboard parks, and rock climbing centers.[75]
- A variation in soil level, surface materials, seating options, foliage, artwork, colors, textures, and sources of shade.[76] According to one researcher, children's exploration of outdoor spaces can be encouraged by varying the ground cover to include elements such as grass, sand, different paving materials, and stones; this can include varying the height, shape, and type of plants and trees to create contrasting textures, colors, and scents.[77]
- Spaces that promote adventure, inspire mystery, and support intrigue.[78]
- Natural elements such as sand, dirt, water, trees, bushes, mud holes, shallow ponds, tall un-manicured grass, and gardens.[79]
- Places children can use to create their own environments (e.g., building a fort).[80]
- Items and areas that support different stages of difficulty and still support challenging yet attainable goals.[81]
- Covered seating areas with tables to support socializing or quiet play activities.[82]

DESIGN APPLICATION. All school yard and playground designs should incorporate a healthy mixture of green spaces, including trees and grass (which are essential for attention restoration)[83, 84] as well as artificial safety material around fixed playground equipment to reduce injury. School yards and playgrounds should be designed to provide sensory stimulation and allow for a variety of play and learning opportunities that promote physical activity such as large green fields, intellectual inspiration stemming from the presence of nature in it's natural habitat such as frogs in a pond, and sensory stimulation associated with the different interpretations of light on the skin that results from playing in wooded areas versus open fields. A school yard, for example, might encompass a wooded area along its periphery that contains trees, grasses, and nontoxic flowering plants; a field of thick grass to be used for sports and games; and two or more small islands surrounding colorful structures or equipment. These islands should have connecting pathways made of sand or wood chips to facilitate the total use of the play space.[85] It is important to note that separating the playground equipment reduces the aggregated black surface. Ideally, an outdoor play space should include play equipment and an uncultivated, natural area (to provide shade and opportunities to explore nature and to promote creativity and inventiveness) as well as hardened

surfaces intermixed with other types of natural spaces to facilitate a variety of activities.[86]

Additionally, up-to-date parks and playgrounds allow for a variety of activities. Just as many senior housing developments include golf courses, housing developments intended for families with children should include a bike course, skate park, and a series of rock climbing options (the rocks should look like rocks). Because of increased development, large expanses for unstructured play are not always possible, particularly within high-density urban environments. In these areas, designers should consider incorporating large and small flower boxes along the edges of school yards and playgrounds, perhaps on or next to fences. They should also consider reserving small areas that can be used as vegetable gardens. Lastly, regardless of the size of the school yard or playground, there should be at least one shade tree surrounded by a patch of grass to facilitate access to nature.

When planning outdoor play areas, designers should involve the primary stakeholders: children, parents, teachers, and care providers.[87] Although their input is important to the design process, stakeholders must first be educated about design initiatives related to child development so that they can make well-informed decisions when making their choices. Other important considerations during the planning stage are the cultural, geographical, and socioeconomic aspects of a community.[88] For example, in a South American–based community, incorporating a soccer field would be more appropriate than incorporating a football field, which would be favored in a North American–based community.

Not surprisingly children learn at an early age to avoid pain, and therefore must feel safe before they will run and play freely. Therefore school yards

Figure 8.4: Playgrounds should have spaces with soft surfaces that can be used for tumbling, games (such as tag), or team sports, and they should also have plenty of trees for shade and relaxing contemplation. Because schools are places for learning, playgrounds in these environments should also contain low-level balance beams and other items that create obstacle courses evoking mystery, inspiring imagination, and inviting exploration. These items should be painted red for maximum visibility and surrounded by sand or other soft ground cover material.

and playgrounds should be appropriate for the children using them and support their various activities. Designers have many means available to them with which to ensure children's safety in playground and school yard settings, including overall design, space planning, safety features, natural elements, and color. Consider designs that are brightly colored, of sufficient size to be seen from a distance, or both. For example, low-level balance beams are excellent for developing balance and coordination, but they are easy to trip over. Painting the beam red will make it highly visible; surrounding it with an "island" of loosely packed fill material (e.g., wood chips, mulch, or sand) will help cushion most falls (Figure 8.4).

Developmental Stages

There is an interactive and symbiotic relationship between individuals and their environments. Environment has an effect on people, which varies from person to person. Therefore, we must first understand young people's developmental stages to gain insights into their perceptions and thought processes and understand how various environments affect them. Children at each stage of development have specific needs and concerns relating not only to their cognitive development but also their overall physical and psychological health. A survey of these age-related needs and concerns, as they relate to the built environment, makes up the rest of this chapter.

Prenatal

People develop faster in the womb during their embryonic and fetal stages than at any other time in life. The prenatal stage (from the eighth week after conception to birth) is marked by three distinct phases: the first, second, and third trimesters. Designing a suitable environment for the expectant mother is in essence designing for the offspring as well; because the womb makes up the prenatal environment, the mother's exposure to environmental agents—both emotional and physical pollutants—has a direct impact on the fetus.

Environmental agents called **teratogens** can produce developmental malformations. If the expectant mother inhales or otherwise absorbs teratogens, then they circulate through her bloodstream and affect the developing fetus. Teratogenic agents include exterior pollutants, such as pesticides, smoke, and vehicle emissions, and interior pollutants, such as emissions from floor coverings and furnishings, and levels of cleanliness. Allergen-producing life-forms (e.g., molds, pollens, dust mites, cockroaches, and pets) are also considered teratogens because *allergens* are often related to both the incidence and the prevalence of asthma.[89] Although the correlation between environmental contaminants and developing fetuses is still being researched, the cause-and-effect relationship has been substantiated by far too many infants who, exposed to crack cocaine in the womb, tend to be hyperactive and overly sensitive to environmental stimulation and have extremely low tolerances to being held.

The first step in designing an environment for an expectant mother is to conduct an environmental analysis to assess potential sources of interior and exterior pollution as well as stress levels incurred from the mother's various environments, including work, home, and community (Box 8.1). This analysis requires a multimodal approach, beginning with a walk-through analysis of known sources of interior pollution. Pollutants include materials such as water-based acrylic wall paints and indoor sealants, nylon carpeting, and PVC (polyvinyl chloride) floor coverings—which all have negative biological and neurological effects on developing humans[90]—and the presence of dampness, mildew, mold, dust, and insects, which have been linked to the prevalence of asthma.[91, 92]

Next, the exterior environment is reviewed for elevated highways, the presence of roadways with heavy traffic, or both, because motor vehicles are the primary source of air pollutants (e.g., benzene, 1, 3-butadiene, diesel particulate matter, carbon monoxide, reactive organic gases, and oxides of nitrogen) that are associated with multiple health issues.[93] For example, vehicular exhaust produces lead dust that penetrates the soil, blows into houses,[94] and causes health risks usually associated with cognitive functioning. Therefore, the presence and penetrability of air pollutants are analyzed in relation to glazing layers (i.e., single-, double-, or triple-paned windows), quality of insulation, and the presence of foliage that can absorb them.

Box 8.1 Environmental Assessment of a Home for an Expectant Mother

Your client (an expectant mother) and her family are the second proprietors of an early 1900s house with very little landscaping located near a moderately traveled street. Most of the rooms have wall-to-wall carpeting and wallpaper above wooden wainscoting. The windows are all original single-paned glazing with painted sills, and much of the tile grout in the primary bathroom shows signs of mold. In answer to your strategic questions, your client says she wants to retain as many of the home's original features as possible, including the windows. She also states that she feels over-whelmed by her recently doubled workload at the office and that her supervisor is micromanaging her but adds that she feels much better when she gets home.

The expectant mother uses her home as a refuge as opposed to a social gathering place and has high levels of both chronic and acute work-related stress, which can negatively affect the developing fetus. Because nature may provide a sense of being away from daily concerns through immersion in a pleasing, restful environment, [95] you should incorporate a variety of natural elements into "safe" zones in and around the home and back yard where the expectant mother can go to get away from daily stressors. These natural elements should coincide with the client's tastes and concepts of soothing décor, not the designer's. For example, she may prefer a water feature over a rock garden.

As for the property itself, first check for the presence of pollutants. Homes this old, especially with only one previous occupant, are likely to have lead paint—a source of various health hazards, including brain damage. Lead-based paints often flake and airborne particles can be inhaled. There is also a strong likelihood that small children will chew on the sweet-tasting chips. Such paints are toxic, so hire a professional to remove all sources. A home on a moderately traveled street, with only singlepaned windows and little or no landscaping, is subjected to increased noise and vehicle pollutants; therefore, encourage foliage and multilayered window treatments to filter out noise and air pollutants. A single heavy drape will also block light, but most occupants will keep them opened, defeating the purpose. Using sheer layers affords protection and still allows in light. Wall-to-wall carpeting provides a soft surface for infants and helps to prevent toddlers from slipping; however, synthetic carpet fibers can be hazardous to their health, especially at close range. Additionally, older carpeting contains many allergens that can damage developing respiratory and immune systems. If the wallpaper and paneling are to be removed and replaced, the work should be done when the expectant mother is not around and the home can be properly aired for at least one week; careful monitoring will then be needed, as chemical fumes may return when the room is closed up.

Finally, a stress assessment is conducted using strategic questions to determine which environment has the most stressful agents and whether the primary stressors are *internal* or *external* and *acute* or *chronic*.

DESIGN APPLICATION. Clearly, design can do much more than simply fulfill aesthetic needs, and designers and planners can contribute to society in profound and fundamental ways. As shown in Box 8.1, by using thorough environmental assessments, designers can take proactive roles in ensuring the physical and mental health of their clients. When renovating a room in a home into a nursery or infant's bedroom, add electrical sockets for reflector spot lamps or wall lamps that emit soft glows; dimmer switches are also useful. Windows require treatments that block strong bright light, but avoid heavy floor-to-ceiling draperies, which collect allergens and can be dragged down by the child when he or she is older. Consider multiple methods of sound absorption if the infant's room is subjected to external sources of noise (e.g., street traffic, sirens, or neighbors). Once the infant reaches nine months of age, it is much safer to expose him or her to varying environmental stimuli in gradual increments.

Infancy

The infancy stage, from birth to about one year, is different from toddlerhood because children in the infancy stage cannot walk. One of an infant's primary lessons is cause and effect.[96] Each time an infant witnesses an effect of an action, the brain forms new synapses (e.g., when they cry until someone comes, they gain a rudimentary understanding of the relationship between crying and being comforted). This is why squeaky toys and mobiles are important in the design of spaces for infants. Since the developmental effect of a mobile is maximized only when the object is low enough for the infant to swat or kick at it, mobiles should be suspended from retractable cords so they can be raised to accommodate adult interaction and lowered for play. The goal of the designer for this age group is to incorporate as many items as possible that show a direct cause-and-effect relationship (Figure 8.5)

Researchers suspect that while infants do store memories, they have difficulty retrieving them.[97] This means that most cause-and-effect situations seem new to them regardless of how many times a situation has been encountered. Experts have speculated that the experience is similar to déjà vu or that the association is more of a hardwired response as opposed to a cognitive response. While the infant forms an association between crying and being held, the effect (being held) of the cause (crying) could be one of instinct (a hardwired response) or one of déjà vu. Regardless, the cause-and-effect relationship is an important process in the development of both the brain and the infant's ability to learn.

The ability to see color and understand depth begins to develop during mid- to late infancy (between 6 and 12 months), and bright, bold, and contrasting colors are important during this period. However, the use of color in relation to infants has more to do with adults and the early socialization of gender roles, which are developed through language (words, tone, and volume) and the way the child is handled. For example, adults respond differently to an infant based on the colors that surround that infant (clothing and environmental décor): Adults will speak in deeper voices and stronger tones to an infant dressed in blue and hold that infant upright, encouraging it to use gross motor skills; adults will speak in higher-pitched voices and softer tones to an infant dressed in pink and cradle that infant in their arms.

The way in which adults respond to infants, no matter how subtle, provides the earliest basis of how that child is expected to behave in later years.[98, 99] The behavioral nuances that we direct at infants tend to be passed down from generation to generation through cultural norms, values, and expectations. As illustrated in this paragraph, one almost universal behavioral norm is how we hold, speak to, and treat infants based on gender.

DESIGN APPLICATION. An infant's environment is typically made up of a crib, a bassinet, a playpen, and play objects. To facilitate learning and the formation of new neural synapses, infants should be exposed to objects and situations that show cause-and-effect relationships. Objects that illustrate three-dimensionality will help the infant develop depth perception.

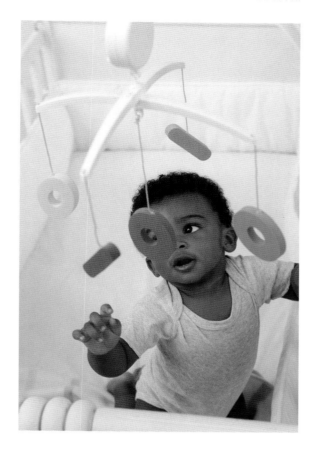

Figure 8.5: Mobiles and toys that rattle or squeak are important for the cognitive development of infants; the cause-and-effect relationship between an infant's action and a toy's reaction help establish neural pathways in the infant.

Choices and uses of color during early infancy, however, are functions of adult socialization and early formation of gender roles and expectations because infants cannot see color that well until after they reach six months of age.

Common sense dictates many design elements in spaces for infants and toddlers. Floors should be suitable for crawling and playing. Cushioned vinyl or cork is easy to clean; area rugs should be secured to the floor with nonslip adhesive strips. Walls should be washable and suitable for repainting or repapering. If a client's heart is set on wallpaper, suggest a single color or a small-scale print that she and her child will not tire of over time. Storage space is an almost limitless design variable; toy boxes, closets, cabinets, baskets, hammocks, and under-bed drawers can store a variety of items while adding to the visual design. Designers must consider the parents' wishes regarding socialization. If they do not wish their children to grow up with gender-related expectations, avoid blues, pinks, and purples and use more gender-neutral colors such as yellows, greens, oranges, and reds.

Designers should be aware of sources of stress and injury that could affect infants. Most infants feel stress from external sources such as excess noise and light or bad or strong smells, and these stressors can be either chronic or acute. Infants who as fetuses were exposed to certain drugs (including alcohol) may suffer from internal stress related to addiction and hypersensitivities. Injuries can occur without proper supervision or as a result of poor environmental design. Because infants lack strength and gross motor skills, their inabilities to rescue themselves from potentially hazardous situations—such as being wrapped in too many blankets, being surrounded by stuffed toys that are too large, or getting caught between the bars of the crib—can be fatal.

Toddlerhood and Preschool Years

This developmental stage encompasses children from about one to five years of age. During this period toddlers begin conforming to gender stereotypes; boys start to gravitate toward trucks and building blocks while girls start to gravitate toward dolls and toy tea sets. As designers we want to accommodate these desires, but we must consult with parents about décor because they may not want to saturate their children's environments with traditional gender-oriented artifacts. Parents may opt for gender-neutral wall coverings, window treatments, and bedding or may wish to saturate the toddler's environment with gender-specific items such as sports-themed wallpaper or frilly canopy beds. Although the parents' wishes must be honored, it is the designer's ethical responsibility to inform clients of alternatives without bias.

Mirrors are an important design feature during this stage. As infants develop into toddlers they start to recognize that they are separate entities. Mirrors encourage toddlers to see themselves as individuals.[100, 101] Early toddlers start to learn that they are not part of a mass collective of thought and feeling, and are starting to see themselves as individual be-

ings with separate bodies. Mirrors fascinate toddlers because they see their reflections move in unison with their movements, yet they can't touch that reflected person. Thus, mirrors help to facilitate analytic skills.

At around age two, toddlers enter an egocentric stage where they understand that their thinking is their own.[102, 103] However, they inappropriately assume that others see and experience what they do. For example, because they don't feel pain when they pull on Fido's ears, they assume that Fido doesn't either. Likewise, when they get hurt and run to their parents for comfort, they assume that the adults know what happened because it must have happened to them as well. It is at this stage that toddlers engage in behaviors of taking and grabbing as they explore their environments and their limitations and form their concepts of self.

An important consideration in designing environments for children at this stage of development is that while toddlers are still developing cognitive skills, they are also developing gross motor skills. They start to form short-term memories, require many new distractions, and start to project their thoughts onto the world. A playroom with various play areas will help accommodate a child's limited attention span. A table covered with paper allows toddlers to project their thoughts in a variety of mediums (crayons, markers, or pencils) and helps them to learn about limits while they explore. Games that involve matching colors, shapes, or images facilitate memory enhancement. However, because toddlers have difficulties differentiating colors (or smells) until about age three, colors need to be highly contrasting. Low, padded balance beams or box springs and mattresses at floor level help developing youngsters learn how to use their muscles for balance and coordination. The ability to maintain eye contact with parents or caretakers from any location in the room is crucial to a toddler's exploration of spaces and interaction with peers.[104] The confidence they get from seeing a protector nearby will encourage further exploration, which is how a child learns.

From ages two to four, toddlers recognize the difference between themselves and other people but still cannot comprehend that others may feel, think, or react differently from them.[105–107] For example, three-year-olds who see someone who is angry or sad will assume that whatever makes them feel better will make the other person feel better too. Toddlers have little understanding of how other living things grow or respond. At this stage they see the world as they would like to see it; therefore, nondescript objects such as empty boxes or broomsticks allow them to foster their imagination. They also start to view actions as having a beginning, a middle, and an end. Although toddlers have little or no concept of past or future, they respond well to routine, which reinforces their understanding of beginning, middle, and end relationships. Using wall art, mobiles, or other design initiatives to depict a progression (in a time line of world history or the construction of a historic building) promotes the formation of neural connections associated with time, especially when these features are positioned at a toddler's level (Figure 8.6).

Between the ages of four and five years, preschoolers explore how to be adults by playing games that mimic adult activities, such as having tea parties or pretending to be firefighters. They still have difficulty with logical deductions such as judging the size of a room or the volume of liquid in a container. This is when children start to project into—and anticipate or dread—the future, e.g., getting excited about visiting Grandma or crying in a doctor's waiting room.

DESIGN APPLICATION. The décor of playrooms in homes or schools should include highly contrasting colors, wall and flooring materials that show progression (a beginning, a middle, and an end), and an assortment of play areas. One of these areas should include a wall-mounted mirror, or some other type of reflecting devise that will not break easily, to help children develop a concept of themselves as individuals. Other areas should be designed to enhance children's memory, analytical skills, and gross motor and coordination skills. Games played at a table or on the floor are often designed to promote memory and analysis, but toddlers have a difficult time sitting for extended periods of time so items that promote physical activity should also be included.

Childhood

By age five children start to understand what others think and comprehend that others may see

Figure 8.6: In the playroom shown here, the mural utilizes sequential images to show how a small seed (*bottom far left*) will one day grow into large tree. The low trampoline with padded edges helps the toddler develop gross muscles, balancing skills, and an understanding of where he or she is in space. Notice that two of the balloons on the wall are composed of reflective material; one is in line with the trampoline to reflect the jumping toddler's image, and the other is at eye level. The low, padded balance beam helps to develop coordination between the toddler's visual cortex and gross muscles, and the rocking horse helps the toddler learn that different movements result in different propulsions.

things differently from them.[108] For example, two children may have the same object but each imagines it to be something different (e.g., a broomstick can be a pony for one child and a motorcycle for the other), and this difference is acceptable. Five-year-old children are keenly aware of their limitations and envious of the power that adults have (freedom, choice, strength, and knowledge). Their imaginative and creative play focus more on adult behaviors and activities as they attempt to grow up as quickly as possible. Ironically, at this age children often can memorize better than adults because they see the world as singular components, whereas most adults see the singular components in relation to other components and must sift through additional information.[109]

This ability to manage multiple thoughts, while diminishing short-term memory, is essential for quick assessments of alternatives in reaction to crises. Designers can assist children to develop their

Figure 8.7: Private areas, such as a tree house or a makeshift fort in a bed loft or closet, are important for the development of children's imaginations. The children pictured here play at being adults or engage in what they perceive as adult activities (e.g., adventures in outer space or far-off lands). This type of play enables children to begin learning how to process multiple thoughts, which is essential for quick assessments of alternatives in crisis situations.

abilities to process multiple thoughts by incorporating places such as clubhouses, tree houses, or other separate areas where children can learn about adult responsibilities by having control over a selected environment. If indoors, these special spaces can be under loft beds, in closets, or in a section of their bedrooms (Figure 8.7). Such spaces should contain a multitude of toys that have meaning for a child. Young children prefer toys that provide them with enjoyment (this preference lasts longer for boys) and that they can personify (this preference lasts longer for girls).[110] For example, a boy may want a clubhouse that can serve as a spaceship or submarine with toys that support his imaginary place, whereas a girl may want a special space that mimics a kitchen or other room in the house with toys that personify her notion of being an adult. Each child will develop attachments to specific objects, and those objects in essence become a part of their notions of self as well as sources of enjoyment and *personification*.

At around age six, children start to reason through simple deductions and superficially analyze situations or circumstances. At this age children are gender sensitive and want their external worlds to match their perceived gender identities.

Gender identity and genitalia are not always congruent. Tomboys, for example, have strong "masculine" gender identities: They like to engage in athletic sports, play with trucks, and roughhouse with boys, and they probably will balk at the notion of a canopy bed, much less wear pink. By age seven, children take their gender identities very seriously and view male and female roles in strictly black-and-white terms, believing, for example, that boys don't dance and girls don't spit. Although many young girls prefer toy kitchen sets or nurseries and boys prefer toy spaceships or time machines, designers must remember that children have individual likes and dislikes and that a girl may desire a spaceship and a boy may desire a kitchen. Clearly, the supports that we offer our children reflect gender expectations and roles; whereas tomboys are often considered to be cute, society is far less tolerant of boys who exhibit "feminine" preferences.

By age 8, children's brains reach 95 percent of their adult size, and their prefrontal cortexes are sufficiently developed to plan and theorize.[111] However, children still have difficulties conceptualizing what has not happened yet or may never happen; when they are included in the design process, they will need to see renderings to understand the big picture (i.e., see objects in relation to the environment).

DESIGN APPLICATION. Children between the ages of five and eight require a variety of environments and objects that will accommodate their imaginations as well as support the active creative play in which they mimic adult behaviors—which designers must consider when designing environments for young people. Children develop attachments to specific objects and places as they explore their notions of self; designers can help to establish favorite places within the home or in children's actual rooms by creating nooks, alcoves, and other small spaces that young children can adopt as play areas and that can be adapted for other uses as they mature. Children at this stage are acutely aware of their places in the world and are both conscious of and sensitive about their gender identities; therefore, they must be consulted when designers are considering gender-specific designs. For example, a boy may not want wall

paper with images of race cars, and a girl may prefer stuffed animals over dolls.

Preadolescence and Adolescence

Between ages eight and nine, children start to take responsibility for their own decisions and are capable of independent thoughts. At this stage in their development, they should be included in the design process so that they can see the relationship between their decisions and the future; however, they will need many pictures to be able to visualize the end results. Because children at this age have not been fully socialized to adult norms, their idea of appealing décor is all their own, and it may vary greatly from that of designers or their parents. By age nine children start to distance themselves from their parents; most of their time is spent with their peers, and they need to be able to control their environment so it conforms to their peers' expectations.

Between ages 10 and 11, gender barriers start to break down, and both genders begin engaging in behaviors previously conceived as gender-specific (e.g., boys cook meals and girls repair bicycles). Eleven is a good age at which to allow children to redecorate their rooms because they can now manage a multitude of thoughts related to colors, shapes, textures, and costs.

The further children progress into adolescence, the more obsessed they become with the image they portray to the world. This is especially apparent in their choice of costume (clothing, accessories, and jewelry), accoutrements (electronic equipment and games), and modes of transportation. For adolescents, possessions are often sources of comparisons and friendly competition and can support their status among their peer groups. Cherished possessions are linked to the self, affecting the development and reflection of self-concept.[112] Such objects have tremendous psychological importance in that they help adolescents relate to the social world and support how they wish to be personified. Therefore, when designing personal spaces for

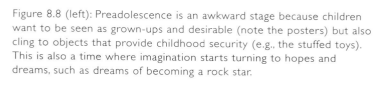

Figure 8.8 (left): Preadolescence is an awkward stage because children want to be seen as grown-ups and desirable (note the posters) but also cling to objects that provide childhood security (e.g., the stuffed toys). This is also a time where imagination starts turning to hopes and dreams, such as dreams of becoming a rock star.

Figure 8.9 (below): Many preadolescents desire objects they can control and master. Video games provide ample opportunity to meet this need; these games allow kids to play again and try to beat their previous scores. Many adults view video games negatively, but they do offer the opportunity for mastery and help develop visual coordination; children make the connection that what they see and do in one place influences what happens at another place.

adolescents, consider how to incorporate their special objects (Figure 8.8).

The nature of attachment to special objects changes as youngsters move through the individuation process, separating themselves emotionally from their primary caretakers, and enter the affiliation stage, in which they begin integrating with others. Preadolescents prefer objects they can control and master, whereas adolescents prefer objects they can acquire and control or contemplate. Boys tend to prefer action or fantasy figures and audiovisual or sports equipment—action and mechanical or instrumental objects related to present experience (Figure 8.9), whereas girls tend to prefer dolls, clothes, and mementos—contemplative and interpersonal objects related to past experiences.[113] These special objects serve not only to support their notions of their places in the world but also as a means of stress reduction. Many youngsters who are upset will retreat to their rooms and use these objects as supports while psychologically working through the stressful event (e.g., a girl may clutch her favorite toy, and a boy may toss a ball repeatedly).

DESIGN APPLICATION. As children move into preadolescence and adolescence, they develop into the people they will become. Throughout this developmental process they become less concerned with their parents' preferences and care more about their peers' expectations. They also gravitate toward special objects that represent their notions of self and their aspirations for the future. For example, an adolescent or preadolescent may embrace extracurricular activities at school and desire paraphernalia associated with their school (pennants; old posters advertising a particular event; or jackets, hats, or other clothing that promote their school). Friends are also important to adolescents and preadolescents. Consider the use of bulletin boards for the display of potentially transitory items of meaning such as a friend's photograph or movie ticket stub. For reasons of development and security, designers must seek ways to incorporate special objects into a young person's space. Ultimately, the occupant must embrace the overall design if it is to create a place where he or she can feel safe and reduce stress levels. Young people will design their spaces in terms of their own and their peers' expectations and even more so as they progress through ado-

lescence. If their environments are constructed without their permission and input, it will not hold the psychological value they need and they will reject it.

Summary Review

Children's relationships with their environments are highly dependent on their stages of development yet the primal need for environmental safety and security can transcend the developmental phases. As such, designers must consider stress; injury and illness; space, place, and privacy; the developmental aspects of play; and housing and green spaces when designing environments for children.

The effects of stress on children are more profound than in adults because children are less capable of considering a stressful event in its entirety or that the event is separate from them. Greater amounts of stress are experienced by children who live in poverty or violent communities and those who are bullied in school. By understanding the causes and manifestations of stress in children, designers can help to develop stress-free or stress-reducing environments.

Injury is the leading health risk for children younger than 15 years. Younger children most often suffer falls, thermal burns, and toy-related injuries. In addition, asthma affects about 3 million children; researchers attribute increases in the rate of childhood asthma and allergies to the increased time children spend indoors and increased exposure to carpeting and other items or places that harbor allergens.

Perhaps not as overt as the presence of a broken limb, or mold and dust, the issues of crowding, the ability for children to develop their senses of place in the world, and lack of privacy can exact results just as detrimental, if not worse. For many children, the violation of privacy needs often results in physical aggression or psychological withdrawal. When chronically exposed to crowding, children's growth, development, and behavior are all negatively affected. One of the possible repercussions is that children are unable to develop a sense of place or bond with a particular place.

Privacy and private places for contemplation and relaxation are important in the developmental process of children. As such, the ability to *personalize* private spaces allows children to express their individuality. Research demonstrates that children

Table 8.2 Developmental Stages of Youth

DEVELOPMENTAL STAGE	PREDOMINANT CHARACTERISTICS	DESIGN RECOMMENDATIONS
Prenatal	The period beginning from the eighth week after conception to birth; fastest growth period of the child's life	Reduce the mother's exposure to teratogens and allergens, which affect the developing fetus.
Infancy	Primary lesson is that of cause-and-effect relationships	Include items that respond to an infant's action (e.g., musical instrument or stuffed toy that squeaks when squeezed or spins when hit).
Toddlerhood and Preschoolers	Cognitive and gross motor skills develop, and children begin conforming to gender stereotypes.	Use objects that foster gross motor skills and that promote temporal associations (beginning, middle, and end).
Childhood	Children start to understand what others think and comprehend that others may see things differently. By age six, children are gender sensitive and want their external worlds to match their perceived gender identities.	Provide places for children to imagine themselves as adults.
Preadolescence	Between ages eight and nine, children start to take responsibility for their own decisions and are capable of independent thoughts.	Designs should combine those items that provided security when they were younger and items that reflect who they would like to become. Starting at age 11, children can be allowed to redecorate their rooms.
Adolescence	Between ages 10 and 18, youths are less concerned with their parents' preferences and more concerned with their peers' expectations. They gravitate toward special objects that represent their notions of self and their aspirations for the future and prefer places where they can feel safe and reduce stress levels.	During this stage, young people start to identify their talents and often desire environments that reflect those talents and who they would like to become.

as young as age three value a room they can personalize. Likewise, adolescents value the freedom and control they feel in their solitary places and the time alone allows for them to make sense of stressful situations and circumstances.

Children's exposure to natural environments is often through school yards and playgrounds. However, the natural aspects of these environments are declining because of safety concerns, the inability of parents to bring their children to parks, and the loss of natural spaces as a result of urban sprawl and mass development. Exposure to well-designed school yards and playgrounds that include natural areas along with fixed play structures and covered areas can enhance positive behavioral patterns and facilitate development of gross motor, cognitive, and social skills, which are linked to greater academic success. Because natural environments provide mental and physical restorative benefits for young people, limiting these spaces to school yards and

playgrounds is insufficient. Studies demonstrate that children engage in significantly more creative play in high-vegetation areas as opposed to barren spaces. Green spaces are an important part of housing and a child's home environment and should be incorporated to the greatest degree possible. Children can be viewed as proceeding through five basic stages of development: prenatal, infancy, toddlerhood, childhood, and preadolescence and adolescence (Table 8.2). Designing an appropriate environment for children at each stage requires an understanding of basic concepts of growth and development.

During the prenatal stage, children develop faster than at any other time in their lives. Designing a suitable environment for expectant mothers is important because a mother's exposure to unhealthy environmental agents (teratogens) will affect her fetus.

Infants need environmental stimulants to help them form new neural pathways and to comprehend their separateness from the people and objects that surround them. Cribs, playpens, and bassinets should include intellectually stimulating objects that reinforce ideas of cause-and-effect relationships, illustrate three-dimensionality, and promote depth perception, all while ensuring physical safety. Because infants cannot discern color differences until about 6 to 12 months of age, their environments should include bright, bold, and contrasting colors. Because infants lack strength and gross motor skills, they are unable to rescue themselves from potentially hazardous situations. Designers therefore need to examine and identify potentially dangerous situations prior to developing of an infant's environment.

Toddlers require diversified environments that will stimulate their developing cognitive and gross motor skills. Depending on their parents' wishes, either gender-specific or gender-neutral décor should be used. Toddlerhood is the stage at which children start to develop and conform to gender stereotypes. Mirrors are an important design feature during this stage because they enable toddlers to see themselves in relation to the world and to recognize that they are separate entities. By age two, toddlers begin to explore their environments and their limitations and see the world as they would like to see it. Design has little meaning for toddlers, as the child relies primarily on his or her imagination to fulfill desires. At this age toddlers are also developing an understanding of sequence: a beginning, a middle, and an end. Timelines can be included to help the child develop sequential understanding and correlations to time. By age four or five, toddlers start to mimic adult activities as they explore their gender identities and social norms.

From ages five to eight, children start to understand what others think and comprehend that others may see things differently. For five-year-old children, imagination and creative play focus on adult behaviors and activities. By age six, children are sensitive to issues of gender and look to reconcile their external worlds with their perceived gender identities. By age seven, children view gender identity in strict black-and-white terms. By age eight or nine, children start to take responsibility for their own decisions and are capable of independent thoughts. When designing for children at this age, it is wise to use pictures of the end results. Children at this age may group items that adults may deem to be uncomplimentary. Therefore, their ideas of beauty are all their own.

During their development, young people learn social values that will serve them as adults. Bedrooms, clubhouses, and lofts often serve as territories where young people explore their senses of self. The further children progress into adolescence, the more obsessed they become with their image, which is contingent on design. For the adolescent, design and possessions are sources of comparisons that support their status among their peers. Within these designs are objects that serve not only to support their notions of their places in the world but also as a means of stress reduction.

As children develop into young adults they require environments that will keep them safe from injury; support physical, social, and cognitive learning; and help them to define who they will become as adults. To create designs that support child and adolescent development, designers need to be cognizant of developmental psychology and its impact on this population.

Discussion Questions

1. Based on the information presented in this chapter, how might the average school day for elementary and middle-school-age children be altered? How would you design an environment for elementary school children to relax in?

2. Discuss ways to evaluate a client's home for potential dangers relating to children. How would you approach subjects that may be personal? How would you evaluate the risks for a particular child? How would you work with the family to rid the home of potential allergens, if necessary? Keep in mind that many people have a difficult time differentiating between needs and wants and are not aware of the many options available.

3. How might you design a playground based on the research presented in the chapter? What elements make a playground soothing and calming to adolescent youths? How would you incorporate these features without increasing any hazards?

4. How would you design low-income housing for families to minimize internal crowding? What features can be added to maximize privacy inside the home?

5. A current theory on the care of newborns suggests that silence is an unnatural phenomenon for them. Consider that a developing

fetus is engulfed in liquid (recall the sounds you hear when underwater) and constantly hears its mother's heartbeat, as well as any sounds that penetrate the womb. How would you create an environment that allows a newborn to adjust to a new world of sounds, without completely removing the sounds it is accustomed to?

6. Discuss the effects of expected gender roles versus child preferences. In your own experience, did societal norms cause your parents (or others you have witnessed) to prohibit certain behaviors that were acceptable for the opposite gender, for example, sending a girl who wants to play army with her brothers inside to play house instead. What are the potential long-term effects of this behavior? How, as a designer, can you help encourage moderation while still respecting the parents' wishes? What questions do you need to ask to understand parents' expectations for their children?

7. How might you involve a child between the ages of five and seven in your design process? How would you work with such children to help give them a sense of control over their space? What techniques could be used to help them understand what is happening and what role they are to play?

8. How would you change your design techniques to deal with a preadolescent compared with a young child? What questions would you ask, and what role would the older child play in the design process? What materials and illustrations would you use to keep the preadolescent involved and engaged?

9. Discuss microenvironments in relation to children. What importance do they have in social, intellectual, and personal development? What similarities do you see in adult life (e.g., work cubicles, studio space, and so on)?

10. How can you apply the information in this chapter about stress, environmental agents, and green spaces to your current life? What aspects about your living space can you alter to better suit your stress and health levels?

Learning Activities

1. Research the clinical diagnosis for attention deficit/hyperactivity disorder (ADHD) and develop a plan for creating a study and play space that would help to minimize negative stimuli for a child diagnosed with ADHD.

2. Spend 30 minutes pretending you are a child who is seven years old or younger. Spend time at the average seven-year-old's height, and minimize your physical characteristics to approximate those of an average child. What dangers do you find in your living space? What temptations exist? Sketch your living space and highlight areas of potential danger, and overlay adaptations to make your living space child-friendly.

3. Design a residential neighborhood made up of 20 single-family homes and 10 town houses that is located one block away from an elementary school. Show the housing plots, public spaces, and circulation for the entire neighborhood. What factors must be considered in laying out the neighborhood? How would you minimize perceived crowding? How would you increase the *sense of community* while still providing for *personalization*? How much green space is necessary? How would you maximize property values based on views of and access to open land?

4. You have been hired to design an addition to an existing family home that will accommodate the family's two children (ages seven and ten) as well as future newborn twins. Devise a step-by-step approach to evaluating the children's currents needs and wants as well as planning for their future needs. Consider information learned in previous chapters about territoriality as well as the stress expected from a major change in family structure. Devise methods for ensuring privacy for the older children and for allowing the twins to develop as individuals.

5. Design a playground. Draw sketches of different enclosures, statues, and interactive objects. What type of layout would peak children's interests, while still providing a safe place where they can indulge their imaginations?

6. Based on the material in the text, draw a full-color site plan for a one-acre playground located in a suburban neighborhood. The playground is bordered on one side by a thoroughfare with a 40-mile-per-hour speed limit and on the other three sides by residential

areas where the streets have stop signs and crosswalks.

7. Visit a local playground, and sketch the layout accurately. Create a new drawing that shows adjustments to improve the use of the facility for all potential users. Write a brief description of your modifications and reasons for those changes.

8. Spend 30 minutes evaluating your living space as if it were to be inhabited by a woman who is three months pregnant. Assume that she will live there for the rest of her pregnancy. What possible teratogens are present? How can they be minimized or neutralized? What physical challenges does your residence pose? Can these be easily modified, or are there structural issues?

9. Design and build a mobile or other tactile and sound-producing toy for an infant. Use the information in this chapter to determine what features are necessary to encourage activity and stimulate synaptic connections. Not all features of the toy must work, but you must write a brief description explaining any nonworking aspects of the toy.

10. Design a playroom that is appropriate for both a toddler and a child. Consider intellectual stimulation, safety, shared space, spaces with multiple functions, and so on. Describe the key features of the room, and explain how they are appropriate for each age.

11. Develop a questionnaire for children ages 7 to 16 to use to assess their wants and expectations for their living, sleeping, study, and play spaces. What types of questions will help gauge current levels of maturity and desired levels of involvement in the process? What questions will give you insight into their likes and dislikes?

12. Research the five most common illnesses in your area. What symptoms do they present? How might environmental agents cause these symptoms? How can design be used to decrease the rate of occurrence? What research is being done to quantify the environment's role in these illnesses?

13. Create a book or poster for a seven-year-old child whose room you are redesigning that will introduce the new materials and colors.

Include sketches of what the space will look like when completed. Incorporate items the child will recognize and finds important. Make sure the textures and colors of the room are properly represented. Develop a fun and interesting presentation.

Terminology

self-regulation Behavioral limitations or boundaries that we set for ourselves in either physical or social environments

teratogen Environmental agent that causes developmental malformations

References

1. Gunnar, M. R., and Barr, R. G. (1998). Stress, early brain development, and behavior. *Infants and Young Children, 11-1*, 1–14.

2. Lombroso, P. J., and Sapolsky, R. (1998). Development of the cerebral cortex: XII; Stress and brain development: I. *Journal of the American Academy of Child and Adolescent Psychiatry, 37-12*, 1337–1339.

3. Monk, C. F., Fifer, W. P., Myers, M. M., Sloan, R. P., Trien, L., and Hurtado, A. (2000). Maternal stress responses and anxiety during pregnancy: Effects on fetal heart rate. *Developmental Psychology, 36-1*, 67–77.

4. McLoyd, V. C. (1998). Socioeconomic disadvantage and child development. *American Psychologist, 53-2*, 185–204.

5. Stansbury, K., and Harris, M. L. (2000). Individual differences in stress reactions during a peer entry episode: Effects of age, temperament, approach behavior, and self-perceived peer competence. *Journal of Experimental Child Psychology, 76-1*, 50–63.

6. See note 5.

7. Fallin, K., Wallinga, C., and Coleman, M. (2001). Helping children cope with stress in the classroom setting. *Childhood Education, 78-1*, 17–24.

8. Marion, M. (2003). *Guidance of young children* (6th ed.). Upper Saddle River, NJ: Prentice Hall.

9. Dacey, J. S., and Fiore, L. B. (2000). *Your anxious child*. San Francisco: Jossey-Bass.

10. Allen, K. E., and Marotz, L. R. (2003). *Developmental profiles* (4th ed.). Albany, NY: Delmar.

11. Kochenderfer-Ladd, B., and Skinner, K. (2002). Children's coping strategies: Moderators of the effects of peer victimization? *Developmental Psychology, 38-2,* 267–278.

12. See note 5.

13. See note 5.

14. Bullock, J. (2002). Bullying. *Childhood Education, 78 (3),* 130–133.

15. National SAFE KIDS Campaign (January 28, 2003). Washington, DC. www.safekids.org.

16. See note 15.

17. U.S. Consumer Product Safety Commission, Office of Information and Public Affairs. (2003). Washington, DC. www.cpsc.gov.

18. Haynes, R., Reading, R., and Gale, S. (2003). Household and neighborhood risks for injury to 5- to 14-year-old children. *Social Science and Medicine, 57-4,* 625–636.

19. National Institute of Environmental Health Sciences (July 1997). Asthma and its environmental triggers: Scientists take a practical new look at a familiar illness. In NIEHS Fact Sheet #9: Asthma. www.niehs/nih/gov.

20. Freeman, N. C. G., Schneider, D., and McGarvey, P. (2003). Household exposure factors, asthma, and school absenteeism in a predominantly Hispanic community. *Journal of Exposure Analysis and Environmental Epidemiology, 13-3,* 169–176.

21. See note 19.

22. Levine-Coley, R., Kuo, F. E., and Sullivan, W. C. (1997). Where does community grow? The social context created by nature in urban public housing. *Environment and Behavior, 29-4,* 468–494.

23. Bixler, R. D., and Floyd, M. F. (1997). Nature is scary, disgusting, and uncomfortable. Environment and Behavior, 29, 443–467.

24. Korpela, K. M. (1992). Adolescent's favorite places and environmental self-regulation. *Journal of Environmental Psychology, 12,* 249–258.

25. Evans, G. W., Saegert, S., and Harris, R. (2001). Residential density and psychological health among children in low-income families. *Environment and Behavior, 33-2,* 165–180.

26. Evans, G. W., Maxwell, L. E., and Hart, B. (1999). Parental language and verbal responsiveness to children in crowded homes. *Developmental Psychology, 35,* 1020–1023.

27. Zuravin, S. J. (1986). Residential density and urban child mistreatment: An aggregate analysis. *Journal of Family Violence, 1,* 307–322.

28. Maxwell, L. E. (1996). Multiple effects of home and day care crowding. *Environment and Behavior, 29-4,* 494–511.

29. Korpela, K. M. (1989). Place-identity as a product of environmental self-regulation. *Journal of Environmental Psychology, 9,* 241–256.

30. Matthews, M. H. (1992). *Making sense of place: Children's understanding of large-scale environments.* London: Harvester Wheatsheaf.

31. Kaiser, F. G., and Fuhrer, U. (1996). Dwelling: Speaking of an unnoticed universal language. *New Ideas in Psychology, 14,* 225–236.

32. Malinowski, J. C. and Thurber, C. A. (1996). Developmental shifts in the place preference of boys aged 8–16 years. *Journal of Environmental Psychology, 16,* 45–54.

33. Van Andel, J. (1990). Places children like, dislike, and fear. *Children's Environments Quarterly, 7-4,* 24–31.

34. See note 32.

35. Laufer, R., and Wolfe, M. (1976). The interpersonal and environmental context of privacy invasion and response. In P. Korosec-Serfaty (Ed.), *Appropriation of space* (pp. 516–535). Strasbourg, France: Institut Louis Pasteur.

36. Newell, P. B. (1994). A systems model of privacy. *Journal of Environmental Psychology, 14,* 65–78.

37. Newell, P. B. (1995). Perspectives on privacy. *Journal of Environmental Psychology, 15,* 87–104.

38. Rivlin, L. G. (1990). Home and homelessness in the lives of children. *Child and Youth Services, 14,* 5–17.

39. Sobel, D. (1990). A place in the world: Adults' memories of childhood special places. *Children's Environments Quarterly, 7-4,* 5–12.

40. Chawla, L. (1991). Homes for children in a changing society. In E. H. Zube and G. T. Moore (Eds.), *Advances in environment, behavior, and design* (3), pp. 187–228. New York: Plenum Press.

41. Owens, P. E. (1988). Natural landscapes, gathering places, and prospect refuges: Characteristics of outdoor places valued by teens. *Children's Environmental Quarterly, 5,* 17–24.

42. Owens, P. E. (1994). Teen places in Sunshine, Australia: Then and now. *Children's Environments, 11*, 292–299.

43. Lieberg, M. (1994). Appropriating the city: Teenagers' use of public space. In S. J. Neary, M. S. Symes, and F. E. Brown (Eds.), *The urban experience: A people-environment perspective* (pp. 321–333). London: Spon.

44. Hadjiyanni, T. (2000). Children and their housing: Insights from the island of Cyprus. *Housing and Society, 27-2*, 19–30.

45. Evans, G. W., Saltzman, H., and Cooperman, J. (2001). Housing quality and children's socioemotional health. *Environment and Behavior, 33-3*, 389–399.

46. Taylor, A. F., Wiley, A., Kuo, F. E., and Sullivan, W.C. (1998). Growing up in the inner city: Green spaces as places to grow. *Environment and Behavior, 30-1*, 3–27.

47. Lindholm, G. (1995). Schoolyards: The significance of place properties to outdoor activities in schools. *Environment and Behavior, 27,3*, 259–293.

48. Wells, N. M. (2000). At home with nature: Effects of "greenness" on children's cognitive functioning. *Environment and Behavior, 32-6*, 775–795.

49. Taylor, A. F., Kuo, F. E., and Sullivan, W. C. (2001). Coping with ADD: The surprising connection to green play settings. *Environment and Behavior, 33-1*, 54–77.

50. See note 19.

51. Malone, K., and Tranter, P., (2003). Children's environmental learning and the use, design and management of schoolgrounds. *Children, Youth and Environments, 13*, 2 online. Available at: www.colorado.edu/journals/cye/13_2/Malone_Tranter/ChildrensEnvLearning.htm

52. Carnegie Corporation of New York (1994). *The quiet crisis. Starting points: Meeting the needs of our youngest children* (abridged text). New York: Carnegie Corporation.

53. Stratton, G., (2000). Promoting children's physical activity in primary school: an intervention study using playground markings. *Ergonomics, 43,10*, 1538-1546.

54. See note 51.

55. See note 53.

56. Scott, J., (July 15, 2000). *When child's play is too simple; Experts criticize safety-conscious recreation as boring.* Arts & Ideas/Cultural Desk.

57. Lindholm, G. (1995). Schoolyards: The significance of place properties to outdoor activities in schools. *Environment and Behavior, 27-3*, 259–293.

58. Taylor, A. F., Wiley, A., Kuo, F. E., and Sullivan, W. C. (1998). Growing up in the inner city: Green spaces as places to grow. *Environment and Behavior, 30-1*, 3–27.

59. Herrington, S. (1997). The received view of play and the subculture of infants. *Landscape Journal, 16-2*, 149–159.

60. Kaplan, R. and S. Kaplan. 1989. *The experience of nature: A psychological perspective.* Cambridge University Press, New York, NY

61. Ulrich, R. S. (1984). The psychological benefits of plants. *Garden, 8(6)*, 16–21.

62. See note 51.

63. See note 47.

64. See note 51.

65. See note 51.

66. Schwebel, D. C., Binder, S. C., and Plumert, J. M. (2002). Using an injury diary to describe the ecology of children's daily injuries. *Journal of Safety Research, 33-3*, 301–319.

67. Ramsey, L. F., and Preston, J. D. (1990). *Impact attenuation performance of playground surfacing materials.* Washington, DC: U.S. Consumer Product Safety Commission.

68. Black, C., Grise, K., Heitmeyer, J., and Readdick, C. A. (2001). Sun protection: Knowledge, attitude, and perceived behavior of parents and observed dress of preschool children. *Family and Consumer Sciences Research Journal, 30-1*, 93–109.

69. Read, M. A., Sugawara, A. I., and Brandt, J. A. (1999). Impact of space and color in the physical environment on preschool children's cooperative behavior. *Environment and Behavior, 31-3*, 413–428.

70. Project For Public Spaces (2005). *What makes a great playground? Elements of a successful play space: Enhancing physical, cognitive and social experience.* Developed By Urban Parks www.pps.org.

71. See note 51.

72. See note 70.

73. Beckwith, J., (May 2000). Why our playgrounds are boring to today's wired child.

Speech at Minnesota Recreation and Parks Association 63 rd Annual Conference, May 2000. www.bpfp.org/PlaygroundDesign/WiredChild.htm

74. See note 73.

75. See note 73.

76. See note 70.

77. See note 59.

78. See note 70.

79. See note 70.

80. See note 70.

81. See note 70.

82. See note 51.

83. Kaplan, S. (1995). The restorative benefits of nature: Toward an integrative framework. *Journal of Environmental Psychology, 15*, 169–192.

84. Kaplan, R., and Kaplan, S. (1989). *The experience of nature: A psychological perspective.* Cambridge: Cambridge University Press.

85. See note 59.

86. See note 57.

87. See note 59.

88. Dierkx, R. (2003). Toward community-based architectural programming and development of inclusive learning environments in Nairobi's slums. *Children, Youth and Environments, 13-1.* Retrieved 072204 from http://colorado.edu/journals/cye.

89. See note 19.

90. Sakr, W., Knudsen, H. N., Gunnarsen, L., and Haghighat, F. (2003). Impact of varying area of polluting surface materials on perceived air quality. *Indoor Air, 13-2,* 86–91.

91. See note 18.

92. See note 19.

93. Gunier R. B., Hertz A., von Behren J., Reynolds P. (2003). Traffic Density in California: Socioeconomic and ethnic differences among potentially exposed children. *Journal of Exposure Analysis Environment Epidemiology, 13-3,* 240–246.

94. Adgate, J. L., Wills, R. D., Buckley, T. J., Chow, J. C., Watson, J. G., Rhoads, G. G., and Lioy, P. J. (1998). Chemical mass balance source apportionment of lead in house dust. *Environmental Science Technology, 32,* 108–114.

95. Wells, N. M., and Evans, G. W. (2003). Nearby nature: A buffer of life stress among rural children. *Environment and Behavior, 35-3,* 311–330.

96. Piaget, J. (1969). *The theory of stages in cognitive development.* New York: McGraw-Hill.

97. Rovee-Collier C. (2000). Memory in infancy and early childhood. In E. Tulving & F.I.M. Craik (eds.), *The oxford handbook of memory.* New York: Oxford University Press.

98. Eccles, J. S., Jacobs, J. E., & Harold, R. D. (1990). Gender roles stereotypes, expectancy effects, and parents' socialization of gender differences. *Journal of Social Issues, 46,* 186-201.

99. Witt, S. D., (1997). Parental influence of children's socialization to gender roles. *Adolescence, 32 (126),* 253-259.

100. Courage, M. L., Edison, S. C; Howe, M. L., (Dec 2004). Variability in the early development of visual self-recognition. *Infant, Behavior, and Development, 27 (4),* 509–532.

101. Loveland, K. A., (1986). Discovering the affordances of a reflecting surface. *Developmental Review, 6 (1),* 1–24.

102. Piaget, J. (1963). *The origin of intelligence in children.* New York: Norton.

103. See note 96.

104. Legendre, A. (2003). Environmental features influencing toddlers' bioemotional reactions in day care centers. *Environment and Behavior, 35-4,* 523–549.

105. See note 96.

106. See note 102.

107. Piaget, J. (1973). *The psychology of intelligence.* Totowa, NJ: Littlefield, Adams & Co.

108. See note 96.

109. Yussen, S. R., & Santrock, J. W., (1982). *Child development* (2nd ed.), Iowa: Wm. C. Brown Company.

110. Dyl, J., and Wapner, S. (1996). Age and gender differences in the nature, meaning, and function of cherished possessions for children and adolescents. *Journal of Experimental Child Psychology, 6-3,* 340–377.

111. See note 109.

112. See note 109.

113. See note 110.

NINE

Environments for Disabled and Elderly Populations

Accessibility, utility, and safety are important considerations in every built environment, particularly for environments used by people whose abilities are impaired by age, disease, or genetic issues. When many Americans hear the words *disabled* or *handicapped*, the first image they conjure is of a person in a wheelchair. However, the term *disability* is a broad classification referring to various conditions that hamper or make difficult a person's everyday life. It can refer not only to limited mobility, vision, and hearing, but also to general conditions of mentality (e.g., cerebral palsy, dementia, and obsessive-compulsive disorders), physicality (e.g., obesity, dwarfism, and gigantism), and health (e.g., chronic fatigue syndrome, arthritis, and HIV/AIDS). Understanding user needs within the built environment is crucial to meeting those needs.

Living with physical limitations can be psychologically debilitating, particularly when a person's ability to function is further impeded by the environment. Growing old, living with a disability, and especially both can have a tremendous impact on a person's psych; feelings of inadequacy, dependency, and loss or lack of control can manifest themselves as anger, depression, or learned helplessness. Being challenged or stymied while trying to perform **activities of daily living (ADLs)**—routine functional tasks such as grooming and dressing—can significantly damage a person's sense of self-worth, not to mention quality of life. Many everyday items, such as vending machines, are problematic for physically impaired people: Wheelchair users cannot reach the higher buttons or gather their selections comfortably, people who lack manual dexterity may have trouble inserting coins and bills, and blind people will not know what selections are

available if there is no Braille signage. These types of everyday challenges, along with limited access to public marketplaces and accommodations, can decrease feelings of independence and autonomy, which in turn reduce self-esteem.[1] Implementing compensatory and adaptive strategies can create positive perceptions that lead to feelings of power, self-sufficiency, and mastery (i.e., autonomy).

Autonomy has been shown to be crucial to intrinsic motivation. Autonomy-supportive events are defined as those that encourage the process of choice and the experience of self-determination. Autonomy support is associated with a more positive emotional tone, higher self-esteem, more intrinsic motivation, greater interest, better conceptual learning, more cognitive flexibility, greater persistence of behavior change, more trust, and better physical and psychological health; it is also associated with less pressure, tension, and aggression than control support,[2] which is support that is dependent on others. Therefore, autonomy-supportive environments promote positive or desired outcomes much more readily than *control environments* (i.e., settings that limit or restrict an occupant's behavior).

Psychologist Martin Seligman noted that helplessness is a central construct of personal control and that protracted *learned helplessness* amounts to depression.[3] Learned helplessness can develop when a person is put repeatedly in a position where there is no possibility of success; eventually, the person responds by doing nothing, in the belief that he or she is powerless to improve the situation. Seligman noted that helplessness is a useful predictor of depression, low achievement, and poor physical health. He cited numerous reports of the sudden deaths of men and women of various ages, backgrounds, and levels of health, all of whom

For more information about learned helplessness, check out Chapter 2.

were found after autopsy to have had no discernible pathological cause and who reportedly had feelings of overwhelming helplessness and hopelessness. However, Seligman also noted that much study supports evidence that independence is a modifying variable for future dependence. In other words, a person may simply give up and die, but such a fate is by no means inevitable and can be prevented by measures that include the implementation of autonomy-supportive design.

Concerns that exist for most people living with disabilities have been identified: having well-defined but different needs; achieving and maintaining independence; and the experiences of being labeled and of receiving unwanted assistance.[4] Planners and designers can best serve physically challenged people by identifying their clients' specific needs and ADLs and by working with them to create environments that support their clients' feelings of autonomy. Interior designers can best contribute to residential environments for the elderly by supporting their personal expressions of identity to facilitate place attachment through interior features.[5]

Many issues of disabilities such as mobility, vision, and hearing affect not only those who are developmentally or physically challenged but also many in the geriatric population. Therefore, when we consider designs for the disabled we must also consider the elderly population who, like the disabled population, have a range of abilities, as well as significant impairments, such as Alzheimer's and Parkinson's diseases.

Issues of Disability

Construction of the built environment is based on the assumption that there is an average person. In the past, people dealt with problems of accessibility by using an itemized approach intended to reduce

the disadvantages of specific groups by way of special features such as ramps and special doors, handrails, and Braille signage (Figure 9.1). Individuals with disabilities were incorrectly and unfairly perceived as exceptions to the norm and were therefore stigmatized and further disenfranchised. Most residential designs are based on the measurements of only a fraction of the population—a so-called average-size adult male—and guidelines and regulations concerning housing design and accessibility do not apply to single- or two-family homes, which make up most residences.[6]

The Americans with Disabilities Act (ADA), a federal civil law, was enacted in 1990 to end discrimination against people with disabilities. Title III of the ADA guarantees individuals with disabilities equal access to places of public accommodation. Today, more buildings incorporate **universal design** features (i.e., those that are accessible and useable for all people regardless of age or ability). However, social institutions and attitudes, as well as government legislation, often hamper further advancement toward universal accessibility. For

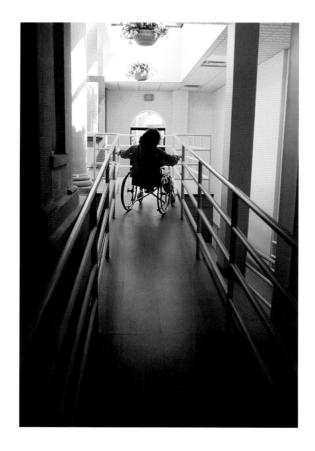

Figure 9.1: The ramp and handrail positioned to the side of the entryway steps create two accessibility issues for this library. First, universal design principles hold that entry, utilization, and departure must be identical for all users; however, in this case, people who use wheelchairs must enter the building from the side. Second, it is difficult for people who rely on canes, walkers, or crutches to navigate up an incline that forces them not only to lift their assistive devices but also to lean backward.

example, trying to meet certain accessibility requirements may offset others;[7] because users have a wide range of ability levels, meeting the needs of some individuals may compromise the needs of others.[8] For example, installing hotel room light switches at heights that accommodate wheelchair-bound people can confuse and frustrate those hotel guests whose vision is limited.

Although well-intentioned, the ADA's accessibility guidelines are not well aligned with universal design principles. A study of a university campus that evaluated the adequacy of the guidelines from a user's perspective noted many areas where these requirements were found to be insufficient: entrances, lecture halls, libraries, **accessible routes** doors, elevators, stairs, restrooms, tables and seating, computer workstations, and signage.[9] When considering an *accessible route* we must regard it as a continuous, unobstructed path that connects all accessible elements and spaces of a building or facility. For example, interior accessible routes may include corridors, floors, ramps, elevators, lifts, and clear floor space at fixtures, and exterior accessible routes may include parking access aisles, curb ramps, crosswalks at vehicular ways, walks, ramps, and lifts. In the ADA's accessibility guidelines study, subjects gave highest priority to providing at least one universally accessible entrance to every building, followed by improving communication barriers (e.g., signage), replacing hard-to-use hardware, and modifying restrooms and classrooms. The researchers' recommendations included decreasing reach ranges by 6 to 12 inches on vending machines, photocopiers, shelves, coat hooks, and drinking fountains so as to improve access, and increasing knee space under tables from 27 inches

Table 9.1 Universal Design Solutions to Common Environmental Challenges of Disability

ISSUE	ENVIRONMENTAL CHALLENGE	UNIVERSAL DESIGN SOLUTION
Mobility	Stairs create multiple challenges for people who use mobility assistive devices.	One-story living accommodations; stairless entryways; gradually inclined ramps with secure handrails; elevators
	Threshold elevation changes often lead to trip-and-fall injuries.	Thresholds built flush with floors
	People who use walkers and wheelchairs need sufficient room in entryways and hallways.	Pocket doors; doorway widths of at least 32–36 inches; hallways widths of at least 36–42 inches
	People who use walkers and wheelchairs need sufficient room to move around furnishings.	Floor space of at least 32 inches around furnishings
Stability	Smooth, wet surfaces are slippery.	Nonslip surfaces on floors, bathtubs, and ramps
	People who experience dizziness need to feel like they are stabilized and not in danger of falling.	Grips or handrails in hallways and bathrooms
	Dim lighting is problematic for people who have limited vision, and indirect lighting causes shadows that affect depth perception.	Bright direct lighting, particularly in stairways and entranceways.
Grip	Globe door handles pose a challenge for people who lack strength or dexterity.	Lever door handles
	Toggle- and twist-type light switches require manual dexterity.	Rocker light switches
Height	Fixed shelving may require the use of stepstools and reaching devices.	Adjustable shelving and brackets
	Electrical outlets installed at standard heights are inconvenient for wheelchair-bound people and others who cannot bend or kneel.	Electrical outlets installed 2 to 3 feet above floor level

deep to 29 to 30 inches to accommodate users of motorized wheelchairs.

DESIGN APPLICATION. Environments that are disability-compatible support development and everyday functioning for all occupants. Therefore, it is essential to determine during intake interviews if there is or will be a need for special or modified designs, constructions, or materials. Many people may think, why consider universal design features if they are currently healthy and mobile? However, incorporating features of universal design in a residence from conception can decrease long-term housing costs and make homes safer and more accessible for residents of all ages and abilities over time.[10] Table 9.1 provides examples of universal design solutions to common disability-related issues.

Issues of Mobility

Mobility impairment can result from age, disease, genetics, injury, or amputation. More than 14.2 million Americans have physical impairments[11] that may call upon the use of mobility aids or **assistive devices**, such as canes and walkers, yet they and their significant others often find built environments to be problematic, particularly in the design of housing and transportation systems. Although design features that serve to maximize mobility are often implemented for wheelchair-bound people, disabled people who can walk tend to receive far less consideration. For example, stairs are obstacles

that wheelchair users easily overcome with ramps. However, a ramp can be as challenging as stairs for individuals who require assistive devices that must be lifted higher to correspond with a ramp's incline; users may lack the strength, balance, or depth perception to do so. Ramps can also be problematic for visually impaired people.

DESIGN APPLICATION. Consider incorporating low and wide landings in the design of entrance stairways, as people with poor depth perception will typically see the rise of a landing more clearly than the incline of a ramp. If a ramp is needed, a very gradual incline will minimize the height that a user will need to lift an assistive device as well as minimize slip-and-fall accidents. In either circumstance, a sturdy, easy to grip handrail should parallel the entrance path, which should itself be as easily navigable as possible. Designers should also consider that attractive landscaping from the street to the entrance can be best savored by people who travel slowly (Figure 9.2).

In a survey of features available in homes designed for wheelchair-bound people many of these features were found deficient in basic needs such as maneuvering space in entryways, lower counter heights in kitchens and bathrooms, and easily operable windows and doors. Designers must consider that this population requires wider doorways and doors that will not obstruct their access to or use of spaces (ideally, pocket doors that slide back into walls, or doors that swing into spaces and stop against walls). These individuals need significant distances both between pieces of furniture and between furnishings and the walls and probably will be unable to utilize wall cabinetry and closet rods hung at standard heights. Designers should be aware of accessibility features that will assist people in the bedroom and bathroom, such as grab bars and handrails, hydraulic or wheelchair lifts, built-in tub transfer seats, roll-in or transfer showers, and adequate space under sinks and counters[12] (Figure 9.3).

Figure 9.2: Notice the handrails positioned on either side of a ramp that comply with universal design principles. All visitors can enter the building from the same direction, which affords easy access to people who use assistive devices. For those who travel slowly, the landscaping affords a pleasant tableau.

Researchers of a college campus study advocate providing approximately 60 inches between furnishings and structures—which will allow wheelchair users a clear turning space and allow blind people to walk next to a guide dog or another person comfortably—and replacing round globe hardware (which requires wrist twisting) with lever hardware to allow people who have prosthetic devices or poor grip strength or coordination to open doors easily.[13]

Interior spaces must provide not only for safety and ease of use but also for ease of cleaning and maintenance.[14] Designers should avoid using flooring materials with inconsistent surfaces, such as slate, flagstone, and tile with dramatic grout lines, as well as high-piled, heavily textured, and sculptured carpeting. If disabled clients desire area rugs, then the rugs must be firmly affixed. Electrical outlets and light switches placed at between three and four feet above floor level will allow people who require mobility assistive devices to access them easily.

Figure 9.3: This bathroom is designed to maximize wheelchair-bound people's autonomy. The grab bars and handrails facilitate movement between the wheelchair and the commode, and the low position keeps people from having to lift themselves as high.

Issues of Vision and Hearing

Universal design practices are intended to reduce the difficulty of performing activities of daily living as much as possible, and people who suffer from visual and hearing impairments make up two populations that require such accommodation. Both populations endure varying degrees and manifestations of disability. The term visual impairment, for example, can refer to total or partial blindness, a slow and progressive loss of eyesight due to age or degenerative disease, or even a difficulty in decoding visual images (i.e., dyslexia). Depending on the severity and the manifestation of the disability, attempting to devise universal design solutions for these populations can pose creative challenges.

Vision

Blind and partially sighted people have different needs from people who have other impairments. Designing hotel rooms according to ADA principles can be inconvenient for visually impaired people who are not accustomed to light switches and handles placed at lower heights. Blind and partially sighted people may use guide dogs, which designers must consider when designing and spec-

ifying materials for hotels and retail spaces.[15] People who have visual impairments prefer deep counters (to avoid spilling), whereas those with mobility problems prefer shallow ones.[16] Restricted vision also serves to limit locomotion; elderly people's mobility can be further hindered by their decreased depth perception and by their decreased ability to detect objects peripherally when they are focused on targets in front of them.[17]

Wayfinding in unfamiliar spaces is a labor-intensive task for visually impaired people. To successfully navigate a constantly changing environment, people must continually reassess and respond to different stimuli and objects. However, research conducted on healthy, older visually impaired adults found that the people who were better able to maintain attention, to selectively attend to relevant stimuli, and to "flexibly and efficiently problem solve" were better able to avoid obstacles.[18] Blind people in particular require suitable strategies for acquiring, processing, and recalling spatial information that promote safety and independence and minimize wayfinding time and effort.[19]

DESIGN APPLICATION. Consider incorporating easily accessible routes to enhance the mobility of visually impaired people and their service

Figure 9.4: This sign allows a blind person to navigate from office to office. Note the raised numbering and Braille.

dogs,[20] tactile maps to help them navigate unfamiliar public environments,[21] and directional signage with raised letters for people who cannot read Braille[22] (Figure 9.4).

A recent study demonstrated that not only direct vision but also **peripheral vision** (outer part of the field of vision), depth perception, and color discrimination all decline with age, and that elderly people take much longer to adapt to changes in light levels.[23] This study also found that by age 75 a person needs twice as much contrast to see as well as a younger person and by age 90 a person needs six times as much. The researchers noted that contrast impairments not only impede reading ability, but also are problematic when detecting curbs or stairs. Additionally, elderly people's attentional impairments are worsened in low-light, low-contrast, and glare conditions.

DESIGN APPLICATION. As the overall population ages, the percentage of visually impaired people is likely to grow due to the increased incidence of macular degeneration, glaucoma, and cataracts among the elderly.[24] This change will have important implications for designers and planners. When designing spaces for visually impaired older people, designers should increase lighting levels and contrast and avoid sudden changes in light levels (e.g., in building entrances) and the use of washed-out colors in interiors, signage, and environmental markers.[25] Designers should also be aware of glare issues, especially those created from using white on white.

Hearing

Title III of the ADA requires businesses and service agencies to provide auxiliary aids and services to enable deaf and hard of hearing people to communicate effectively. Aids include devices such as teletypewriters, now commonly referred to as text telephones (TTYs), as well as visible doorbells and captioning decoders. Services include interpreters or note takers and written informational materials. The ADA also requires the installation of flashing alarm systems, permanent signage, and adequate sound buffers and the removal of structural communication barriers in existing facilities.

Hearing ability and general slowing of the brain affect our abilities to understand spoken language in noisy environments as we age, but older adults also have more difficulty recognizing words in quiet conditions due to age-related changes in the ability to hear words distinctly.[26] Researchers have found that listening performance, particularly the ability to hear clearly in all directions, is also affected by age and that age-related differences in language processing can be magnified due to distracting sounds (e.g., music streams, competing speakers, white noise, or background babble).

DESIGN APPLICATION. Planners and designers must carefully consider structural and layout choices when designing interiors to accommodate hearing-impaired individuals. Interpreters, for example, must be clearly visible to those they serve; therefore, seating arrangements and lighting systems must provide clear lines of sight to interpreters.[27] White noise should be eliminated or significantly reduced, and the environmental acoustics (increased sound quality) designed to enable people of all ages to comprehend, understand, and process language regardless of distracting sounds.

Geriatric Populations

Multiple factors contribute to successful aging, including a healthy diet, adequate sleep and exercise, a participatory social network, and engaging in enjoyable activities and projects. The most important factor, however, is *attitude*; people who accept the aging process as an integral part of the life cycle with unique characteristics[28] are more likely to remain vital and active; those who cannot may literally give up on life.

People who are beyond the age of 80, referred to as the *oldest old*, make up one of the fastest-growing population segments in industrialized countries. Many of these people may have full mental acuity and clear memories of their once independent lifestyles, so the sense of having a young mind trapped in a frail old body can foment feelings of anger, despair, and helplessness. Social factors (family, friends, and caregivers) can provide emotional support and physical assistance, but living in a culture in which youth is prized for its productivity while old age is dishonored and often regarded as burdensome can have devastating psychological effects, including feelings of worthlessness.

Motor and cognitive limitations influence every aspect of elderly people's daily lives and determine the amount and type of activities in which they can participate. Minds and bodies react and function slower the older people get. One or more of the five senses are often compromised, as is the ability to stay asleep. Movement, coordination, and balance are significantly affected, and even simple mental processes take longer. After a lifetime of self-sufficiency and relative freedom, being unable to perform routine ADLs (e.g., driving, cooking, reading, rising from a chair, taking a stroll, bathing, grooming, dressing, or even eating) can be frustrating to the point of severely damaging an older person's self-esteem. The difficulties associated with advanced age are often compounded by greater risk and incidence of injury, physical or mental illness, or a combination of these. Keeping this in mind, designers can alleviate some of these difficulties for the elderly by adding components such as grab bars in elevators (Figure 9.5).

In a study conducted to determine if older adults with chronic illness or disabilities used different strategies to adapt to everyday activities and how these strategies affected feelings of independence, dependence, helplessness, emotional reactivity, and coping ability, study subjects demonstrated a wide range of coping strategies to manage their disabilities. These strategies include the following:

Figure 9.5: Although handrails should be considered in all public buildings according to universal design principles, they should be placed against contrasting backgrounds. Note the copper-plated rail in front of the stainless steel background in this elevator. In this case, the contrast is so subtle that for some they may blend together. Moving elevators can cause vertigo (dizziness) in older people, especially older people who have slower cognitive functioning and reactions; instantly detectable handrails would help to reduce falls.

- Giving up or restricting an activity or performing it less frequently
- Optimization (i.e., spending more time on an activity, planning an activity to avoid problems, using movement to avoid pain or stiffness, and taking rest periods)
- Compensation (i.e., substitution, modification, or use of furniture or equipment for assistance)
- Accepting help from others[29]

Because older adults fear losing their independence, negative psychological impact is inherent to these coping strategies, all of which are associated with feelings of dependence and helplessness, loss of independence, and lower coping efficacy. The optimization techniques also heighten emotional reactivity or a person's response to an event. To maintain an active and independent lifestyle, older adults must be able to perform daily activities such as bathing, eating, and taking medications without active external support.[30]

Elderly individuals often experience problems with coordination, which results in balance problems.[31] Attention, problem solving, and general anxiety have a strong relationship to tripping, and the elderly may be more prone to tripping when contradictory or changing verbal and visual information is presented simultaneously.[32] As we age, our internal systems that maintain balance deteriorate (and some completely fail), and this change results in greater dependence on visual cues to maintain balance.[33] Researchers advocate providing visual spatial cues (i.e., objects or elements in the space) in environments used or occupied by older adults to help them maintain balance—noting, however, that such cues can become compromised when a person is moving (e.g., walking through a mall) or when an environment is moving (e.g., going up an escalator) and that individuals with balance problems become unstable more easily and take longer to regain balance in environments that have moving visual cues (e.g., standing on a moving bus, walking down stairs, or riding a moving sidewalk at an airport).[34]

When we are younger our visual acuity is sharper and the degree of contrast needed to distinguish objects is minimal. As we age, the ability to differentiate between colors decreases, and many older people need a higher degree of contrast to notice such differences. Pastel colors from the cooler end of the spectrum (blues, greens or purples) become much harder to discern; to many elderly people, pastel blues, greens, and purples all appear gray. This becomes an important consideration for designers, particularly as it applies to changes in elevations. Although older people require more contrast between colors, it is important that designers avoid creating too much contrast (i.e., black and white, black and yellow, and so on), particularly within patterns, which could lead to a three-dimensional illusion.

Visual cues in the environment can make older people less stable by interfering with their visual perception, which makes them more susceptible to falls. When young people become unstable they move their ankles to retain their balance, but older people move their hips, which is more likely to cause a fall (and indicates balance problems linked to posture control).[35] Falls are a leading cause of death among the elderly, and participants in one research study reported that the mere fear of falling could cause them to avoid everyday activities such as going outdoors in slippery conditions and reaching overhead for something.[36]

DESIGN APPLICATION. Be aware of design elements that may increase elderly people's fears of falling, such as angles, distances, and surface textures. Provide railings and other supports to stabilize people with balance problems in places where floor and wall cues are confusing and mismatched.[37]

Dominant medical approaches view aging as a curable disease and ignore the social, environmental, and quality-of-life needs of the oldest old, whose well-being can thus be compromised.[38] Designers and caregivers alike should provide means for the oldest old to adapt and utilize the psychosocial resources that will help them compensate for a decline in their physical health. A longitudinal study found that oldest old individuals who were living independently and with better perceived health and mastery beliefs displayed greater stability in ADL functions during the first two years of the study. The study also found that age, marital status, grip strength, and mastery were significant predictors of mobility status after four years.[39] The researchers noted that ADL functioning is dependent not only on age but also on individual physical, psychological, and social characteristics, and environments that promote a sense of mastery over challenging situations help to avert passive and dependent behaviors, which precludes disabilities. Other researchers found that although older adults experience difficulties with new technology, they are eager to learn how to use technology that will enrich their lives and help them to remain independent.[40]

An initial study of institutionalized elderly people demonstrated that residents who received autonomy support experienced improved overall well-being;[41] the follow-up study 18 months later of the same residents found them to be healthier than their peers who did not receive such support.[42] Additional studies have demonstrated that some of the oldest old can remain stable over time, that psychosocial factors play a critical role in improving or maintaining health, and that a sense of dependence and a lack of control—typical within long-term care facility environments—contribute to physical decline.[43] If at all possible, the elderly should be allowed to remain in their homes. When this is not possible, long-term care facilities designed in ways that encourage feelings of usefulness and independence can help to maintain the occupants' psychological health and thereby reduce the incidence of debilitating illnesses.

DESIGN APPLICATION. Design elements should serve to compensate for the physical and energy limitations of elderly individuals. Many older adults require easily accessible storage because they have trouble reaching into upper wall cabinets and the lower shelves of base cabinets or refrigerators. Moreover, they do not cook extensively, cannot use the back burners on stoves safely, and prefer to use smaller appliances (e.g., microwaves, toaster ovens, or Crock-Pots).[44] Consider incorporating an L-shaped kitchen layout that provides a corner where people with limited stamina can lean and a small work triangle (the area between the refrigerator, sink, and oven or range) to reduce the effort involved in meal preparation[45] (Figure 9.6).

Design should also provide both storage and display areas for personal objects, memorabilia, and heirlooms, which can evoke pleasant feelings and symbolize the self and specific memories for older individuals who may depend on those objects for their well-being.[46] One researcher, citing earlier findings that possessions can trigger memories, give meaning to a home, and reinforce self-identity, found that *place attachment* is more likely to occur when personal artifacts are incorporated into an otherwise anonymous space where they can be seen and touched; this researcher recommended using personal possession criteria in design programs to determine how individuals feel about their personal possessions.[47] Some people may not wish to be reminded of their past experiences or lost youth.

Figure 9.6: In this kitchen the island stove creates room to manuever but does not allow much counterspace for people to lean against.

See Chapter 11 for more on the design of long-term care facilities and the psychological health of the elderly.

Dementia of the Alzheimer's Type

It is estimated that dementia of the Alzheimer's type (DAT) will affect up to 16 million Americans by 2050.[48] Currently, about 5 to 10 percent of people who are age 65 and older have DAT, an incurable condition that affects the nervous system by reducing cognitive abilities and increasing spatial disorientation.[49] The disease causes progressive cognitive degeneration, which usually advances even faster in the later stages. Affecting different parts of the brain at different times, DAT is associated with memory loss, confusion, language problems, lack of identity, emotional and personality changes, sleep and sexual disorders, and disruptive behaviors.[50–52] These last include abnormal motor and verbal activity, hallucinations, incontinence, agitation and irritability, aggression and violence, social withdrawal, and wandering.[53] Motor skills, social processes, and habitual personality traits are least affected.[54] Additionally, DAT often causes sufferers to regress psychologically to a very young age; such regression can extend to the use of native languages and cultural behaviors, depending on how different a person's adopted culture is from the native one, how well the person has dealt with biculturalism, and to what extent the person has integrated the new culture into his or her identity.[55] Table 9.2 outlines characteristic changes associated with mild, moderate, and severe DAT.

Dementia sufferers who are aware of their impairment and deterioration respond with feelings of helplessness and depression,[56] and the stage of the disease, as well as a sufferer's circumstances, can either speed or slow the cognitive degeneration. Privacy that relates to the control and freedom of choice regarding accessibility to ourselves[57] is a fundamental human need; therefore, thwarting people's abilities to control privacy in the early stages of DAT can facilitate the disease's progression.

One of the most challenging decisions for family members to make is when to place a loved one in an institution such as a nursing home or other type of long-term care facility. Families can delay this decision by having their home environments designed to be more compatible with both the dementia sufferer and the symptom manifestation.[58] Although eventually inevitable for many dementia sufferers (especially those who wander), institutionalization has significant negative physical, psychological, and communicative implications.[59] The mere transition from an environment associated with familiarity and privacy into one of unfamiliarity and higher density will evoke natural feelings of insecurity. Numerous studies indicate that institutionalized people have higher mortality rates than those who receive care in their home environments. However, researchers have found that residents who had bet-

Table 9.2 Stages of Dementia of the Alzheimer's Type (DAT)

STAGE OF DISEASE	COMMON CHANGES
Mild DAT	Loses spark or zest for life; does not start anything Loses recent memory without a change in appearance or casual conversation Has trouble finding words; may stop talking to avoid making mistakes Has shorter attention spans and less motivation to keep doing an activity Easily loses way going to familiar places Has trouble organizing and thinking logically Asks repetitive questions Withdraws, loses interest, becomes irritable, insensitive to others' feelings, and becomes uncharacteristically angry when frustrated or tired Loses or misplaces things by hiding them in odd places or forgets where things go, such as putting clothes in the dishwasher
Moderate DAT	Changes in behavior and concern for appearance, hygiene, and sleep become more noticeable Confuses people's identities Poor judgment creates safety issues when left alone; may wander and risk exposure, poisoning, falls, self-neglect, or exploitation Continuously repeats stories, favorite words, statements, or actions like tearing tissues Has restless, repetitive movements in late afternoon or evening, such as pacing, trying doorknobs, or touching draperies Makes up stories to fill in gaps in memory; for example, a person might say, "Mama will come for me when she gets off work."
Severe DAT	Doesn't recognize self or close family Speaks in gibberish, is mute, or is difficult to understand May refuse to eat, chokes, or forgets to swallow May repetitively cry out, pat, or touch everything Loses control of bowel and bladder May look uncomfortable or cry out when transferred or touched

Source: Stage of Disease. Modified from: www.alzheimers.org/pubs/stages.htm

ter cognitive and physical functioning, expressive language, and less agitation had experienced more overall decline one year after being admitted into a long-term care facility.[60] These findings suggests that the transition itself accelerates patient decline, and those who decline less are usually at a point in which there isn't much further to go.

DAT sufferers have different environmental needs than other older adults and are less able to adapt to environmental stress.[61] They have even more difficulty staying asleep than their peers, and those who wander may do so at all hours.[62] Harsh lighting and loud or sudden noises can cause sensory overstimulation, which can increase the confusion, distraction, and agitation associated with dementia;[63] however, sensory deprivation can be equally problematic (e.g., inadequate lighting can hamper dining and wayfinding).[64] Design can serve to maintain a healthy balance. Facilitating spatial orientation and wayfinding can be therapeutically beneficial[65] because being able to reach a desired destination is critical to a person's sense of autonomy and quality of life.[66] Therefore, redundant *wayfinding mechanisms* should be available throughout the environment.

DESIGN APPLICATION. Designers should provide visual cues, such as signs on doors and exits, to discourage wandering in locations where dementia sufferers live.[67] Marking a residence with the occupant's personality has been shown to bolster self-esteem.[68] Consider modifying dementia patients' environments so they can better adjust to their lives,[69] as this behavioral approach is, essentially, the only "treatment" that will benefit sufferers (Figure 9.7)

Environmental design can greatly benefit people who suffer from various forms of dementia, especially when implemented so as to aid both sufferers and caregivers in mitigating and managing symptom manifestation.[70] In many ways, the impact of design for dementia sufferers has spread far

beyond serving the needs of cognitively impaired individuals and is considered supportive for all residents of long-term care facilities.[71] Such design concepts include recognizing the importance of the physical environment, including sunlight and fresh air; improving patient quality of life while mitigating problematic behaviors; and providing interior and exterior environments that are diverse and user-appropriate and minimize sensory overstimulation. Design features include special care units; simplified building configurations; smaller residential spaces that incorporate kitchen areas and personal possessions; the use of personalized cues for patient orientation; and the provision of outdoor spaces, natural views, and landmarks. A paradigm shift in treatment is occurring as more is discovered about dementia of the Alzheimer's type, and researchers are studying how the designed environment supports the unaffected abilities of dementia patients.[72]

Research has identified these crucial components for designers to consider when designing facilities for people who suffer from DAT:[73]

- Use or nonuse of restraints (physical and chemical)
- Flexible care routines (client-relevant activities)
- Specialized environmental design
- Facility adaptation

Designers can help to ensure the most appropriate environments for client-relevant activities in both a

For more on issues that designers face regarding people who have dementia, read Chapter 11.

Figure 9.7: Hospital rooms should be designed to resemble as closely as possible spaces in a home and should have exterior views. However, people who have DAT often become more agitated late in the day (an affliction commonly referred to as *sundowner's syndrome*); therefore, their views should not face west because the sun from this perspective serves as an agitator.

primary role (e.g., environmental design, and facility adaptation) and a complementary role (e.g., the design of communication and restraint systems). DAT affects behavioral, emotional, and cognitive functioning,[74] particularly memory,[75] as well as physical functions, often to the point where sufferers can no longer control their bodily functions.[76] Incidents of incontinence are acutely distressing to both patients and caregivers;[77] therefore, designers can support sufferers' sense of personal control by strategically positioning—and clearly marking—toilet facilities (Figure 9.8).

Cognitive impairments have been linked to decreased response time when avoiding obstacles; tripping over objects is a frequent cause of falls among the elderly. Therefore, when designing interior environments consider the longer reaction times of older adults and dementia patients and avoid using architectural features that become obstacles.[78] Older people (mostly those with DAT) are susceptible to a phenomena called *visual cliffing*, which stems from the inability to differentiate between colors and textures. Thus, a dark mat in front of a door may appear to be a deep hole. This illusion can have positive or negative consequences for older people. The dark mat, by resembling something like a mote, can serve as a restraint, preventing a resident from preceding any further. However, the presence of this "hole" may prompt the resident to attempt jumping over it, thus risking a fall and serious injury. Another problem with visual cliffing is that residents often stop suddenly when they perceive inconsistencies in their paths,

such as a black tile intermixed with lighter color tile. Known as *stalling*, this sudden stopping often results in falls. Visual cliffing can be a problem not only with flooring but also with wall surfaces, such as when a dark-colored wall appears to be an empty space. In one study, people with DAT fell more frequently than those with Parkinson's disease and twice as often as healthy adults.[79] Parkinson's sufferers exhibited balance problems across all test situations, indicating general balance problems, but frequent falls by people with DAT were not due to poor motor (body) control; rather, they resulted from people's inabilities to process and control information gained from the senses. This suggests that dementia sufferers may have trouble breaking attention away from conflicting visual cues when situations require concentration to maintain balance.

DESIGN APPLICATION. The design of facilities for people suffering from dementia depends greatly on the disease stage. Those in the early and middle stages of DAT, for example, can still make decisions based on environmental information and routine sets of behavior,[80] and appropriate designs can help to slow the disease's progression. For patients in the late stages, who are less aware of their environments,[81] design is less influential.

Parkinson's Disease

According to the Parkinson's Disease Foundation, after Alzheimer's disease, Parkinson disease is the most common neurodegenerative disease in the United States. Approximately 1.5 million Americans are affected by Parkinson's disease, with about 60,000 new cases appearing each year.[82] Approximately 90 to 95 percent of those who develop Parkinson's disease do so after the age of 60. The remaining 5 to 10 percent, referred to as "young onset" patients, develop symptoms before the age of 40.

In people with Parkinson's disease, the neurons

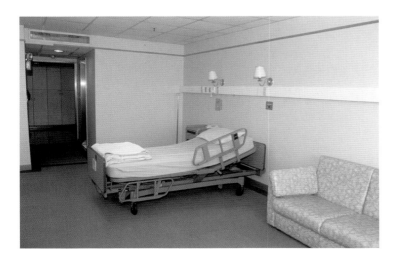

Figure 9.8: Positioning the bed in a direct line of sight from the bathroom affords easy access to people who suffer from DAT, which can reduce episodes of incontinence. In this case the bed is placed to the left of the bathroom and is visible to a patient lying down.

Table 9.3 Primary Symptoms of Parkinson's Disease

SYMPTOM	DESCRIPTION
Tremors	Early in the disease, about 70 percent of people experience a slight tremor in the hand or foot on one side of the body, called a resting tremor because it appears when the muscles are relaxed and disappears with action. As the disease progresses, the tremor often spreads to the other side of the body but remains most apparent on the original side.
Rigidity	Normally, muscles contract with movement and relax at rest. Rigidity causes the muscle to remain contracted and can result in decreased range of motion as well as pain and cramps at the muscle site.
Bradykinesia	Bradykinesia refers to slowing or incompleteness of voluntary muscular movements. Patients often experience difficulty initiating movements and may begin to walk with short, shuffling steps (festination). Patients may have difficulty making turns or abrupt movements or may experience periods of freezing (i.e., becoming stuck and finding it difficult to stop or start walking). The slowness and incompleteness of movement can also negatively affect balance, speaking, and swallowing.

in the brain that are responsible for producing the neurotransmitter dopamine become impaired or die.[83] Dopamine is needed for the smooth control and coordination of voluntary muscle groups. Symptoms of Parkinson's disease typically develop once 80 percent of the dopamine-producing cells have ceased to function. Researchers suspect that the cause of Parkinson's disease reflects a combination of genetic factors and environmental exposures.

The most common symptoms of Parkinson's disease include tremors, rigidity, and bradykinesia (Table 9.3). The many secondary symptoms include speech changes, loss of facial expression, micrographia (small, cramped handwriting), difficulty swallowing, drooling, pain, dementia or confusion, memory difficulties and slowed thinking, fatigue and aching, and loss of energy.

DESIGN APPLICATION. Because tremors are more likely to occur when muscles are relaxed, many patients with Parkinson's disease prefer to grip or hold onto something. Consider placing rails or bars at key locations, such as hallways, bathrooms, and along outdoor paths, and including chairs with armrests in all sitting areas. Be aware that rigidity can greatly decrease an individual's range of motion, to the point where lifting a hand over the head to reach for something can be problematic. Mechanical storage shelves that raise and lower reduce the need to bend down low or reach up high.

Summary Review

Most of the built environment is based on the height, weight, and mobility of the so-called average adult male; however, these measurements and capabilities apply to only a fraction of the population. People who have disabilities have often incorrectly or unfairly been perceived as exceptions to the norm. In an attempt to address such discriminatory attitudes, the Americans with Disabilities Act (ADA), enacted in 1990, mandated access to public places for people with disabilities. In addition to the ADA's accessibility guidelines, designers also rely on principles of universal design to ensure that the built environment is as accommodating as possible to people with all other forms of limitations. Universal design principles consider the multitude of users of an environment and develop ways for everyone to have equal access without creating a hardship or challenge for any population. At times, however, these two sets of guidelines can be at cross-purposes.

Currently, more than 14.2 million Americans use mobility aids or some form of assistive device ranging from wheelchairs to canes and walkers. Many of the design features intended to maximize mobility are directed toward the wheelchair-bound person, and people who are able to walk to some degree receive less consideration. Stairs are easily augmented with ramps; however, ramps can be challenging for the visually impaired or people who use walkers. For these reasons, universal design

For more on the brain and the effects of dopamine, read Chapter 3.

principles are often more advantageous than strict compliance with ADA accessibility guidelines.

Universal design practices are intended to enhance activities of daily living. In performing such daily activities, most of us take for granted the ability to see and hear. However, many Americans have vision and hearing disabilities, ranging in degree from only slight impairment to being completely blind or deaf. Among common issues of concern for those who are partially sighted are issues of depth perception, color discrimination, and peripheral vision. The impairment of one or more of these aspects of vision can make navigation a challenge. Likewise, those who have partial hearing have unique challenges, which include difficulty recognizing words and filtering background sounds and an inability to hear equally in all directions.

Many factors contribute to successful aging, among them a healthy diet, adequate sleep and exercise, and participation in social networks. Because of healthier lifestyles and advances in medical technology, adults who are 80 years and older are now one of the fastest-growing population segments in industrialized countries. However, as we age, vision, hearing, and coordination all diminish to some degree, causing us to become somewhat impaired. Slowed reactions of both mind and body make it more difficult to process a potential threat. One consequence is an increased risk of falls, which are the leading cause of death among the elderly. Another, equally important consequence is loss of independence, which has negative psychological implications for older people, who may begin to feel dependent and helpless.

With increased age comes an increased incidence of neurodegenerative diseases such as dementia of the Alzheimer's type and Parkinson's disease. Currently, about 5 to 10 percent of people age 65 years or older have DAT, and 1.5 million Americans are affected by Parkinson's disease. DAT produces cognitive and behavioral symptoms that include memory loss, confusion, language problems, lack of identity, emotional and personality changes, sleep and sexual disorders, and disruptive behaviors. Patients with Parkinson's disease develop physical symptoms that usually include tremors, rigidity, and bradykinesia (slow or incomplete movements).

Placing a loved one in an institution such as a nursing home or other type of long-term care facility can be one of the most challenging decisions that families face. This decision can be delayed by designing home environments to be more compatible with limitations imposed by diseases such as Alzheimer's and Parkinson's diseases. Eventually, however, most individuals with severe symptoms (especially those who wander or routinely choke when eating) will require 24-hour care. The transition from a familiar and private environment to an environment of unfamiliarity and higher density can evoke feelings of fear and insecurity. Designers and planners must therefore be creative in incorporating design features within long-term care facilities that help alleviate those fears while facilitating ways for cognitively or physically impaired people to master their new environments.

Design is the best source of practical solutions to environmental problems encountered by a wide range of people. Neglect by design professionals has made disabled individuals feel anger, frustration, learned helplessness, and apathy. Concerted efforts must be made to establish direct communication among challenged people, their significant others, healthcare providers, designers, planners, architects, and contractors early in the design process. Consider strategies that will increase feelings of autonomy for people with disabilities, always remembering that their individual needs will vary and change over time. This is especially true for dementia patients, whose disease slowly strips them of their senses of self, and for which there is no known medical means of prevention, reversal, or cure. Design can help to compensate for elderly and disabled individuals' limitations and increase their feelings of well-being. When designing environments for impaired populations, strive to create spaces appropriate to their needs wherein they can enjoy as much comfort, personal control, and self-sufficiency—and therefore relative freedom—as possible.

Discussion Questions

1. Discuss what is meant by *ADLs*. What are some examples of daily activities you may take for granted that could pose a challenge for people with disabilities?

2. Discuss the psychological and physiological

effects of aging, and compare those effects with how elderly individuals might view their surroundings.

3. Discuss the concept of *learned helplessness*. What are examples of activities where a person might learn to be helpless, even if that person does not have a disability?

4. This chapter mentions many specific issues in which the ADA accessibility guidelines conflict with universal design principles. How does this knowledge inform and affect your future design decisions?

5. Discuss the effect of incorporating designs for individuals with mobility issues into your standard designs. What effect does this have on visibility through a space, traffic flow, and aesthetics?

6. Discuss how a visually impaired individual with a guide dog would respond to the environment you currently occupy. Is there easy ingress and egress? Are there many distractions for the dog? Do people regularly leave food where the dog may find it?

7. Similarly, discuss how an individual with hearing difficulties might perceive your current environment. What would happen in case of emergency (e.g., fire, flood, or tornado)? Would they be able to tell immediately from visual cues? Are there visible maps of the space available?

8. Discuss the psychological impacts of aging. Consider the design issues mentioned in the chapter, but also investigate and consider the social consequences of aging. Consider ways that design may be used to help minimize the age stereotypes.

9. Consider the idea that *learned helplessness* is a disability. How might design help minimize the condition in elderly people? The elderly are more likely to learn new technology if it improves their quality of life; how might you incorporate technology in your designs to improve the quality of life of the geriatric population? Keep in mind that many elderly individuals enjoy visits to the bank, grocery store, and pharmacy simply for the social interaction.

10. As the American population ages, dementia and DAT will continue to influence design decisions. How might residential designers adapt ideas about orientation and privacy to allow a family to care for their aging loved ones?

11. Improving the line of sight to the restroom may decrease incidents of incontinence in patients suffering from dementia. Discuss other issues that could help caregivers lessen some of the effects of DAT.

Learning Activities

1. Spend a day with a friend who is willing to act as your caregiver as you attempt to "live with" one or several disabilities. Record the difficulties you experience throughout the day, and list ways to make the obstacles you encountered less problematic for someone who really suffers from those disabilities.

2. Redesign the room where you live or study for a person who has lost the use of both legs. What factors do you need to consider? What aspects of standard design are no longer functional? Draw complete before-and-after floor plans, using the blueprint of your actual room.

3. Draw an elevation of a wall with a door, light switches, electrical outlets, exit signage, and a fire alarm. You are designing for five different disabled conditions: blindness, deafness, wheelchair-bound, and limited joint mobility. Ensure that an individual with any one or more of these impairments can access or utilize all items. Show dimensions and include comments about functionality or feasibility. (Some items may need to be duplicated in different locations on the wall to make them accessible to all parties.)

4. Lighting design can aid or hinder a partially sighted individual. Draw two diagrams of a hallway or lobby: one illustrating constructive lighting and the other illustrating destructive lighting.

5. Consider how a blind individual might navigate through a crowded retail space (e.g., a mall or grocery store), and what services might be made available to aid accessibility. Contact the manager of a local grocery store or mall and discuss the methods their establishment uses. What ideas were new to you?

Did you have novel ideas? Present your data in a table, listing all comments and opinions next to each method.

6. How might lighting affect a deaf person? Draw three diagrams showing how poor light placement may hinder his or her communication.

7. Research the most common injuries to individuals who are 70 years or older. Write brief summaries of the top three injuries, and suggest methods by which design can lessen the severity or frequency of these injuries. Make note of any mention of the location where the accident occurred (e.g., home, office, car, or retail setting). List all sources using proper bibliographic format. Use images only if necessary.

8. What built-environment factors discussed in other chapters affect elderly individuals? Considering issues of mobility, access, privacy, and independence, design a housing scheme that would support the overall physical and mental health of the oldest old.

9. How might the design of a space encourage healthy activities for independent, oldest old people? Design a room that promotes independence, physical health, and psychological health for an individual living alone.

10. Design a room for a patient suffering from DAT, incorporating all of the information included in this chapter as well as any research you perform online or in the library. Present your design in a way that highlights any adjustments made specifically for a DAT patient and explain how these modifications are beneficial. Cite your research sources, including the specific pages in the chapter, that informed your design decision.

Terminology

accessible route   Continuous, unobstructed path connecting all accessible elements and spaces of a building or facility; interior accessible routes may include corridors, floors, ramps, elevators, lifts, and clear floor space at fixtures, and exterior accessible routes may include parking access aisles, curb ramps, crosswalks at vehicular ways, walks, ramps, and lifts

acoustics   Increased sound qualities of an environment; design elements that affect the sound characteristics of a space through transmission, absorption, and reflection

activities of daily living (ADLs)   Routine functional activities such as bathing, grooming, dressing, dining, cooking, light housekeeping, and taking medication

assistive device   Physical mobility aid that assists users' movements, such as a brace, cane, crutch, walking frame, wheelchair (standard or motorized), prosthetic limb, or service animal

peripheral vision   Outer part of the field of vision

universal design   Approach to the design of products and spaces that emphasizes usability by people with a wide range of needs; intended to enable people of all ability levels to achieve maximum environmental independence

References

1. Baker, S. M., Stephens, D. L., and Hill, R. P. (2002). How can retailers enhance accessibility: Giving consumers with visual impairments a voice in the marketplace. *Journal of Retailing and Consumer Services, 9*, 227–239.

2. Deci, E. L., and Ryan, R. M. (1987). The support of autonomy and the control of behavior. *Journal of Personality and Social Psychology, 53*, 1024–1037.

3. Seligman, M. E. P. (1991). *Helplessness: On depression, development, and death* (2nd ed.). New York: W.H. Freeman and Company.

4. See note 1.

5. Eshelman, P. E., and Evans, G. W. (2002). Home again: Environmental predictors of place attachment and self-esteem for new retirement community residents. *Journal of Interior Design, 28-1*, 3–9.

6. DeMerchant, E. A., and Beamish, J. O. (1995). Universal design in residential spaces. *Housing and Society, 22-1/2*, 77–91.

7. Mazumdar, S., and Geis, G. (2002). Accessible buildings, architects, and the ADA law: The MCI Center Sports Arena case. *Journal of Architectural and Planning Research, 19-3*, 195–217.

8. Osterberg, A. E., Davis, A. M., and Danielson, L. D. (1995). Universal design: The users' perspective. *Housing and Society, 22-1/2,* 92–113.

9. See note 8.

10. Femia, E. E., Zarit, S. H., & Johansson, B. (1997). Predicting change in activities of daily living: A longitudinal study of the oldest old. *Journal of Gerontology: Psychological Sciences,* 52B, P292-P304.

11. Gray, D. B., Gould, M., and Bickenbach, J. E. (2003). Environmental barriers and disability. *Journal of Architectural and Planning Research, 20-1,* 29–37.

12. Connell, B. R., and Sanford, J. A. (2001). Difficulty, dependence, and housing accessibility for people aging with a disability. *Journal of Architectural and Planning Research, 18-3,* 234–242.

13. See note 8.

14. See note 12.

15. See note 1.

16. Boschetti, M. A. (2002). An observational study of older people's use of standard U.S. kitchens. *Housing and Society, 29-1/2,* 1–12.

17. Brabyn, J. A., Haegerström-Portnoy, G., Schneck, M. E., and Lott, L. A. (2000). Visual impairments in elderly people under everyday viewing conditions. *Journal of Visual Impairments and Blindness, 94-12,* 741–755.

18. Persad, C. C., Giordani, B., Chen, H. C., Ashton-Miller, J. A., Alexander, N. B., Wilson, C. S., Berent, S., Guire, K., and Schultz, A. B. (1995). Neuropsychological predictors of complex obstacle avoidance in healthy older adults. *Journal of Gerontology: Psychological Sciences,* 50B-5, P272–P277.

19. Espinosa, M. A., Ungar, S., Ochaita, E., Blades, M., and Spencer, C. (1998). Comparing methods for introducing blind and visually impaired people to unfamiliar urban environments. *Journal of Environmental Psychology, 18-3,* 277–287.

20. See note 1.

21. See note 19.

22. See note 8.

23. See note 17.

24. See note 1.

25. See note 17.

26. Tun, P. A., and Wingfield, A. (1999). One voice too many: Adult age differences in language processing with different types of distracting sounds. *Journal of Gerontology: Psychological Sciences,* 54B-5, P317–P327.

27. National Association of the Deaf Law Center. Title III of the ADA: Provision of Auxiliary Aids. Retrieved May 2004 from www.nad.org /infocenter/infotogo/legal/ada3aux.html.

28. Schwarz, B. (1997). Nursing home design: A misguided architectural model. *Journal of Architectural and Planning Research, 14-4,* 343–359.

29. Gignac, M. A. M., Cott, C., and Badley, E. M. (2000). Adaptation to chronic illness and disability and its relationship to perceptions of independence and dependence. *Journal of Gerontology Series B: Psychological Sciences and Social Sciences,* 55B-6, P362–P372.

30. Rogers, W. A., Meyer, B., Walker, N., and Fisk, A. D. (1998). Functional limitations to daily living tasks in the aged: A focus group analysis. *Human Factors, 40-1,* 111–125.

31. See note 30.

32. See note 18

33. Sundermier, L., Woollacott, M. H., Jensen, J. L., and Moore, S. (1996). Postural sensitivity to visual flow in aging adults with and without balance problems. *Journal of Gerontology: Medical Sciences,* 51A-2, M45–M52.

34. See note 33.

35. See note 33.

36. Lachman, M. E., Howland, J., Tennstedt, S., Jette, A., Assman, S., and Peterson, E. W. (1998). Fear of falling and activity restriction: The survey of activities and fear of falling in the elderly (SAFE). *Journal of Gerontology: Psychological Sciences,* 53B-1, P43–P50.

37. Chong, R. K. Y., Horak, F. B., Frank, J., and Kaye, J. (1999). Sensory organization for balance: Specific deficits in Alzheimer's but not in Parkinson's disease. *Journal of Gerontology: Medical Sciences,* 54A-3, M122–M128.

38. See note 28.

39. Femia, E. E., Zarit, S. H., and Johansson, B. (1997). Predicting change in activities of daily living: A longitudinal study of the oldest old in Sweden. *Journal of Gerontology: Psychological Sciences,* 52B-6, 294–302.

40. See note 30.

41. Langer, E. J., and Rodin, J. (1976). The effects of choice and personal responsibility for the aged: A field experiment in an institutional setting. *Journal of Personality and Social Psychology, 34*, 191–198.

42. Rodin, J., and Langer, E. J. (1977). Long-term effects of a control relevant intervention with the institutionalized aged. *Journal of Personality and Social Psychology, 35*, 897–902.

43. Boschetti, M. A. (1995). Attachment to personal possessions: An interpretive study of the older person's experience. *Journal of Interior Design, 21-1*, 1–12.

44. See note 43.

45. See note 43.

46. See note 43.

47. See note 43.

48. Alzheimer's Association (2004). Statistics fact sheet, retrieved 06 Aug 2004 from website www.alz.org.

49. Passini, R., Rainville, C., Marchand, N., and Joanette, Y. (1998). Wayfinding and dementia: Some research findings and a new look at design. Journal of Architectural and Planning Research, 15-2, 133–151.

50. Zeisel, J. (2000). Environmental design effects on Alzheimer symptoms in long-term care residences. *World Hospitals and Health Services, 36-3*, 27–31.

51. Cohen, U., and Weisman, G. D. (1991). *Holding on to home: Designing environments for people with dementia.* Baltimore, MD: Johns Hopkins University Press.

52. Rabins, P.V. (1989). Behavior problems in the demented. In E. Light and B.D. Lebowitz (Eds.), *Alzheimer's disease treatment and family stress: Directions for research* (pp. 322–339). (DHHS Publication No. ADM 89-1569). Washington, DC: U.S. Government Printing Office.

53. Day, K., and Calkins, M. P. (2002). Design and dementia. In Robert B. Bechtel and Arza Churchman (Eds.), *Handbook of environmental psychology*, pp. 374–393. New York: John Wiley & Sons.

54. See note 50.

55. Valle, R. (1989). The emergence of transpersonal psychology. In E. Light and B.D. Lebowitz (Eds.), *Alzheimer's disease treatment and family stress: Directions for research* (pp. 322–339). (DHHS Publication No. ADM 89-1569). Washington, DC: U.S. Government Printing Office.

56. Brannon, L., and Feist, J. (1997). *Health psychology: An introduction to behavior and health* (3rd ed.). Pacific Grove, CA: Brooks/Cole.

57. Morgan, D. G., and Stewart, N. J. (1998). Multiple occupancy versus private rooms on dementia care units. *Environment and Behavior, 30-4*, 487–503.

58. See note 49.

59. Passini, R., Pigot, H., Rainville, C., and Tetreault, M. H. (2000). Wayfinding in a nursing home for advanced dementia of the Alzheimer's type. *Environment and Behavior, 32-5*, 684–710.

60. Chappell, N. L., and Reid, R. C. (2000). Dimensions of care for dementia sufferers in long-term care institutions: Are they related to outcomes? *Journal of Gerontology: Social Sciences*, 55B-4, S234–S244.

61. See note 57.

62. See note 56.

63. See note 53.

64. See note 51.

65. See note 49.

66. See note 59.

67. Logsdon, R. G., Teri, L., McCurry, S. M., Gibbons, L. E., Kukull, W. A., and Larson, E.B. (1998). Wandering: A significant problem among community-residing individuals with Alzheimer's disease. *Journal of Gerontology: Psychological Sciences, 53B-5*, P294–P299.

68. Eshelman, P. E., and Evans, G. W. (2002). Home again: Environmental predictors of place attachment and self-esteem for new retirement community residents. *Journal of Interior Design, 28-1*, 3–9.

69. See note 52.

70. Day, K., and Cohen, U. (2000). The role of culture in designing environments for people with dementia: A study of Russian Jewish immigrants. *Environment and Behavior, 32-3*, 361–399.

71. See note 70.

72. See note 50.

73. See note 60.

74. See note 70.

75. See note 51.
76. See note 49.
77. See note 56.
78. Chen, H. C., Schultz, A. B., Ashton-Miller, J. A., Giordani, B., Alexander, N. B., and Guire, K. E. (1996). Stepping over obstacles: Dividing attention impairs performance of old more than young adults. *Journal of Gerontology, 51A-3*, M116–M122.

79. See note 37.
80. See note 49.
81. See note 57.
82. Avicena (n.d.). Disease Targets. retrieved June 20, 2005 from www.avicenagroup.com/disease_targets/neurology/parkinsons.php#2.
83. Parkinson's Disease Foundation, (n.d.). Symptoms. Retrieved June 20, 2005 from www.pdf.org.

TEN

Schools and Learning Environments

Much of contemporary school design and education practices within the United States is based on design and education reform concepts that marked the culturally creative period of Germany's Weimar Republic (1919–1933). Today's trend in school design is toward consolidation: larger, more centralized schools that accommodate more students. This trend is driven primarily by costs; with only one building, money that would have been spent on maintaining several buildings can be reallocated to education. As a result, the student populations of many urban middle and high schools rival those of some larger universities; some studies indicate that what we save in financial resources we lose in social development.[1]

The Weimar design disciplines, such as the Bauhaus school, developed from a collaboration among professionals of various specialties who were seen as an extension of the community.[2] These professionals studied the effect of environmental factors such as natural lighting and air circulation on a child's ability to learn. Today, it is still generally theorized that a significant part of children's development depends on the physical environment.[3] Learning environments therefore need to support development by providing a variety of stimuli, accommodating many activities, and furnishing ample opportunities for privacy.

Children constantly receive enormous amounts of complicated information within educational environments, and how they interpret and aggregate this information will affect their learning and subsequent behaviors.[4] In fact, researchers confirm that the design of physical environments will affect children's perception, learning, and behavior[5] as do experts who found that early development of motor, cognitive, and social skills can be supported by the design of children's play spaces.[6] Understanding which characteristics of the physical environment affect young people's behaviors will help designers create more developmentally appropriate environments.[7]

The design of learning environments involves many factors and considerations—there is extensive literature devoted to this topic. This chapter surveys some of the underlying issues that affect the design of learning environments and explores considerations in the design of the following educational settings: day-care centers and preschools, primary and secondary schools, and colleges and universities. Specific topics addressed in this chapter include psychological issues such as crowding, density, and personal space, and issues related to the physical aspects of the learning environment, such as lighting types and levels; color, acoustics, and noise; and temperature, humidity, and ventilation.

Learning and Environment

A learning environment is a system of complex relationships that exists among the physical structure (size and arrangement of a room), a teacher, and a student.[8,9] The physical aspects of a learning environment can have a direct influence on learning, behavior, and productivity.[10] The ideal learning environment contains appropriate and comfortable furnishings, provides a variety of tools for learning, facilitates individual learning, and contains design features that are interesting and novel.[11] Also included in the physical environment are ambient features such as color, noise, lighting, temperature, and odor. These ambient features of an environment tend to influence mood, emotions, behavior, and learning capabilities.[12]

Modes of Learning

The primary purpose of a learning environment is to support the acquisition of new cognitive skills through three modes: visual, auditory, and kinetic.

- **Visual learners** process information from what they see and think in terms of pictures.
- **Auditory learners** process information from what they hear; they listen carefully and reason through discussion.
- **Kinesthetic learners** process information by experiencing, doing, and touching. They are more inclined to try things out and manipulate them.

To learn more about personal space zones and their dependence on culture, gender, and age, see Chapter 4.

Most people learn employing all three modes to a certain degree; however, each individual has a preferred mode that they use more than the other two. Approximately 35 percent of the population learns visually, 25 percent learns auditorily, and the remaining 40 percent learns kinesthetically.[13] By understanding how people learn, designers can customize environments to optimize the particular learning process. Table 10.1 summarizes design strategies based on the modes of learning.

Physical Environment for Learning

Some of the issues that affect the physical environment and therefore learning include crowding, density, and personal space. Included in the school environment are ambient conditions, which are the nonvisual qualities of an environment that determine people's moods and memories.[15] These qualities include color, noise, lighting, and temperature; color and noise, in particular, have distinctive influences on individuals. Crowding and density are closely related and often occur together: High density typically promotes feelings of crowding, and feelings of crowding are usually, but not always, related to high density.

Crowding, Density, and Personal Space

Perhaps the most notable effects of crowding are aggressive behaviors, lower task performances, poor memory, and feelings of anxiousness.[16] However, during times of competition, which could include the classroom environment, feelings of crowding lead to social and psychological withdrawal.[17] Both crowding and density will have a direct impact on students emotionally and behaviorally.[18] Students who feel crowded will be less likely to develop relationships and may not perform as well in school.[19]

Personal space zones are highly individual because they stretch and shrink depending on many factors, including culture, gender, and age. Most people will react when personal space is violated.[20] Research suggests that children's personal space requirements increase as they get older and until they reach puberty; females tend to use smaller personal space zones when they relate to familiar individuals, and males tend to be more sensitive and reactive to invasions of their personal space.[21]

Structure of the Learning Environment

The learning environment's physical structure includes the arrangement of space and furniture as well as the materials used in it and is vital to its effectiveness (i.e., the amount of learning that takes place).[22] The learning environment's struc-

Table 10.1 Design Strategies Based on Mode of Learning[14]

MODE OF LEARNING	METHOD OF INVOLVEMENT	IMPLICATION FOR DESIGN
Reading and hearing words	Auditory receiving	Ensure noise control and proper classroom acoustics.
Looking at pictures or watching a demonstration, movie, or exhibit	Visual receiving	Provide multimedia, posters, paintings, and drawings of significance and visual penetration.
Participation in a discussion	Kinesthetic receiving	Use semicircular seating arrangements and include features that facilitate small group discussions.
Simulating the real thing	Kinesthetic receiving	Provide laboratory space.

ture includes the size, shape, and scale of the actual classroom. In most circumstances a larger, more spacious classroom is more flexible and accommodates more uses than smaller classrooms. However, smaller classrooms allow for more class participation and group discussion. Research shows that rectangular-shaped rooms afford more interactive visibility, L-shaped rooms or those that have alcoves accommodate the various privacy needs of individual learners, and rooms that have movable wall partitions enable teachers to reconfigure rooms into many different shapes.[23] When designing classrooms, designers must consider the course that will be taught in the room. Likewise, designers should consider the room's size and location as well as the presence and location of windows, furniture, and storage elements.

The size of a classroom can have a direct relationship to density levels and students feeling crowded. Unfortunately, many classrooms that were already too small are becoming denser with the consolidation of schools and increased enrollment.[24] Higher densities in classrooms result in limited spatial arrangements, more aggressive behavior, and greater demands for resources.[25]

Another issue affecting the physical environment of classrooms is ergonomics, particularly as it relates to the types of seating available to students. The poor ergonomic design of the chairs, coupled with the length of time students are expected to remain seated, can lead to lower back pain, which has become a major health concern in industrialized nations.[26] Musculoskeletal fatigue and pain can cause students to focus more on easing their discomfort than on the subjects they are learning because the human brain is configured to satisfy physiological needs before cognitive needs. Because of the limited amount of studies, little is currently known about the use of ergonomically designed furniture in schools.

Lighting

Lightning is an important consideration within the educational environment.[27] Because children spend a significant portion of their days inside school buildings, it is important to expose them to high-quality, full-spectrum lighting as a means of enhancing their general well-being[28] and to counter symptoms related to light deprivation (e.g., fatigue,

irritability, and general malaise). Researchers report increases in student attendance, academic achievement, and physical and cognitive growth and development in schools that use full-spectrum lighting and ultraviolet enhancements.[29,30] Full-spectrum lighting is also associated with a decrease in the incidences of hyperactivity.[31]

The quality and quantity of lighting directly impacts a student's performance. An early study of fifth- and sixth-grade students showed that test scores were higher for students who were taught their subjects in well-lit classrooms.[32] Likewise, students demonstrated better concentration levels in rooms with better quality and greater quantity of lighting.[33]

DESIGN APPLICATION. The human need and desire for natural sunlight and for views to adjacent spaces (for orientation) requires a balance of natural and artificial sources of illumination.[34] The illumination provided by sunlight varies with the season, time of day, weather, and glazing of windows; therefore, designers must consider measures to control its entry into classrooms. Such measures may include the use of window tinting, retractable awnings, and adjustable blinds. Even so, teachers can obviously control artificial light sources better than sunlight, but they must avoid glare that bounces off reflective surfaces (e.g., marker boards or computer monitors) caused by the imbalance of light sources. The reflectivity of surface finishes, arrangement and location of light sources, and their methods for diffusion within the classroom all influence the comfort of students and teachers.[35]

Color

The use of color within schools and other learning environments has been shown to influence students' attitudes, behaviors, and learning comprehension by affecting their attention spans and the teachers' perceptions of time.[36] Likewise, the use of color in schools significantly affects students' perceptions of the environment. It can transform a dull and drab environment into one that is pleasing, exciting, and stimulating, which has been implicated in the reduction of absenteeism and promotion of greater school affiliation.[37] A bright room with light colors is preferred over a room with dark colors.[38]

Both physiological and emotional reactions have been linked to room color, including respiratory rate and blood pressure,[39] as well as the release of hormones within the brain and hypothalamus,[40] which in turn affect mood, mental clarity, and energy levels. The transmission of light energy to the brain also affects the functioning of the cerebral cortex (where thought occurs) and the central nervous system (responsible for muscle control, eyesight, breathing, and memory).[41] While the use of warm colors in classroom environments appears to stimulate the optic nerve (and when combined with bright lighting, people have increases in blood pressure, heart and respiratory rates, muscle tension, and brain activity[42]), the reverse physiological response is noted with the use of cool colors and dim lighting.[43,44] Interestingly, white and off-white decrease human efficiency by an average of 25 percent.[45]

Studies indicate that one-fourth of the population views or perceives color differently from the majority.[46] This finding has important implications for designers: people's perceptions and reactions to color are linked to cultural style but have historic and symbolic references as well.[47]

DESIGN APPLICATION. Based on their own research, Frank Mahnke and Rudolf Mahnke offer the following guidelines for how to integrate color into learning environments:

- **Preschool and primary school: Warm, bright color scheme**
- **Secondary school: Cool colors**
- **Hallways: Diverse color range**
- **Libraries: Pale or light green[48]**

Further to these guidelines, designers should use mild colors for the walls and floors to minimize glare and brightness and use contrast between workstations and the overall environment to create appropriate focal points. Bright and light colors tend to advance, and dim or dark colors tend to recede.[49] In classrooms designed for young children, consider using stronger colors with warm tones. Other environments in a school include gymnasiums, auditoriums, and lunchrooms; designers should use warmer colors with lighter tones for each of these environments. Hallways, doors, and stairwells should be painted in a variety of color to enhance stimulation while students pass through.[50]

Acoustics and Noise

Noise is an environmental variable that can cause a variety of detrimental effects. The effects of noise in learning environments are controversial. Some researchers believe that noise causes distraction and interferes with learning, while others insist that becoming distracted can be traced to gender, age, and academic ability.[51] The effects of noise in educational settings can range from impairment of psychomotor performance,[52] language acquisition and understanding,[53] and reading skills[54,55] to a greater likelihood of having elevated blood pressure.[56] Researchers seem to agree, however, that learning is compromised when students can't hear clearly.[57]

The three most common sources of classroom noise are reverberation, internal noise, and external noise. Reverberation (also termed *acoustical liveliness*) occurs when sound waves rebound from hard flat surfaces. Imagine throwing a tennis ball; it will bounce off a wall but not off a pillow. Hard surfaces reflect sound, and soft surfaces absorb or diffuse it. Reverberation reduces audial (i.e., hearing) perception because it creates extra noise, which students must filter out. In tennis, players devote all their energy to the ball in play, but if additional balls keep coming at them eventually there will be too many bouncing around for players to be able to focus on just one of them (Figure 10.1). Reverberation is a product of room configuration (parallel walls), surface finishes (hard or soft), material density (solid or hollow), and air tightness (sound transfer)[58] and can be either enhanced or reduced by changes to room size, internal surface dimensions (walls, ceilings, floors, and windows), and surface materials (chairs, desks, flooring, wall coverings, and ceiling treatments).

External noise typically derives from machines: cars, trucks, trains, airplanes, lawn mowers, and so on. School and child-care facilities must be constructed with these concerns in mind, and should not be placed near areas of heavy transportation (e.g., along flight paths, railways, or highways) and industry. Sound-dampening zones built into walls and ceilings, double- and triple-paned windows, and tall greenery can all help to reduce, but will

For more on how people's perceptions of color are related to cultural style, see Chapter 5.

See Chapter 6 for more on noise as a risk factor for physical illnesses related to stress and hearing loss.

Figure 10.1: Sound works very much like the depiction in this illustration. If there were one tennis ball, the man would probably be able to move out of the way. However, as the number of tennis balls increases, his ability to concentrate decreases until he finally reaches his saturation point and simply recoils and tries to protect himself. Similarly we can concentrate or screen out a limited number of sounds. Each of us has our own limit as to how many and what kinds of sounds we can successfully screen out. For children with limited screening abilities, excessive and varying sounds can cause frustration and even lead to behaviors of learned helplessness.

Figure 10.2: There are many ways to soundproof a facility. The trees planted around the base of the office building shown in this picture help shield noise from nearby traffic.

not eliminate, external noise (Figure 10.2). Thick walls and those with sound insulation prevent exterior noise transfer only if there is no air gap (ie, walls that reach to only the bottoms of suspended ceilings are ineffective).[59] Community measures can be taken to reduce noise deriving from air and road traffic. Setting buildings back from streets will help reduce roadway noise; mandating appropriate airport flight paths can reduce the negative effects of air traffic; and placing schools far from public and private rail lines, manufacturing plants, and warehouses will reduce these external noise sources. Additionally, groundskeeper activities (e.g., lawn mowing and tree trimming) can be done when school is not in session.

Internal noise is harder to mitigate because much of it derives from human actions. Sources of classroom noise include dozens of voices; the movement of chairs and desks on hard floors as students fidget in their seats; the tapping of pens or pencils against desks; and mechanical devices such

as computers, printers, copiers, cell phones and pagers, older lighting fixtures, and heaters or air conditioners.

DESIGN APPLICATION. One of the best methods to reduce noise is to use sound-absorbent cladding on a low ceiling. Other measures include window treatments in lecture rooms (which may not be safe in science labs), pads applied to the feet of chairs and tables, and rubber strips affixed to desks (thicker rubber absorbs sound better). Rooms where group activities are more prevalent than lecturing should absorb more sound.[60] Where necessary, designers should encourage the use of low-frequency sound to mask conversations or exterior noise. Flooring should be of soft material (e.g., cork, linoleum, or carpeting) to minimize noise caused by foot traffic, dropped objects, and the movement of chairs and tables; at the very least, designers can incorporate carpet strips into their design schemes (Figure 10.3).

Figure 10.3: In this classroom, the flooring is composed of cork to reduce excessive noise caused by everyday foot traffic; the tables have thin rubber laminate on their surfaces to limit noise from tapping pencils or dropped items; the pressed-fiber bulletin boards on the wall help to absorb ambient noises; the mesh screen on the windows can be pulled down to minimize noise without completely obstructing the natural views; and the ceiling is composed of sound-absorbent cladding.

Carpet on floors and acoustical ceilings can also cut down on reverberation. Hard walls (e.g., glass) or marker boards should be positioned opposite to open storage areas of differing heights and depths. Angling walls at least 5 degrees out from their original parallel plane can also reduce reverberation.[61]

Temperature, Humidity, and Ventilation

The results of several studies show that temperature fluctuations within classrooms affect teachers more so than students and that students generally like the temperature slightly cooler (5 to 10 degrees) than do teachers.[62] Early studies of classroom temperature found that when learning environments included air-conditioning, the incidences of classroom annoyances were reduced,[63] and attitudes, performance, and student behavior improved.[64] One study found that at temperatures higher or lower than 72 degrees Fahrenheit, students showed decreases in memory, suggesting that the optimum temperature for learning is 72 degrees.[65]

The ability to maintain ideal classroom environments has been shown to affect the mental efficiency of students, especially in situations that require quick recognition and response. When temperatures exceed 80 degrees, there is a significant decrease in students' work efficiency and productivity levels.[66] Likewise, human beings work most efficiently at psychomotor tasks when the environment is at a comfortable temperature,[67] and The New York State Commission on Ventilation found that temperatures higher than 75 degrees produced harmful effects such as increased respiration, decreased amount of physical work, and conditions conducive to the spread of disease.[68] Designers must consider and allow for the regulation and maintenance of temperature because of its role as a contributor to the ambient environment in classroom settings.

One of the predominating issues with temperature is the lack of adequate ventilation; poor ventilation interferes with the body's ability to dissipate heat. Temperature, humidity, and ventilation depend on a number of factors, including the configuration and materials in a building, amount of glazing on windows, size and volume of the space, number of occupants, and their current state of activity, as well as the heating and cooling systems.[69] To ensure the comfort of occupants, flexibility in manipulating this system is extremely important, and designers should consider including independent controls for each space that are simple to operate.[70]

Day-Care Centers and Preschools

Children spend most of their time at home, in school, or in day-care centers.[71] Although one parent used to remain at home to provide child care, by 1998, 59 percent of mothers with children younger than three years, and 60 percent of mothers with children ages one to five went back to work.[72] Current estimates suggest that 48 percent of children ages five years or younger whose mothers are employed outside the home receive care in either a family-based or center setting.[73] Day-care and preschool settings can be found in homes, workplaces, campuses, and community parks and recreation centers, such as YMCAs, JCCs, and 4-H Clubs, throughout the United States. Settings vary significantly according to financial resources, as do size and social density. Inadequate public resources for day-care centers and schools result in increasingly crowded classrooms,[74] especially in communities where parents cannot afford private care.

Toddlers' behaviors and emotional well-being are influenced by their social and physical environments. Their interaction with peers in day-care centers helps them develop their sociocognitive skills, but when such interaction is too demanding, it becomes stressful.[75] Crowding in these settings can have many negative implications for children's emotional, psychological, and cognitive development,[76] which can manifest as increased aggression, lower task performance, poor memory, anxious feelings, physiological responses related to high blood pressure, and nervous habits (such as nail biting, hair pulling, skin picking, and other symptoms of stress). If left unattended, such habits can lead to obsessive-compulsive disorders that last into adulthood and possibly for a person's entire life.

The combination of crowded day-care and residential settings has been shown to increase a child's propensity for behavior problems.[77] A well-designed day-care setting is divided according to homogenous age groups and has at least 5 square meters, or 16.4 feet, of play space (not total floor space) per child.[78] Facilities that operate at these density levels have fewer incidences of negative behaviors resulting from crowding and stress. Lower social density levels in day-care and school settings may provide the additional benefit of easing the effects of crowding at home,[79] since the detrimental effects of crowding do carry over from one environment to the other.

Day-care and preschool settings should contain safe, small spaces in which children can seclude themselves. Such intimate environments are valued by children because they fulfill needs for both privacy and exploration.[80] Several studies have shown that children's psychological development can be affected by how much control they have over their environments. Children take the initiative, explore their surroundings, and engage in more social interaction when they feel they have control. Portable private spaces within open-plan settings enable children to *self-regulate* their privacy needs, which gives them more control over their environments.

DESIGN APPLICATION. When designing daycare and preschool settings, spaces should not restrict a child's visual access to the caregiver.

Designers should use colors, textures, and lighting (*symbolic edges*) to delineate spaces, rather than solid barriers (*physical edges*). Symbolic edges allow young children to maintain eye contact with caregivers, which not only allows them to feel safe and more confident about trying new things but also encourages them to explore spaces and interact with their peers.[81]

Open play areas allow caregivers to maintain supervision no matter how close or far they are from the children.[82] However, open spaces are not conducive to educational activities related to counting or reading; therefore, designers should incorporate a variety of smaller spaces within open environments.[83] These smaller spaces do not require fixed walls; for example, children can be quite content in a table tent. Spaces can also be separated visually by lowered or differentiated ceiling heights and contrasting wall colors and textures. These methods help to facilitate cooperative behavior in children; however, using of both wall and ceiling strategies within a single space may be overwhelming to children and thus defeat a designer's purpose.[84] If designers implement both strategies, reducing the contrast will help to avoid sensory overload; varying paint, fabric, or netting on walls and ceilings are three methods of differentiating spaces.[85] For example, in a space with varied ceiling heights and designs, the wall décor could include large fishing nets, tapestries, or posters with low color contrast.

Primary and Secondary Schools

Of all the educational settings, the primary school classroom requires the greatest diversity in terms of its physical environment. Most are set up with the traditional row of desks facing the front of the room; some have open settings with movable partitions for separating spaces and smaller class groups; and some are soft classrooms complete with carpeting, incandescent lighting, sofas and tables (instead of desks), and potted plants. Soft classrooms have also been effective in postsecondary educational settings and in smaller courses that involve discussion and philosophical reasoning. Primary schools should be designed to enhance gross motor skills, with facilities for grades five and higher that promote concentration as well as tactile learning.

During most of the early 20th century, school

buildings were designed to admit as much fresh air and direct sunlight as possible.[86] Both the design and teaching styles of the period derived from educational reforms that took place in Germany during the Weimar Republic; however, much of the original intent and breadth has been lost over time.[87] Following these reforms, school buildings were limited to one or two stories to improve air circulation and increase natural light and therefore promote health.[88] Unfortunately, by the 1970s many of these reform principles had been rejected. Windowless classrooms became popular when windows came to be perceived as sources of distraction and excess heat.[89] This, in conjunction with larger facilities, especially in secondary schools, all but eradicated the benefits of natural lighting and fresh air circulation within classroom settings.

Teachers experience more visual and kinetic distractions in large rooms with high ceilings, most likely because there is simply more space to supervise and the larger space inhibits focused attention. Paradoxically, students tend to experience more kinetic distractions but fewer visual distractions in rooms with lower ceilings, presumably a result of focusing attention on one person at the front of the room. Overall classroom satisfaction is associated positively with greater space, ceiling height, and more square footage per person.

Research spanning nearly one century shows that schools should provide sufficient access to green spaces, fresh air, and natural light and that classrooms should minimize noise, provide optimum levels of stimulation for learning, and contain attention-restoration attributes. Learning for children is often thought of in terms of cognitive learning, but developing gross motor skills is also a means of learning, which can be promoted through well-designed playgrounds as well as a diverse physical education program.

Classrooms should be designed for specific uses (e.g., science laboratories) and equipped with furnishings and other components that promote and facilitate those uses.[90] The increasing use of technology in classrooms has far outpaced the design of workstations and building featuress (i.e., chairs that aren't adjustable and inadequate desks for laptops to rest upon) that cause distractions and discomfort—both of which are detrimental to learning.[91] Deficiencies in the physical

See Chapter 8 for more on the developmental considerations and design strategies involving playgrounds and school yards.

environment can have a negative effect on students' task orientations, class cohesiveness, and feelings of support autonomy.

Classroom environment, including seating, is an issue of comfort, safety, and learning.[92] Yet furnishings are an important aspect of design that is often overlooked. Research indicates that types of classroom furnishings relate to the children's health, behavior, and education.[93] One fifth-grade soft classroom teacher stated, "These students have some soft-cushioned furniture to provide a comfortable place for them to do their work. At their age, their growth and development does not allow for them to sit on hard furniture all day."[94] Researchers support this concept that young people who sit for long periods of time accumulate stress to their back muscles, ligaments, and discs and that the incidence of back pain correlates to increased sitting time.[95] Again, students who move around in their seats attempting to find comfort are not paying attention to schoolwork because their physiological needs supersede their cognition demands (Figure 10.4).

DESIGN APPLICATION. When designing a school, one of the greatest challenges is to maximize space without creating long hallways. The overall design should not only eliminate long hallways but also maximize views while clustering similar classes. If the climate allows, consider connecting separate buildings via covered walkways. This would direct students to walk along pathways through mini-gardens, which are believed to promote learning.[96] In harsher climates, glass-covered pathways still would allow students to enjoy unencumbered views of the natural world. Regardless of climate, where wall space allows, incorporate double-paned windows to allow natural light into the facility, and consider using reflective exterior window tinting to prevent students on the inside from being distracted by those outside.

A ceiling that slopes gradually so that it is higher in the front of the room and lower in the rear will not only reduce the teacher's visual distraction but also increase the students' perceptions of the space in front of the room and decrease their feelings of crowding. Designers should use soft flooring material such as linoleum or carpeting to minimize noise. Potted plants at the fronts and rears of classrooms can serve as vital attention-restoration features for the instructor and the students, respectively.

Furnishings should support students comfortably in their two main seated positions: leaning forward to write, read, or draw and leaning back to listen or watch.[97] School furniture should allow for natural body positions (e.g., trunk and thighs at 120-degree angles);[98] a seat that tilts forward will help alleviate strain on the spine by increasing the trunk-thigh angle.[99] Furnishings should be moveable and scaled for students of different ages and needs.[100] Chair seat height should not exceed a student's popliteal height, which is measured from the back of the knee to the floor.[101] When integrating seating at the front and back of lecture halls and other locations for students who use wheelchairs, ensure that the seating surface is flat and out of the traffic path.[102] One research team eschews standard rows of desks facing the teacher, recommending instead nontraditional seating patterns such as horseshoe or circular arrangements to increase student interest, participation, and performance.[103]

Horseshoe or circular seating arrangements provide many benefits, including increased student visibility, attentiveness, and participation rates. Take a look at the floor plan shown in Figure 10.5 so you can see that such room configurations afford much lower desk-to-floor-space ratios; more desks and chairs can be placed in a room by using traditional row layouts.

Figure 10.4 (top): Soft furnishings are used in the science class for primary school children pictured here to provide comfort and organize the children in a way that promotes and facilitates discussion.

Figure 10.5 (bottom): This classroom floor plan tries to utilize space in the most ideal way.

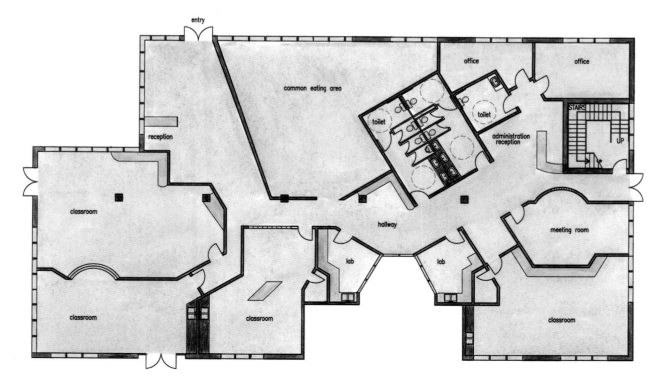

Figure 10.6: Students' athletic and academic achievements are displayed in this school hallway as a means to honor them.

Encouraging students to develop ownership, territoriality, and school pride can help prevent negative behaviors such as bullying, which is a significant problem in most schools (Box 10.1). Incorporating the students and their works into the school's décor increases a student's sense of ownership.[104] Permanent displays of students' artwork or large photos of theatrical, musical, and athletic performances should be part of the wall décor. The school's hallway should showcase significant student accomplishments (Figure 10.6). Placing small concrete slabs bearing students' names and accomplishments in walkways that lead to the main entrance (resembling the Hollywood Walk of Fame) shows the school's pride in its students and encourages students to develop a sense of ownership in the learning process and the development of their learning environment.[105]

Box 10.1 Bullying in Schools

Bullying can be any type of recurring abusive behavior, from verbal indirect bullying (spreading rumors) to physical direct abuse, such as assault or sexual harassment.[106] Physical bullying is most common among boys; girls are most prone to verbal taunts, segregation, and rumor-spreading, which may be reported less frequently.[107] According to the U.S. Department of Justice and the Department of Education, while the incidence of school violence has reportedly decreased, cases of bullying and weapons charges have increased.[108] It is estimated that between 15 and 30 percent of students in the United States are involved in bullying, either as the aggressor, the victim, or both.[109]

Causes of Bullying

There are many hypotheses as to why bullying occurs, but the predominant instigators appear to fall into one of three categories: familial factors, school factors, and peer pressure.[110] Children who engage in bullying often experience violence in the home, lack of adult supervision, lack of discipline with specific and consistent consequences, and bullying from older siblings or other family members; therefore, these children have inadequate social skills. Children who are victimized tend to have overprotective parents or teachers, which inhibits their abilities to cope with bullying.[111] Causes of bullying associated with problems at school can include lack of supervision, feeling that no one will intervene,[112] believing that teacher intervention will be ineffective, facilities that are poorly designed, and poor social environments.

Long-Term Effects of Bullying

Children who are victims of bullying show long-term effects such as lower self-esteem and greater incidences of depression, loneliness, feelings of isolation, anxiety, and frequent thoughts about suicide.[113] Adults who experienced bullying as children tend to be more susceptible to severe depression, poor interpersonal relationships, misplaced aggressions, academic underachievement, and higher predisposition toward suicide.[114, 115] Victims are also more likely to report headaches, sleeplessness, nightmares, and upset stomach, which can result in poor school attendance and lower grades.[116] Many of the perpetrators of the school shootings that have occurred since 1974 in the United States were reportedly victims of bullying who struck out violently and vengefully against their peers.[117–119]

Children who are bullies also experience numerous negative side effects. They often exhibit low self-esteem, which they remedy by taunting smaller, weaker children or children they deem to be different. Often the bullying occurs in groups, which enables bullies to feel powerful and important. In some cases, children participate in bullying to fit in. Statistics show that one quarter of the children who bully others will be convicted of a crime by the time they are 30 years old.[120, 121] Children who bully others on a routine basis engage in other destructive activities, such as drug use, alcoholism, smoking, vandalism, theft, and other violent acts. Truancy, low achievement in school, and dropping out of school are also common.[122–124]

Design Strategies to Prevent Bullying

Most schools in the United States are at least 40 years old and therefore have severely antiquated designs that are no longer appropriate for today's society or technological requirements. Schools that are able to upgrade their designs should strongly consider using CPTED (crime prevention through environmental design) guidelines to assist in raising positive feelings in schools, which can increase students' senses of place attachment, territoriality, and safety.[125] Studies have shown that police presence, metal detectors, and Zero Tolerance policies don't reduce bullying effectively because they increase negative feelings in schools.[126] Although these measures may make facility users feel more secure, they do not address deeper social issues because they tend to reinforce fear and restriction.[127] Research has shown that encouraging positive interaction in schools has a more long-lasting effect on general morale improvement.[128] Therefore, CPTED is most effective because it focuses on positive and desirable behaviors.[129]

Reducing visual boundaries by using more windows effectively prevents behavioral problems in schools. Open spaces and a greater number of windows allow "passive surveillance" (teachers can supervise their students in a less intrusive or overt manner), which increases the sense of community and reduces the number of secluded places where negative behaviors can occur. Keeping vegetation trimmed also increases opportunities for "natural surveillance," as does moving the instructors' lunch areas closer to the students' cafeterias.[130] Experts recommend that round tables be used in lunchrooms instead of the standard long rectangular tables. Sitting at round tables promotes group interaction and reduces the need for students to yell to one another across large distances.

An experimental program in England has been under way for several years in which schools are being renovated to stimulate learning while giving students, teachers, and the community as a whole a greater sense of ownership of the facilities. This sense of ownership has been shown to reduce incidences of violence, theft, and vandalism and has in-

creased school attendance. Some of the steps taken to improve the schools include widening the hallways and removing old lockers, which are replaced with newly designed lockers or walk-in closets assigned to small groups of students. Closed-circuit television has also been installed for greater security, and restroom facilities have been upgraded to ensure cleanliness and safety.[131]

Colleges and Universities

The predominant physical difference between primary and secondary schools and postsecondary schools (colleges and universities) is that the latter usually have large campuses with multiple buildings and provide student residential housing. Because most of the same classroom design principles apply, this section focuses on the design of libraries, residential dormitories, and the campuses themselves.

Libraries

Because most students work alone in libraries, designers must consider many personality variables when developing library designs, including differences between individuals who are *screeners* and those who are *nonscreeners*. Screeners (people who can screen or block out distractions) are able to concentrate while people are moving or talking around them; therefore, an open library plan neither enhances nor impedes their learning. For nonscreeners and visually impaired students, however, such stimulation is distracting. For these individuals, small private rooms with reflective film on the interior glass would minimize both visual and audial distractions for nonscreeners while still allowing the library staff to supervise them (Figure 10.7). Like the workplace environment, open-plan libraries better accommodate individuals who are not performing challenging tasks, and private environments better accommodate individuals who are performing more complex tasks.[132] Because nonscreeners tend to be more introverted, they will benefit more from green spaces as a means of attention restoration; therefore, private rooms should have windows that face green spaces and allow natural light to enter. Such rooms are ideal places for visually impaired students to listen to recorded textbooks and lectures. Research suggests that reading conducted in blue or pale green

See Chapter 6 for further discussion on CPTED.

See Chapter 2 for more information about screeners and nonscreeners.

Figure 10.7 (right): Library spaces should contain private rooms where visually impaired individuals can listen to recorded lectures or books and where study groups can meet and discuss projects freely. As illustrated here, one wall should be glass so that outsiders know when the room is occupied and librarians can supervise people in the rooms as well as the main parts of the library.

Figure 10.8a and b (below): Ideally, libraries should include private, semiprivate, and public spaces as well as natural scenes. (a) These various seating arrangements provide semiprivate spaces, and the expansive space affords opportunities for *attention restoration*. (b) Varying the desk configuration in a library's computer center not only ensures students greater personal space but also offers them a degree of privacy.

a

b

environments will yield greater comprehension and retention than in red environments.[133, 134]

DESIGN APPLICATION. A well-designed library should have a large open space in the center, and large potted plants dispersed throughout. Sound-dampening ceiling and window treatments will minimize noise, and retractable skylights will allow natural light and air into the space. All west-facing windows should be tinted to reduce direct sunlight, glare, and associated heat. Rooms of various sizes should accommodate both individual and group study (Figure 10.8a and b). The floor should be carpeted, and the color schemes should be made up of different shades of blues or pale greens. The central open space should include both individual desks with privacy barriers and large tables for pairs and groups. Each of these study areas should include a study lamp as well as the option for dim ambient lighting that will allow students with specific disabilities to maximize their visual attention to materials.[135] Knee space under tables and desks should be increased from the standard 27 inches to 29 or 30 inches deep to accommodate wheelchair users.[136] Figure 10.9 shows a floor plan for an ideal library setting.

Residential Dormitories

Although not all college students live in residential dormitories and some primary and secondary students do, many of the same principles apply to dor-

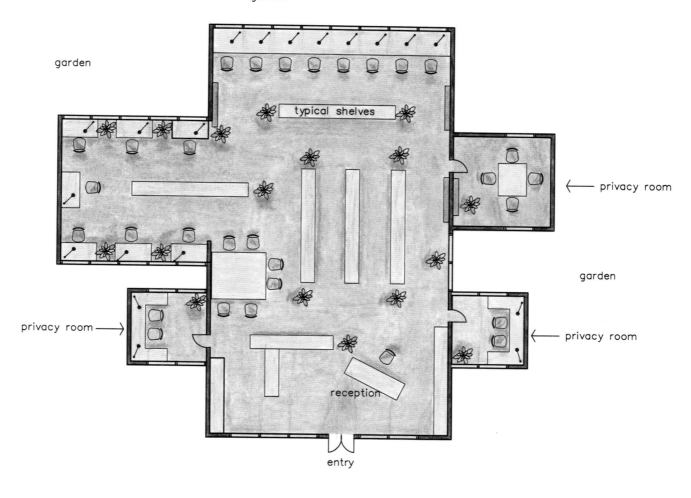

garden

garden

typical shelves

← privacy room

garden

privacy room →

← privacy room

reception

entry

Figure 10.9 (top): In this library plan, different configurations accommodate the various working styles of library users: two small private rooms, one large private room, open area seating, small cubicle seating, and independent tables. Note that each seating area has its own lamp for illumination control.

Figure 10.10 (left): In a well-designed dorm room, spatial delineation divides the room so that roommates each have their own territory complete with a bed, desk, storage space, and soft seating. The dorm room configuration pictured here holds the real possibility of roommate territorial invasion. Spatial delineation is not as clear, although each occupant has a study area and bed. It is important to note that rooms on higher floors with open views decrease perceptions of crowding.

mitory settings at all three levels. Occupants' perceptions of room size and their feelings of crowdedness can affect their senses of privacy and satisfaction as well as the quality of their social interactions.[137] Residential crowding significantly and negatively affects psychological well-being by causing residents to withdraw socially from their supportive relationships with other residents.[138] Although gender (and race) does not influence the relationship between crowding and psychological well-being, young and adult men seem to be more affected by perceptions of crowding than boys, who do not seem as bothered.[139] Dormitory residents desire time to be alone and time when they can control personal interactions with others[140] (Figure 10.10).

Dormitory residents who occupy higher floors seem to be more satisfied with their individual rooms, perceive the dormitories as less crowded, and believe they have more privacy and better views than residents of lower floors.[141] This may be due to the absence of the built environment directly outside their windows and the reduced flow of people by their spaces.

DESIGN APPLICATION. Designers can take active measures to reproduce these ideal effects that residents of higher floors report having for residents of lower floors. Tall greenery between structures will limit views from adjacent buildings, and cascading planters and automatic water systems can be incorporated into the architectural design of high-rises. Elevators and stairs placed at entry and exit points will minimize pedestrian traffic. Consider providing a common area between the main corridor and the entry point into the dorm rooms, rather than just a corridor that leads directly into the dorm rooms.[142]

Campus Wayfinding

Wayfinding difficulties typically arise when maneuvering through large buildings or grounds.[143] Large, well-designed facilities and complexes accommodate the various ways in which humans cognitively interpret an environment. Whether a campus is made up of several buildings or a single large structure, designers should proactively implement optimum wayfinding strategies. The ability to navigate through campus depends in part on a

See Chapter 6 for more on how design can minimize opportunities for criminality and increase perceptions of safety.

person's experience with the environment; new students will naturally experience greater feelings of confusion and vulnerability. However, all students can have problems with reaching various destinations quickly and efficiently unless good wayfinding measures are built into the design.[144] Wayfinding increases in importance as campuses increase in size and student population. Minimizing spatial complexity and varying the size, form, color, or architectural style of buildings enhance wayfinding.[145] In a row of buildings, each could either be painted a different color overall or simply have a different accent stripe. Key areas in complexes and buildings on large campuses should be named, and the signage for each unit or group should be painted a different color.

Wayfinding maps that combine pictorial representations of architecturally diverse buildings with diagrams, name lists, and color keys will accommodate people who rely on either *scenographic* or *abstract representations*. People who prefer pictures will quickly discern visual differences in architectural style, and people who prefer maps will be able to pinpoint named areas or structures easily. Color coding supports wayfinding for both types of people but is often useless for the 10 percent of the male population who is colorblind.

Campus Crime

The rising incidence of violent crime on college campuses is increasing fear of crime, especially among female students. Campus activities occur around the clock, and designers must give special consideration to how spaces will be perceived and used during the day and night and to the connections among those spaces. For example, the uniform illumination of potential nighttime hiding places (e.g., trees, shrubbery, parked cars, and low walls) allows greater user supervision and discourages potential criminals. In spaces with many pathways, consider lighting along select paths at night so as to concentrate pedestrian traffic[146] and increase activity and overall safety.

Summary Review

Nearly a century's worth of research shows that the learning process is enhanced by abundant natural elements (fresh air, sunlight, green spaces, and natural views), adequate personal space, and minimal noise levels. Modern designers have the opportunity to enhance each of these components and improve the quality of education for children and adults. Over the years, schools evolved from buildings that captured natural light and facilitated natural ventilation to buildings with few windows and minimal climate control systems. School designs are at long last reverting to buildings that incorporate many windows to allow in natural light and have appropriate ventilation systems.

The learning environment supports the acquisition of new knowledge. Although most learners call on all of the learning modalities (visual, auditory, and kinetic), each individual favors one mode over the other two. By understanding the different learning modalities, designers can develop environments that foster the learning process.

Aggressive behaviors, lower task performances, poor memory, and feelings of anxiousness are all symptoms of crowding, which can lead to social and psychological withdrawal. When a person's personal space is routinely violated, perceptions of crowding are likely to follow. However, personal space is highly individual and depends on many factors, including culture, gender, and age. Current research on the personal space requirements of children show that personal space requirements increase with age until adolescence. Although females tend to prefer smaller personal space zones, males tend to be more reactive to invasions of their personal space.

The structure, arrangement, and materials used in the learning environment affect the level of learning. Designers must consider the size, shape, and scale of classrooms when designing them. Larger classrooms allow for greater flexibility of use, and smaller classrooms allow for more interaction. The shape of the classroom also accommodates a variety of learning activities. Rectangularly shaped rooms allow for more interactive visibility, while rooms with movable wall partitions allow for various configurations. The manner in which a classroom is designed should be determined by the course being taught along with the room's architectural features such as windows, furniture, and storage elements.

The interiors of school buildings are often de-

void of significant sources of natural light. Therefore, it is important to include high-quality, full-spectrum lighting as a means of mitigating symptoms related to light deprivation (e.g., fatigue, irritability, and general malaise). Research has shown improved attendance, academic achievement, and physical and cognitive growth along with a decrease in hyperactivity in students who are exposed to full-spectrum lighting with ultraviolet enhancements. Better quality and quantity of lighting in classrooms also allow students to concentrate more.

Color is a key element in educational settings for both students and instructors. Bright colors tend to induce hyperstimulation (i.e., increase arousal), which can lead to more fidgeting and less concentration. Conversely, dark and drab colors induce hypostimulation, which may decrease the efficiency of comprehension and retention processes. Many studies indicate that color also affects mood and fatigue levels, which in turn affect stimulation levels.

Noise is an environmental variable with many different and detrimental effects related to physical illnesses, elevated levels of stress, decreased levels of perception and satisfaction, and impairment of psychomotor performance, language acquisition and understanding, and reading skills in general. Many young children are exposed to greater densities and noise levels from an early age in day-care centers and preschools. Therefore, these environments must be carefully considered so that they maximize child learning.

A stable climate control of 72 degrees Farenheit has been shown to reduce the incidences of classroom disturbances and improve student attitudes, performance, and behaviors. Classroom performance significantly decreases when temperatures exceed 80 degrees. Lack of adequate ventilation is one of the predominating issues with temperature because it interferes with the body's ability to dissipate heat. Designers can ensure the comfort of occupants by including easy-to-operate climate control systems for individual spaces.

More than half of all children ages five and younger whose mothers are employed outside the home attend either a family-based or center-based setting. Crowding in child-care settings can negatively affect a child's emotional, psychological, and cognitive development, which can manifest as a variety of behaviors that last into adulthood and possibly for a person's entire life. As such, day-care and preschool settings should provide for a multitude of safe, small spaces where children can fulfill needs for privacy and exploration and enjoy opportunities to assert control over their environments. Mastery and control over the environment often result in greater initiative, exploration, and the promotion of positive social engagement.

It is crucial that each school be designed to accommodate the developmental capabilities of its student populations. Schools must support not only cognitive learning but also the development of gross motor skills, which are especially important for children attending primary school. Students in grades five and higher should be provided with opportunities to develop concentration skills as well as mechanisms for tactile learning; this includes using furnishings and other components that are optimal for learning. One of the new phenomena facing the educational environment is the increased use of technology, which requires that classroom space and facility design be modified to include adequate power sources and appropriate desks to accommodate laptops and other electronic devices.

College and university campuses differ from most high school campuses not only in their libraries, but also in their abilities to offer residential housing. Libraries, in particular, require special attention from designers because of the need to accommodate many personality variables, learning styles, and possible user disabilities and because these facilities must provide an optimal environment for the storage of books, microfiche, and other printed items. Dormitories serve as the home away from home for many students while they attend college. Issues of spatial density, crowding, and privacy can support or detract from a student's ability to attain a degree of comfort within his or her environment. Therefore, designers of residential housing for college students must be aware of design features that reinforce and support comfort and privacy.

Another aspect that tends to differentiate a high school campus from a college or university campus is size. Because college and university campuses tend to be larger than high school campuses, designers of these environments must be conscious of wayfinding. Varying the size, form, color, or archi-

tectural style of various buildings can aid wayfinding, enabling students to easily distinguish one building from another while navigating the campus. With the size of many college and university campuses also comes an increase in campus crime. Designers must therefore give special consideration to the perception of danger during the day and night as well as within buildings and along walking paths that connect buildings.

As we progress in our education, we find ourselves calling more upon our cognitive capabilities and less upon our gross motor skills; our learning environments must provide for these changing needs. Designers can use exterior design, architectural layout, and interior décor not only to develop safe and pleasurable learning environments but also to enhance concentration, collaboration, and tactile learning abilities.

Discussion Questions

1. Based on your personal experience, discuss the effects of sitting in a work space or waiting room that is not designed for your body type. What reactions did you have, and how did this affect your attention level, productivity, or satisfaction?

2. What wayfinding techniques are used in your campus or educational environment?

3. Consider the colors used in different educational environments (e.g., classrooms, libraries, and dormitories). How is color used to enhance or alter moods?

4. Discuss ways to improve the acoustics of primary and secondary school classrooms. How might this differ from the ideal acoustics of a large university?

5. What new technologies can be incorporated into the design of schools to help control noise and reverberation?

6. Discuss the design of indoor play areas in elementary schools. Consider a location where poor weather conditions keep children indoors for much of the school year. How might that play area differ from one in Hawaii?

7. Discuss the need for privacy in preschool or day-care settings. What design ideas can help create educational and soothing private spaces for young children?

8. Discuss the concept of the soft classroom. Would you be able to focus better in that type of environment? Why or why not?

9. Discuss the pros and cons of classroom windows. Consider the style and placement of the windows. Are small, high windows as effective in increasing enjoyment and satisfaction in the room as large, eye-level windows?

10. What design concepts does your school library employ to enhance the space's functionality for all its users? How much control over study or research space does a user have? Does the library accommodate individuals with disabilities as well as different groups of people?

Learning Activities

1. Based on the information in the text, design a chair and desk that would be most effective for school-age children. List all design features and reference information that supports your design.

2. Draw a map of your campus and the surrounding area using the text's suggestions to help users differentiate areas and quickly locate both where they are and where they are going.

3. Design a study that you can perform to analyze the effect of color on a specific educational skill (e.g., reading comprehension, math computation, or spelling). Write an outline of the research techniques and your hypothesis, and gather supporting research and documentation.

4. Create a survey to help analyze your classmates' study preferences regarding noise and ambient sound. Consider using a medley of sounds and asking your classmates to rate the sounds as annoying or pleasing. Administer the survey to 20 people, present your results in graphic format, and show answer ranges for each question.

5. Draw a floor plan for an ideal preschool activity room, based on the text's criteria. Color the different areas and functions of the room and write a brief essay explaining how your design enhances the room's function.

6. Create a study to determine if fresh air and natural daylight enhance cognitive function-

ing. Gather supporting research to validate your hypothesis.

7. What systems are in place on your campus to prevent various types of crime? What methods does the administration use to keep students informed about their safety and the measures taken to protect them? Using information from the text, how might your campus improve security?

8. If you live in a dormitory, sketch your room, and create an overlay showing ways to modify the space and improve its efficiency. Visit a local dormitory if you don't live in one, and interview several residents to discern the pros and cons of their living situations.

Terminology

auditory learners People who process information by what they hear and reason through discussion

kinesthetic learners People who process information by experiencing, doing, and touching

visual learners People who process information by what they see and think in terms of pictures

References

1. Yamamoto, T., and Ishii, S. (1995). Developmental and environmental psychology: A microgenetic developmental approach to transition from a small elementary school to a big junior high school. *Environment and Behavior, 27-1,* 33–42.

2. Henderson, S.R. (1997). "New buildings create new people": The Pavillion schools of Weimar Frankfurt as a model of pedagogical reform. *Design Issues, 13-1,* 27–9.

3. Lindholm, G. (1995). Schoolyards: The significance of place properties to outdoor activities in schools. *Environment and Behavior, 27-3,* 259–293.

4. Gibson, J.J. (1996). *The ecological approach to visual perception.* Hillsdale, New Jersey: Lawrence Erlbaum Associates

5. Read, M.A., Sugawara, A.I., and Brandt, J.A. (1999). Impact of space and color in the physical environment on preschool children's co-

operative behavior. *Environment and Behavior, 31-3*, 413–428.

6. Legendre, A. (1999). Interindividual relationships in groups on young children and susceptibility to an environmental constraint. *Environment and Behavior, 31-4*, 463–496.

7. See note 5.

8. Martin, (1976) In Prohansky, H.M., Ittelson, W.H., and Rivlin, L.G. (Eds). *Environmental psychology: People and their physical settings*. New York: Holt, Rinehart & Winston.

9. Rivlin, Leanne G. and Rothenberg, M., (1976). *The use of space in open classrooms*. New York: Holt, Rinehart, Winston.

10. McAfee, J.K. (1987). Classroom density and the aggressive behavior of handicapped children. *Education and Treatment of Children, 10, (2)*.

11. Maxwell, L.E. (2003). Home and school density effects on elementary school children: The role of spatial density. *Environment and Behavior, 35(4)*: 566–578.

12. McAndrew, F.T., (1993). *Environmental psychology*. Pacific Grove, CA: Brooks/Cole Publishing Company.

13. Ngee Ann Polytechnic (2001). Sensory Learning Styles. Produced by Ngee Ann Polytechnic at http://tlcweb.np.edu.sg/esprit /tb-lc-eAudience-VAK-learning-styles.htm. Retrieved June 21, 2005.

14. Haroun, L., and Royce, S.R. (2004). *Teaching ideas and classroom activities for healthcare*. Delmar Publishing, Delmar, CA.

15. See note 12.

16. See note 12.

17. See note 12.

18. See note 12.

19. Cooper, J., Prescott, S., Cook, L., Smith, L., Mueck, R., Cuseo, J. (1984). Cooperative learning and college instruction: Effective use of student learning teams. California State University Foundation publication.

20. See note 12.

21. See note 12.

22. See note 12.

23. Lang, D. (1996). *Essential criteria for an ideal learning environment*. Seattle, WA: New Horizons for Learning. Available at: http://www .newhorizons.org.

24. See note 12.

25. See note 12.

26. Troussier, B., Tesniere, C., Fauconnier, J., Grison, J., Juvin, R., and Phelip, X. (1999). Comparative study of two different kinds of school furniture among children. *Ergonomics, 42-3*, 516–526.

27. Dunn, R. Krimsky, J.S., Murray, J.B., and Quinn, P.J. (1985). Light up their lives: A research on the effects of lighting on children's achievement and behavior. *The Reading Teacher, 38(19)*, 863-869.

28. Hathaway, W.E., and Fielder, D.R. (1986). A window on the future: A view of education and educational facilities. Columbus, Ohio: Paper presented at the meeting of the Council of Educational Facility Planners.

29. Hathaway, W.E. (1994). Non-visual effects of classroom lighting on children. *Educational Facility Planner, 32(3)*, 12-16.

30. Lexingtron, A. (1989). Healthy offices: Hard to define, but we need them. *The Office*, 73-75.

31. King, J., and Marans, R.W. (1979). The physical environment and the learning process. (Report No. 320-ST2). Ann Arbor: University of Michigan Architectural Research Laboratory.

32. Luckiesh, M., and Moss, F.K. (1940). Effects of classroom lighting upon the educational progress and visual welfare of school children. *Illuminating Engineering, 35*, 915-938.

33. Horton, C.D. (1972). Humanization of the learning environment. Arlington, VA. (ERIC Document Reproduction Service No. ED066929).

34. See note 23.

35. See note 23.

36. Sinofsky, E.R., and Knirck, F.G. (1981). Choose the right color for your learning style. *Instructional Innovator, 26(3)*, 17-19.

37. Papadotas, S.P. (1973). Color them motivated-color's psychological effects on students. *National Association of Secondary School Principals Bulletin, 57(370)*, 92-94.

38. See note 12.

39. See note 12.

40. Engelbrecht, K. (2003). *Impact of color on learning*. (W305). Chicago IL: NeoCon.

41. Birren, F. (1997). *The power of color*. Secaucus, NJ: Carol Publishing Group.

42. Wohlfarth, H. (1986). *Color and light effects on students achievement, behavior and physiology*. Edmonton, Alberta: Planning Services Branch, Alberta Education.

43. Failey, A., Bursor, D.E., and Musemeche, R.A. (1979). The impact of color and lighting in schools. *Council of Educational Facility Planners Journal*, 16-18.

44. Hathaway, W.E. (1988). Educational facilities: Neutral with respect to learning and human performance. *CEFPI Journal, 26(4)*, 8-12.

45. See note 41.

46. See note 23.

47. See note 23.

48. Mahnke, F.H. (1996). *Color, environment, and light in man-made environments*. New York, Van Nostrand Rheinhold.

49. See note 23.

50. Pile, J. (1997). *Color in interior design*. New York: McGraw Hill.

51. See note 12.

52. Hambrick-Dixon, P.J. (1986). Effects of experimentally imposed noise on task performance of black children attending day care centers near elevated subway trains. *Developmental Psychology, 22*, 259–264.

53. Maxwell, L.E., and Evans, G.W. (2000). The effects of noise on pre-school children's pre-reading skills. *Journal of Environmental Psychology, 20-1*, 91–97.

54. Bronzaft, A.L. (1981). The effect of noise abatement program on reading ability. *Journal of Environmental Psychology, XX-1*, 215–222.

55. See note 52.

56. Evans, G.W., and Lepore, S.J. (1993). Nonauditory effects of noise on children: A critical review. *Children's Environments, 10-1*, 31–51.

57. See note 23.

58. See note 23.

59. See note 23.

60. See note 23.

61. See note 23.

62. See note 23.

63. McDonald, E.G. (1960). Effect of school environment on teacher and student performance. *Air conditioning, Heating, and Ventilation, 57*, 78-79.

64. Stuart, F. & Curtis, H.A. (1964). Climate controlled and non-climate controlled schools. Clearwater, Florida: The Pinellas County Board of Education. *Air conditioning, Heating, and Ventilation, 57*, 78 – 79.

65. Pilman, M.S., (Dec 15, 2001). The effects of air temperature variance on memory ability. Missouri Western State College http://clearinghouse.mwsc.edu/manuscripts/306.asp.

66. Herrington, L.P. (1952). Effects of thermal environment on human action. *American School and University, 24*, 367-376.

67. Canter, D.V. (1976). *Environmental interaction psychological approaches to our physical surroundings*. New York: International University Press.

68. New York State Commission on Ventilation. (1931). School Ventilation and Practices. New York: Teachers College, Columbia University.

69. See note 23.

70. See note 23.

71. Maxwell, L.E. (1996). Multiple effects of home and day care crowding. *Environment and Behavior, 29-4*, 494–511.

72. U.S. Bureau of the Census (2001). Record share of new mothers in labor force (data from the June 1998 supplement to the Current Population Survey). Washington, DC: U.S. Department of Commerce News.

73. Capizzano, J., Adams, G., sonen-Stein, F.L., (2000). Childcare Arrangments for Children under Five. Washington, D.C.:Urban Institute. www.urban.org.

74. See note 23.

75. Legendre, A. (2003). Environmental features influencing toddlers' bioemotional reactions in day care centers. *Environment and Behavior, 35-4*, 523–549.

76. See note 23.

77. See note 23.

78. See note 73.

79. Cohen, S., Evans, G., Krantz, D.S., and Stokols, D. (1996). *Behavior, health, and environmental stress*. New York: Plenum.

80. Boschetti, M.A. (1987). Memories of childhood homes: Some contributions of environmental autobiography to interior design education and research. *Journal of Interior Design, 13-2*, 27–36.

81. Legendre, A. (1995). The effects of environmentally modulated visual accessibility to care

givers on early peer interactions. *International Journal of Behavioral Development, 19*, 297–313.

82. See note 6.

83. Friedmann, S., and Thompson, J.A. (1995). Intimate space issues in preschool environments. *Journal of Interior Design, 21-1*, 13–20.

84. See note 5.

85. See note 5.

86. Wu, W., and Ng, E. (2003). A review of the development of daylighting in schools. *Lighting Research and Technology, 35-2*, 111–125.

87. See note 2.

88. See note 2.

89. See note 5.

90. See note 2.

91. Zandvliet, D.B., and Straker, L.M. (2001). Physical and psychosocial aspects of the learning environment in information technology–rich classrooms. *Ergonomics, 44-9*, 838–857.

92. See note 5.

93. Knight, G., and Noyes, J. (1999). Children's behavior and the design of school furniture. *Ergonomics, 42-5*, 747–760.

94. Sugameli, J. (November 12, 2001). Classrooms find comfort. *The Detroit News.* http://www.detnews.com/2001/schools/0111/12/index.htm.

95. See note 26.

96. See note 2.

97. See note 26.

98. See note 91.

99. See note 26.

100. See note 2.

101. See note 91.

102. Osterberg, A.E., Davis, A.M., and Danielson, L.D. (1995). Universal design: The users' perspective. *Housing and Society, 22-1/2*, 92–113.

103. Sommer, R., and Olsen, H. (1990). The soft classroom. *Environment and Behavior, 12*, 3–16.

104. Killeen, J.F., Evans, G.W., and Danko, S. (2003). The role of permanent student artwork in students' sense of ownership in an elementary school. *Environment and Behavior, 35-2*, 250–263.

105. See note 102.

106. National Association of State Boards of Education (NASBE). (2004). Policy Update: Bullying In Schools, 11. Retrieved June 22, 2005, from http://www.nasbe.org/Educational_Issues/Policy_Updates/11_10.html.

107. Crawford, N. (2002). New Ways to Stop Bullying. *APA Monitor On Psychology, 33*. Retrieved June 22, 2005, from http://www.apa.org/monitor/oct02/bullying.html.

108. Lokeman, R. C. (2005, April 1). Echoes of Torment: Damage From Bullying Can Last Into Adulthood. Kansas City Star. Retrieved June 22, 2005, from http://stopbullyingnow.hrsa.gov/news/KansasCityStar-Column.gif.

109. See note 107.

110. See note 107.

111. See note 107.

112. See note 107.

113. Stop Bullying Now! What Adults Can Do. Retrieved June 22, 2005, from http://stopbullyingnow.hrsa.gov/indexAdult.asp?Area=shouldadultscare.

114. See note 106.

115. See note 104.

116. See note 111.

117. See note 102.

118. See note 107.

119. Dunn, M. J. (2001). Security Solutions: Break the Bullying Cycle. American School and University. Retrieved June 22, 2005, from http://asumag.com/mag/university_security_break_bullying/index.html.

120. See note 106.

121. See note 104.

122. See note 107.

123. See note 102.

124. See note 107.

125. Schneider, T. (2001). Safer Schools Through Environmental Design. *ERIC Digest*. Retrieved June 22, 2005, from http://www.ericdigests.org/2001-4/safer.html.

126. See note 107.

127. See note 102.

128. See note 107.

129. See note 102.

130. See note 102.

131. DesignCouncil.org (2005). Case Study: School Works - Kingsdale School. Retrieved June 22, 2005, from http://www.designcouncil.info/webdav/servlet/XRM?Page/@id=6048&Ses

sion/@id=D_x7FuUtp5a5ODJwYd9F3C &Document/@id=2596.

132. Stone, N.J. (2001). Designing effective study environments. *Journal of Environmental Psychology, 21-2,* 179–190.

133. See note 102.

134. Mahnke, F.H., and Mahnke, R.H., (1996). *Color, environment and human response.* New York: Van Nostrand Rheinhold.

135. Erin, J.N., and Koenig, A.J. (1997). The student with a visual and a learning disability. *Journal of Learning Disabilities, 30-3,* 309–320.

136. See note 2.

137. Kaya, K., and Erkip, F. (2001). Satisfaction in a dormitory building: The effects of floor height on the perception of room size and crowding. *Environment and Behavior, 33-1,* 35–53.

138. Evans, G.W., Lepore, S.J., and Schroeder, A. (1996). The role of interior design elements in human responses to crowding. *Journal of Personality and Social Psychology, 70-1,* 41–46.

139. See note 2.

140. See note 136.

141. See note 136.

142. See note 2.

143. Abu-Ghazzeh, T.M. (1996). Movement and wayfinding in the King Saud University built environment: A look at freshman orientation and environmental information. *Journal of Environmental Psychology, 16-4,* 303–319.

144. See note 136.

145. See note 136.

146. Nasar, J.L., Jones, K.M., and Chin, B. (1997). Landscapes of fear and stress. *Environment and Behavior, 29-3,* 291–323.

ELEVEN

Healthcare Environments

Hospital design has changed significantly over the past century as a result of social and political influences and advances in medical technology. In the 1880s hospitals began to evolve from "death houses for the poor" to models of scientific and medical excellence; however, it was not until the late 1970s that hospitals became warmer and more inviting environments[1] (Figure 11.1a and b). Hospitals of the 19th century usually were made up of large open spaces that housed many beds arranged in long rows, wherein the lack of sanitation and privacy dehumanized patients and their loved ones. By the 1960s most hospitals reeked of disinfectant and utilized sterile designs and materials almost exclusively, harsh lighting, and the color white; they became cold, impersonal environments that disaffected even the caregivers.

In the late 1970s, a radical new approach to hospital design emerged. Termed the *Planetree model* (Box 11.1), this holistic approach promotes healing by simultaneously addressing a patient's physical, psychological, emotional, spiritual, and social well-being. Consistent with this model is the development of a more inviting, home-like environment with softer furnishings, warmer colors, and barrier-free designs that maintains the patient's dignity and promotes family participation in care. (Figure 11.2)

Types of Healthcare Environments

Different types of public and private healthcare environments accommodate different patient needs, and it is important to note that chronic (long-term) diseases are far more common in the United States than are acute (short-term) diseases.[2] **Acute care facilities** are equipped to deal with emergencies, life-threatening illnesses and injuries, and surgical

a

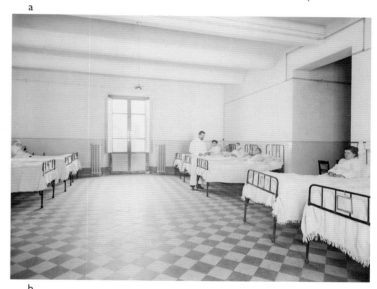

b

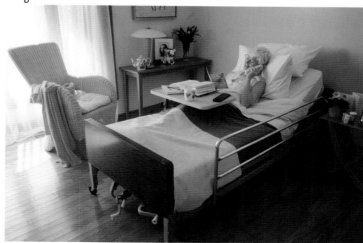

Figure 11.1a and b: Hospitals used to be places designed specifically for the confinement of illness (a). They have come a long way as far as overall ambiance: from sterile and austere settings that reeked of disinfectant to modern environments with spaces that resemble areas in private homes (b).

Box 11.1 The Planetree Model of Healthcare Design

Planetree is a nonprofit organization that was founded in 1978 by Angelica Thieriot and promotes an alternative to the traditional healthcare experience. The Planetree model encourages healing in multiple dimensions (e.g., physical, psychological, emotional, spiritual, and social), emphasizing a patient-centered approach—medical care from the patient's perspective—rather than provider-focused medical care. A key component of the model is its focus on empowering patients.

The model relies on nine components that provide a holistic experience to maximize healthcare outcomes through the integration of complementary therapies with conventional medical therapies. These nine components are as follows:

- Human interaction
- Family, friends, and social support networks
- Empowerment of patients through information and education
- Architectural design conducive to health and healing
- Spirituality: the importance of inner resources
- Nutritional and nurturing aspects of food
- Healing arts
- Human touch
- Complementary therapies that expand the choices offered to patients (e.g., mind/body medicine, therapeutic massage, acupuncture, yoga, and energy therapies such as therapeutic touch and Reiki)

Of particular importance to designers is the model's focus on architectural and environmental design in the healing process. Researchers have revealed the importance of the physical environment as a contributing force to positive patient outcomes. The Planetree model advocates facility design conducive to the healing process: efficient layouts that support patient dignity; warm, home-like, noninstitutional designs; and the removal of unnecessary architectural barriers. Art, aesthetics, and elements that connect patients with nature are emphasized.[3]

Increasingly, healthcare facilities have incorporated similar features into their design, and the present-day hospital, with its patient suites, gift shops, community meeting rooms, and greenscaping, looks and feels very different from the facilities endured by our great-grandparents. As designers consider various designs for the healthcare environment, they will need to develop designs that help reduce stress and anxiety; foster place attachment, facilitate patients', caretakers', and visitors' abilities to find their way around the facility; and be aware of the symptom manifestations for various diseases to use design as a proactive measure for health and safety. Some of the specific issues that designers consider include natural and artificial lighting levels and lighting transitions (lighting levels from indoors to outdoors), facility layout (corridors and intersections), surface materials, themes, and the relationship of nature to human health and satisfaction. Today's healthcare environment is no longer the sterile environment of our not so distant past; instead, it is a complex environment involving people, nature, and the designs that bring them together.

operations; stays in these facilities are relatively short, ranging from a few hours to a month or so. **Rehabilitation facilities** provide for extended stays of weeks or months during which patients work to regain their health following accidents, amputations, strokes, and so on. **Long-term care facilities**, also called nursing or convalescent homes, serve as residences for individuals whose chronic conditions require routine medical care or assistance (i.e., those who, living on their own, pose a threat or hazard to themselves or others). The residents of most long-

Figure 11.2: Many modern hospital lobbies are designed more explicitly for comfort than they were in the past. Aquariums and plants are often incorporated for their soothing effects.

term care facilities are generally elderly people, but such facilities often accommodate younger patients. **Continuing care retirement communities** provide independent-living apartments, assisted-living facilities, and skilled nursing facilities within campus-like environments that allow residents to "age in place" as their health deteriorates. Such institutions, which provide both homes and workplaces for residents, have become increasingly popular over the past 50 years and are expected to continue to do so to meet the needs of the baby boom generation. Both long-term care facilities and continuing care retirement communities provide assistance for residents who need help with activities of daily living. Some healthcare facilities accommodate different patient populations with specific needs in separate **special care units** that provide, for example, emergency, pediatric, and rehabilitation services within a single building or complex. Other patient-specific healthcare environments include **birthing centers**, **behavioral health facilities** such as psychiatric hospitals and mental health institutions, **pediatric hospitals** for infants and children, and **hospices** for terminally-ill patients.

Understanding the specific purposes of different facilities is crucial to effective design because each plan, scheme, and feature must support the overall function of the facility as well as the requirements of the individuals who occupy it

(Table 11.1). Although federal and state regulations intended to prevent the mistreatment of elderly people and to control costs have dictated minimum and maximum requirements for long-term care facility design since 1954, such facilities still suffer from the stigma of being considered poorhouses for the elderly and from the elder-abuse scandals of the 1970s.[4]

Issues in Healthcare Environments

Every healthcare setting, whether a room in a family residence or a housing complex designed to care for hundreds of patients, requires healthcare providers. This human support system has many of the same physical and psychological needs as the individuals it serves. Facilities should be designed with both patient populations and healthcare staff members (e.g., caregivers, administrators, or maintenance workers) in mind because staff discord and negative attitudes often transfer to residents,[5] and the safety and comfort of visitors and guests must be ensured. Patients and their families and healthcare providers participated in focus groups for a recent study and identified wayfinding, privacy, and accommodations for family members as important features of healthcare environments.[6]

Other issues of concern within the healthcare environment include stress, place attachment, and

Table 11.1 Types of Healthcare Facilities

TYPE OF FACILITY	SCOPE OF CARE	PRIMARY DESIGN CONSIDERATION
Acute care facility	Emergencies, surgeries, short-term stays, or any combination of these	Relief of anxiety that contributes to a fight-or-flight response in patients
Rehabilitation facility	Traumatic injuries requiring rehabilitation; stays of 6 to 12 months	Provisions for inspiration and motivation during lengthy recovery of patients
Long-term care facility	Chronic disease or debilitation; the inability to control the body or mind	Promoting of feelings of homeyness, safety, and security for residents
Continuing care retirement community	Minimal assistance for prolonged periods of time	Promoting feelings of homeyness, ownership, and environmental control for residents
Special care unit	Specialized facility for short- or long-term stay (e.g., birthing center, behavioral health facility, pediatric hospital, or hospice).	Depends on the facility's area of specialization, such as care of patients with acquired immunodeficiency syndrome (AIDS).

wandering. Stress is a biological reaction to any adverse stimulus—physical, mental, or emotional, internal or external—that can affect a person's normal state of well-being. For most people, illness is a source of stress that is elevated when they are placed into a hospital setting. The bonds of place attachment can also be a source of stress when abruptly severed. Defined as an affective connection between people and a particular place or setting,[7] place attachment involves a person's interpretive and cognitive perspective toward an environment and his or her subsequent emotional reaction to it.[8] Stress brought about by the severing of place attachment bonds usually arises when a person is forced to leave his or her home and enter an institution.

People with dementia of the Alzheimer's type tend to wander—a behavior that inadvertently places them at risk and often leads to their being placed in a long-term care facility. Healthcare environments designed to accommodate such patients must therefore address the special safety and behavioral needs of this population.

Stress

Many people tend to experience strong emotions related to fear and anxiety when they are required to stay in a healthcare environment. Once hospitalized, nearly everything about patients, with the exception of their illnesses, becomes invisible, and the psychological loss of control that results from not being allowed to make decisions about their lives and the activities they can partake in reduces patients' desires to be proactive about their health.[9] Institutionalized elderly people, the most debilitated of the aging population, have a higher risk of death and depression, which contributes to the shortened length of their lives.[10]

Most patients stress derives from feelings generated by negative experiences—losing control of privacy and normal routines, feeling vulnerable because their condition diminishes their sense of mastery, fearing an unknown outcome—and is exacerbated by the separation from home. This devastating combination often leads to tremendous levels of stress, especially for new patients. Children, especially, are affected by the separation from the safety of their families and their own rooms. Teens and adults in rehabilitation hospitals struggle with fears about their future. For many elderly people, leaving home for a long-term care facility represents life's final stage before death. Relocation is stressful for older adults partly due to its association with the loss of mobility, possessions, social relationships,[11] and independence and partly due to the transition from a place with many memories to one with none. Lack of control can decrease a person's capacity to concentrate and increase a person's tendency to report physical symptoms.[12] In short, power and control are important to the psychological health of patient populations.[13]

Stress reduces the efficiency of the human immune system. When under stress, older adults (who require the services of healthcare facilities most) are particularly vulnerable to decreased **immunocompetency**, the ability or capacity for the immune system to respond or function adequately.[14] Incorporating aspects of nature within healthcare environments can help establish a semblance of familiarity and evoke feelings of relaxation,[15] as can allowing patients to personalize their rooms and incorporate their personal artifacts into public spaces.

The people in charge of designing healthcare settings are often administrators who tend to select designs from their perspective: that of a workplace environment. However, to the patients occupying rehabilitation facilities, continuing care retirement communities, and long-term care facilities, these places are homes. Our society needs to make a paradigm shift from perceiving such facilities as institutions and workplaces to regarding them as homes. Users of a long-term care facility's sitting area should be able to view green spaces from both inside and outside the facility. Nature settings help to reduce the anxiety patients are likely to experience as they make the transition from private homes to assisted care environments. Allowing personal items to be brought into a long-term care facility, such as a bed and dresser, will convey a familiarity with the space and help patients feel more comfortable in their new homes because they evoke personal, often happy, memories. Also, designs should provide opportunities for occupants to control their environment by being able to open or shut blinds, make their beds, and merge items that reflect their personal tastes with the designs of their new homes.

Patient rooms housing multiple roommates often evoke feelings associated with being over-whelmed by unwanted noise and social interaction; resident physicians and family members indicate that private rooms allow for more control over unwanted interaction, and therefore facilitate visits with family and friends.[16] Many individuals from Western cultures value privacy, especially when they feel vulnerable, but members of large families or other cultures may prefer shared rooms over private ones.[17] This inconsistency between cultural and individual preferences requires that both designers and caregivers gain intimate knowledge of current and potential patient populations.

Following admission to a healthcare facility, other factors contribute to patients' stress. People tend to conceptualize illnesses as being temporary rather than permanent (which helps us maintain a sense of control), and when we are (or believe we are) sick or injured, we assume the "role" of patient.[18] This sick role is based on three assumptions: Being sick may or may not be our fault and frees us from our normal responsibilities (privilege), and we must take steps to get well (duty). The **sick role**, which is based on *operant conditioning*, does not realistically apply to chronic conditions; being diagnosed as having a chronic illness changes our self-perception and our coping strategies according to our understanding of both the disease and the outcome.[19] This role can lead patients, especially elderly ones, to adopt a passive or defeatist attitude toward both their immediate circumstances and their overall lives.

Negative intrusive thoughts, which can remain with patients for three or more months, can interfere with patients' successful adaptations to new environments; contribute to anxiety, depression, and physical symptoms;[20] and may derive from the patient's own concerns or from overheard conversations among relatives or caregivers. Intrusive thoughts can be kept to a minimum by pleasant distractions, such as those afforded by a private room in which a person may speak freely, enjoy a favorite TV show, or read a book with little interference.

In long-term care facilities, rehabilitation facilities, and behavioral health settings, a garden incorporated into the overall design helps to increase participation in future-oriented exercises (e.g., planning, planting, and tending). Entering hospitals can be a stressful event for both the patient and

their family members. However, the stress levels of family members has been shown to be mitigated by exposure to natural settings and gardens incorporated into the design of healthcare facilities by providing a beneficial distraction and mood enhancement.[21] Likewise, patients who have a view of pleasant landscapes outside their hospital room have shorter postoperative stays, require lower doses of painkillers, and experience lower levels of stress; nursing reports revealed more negative emotions from patients who had a view of a brick wall.[22] Consider the following scenario:

> A young man who suffered a brain injury in a traffic accident is now in a rehabilitation facility. His higher cognitive functions are not affected, but his ability to speak is impaired. This patient is experiencing tremendous stress as a result of the trauma and pain of the injury itself, intrusive thoughts about permanent brain damage and immobility, and the unfamiliar sights, sounds, smells, and activities of his surroundings. If he were healthy, his feelings of anxiety and helplessness would likely cause him to seek the refuge of his home, but his condition prevents that option.

Design can serve to increase this patient's feelings of comfort and control, as well as his rate of recovery, by providing the following features in this new environment:

- A private room with colors, materials, and features typical of a home or hotel
- Comfortable accommodations for visitors
- Various sources of distraction (e.g., TV, radio, reading materials, natural elements, a view)
- Areas in which to mingle with other patients, as well as a garden he can visit or tend when he is able

Exercise rooms are integral to rehabilitation facilities. Inclusion of a sound system is a key design feature in these rooms because music plays an important role in stimulation and motivation. Patients in rehabilitation facilities often suffer from insecurity about the future, and the use of warm colors can promote feelings of safety and security. A mural can be a source of inspiration; plants provide soothing natural elements; and a mirror enables patients to observe their progressive improvement.

Providing environments that help mitigate stress should be a primary concern when developing healthcare institutions. People who are admitted to healthcare facilities often experience a profound sense of loss, particularly in long-term care facility environments. High levels of stress, especially when sustained over time, can have devastating psychological and physical effects.

Studies examining the effects of plants in the workplace showed that they not only helped clean the air, but also contributed to greater office appeal, task performance, and comfort. Likewise, access to nature has been shown to alleviate stress and anxiety, improve psychological function, and increase identification with an environment.[23] Views of nature and access to outdoor areas have many beneficial effects in healthcare environments, including restorative qualities for both patients and healthcare workers. For example, tending and nurturing plants can have many psychologically and physically therapeutic qualities; such activities help to restore patients' feelings of control, give patients a sense of purpose and meaning, and keep patients active. Similarly, Roger Ulrich's findings indicate that psychologically appropriate artwork, such as nature scenes (especially those of water and trees), can substantially affect patient outcomes in an acute care setting, reducing blood pressure, anxiety, intake of pain medication, and length of patients' hospital stays.[24]

DESIGN APPLICATION. Designers should strive to minimize the negative feelings typically associated with institutional environments, which include lack of control (i.e., feelings of powerlessness or helplessness) resulting from perceived financial, physical, and psychological constraints and social factors (e.g., sick role, stereotyping, power or status levels).[25, 26]

Designers can provide specific living components that give residents greater control over their lives, such as layouts that allow them to move easily and freely throughout the environment (Figure 11.3a and b). Feelings of autonomy can be increased by homey, inviting environments that provide various means for residents to increase physical strength, decrease mental stressors, and maintain social connections.[27, 28] Researchers recommend creating a noninstitutional atmosphere that includes

outdoor spaces[29] and advocate using rich colors to enhance social areas, incorporating residents' personal objects into public spaces, providing opportunities for residents to enjoy agreeable aromas (from sources such as cooking, flowers, and herbs), and designing workspaces that enable residents to be involved in the facility's daily operations (e.g., answering telephones) to give them a sense of inclusion and control.[30]

Place Attachment

People who enter an long-term care facility may not embrace or develop an attachment to their new environments, which can lower their self-esteem and raise their stress levels. In a recent study, place attachment was affected by the space's functional aspects (e.g., adequate room for sleeping and socializing) and meaningful aspects (e.g., the appearance of a lived-in home and its reflection of the resident's personality); occupant satisfaction occurred when higher-level needs were met.[31] Other research asserts that as opposed to those who do not, people who have a strong sense of place attachment are more satisfied with their environments, have more positive moods, and are better adjusted—all of which supports mental and physical health—and that access to natural areas not only encourages place attachment for residents, but also can facilitate greater communication, improve moods, increase satisfaction, and possibly provide means of refuge.[32]

Developing place attachment can be particularly difficult for adolescents (12- to 18-year-olds) in healthcare settings. Research has shown that youths have specific developmental and social needs that should be addressed in the design of healthcare facilities; however, members of this age group generally are placed in pediatric or adult wards or units where they feel out of place. The researchers cited earlier findings that adolescent inpatient units improve health outcomes by reducing psychosocial morbidity and improving adherence and behavior, can shorten patient stays and improve control of chronic illness, and should provide peer contact, privacy, mobility, independence, and educational continuity. These researchers advocate providing adolescent units with patient rooms, a day room for common activities, and a schoolroom near the pediatric unit (Figure 11.4).[33]

Place attachment is also important for caregivers,

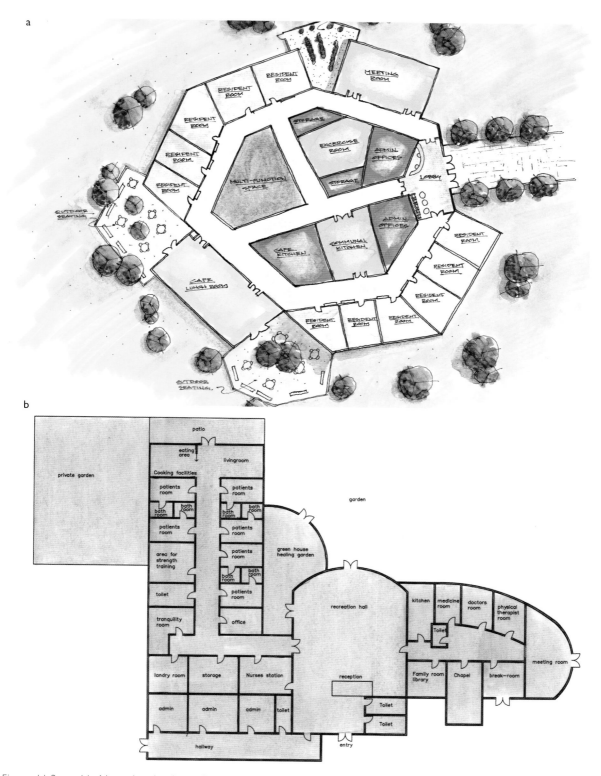

Figure 11.3a and b: Note the circular walking patterns in this floor plan (a) of a long-term care facility. The lack of terminal points is an important feature for patients who wander, such as those who have DAT. The floor plan pictured at the bottom (b) is not ideal because of the terminal hallways which would not be suitable for patients with DAT, although the design works well for other residents of long-term care facilities. This environment is made more attractive by the multiple options available to its residents: opportunities to cook, stretch or exercise, read or meditate, do laundry, garden in the greenhouse or outdoor garden, and fulfill their spiritual needs.

Figure 11.4: Healthcare facilities that serve children should operate with minimal intrusion into their patients' lives and daily activities. Children who suffer from chronic or terminal illnesses or injuries that require rehabilitation feel estranged from their normal lives. As such, children's facilities should encourage them to express themselves and incorporate the results into the environment. Here, a space is set aside to display the artwork of children, which allows them to personalize an area that can feel foreign to them otherwise.

administrators, and maintenance staff. The very nature of emergency care facilities, for example, creates high levels of stress for patients and staff alike, much of which can be mitigated by thoughtful design. Employees who are comfortable in and proud of their workplace provide better service; therefore, the more pleasant and efficient the overall workspace, the better the overall patient care. Yet, the needs of employees and stakeholders should not supersede those of the patient populations.

Wayfinding

Understanding movement within spaces is part of environmental cognition, which we use in wayfinding.[34] To successfully navigate an environment that changes as we move through it, we must continually assess and respond to different stimuli and objects.[35] Because people who occupy healthcare facilities are often cognitively compromised by injury, degenerative disease, or elevated levels of stress, their walking and wayfinding abilities may be impaired. Therefore, it is essential to provide easy access from parking areas to buildings; use an easily navigable floor

plan for patients and visitors, including those who use mobility aids or service animals;[36] and use signage every 50 feet as a back-up system to environmental features that serve as reference points, such as nurses' stations.[37] The design should include simple configurations that allow people to move from one destination to another without having to plan their next move; articulate circulation clearly in the building's or complex's spatial organization (thus minimizing the need for signage); and provide visual access to all spaces and functions so that users can see and understand the environment (thus eliminating the need for maps).[38]

The way in which spaces are connected to one another (i.e., the topological configuration) helps residents find their ways in and form better cognitive maps of an environment; therefore, planners and designers must avoid implementing environmental variables that impede wayfinding efforts, such as the interruption of views (e.g., placing a feature in the middle of a corridor and splitting the path around it), because it is easier to find a destination or connecting point that can be seen from a distance.[39] Conversely, the strategic placement of noise-producing zones will assist wayfinding (e.g., recreation areas have the most noise, and media centers, visitors' areas, libraries or study areas, and healing gardens have the least noise).

All wayfinding information should be designed to fit the needs of the patient population. Dementia patients typically find floor plan–type maps difficult to comprehend; pictographs facilitate more successful wayfinding in dementia-care facilities.[40] Graphic information that facilitates wayfinding (e.g., signage and arrows) should be clear and consistent throughout both the design and the facility so that users know where to look for what they need.[41] Although safety codes require the use of signage, dementia patients may not see wall-mounted signs because their visual field is often the floor.[42] Designers should use color, texture, and patterns that will engage various senses and, in addition to wall décor and window treatments, help orient people to their surroundings (Figure 11.5).

Consider creating spaces based on a particular theme that is meaningful to the majority of residents, as well as microcommunities in which each social area has a distinguishable, appropriate name

Figure 11.5: Bulging areas on doorways, elevators, or in corridors subtly indicate where potential turns may be made into building exits, room entrances, waiting areas, and so on. However, these subconscious indicators can call attention to possible "escape routes," and therefore should not be incorporated into the design of facilities that house patients who have dementia.

and unique architectural feature but is consistent with the overall design scheme of the facility (e.g., design a media center to look like a theater).[43] Keep signs and messages simple and relevant for users to understand; avoid the use of abbreviations because not everyone will understand their meaning; and limit information in corridors to wayfinding information and signage.[44] Expanding on the microcommunity theme, such signage could be made to resemble roadway and street signs.

Wandering

Wandering is a form of restless behavior often engaged in by very young, very old, and cognitively impaired people. In a study of patients with DAT, a wide range of wandering behavior was observed at all levels of impairment, indicating that wandering by these patients is not caused solely by cognitive decline. Subjects who were less cognitively im-

paired, depressed, and functionally impaired wandered less, and no gender, ethnicity, age, or living-situation differences in wandering behavior were found.[45] Wandering patterns fall into four categories: direct, random, pacing, and lapping.[46]

The act of wandering can cause various problems relating to health, safety, and social order, especially within healthcare facilities housing dementia patients. Some facilities still physically or chemically restrain their wandering residents, but the current trend is to alter living environments to help prevent or to accommodate wandering.[47] Adjusting design to accommodate wandering can keep residents safe while providing an environment they can continue to explore freely, encouraging independence and a sense of well-being.

Why dementia patients wander is unclear; they may be unaware of their actions or become lost even if the environment is familiar to them. When they start out to do something, they may forget what they were doing, where they were going, or where they are. The resulting wandering is a by-product of that forgetfulness. One study reports that up to 40 percent of residents in SCUs wander, and the investigators suggest several reasons for this behavior: Residents seek to relieve boredom or stress, they seek escape (exit) or social interaction, or they simply follow others.[48] In many cases the wandering process itself seems to have a calming affect and reduces agitation and verbal disturbances.[49] Wandering can be beneficial for some patients by providing an opportunity for exercise, reducing stress, and filling unstructured time, but unsafe exiting is a serious problem for those suffering from dementia.

Many researchers advocate developing spaces that allow wandering to occur, contending that this will not only decrease the need for staff supervision and search parties but also increase perceived freedom for patients.[50, 51] Others recommend providing rooms, spaces, and facilities for activities and social interaction to engage those who wander due to a lack of environmental stimulation;[52] creating continuous paths that do not lead to a dead-end and that maintain social or visual areas of interest along them; and providing visual and sensory stimulation along these "wandering paths" to encourage users to stop and interact with the environment.[53]

DESIGN APPLICATION. In designing facilities for cognitively impaired patients, keep in mind

that endless corridors will accommodate "lap-ping" wanderers, but should not dead-end into nodes. Interior courtyards provide outdoor space from which residents cannot wander, and circular paths minimize disorientation and fear of getting lost.[54] Such design features encour-age meaningful walks instead of wandering.[55] Recent research indicates that paths that travel through garden areas or even along corridors with much shadowing or mottling (i.e., lacking visual penetration) seem to have a calming ef-fect on dementia sufferers.[56] Wandering paths and endless corridors should pass through ac-tivity areas to encourage social interaction and participation in scheduled activities and to re-duce the staff time dedicated to watching and locating patients. Facility exits must be visible but must not attract dementia patients. Consider placing exits away from wandering paths so they do not become destinations for wanderers and camouflaging exits.[57] Placing vi-sual barriers in front of exits help to prevent escapes by dementia patients.[58]

Interior Design Features in Healthcare Settings

The interior design of healthcare facilities is criti-cal to both patients' and healthcare providers' abil-ities to establish a sense of attachment, belonging, and personal control. Maslow's hierarchy of needs provides a useful perspective: When lower-level needs of physiological and safety are met, higher-level needs of belongingness and self-esteem can be addressed.[59, 60] Remember, too, that aesthetic assessments are influenced by smells, sights, sounds, and tactile sensations—all of which must be addressed.[61]

More on Maslow's hierarchy of needs can be found in Chapter 1.

Those who leave home to stay in healthcare en-vironments, whether for days or years, must be se-lective as to the size and quantity of personal possessions they can or may bring to a limited space. Patients and their well-meaning loved ones often transport a collection of personal objects to the new residence; however, a familiar but disor-ganized display of meaningful yet unrelated arti-facts only accentuates the alien environment[62] (Figure 11.6). Interior components with a home-like aesthetic (e.g., small-scale furnishings, wall

coverings, and lighting fixtures) will create a sense of familiarity and security.[63] Materials, finishes, lighting, furnishings, and decorative objects should also serve to create a more residential atmosphere.[64] Linking artwork to familiar life events can create more resident interest, but do not use items that dementia patients could perceive as toys.[65] Create dedicated space and fixed furniture layouts for eat-ing, sleeping, and leisure activities because re-arrangement can cause confusion.[66] Secure artwork with locks or adhesives, and, when possible, anchor furniture so that patients experiencing vertigo (dizziness) can reach for support without fear of its moving. Design quiet, private areas for residents that can be personalized (e.g., bedrooms, sitting rooms, small areas within a common space) and help trigger residents' memories and facilitate calmness,[67] as well as indoor and outdoor spaces for residents to engage in physical activity because some people remain active into advanced old age.[68] Providing facilities for shared, festive meals can es-pecially benefit residents who lack other opportu-nities for social interaction.[69]

Provide recognizable cues, such as signs and colors, for people to rely on while wayfinding.[70] When using color to decorate social spaces, use enough to promote interest but not so much as to reduce environmental comprehension (i.e., a color scheme that is too dull, too bright, or too busy).[71, 72] Use culturally supportive design ele-ments that focus on activities and relationships with a social and physical context and are easily understood by dementia patients.[73] To help pa-tients distinguish their spaces from others', allow patients to personalize their rooms, especially di-rectly inside and outside of the entries; combine signage with patients' names and photographs of their younger selves; and vary the color of individ-ual doors and frames.[74]

One research team advocates incorporating culturally specific design throughout healthcare facilities serving *homogeneous populations* (i.e., those who make up a particular ethnic or cultural group) and providing space in residents' rooms to accommodate cultural artifacts, activities, or both for *heterogeneous populations* (i.e., those composed of multiple ethnic or cultural groups).[75] These re-searchers recommend including space appropriate for intergenerational family members (because

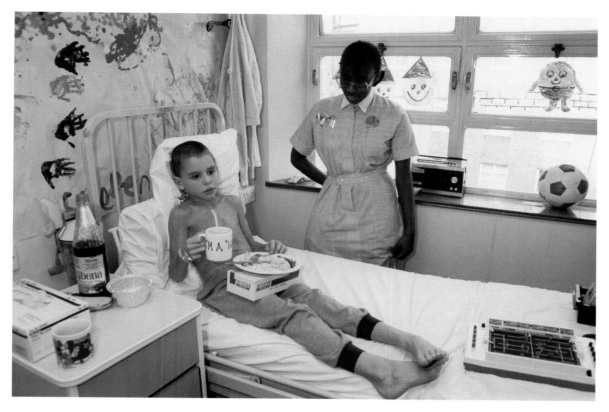

Figure 11.6: Comfortable items that are associated with the home can provide many psychological benefits, but also make an already alien environment feel more so. The young patient pictured here has surrounded himself with games and other familiar objects and has been encouraged to design a "mural" that hangs behind his bed.

even patients in the early stages of dementia may be able to continue caring for grandchildren with help from staff members) and providing culturally appropriate, noninstitutional settings for interaction between staff and residents' families. However, they caution against assuming that members of user groups (especially immigrants) identify with local concepts of ethnicity and culture; for instance, in their study, elderly Russian Jews tended to identify themselves more as Russians than as Jews. The researchers further note that functional ability may also be compromised by social problems experienced by a particular cultural group (e.g., bigotry or lack of resources).

Lighting

Lighting is crucial in healthcare environments, particularly those serving elderly and cognitively impaired people. When designing healthcare environments for older populations, architects and designers must consider building orientation relative to natural light and its seasonal changes. As we age, our pupils dilate and contract more slowly in response to dim and bright light, respectively; therefore, architects should take measures to diminish the brightness and glare brought about from direct sunlight along predominant pathways, and interior designers should incorporate surface materials with flat or matte finishes. An understanding of the relationship between lighting and surface materials throughout the day and year, as well as the interrelationship between architecture and interior design, will lead to the development of environments that enhance occupant satisfaction.

Sunlight is brightest from the south, weakest from the north, most invigorating from the east, and most intense from the west. Also, the color, angle, and intensity of light changes during the day, affecting a person's perception of the environment. Locations receive different levels of light over a 24-hour period as well as seasonally, and changes in lighting can alter the perceived appearance of the environment enough to confuse patients suffering from cognitive impairments. Many healthcare facilities opt for easy-to-clean surfaces; however, the glossier the surface the greater the glare, which can cause temporary blindness and pain and may create a false perception of elevation change or of a solid obstacle.

A recent study found that institutionalized older adults are generally confined to their rooms with very little exposure to sunlight, and inadequate exposure to light is thought to cause changes in brain chemistry and circadian rhythms, leading to depression.[76] The researchers exposed depressed institutionalized adults to bright light treatment for 30 minutes per day for five days, which decreased the patients' depression to that of the normal range for healthy adults and decreased the depression score significantly. Another researcher also found that the presence or absence of natural daylight seems to be related to behavior changes, noting that disruptive behaviors among dementia sufferers are most often associated with mid- to late afternoon (around 2:00 p.m. to 4:00 p.m.) and that, by controlling lighting levels throughout the experimental daycare room, disruptive behaviors such as wandering, repetitive statements, and pilfering by dementia patients can be reduced by 11 percent during the spring months and by 41 percent in the winter months when there is much less natural daylight.[77]

Surface Materials

Another design challenge lies in the selection of surface materials. Materials and adhesives that peel, flake, or crack create not only maintenance issues but also the potential for harm to patients.[78] Floor finishes, wall coverings, and cabinet sheathing and their colors, patterns, or textures may be acceptable in one facility but may cause confusion or hazardous conditions in another.[79] This inconsistency results from differences in light and shadow and from perceptions created by interacting design features. The fully functioning brain can screen out extrasensory information and maintain fairly uniform perception. However, people with cognitive impairment caused by high levels of stress or dementia have less ability to recognize and understand sensory experiences, which can make them hypersensitive to environmental conditions[80] and

Figure 11.7: Handrails in hallways allow patients with little stamina to rest; the contrast of the handrail against the wall makes it easier to see.

therefore able to perceive subtleties that fully functioning people would not. When selecting surface materials, be aware of natural light patterns during the course of the day, as well as patterns generated by artificial light sources at night. Consider that reflected light is often bright enough to "wash out" colors and patterns.

All surface materials must be carefully evaluated to ensure their appropriateness for each facility and unit. Risk of injury from falling is a serious problem for elderly people in general; factors that contribute to falls include disease (e.g., Parkinson's, arthritis), poor balance, and use of psychoactive drugs;[81] even nonslip flooring can be hazardous to patients if it has a strong pattern or a monochromatic color scheme. Brighter colors against darker backgrounds can create the illusion of three-dimensionality, which can lead to disorientation and falls among patients who suffer from cognitive degeneration; therefore, avoid the use of highly contrasting colors (e.g., black and yellow). Similarly, the use of monochromatic colors in areas that change elevation (e.g., stairs and landings, sunken rooms) can be problematic for those whose brains may be unable to recognize or interpret elevation changes. Varying rich colors between elevations will help to minimize this perceptual problem. Incorporate handrails, nonslip flooring, and high-rise toilets into spaces to both encourage and enable patients to function independently.[82] Note, however, that even safety devices can be sources of risk to elderly people and others who have poor depth perception; handrails and grab bars often blend into the background, which is especially problematic in bathing areas. A contrasting background accent (e.g., a gold accent behind brushed steel) will focus attention on the rail (Figure 11.7).

Architectural Features in Healthcare Settings

Design should serve to minimize the institutional feel of healthcare environments and maximize feelings of homeyness. Exterior elements affecting homeyness include supportive protection (i.e., elements that evoke familiarity, enclosure, and care), **human-scale elements** (elements that are neither oversized nor undersized), and naturalness (Figure 11.8). Therefore, designers should avoid massive buildings and long uninterrupted façades, and utilize elements found in single-family homes (e.g., covered entries protected from the weather, detailed window treatments, differentiated roof lines, building materials such as wood or brick) and generous landscaping with elements such as benches to suggest human presence.[83] Additionally, residents may be more comfortable in low-rise buildings because they sense they can exit more easily in case of emergency.[84] Vital institutional elements, such as security systems and **areas of rescue assistance** (spaces that have direct access to an exit, utilized during evacuations), can be blended into the environment to be easily accessible to staff and emergency workers yet not detract from the overall ambience.

Layout Issues

Layout is integral to successful design within any large facility; therefore, design layouts must be consistent and easily understandable. If a person is disoriented within a community, he or she can look for cues from street signs, landmarks, or sounds; but within institutional environments, orientation cues are usually smaller and much less familiar, and this can be especially problematic for cognitively impaired people. A healthcare facility's overall design should attempt to evoke a more residential feel, with flexible spaces (i.e., those used for recreational

Figure 11.8: The exterior of this long-term care facility looks more like a residential estate and affords patients the opportunity to escape into a more expansive setting without moving too far from the facility itself.

and other social activities) that are centrally located[85] and nursing stations that are placed at a distance from them. Designers should incorporate landmarks that have special meaning to the primary patient constituency and can serve as orientation reference points for both patients and visitors.[86] In a facility serving a Catholic constituency, the lobby might contain a large cross; in a Buddhist community, it might contain a prayer shrine. Through such special considerations, design can help compensate for the physical and mental losses of the users.[87]

Some architectural features may be obstacles to certain patient populations (e.g., people whose mobility, vision, or cognitive abilities are impaired). Reduce distractions along circulation pathways when designing for older adults because avoiding obstacles is more difficult when a person's attention is divided or distracted.[88] This advice is applicable to all healthcare environments because patients experience many stressors that can affect their ability to concentrate or function normally. In multistoried facilities, elevator areas used by patients should be distinguishable from one another and include a voice activation system or other alternative measures for users who cannot or do not remember to push buttons.[89] Be aware of crutch users' concerns about slipping on wet floors (especially after their being out in rain or snow), and decrease the size of floor grate openings that could trap wheelchairs, crutches, and canes.[90] Grates serve as points of de-livery for air circulation and heat in older buildings or as drainage points for excess water on the streets and are often found just outside of buildings and along sidewalks.

Creating architecturally diverse environments within the larger facility—with clear sight lines between different areas, visually distinctive fea-tures, and recognizable furniture—provides refer-ence points that serve to improve patient wayfinding.[91] Consider designing long-term care facilities using circulation paths similar to that of public streets,[92] and keep such paths straightfor-ward with visual access to important spaces and functions[93] because these types of designs allow residents to see and be seen.

Corridors, Intersections, and Themes

Corridors (*paths*) require particular attention dur-ing the design process. Shorter corridors in long-term care, rehabilitation, and behavioral health facilities will help to facilitate staff interaction with, and reduce physical distances between, pa-tients.[94] Corridors should have identifiable refer-ence points to counteract the confusion that can be created by symmetrical floor plan designs.[95] Create niches for displaying information (e.g., an-nouncements, invitations, publicity) to avoid con-fusing patients who might be looking for directional signs, and provide alcoves to serve as additional gathering spaces[96] and as temporary storage for cleaning equipment so as to maintain clear circulation pathways.[97] Following the *micro-community* concept described earlier in this chap-ter, corridors could have different names depicted in particular colors on lighted signs suspended from the ceiling, with the names incorporated into transition points denoting the separation of public and semipublic spaces.

Intersections (*nodes*) are often more important than corridors (the spaces connecting nodes) to people trying to find their way in a new environ-ment,[98] who will create orientation reference points for each node containing a unique service or feature. Giving each node its own entrance and façade, with a distinct meaning or theme, makes identification easier for patients.[99] Each separate area of the facility should have its own unifying theme that distinguishes it; for example,

the dining room could be made to resemble a restaurant appropriate to the microcommunity context (e.g., sidewalk café, 1950s-style diner, and so on).

Such variations in themes encourage active engagement with the environment and enhance recognition.[100] Creating social areas with differ-ent aesthetic looks and functions (e.g., media center, recreation room, library) will help to stimulate residents and prevent boredom.[101] De-signs and themes should be culturally appropriate for the intended population because settings that support specific cultural activities and rituals can provide the context and the comfort that pro-mote positive patient outcomes; therefore, create spaces indoors and outdoors for small-group conversations, meals, and game playing.[102] How-ever, planners and designers must be aware that users' varying capabilities can affect specific de-sign initiatives.

The Role of Nature in Healthcare Settings

Architectural features should include elements found in nature. Consider incorporating into the overall facility design a "healing garden" or similar destination to provide patients sanctuary and relief from confinement, and where they may choose to sit quietly amidst the greenery or pursue gardening activities.[103] One research team, noting that gardens can help to reduce stress by providing places for in-dividual reflection and psychological restoration for both staff and patients, recommends that gardens be incorporated along primary pathways (e.g., facilities located in temperate climates could have gardens between buildings; in colder regions, greenhouses could be utilized) and notes that healing gardens provide screened-off areas for privacy, wheelchair access, support for patients' equipment (e.g., IV stands, oxygen tanks), and plants with soothing scents, such as herbs and edible flowers[104] (Figure 11.9). Note, however, that facilities housing demen-tia patients need to incorporate security precautions to prevent patients from wandering off.

Whenever possible, incorporate nature into the facility's interior, using plants and other natural el-ements, as well as window views of nature. Indoor gardens containing features appropriate to the pa-

Figure 11.9: This healing garden's design enables patients to walk through and among greenery. The layout also allows patients to have a view of the garden from their rooms, important for those who are unable to move through the garden itself.

tient population (e.g., at a child's scale for pediatric facilities) and complementary sensory stimulation, such as water features, colorful surfaces,[105] and **music streams** (a constant flow of pleasurable, musical background noise) can be very beneficial to psychological and physical health and help reduce stress associated with the facility itself for patients, visitors, and staff members. Allow visual access to the natural, outside world for bedridden patients to promote their health and maximize their feelings of security.[106, 107]

Other Features and Considerations

When designing corridors and individual living spaces, include niches or other exhibit areas in entryways to living spaces and within those spaces;

such areas can be used by patients to display memorabilia in an organized way.[108] According to healthcare staff and family members, designers should arrange bathrooms so that the toilets can be seen from the patients' beds because this visual cue can help reduce episodes of incontinence;[109] for the same reason, place clearly marked and visible public toilet facilities near congregant activity areas. Incorporate generous lighting so that patients can more easily see and enjoy their personal possessions.[110] Light-dimming controls facilitate relaxation by allowing patients to control their level of stimulation. Lockable cupboards and the use of familiar blankets, pillows, and personal grooming items (e.g., shaving or makeup mirrors) will go a long way toward easing patient stress and providing a sense of control. Features should be appropriate

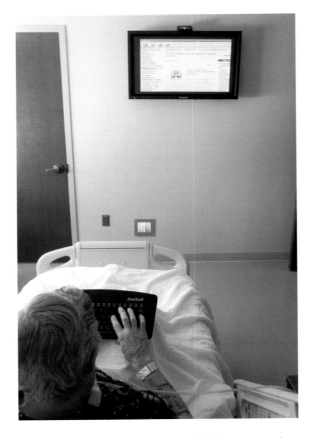

Figure 11.10: Many long-term care facilities are now incorporating Internet access into the rooms of patients who are able to utilize the technology to stay connected to the world outside. While many patients can benefit from this access, it can be inappropriate for others who lack the need or ability to use it.

for the users' needs and abilities. For example, in acute care settings, patients may have telephones in their rooms; long-term care facilities can provide telephones or computers with Internet access in common areas and monitored by the residents (Figure 11.10).

It is important that resident living spaces for older adults and dementia sufferers be modified to compensate for the degenerative process. Dementia sufferers in particular often try to escape and could become lost or injured; therefore, it is important to control all exits.[111] Select architectural designs and materials that will reduce potential injuries, such as rounded walls that prevent injuries that would result from impact with sharp corners and tempered safety glass in windows and doors. Utilize durable yet comfortable materials for spaces occupied by

patients suffering from degenerative diseases who will continue to decline. Such patients often require greater surveillance, but overly close monitoring can lead to reduced autonomy; therefore the use of too many cameras or observation windows can generate feelings of loss of control that may lead to learned helplessness in long-term patients.[112] Decrease the visibility of "dangerous" doors (e.g., exits from the facility and grounds, entries to supply rooms) and increase the visibility and attractiveness of "safe" doors (e.g., entries to patient rooms and social areas) to reduce confusion and frustration and to increase independence.[113]

Summary Review

Many people who enter healthcare environments experience anxiety and stress that impairs their cognitive abilities and leads to greater stress. This applies to short- and long-term patients, visitors, and healthcare providers and staff members, all of whom have various needs that design can accommodate. Everyone who enters a healthcare facility must cope not only with their condition but also with the stress of receiving treatment. Although the predominant constituency requiring the services of healthcare facilities is elderly, planners and designers must consider the numerous special needs and afflictions of all users of healthcare facilities.

Place attachment is an important aspect of any healthcare environment, especially in long-term care settings. Numerous studies have shown that a strong sense of attachment promotes mental and physical health is crucial in care environments. Design can serve to increase the likelihood of place attachment for patients and staff alike by meeting the needs of all users as comfortably, efficiently, and attractively as possible.

Aesthetics, safety, and security are key to successful healthcare facility design. Wayfinding mechanisms are also important considerations, and many architectural features can be incorporated that will aid place recognition for patients who have impaired cognitive functioning, limited wayfinding abilities, or both. The combined use of redundant wayfinding mechanisms (e.g., well-chosen words, strong colors, and patterns that vary in texture) enables patients to better conceptualize and form cognitive maps. Signage, while appropriate for staff and visitors, may not serve certain patient populations.

Design should provide as much natural light as possible within healthcare settings. The materials and design elements used in healthcare facilities must not only be practical and durable in terms of maintenance but also must limit perceptual confusion, glare, and risk of injury. Planners and designers must thoughtfully evaluate the appropriateness of surface materials to be used for each facility or unit to ensure the safety and well-being of patients, visitors, and staff.

Environments that facilitate wayfinding, safety, relaxation, and cultural affiliation are more efficient, secure, comforting, and accessible to the entire population. In short, design can help compensate for patients' physical and psychological losses and allow them as much freedom as possible.

Discussion Questions

1. Discuss the design of a patient room in a long-term care facility, taking into consideration the need for natural elements and privacy.

2. How might emerging technology be used to help ensure the safety of dementia sufferers patients (particularly wanderers) while still affording them privacy?

3. Discuss ways to decrease the perceived "invisibility" of patients in hospitals and long-term care facilities. How can design influence their sense of self and help maintain their identity?

4. Discuss the design and layout of a healthcare facility from a healthy visitor's point of view. What psychological effect does entering the facility have on healthy people? How might the facility's design change their behavior and responses?

5. Consider the previous chapter's information regarding playgrounds. How might indoor and outdoor play areas be incorporated for children and adolescents in healthcare facilities? What effect might a play area for visiting children have for improving patient moods in long-term care facilities?

6. Discuss programs that could help to reduce patient stress in healthcare facilities.

7. Discuss ways to modify the perception of the role of patient. How might healthcare workers help to promote a healthy psychological response to illness?

8. How do you recover from stressful events? How might that knowledge be used to inform your design decisions for healthcare facilities? What role does the natural environment play in your recuperation?

9. What design elements can help control lighting for patients? What technology is available for maintaining a regular lighting schedule to help minimize the effects of the winter and summer solstices?

10. Discuss the concept of home. What makes a location feel cozy and "homey"? How can these qualities be incorporated into healthcare facilities?

11. What materials are most effective for ensuring the safety of patients? How can they be used to make patients feel comfortable and secure without overwhelming them with restraints or other equipment?

Learning Activities

1. Divide into groups of five. Each group member will visit a different healthcare environment. Take notes on the design of these different environments, and report your observations to your group and then the class.

2. Design the lobby of a hospital, paying particular attention to wayfinding mechanisms. Discuss the reasons why you chose certain mechanisms.

3. Illustrate a floor plan for an long-term care facility that houses many patients suffering from dementia.

4. Compare and contrast the purposes and needs of the five different healthcare facilities noted in the text. Be sure to compare average facility sizes, lengths of stay, ages of patients, square footage of patient rooms, available recreational facilities, and so on.

5. Contact a local healthcare facility and arrange to meet with staff members when they are off duty or on break. Discuss the facility's design and determine if the layout of the hospital is conducive to an effective and satisfactory work environment. Are design issues interfer-

ing with patient care? Does the facility itself hamper or improve the staff's emotional responses to daily situations?

6. Design a hospital room for a child. Consider needs for companionship, toys, comfort, privacy, and safety. How might children respond to different styles of rooms?

7. Research interior surfacing and upholstery materials created by new technologies. How might they be used to improve appearances and comfort levels for patients? Keep in mind that, because decreased immunocompetency affects almost all patients, antibacterial and nontoxic materials are particularly effective. Provide proper citations for all articles and papers referenced.

8. Create an "admission" form that will be used to place new patients in appropriate rooms and create décor they will appreciate. Design the form to be easily understood and filled out by prospective residents of long-term care facilities.

9. Design a room in a long-term care facility that addresses the issues mentioned in the chapter. Consider the effects of intrusive negative thoughts, wandering, memory loss, disorientation, loss of balance, and so on.

10. How might a patient in an long-term care facility develop place attachment? What design features can enhance such development? Include drawings or photographs of effective displays and designs for incorporating a patient's personality in the space.

11. Design a hallway system that exhibits effective wayfinding mechanisms and minimizes the dangers associated with wandering behaviors. Create both perspective drawings and floor plans.

12. Design a garden that incorporates spaces for relaxation, stimulation, activity, social interaction, and rehabilitation. Keep in mind the need for patient safety and observation.

13. The text notes the use of architectural features to minimize the institutional feel of a hospital or long-term care facility and support wayfinding. Create a precedent collage depicting modern structures designed to feel more approachable and accessible. Which architects and designers are proving to be effec-

tive with this approach? What techniques are they implementing?

Terminology

acute care facility   Healthcare environment equipped to deal with emergencies, life-threatening illnesses and injuries, and surgical operations

area of rescue assistance   Space that has direct access to an exit where people who are unable to use stairs may remain temporarily in safety and await instructions or assistance during emergency evacuation

behavioral health facility   Psychological healthcare environment, such as a psychiatric hospital or mental health institution

birthing center   Facility that allows women to give birth in a home-like setting

continuing care retirement communities (CCRC)   Campus-like environment that allows residents to "age in place" as their health deteriorates

hospice   Specialized environment that provides care and comfort for terminal (dying) patients

human-scale element   Design element that is neither oversized nor undersized

immunocompetency   Ability or capacity for the immune system to respond or function adequately

long-term care facility   Residential environment for individuals (usually elderly) who require routine medical care and assistance with activities of daily living; also called nursing or convalescent home

music stream   Constant flow or stream of pleasurable, musical background noise

pediatric hospital   Specialized hospital dedicated exclusively to the care of infants and children

rehabilitation facility   Extended-stay environment that provides multidisciplinary physical restorative services in which patients work to regain their health after accidents, strokes, and so on

sick role   Patient role we assume when we are sick or injured that affects our cognitive processes, behaviors, and medical outcomes

special care unit (SCU)   Separate area within a

healthcare facility that provides specific services (e.g., emergency, pediatric, or rehabilitation services)

References

1. Sloane, D. C. (1994). Scientific paragon to hospital mall: The evolving design of the hospital, 1885–1994. *Journal of Architectural Education, 48-2,* 82–98.

2. Brannon, L., and Feist, J. (1997). *Health psychology: An introduction to behavior and health* (3rd ed.). Pacific Grove, CA: Brooks/Cole.

3. Planetree. Available at: www.planetree.org. Retrieved June 21, 2005.

4. Schwarz, B. (1997). Nursing home design: A misguided architectural model. *Journal of Architectural and Planning Research, 14-4,* 343–359.

5. Martin, P.Y. (2002). Sensations, bodies, and the "spirit of a place": Aesthetics in residential organizations for the elderly. *Human Relations, 56-7,* 861–885.

6. Leventhal-Stern, A., MacRae, S., Gerteis, M., Harrison, T., Fowler, E., Edgman-Levitan, S., Walker, J., and Ruga, W. (2003). Understanding the consumer perspective to improve design quality. *Journal of Architectural and Planning Research, 20-1,* 16–28.

7. Tuan, Y. F. 1974. *Topophilia: A study of environmental perception, attitudes, and values.* Prentice-Hall, Englewood Cliffs, N.J.

8. Hummon, D. M. (1992). Community attachment: Local sentiment and sense of place. In I. Altman & S.M. Low (Eds.) *Human behavior and environment; Advances in theory and research: Place attachment.* New York: Plenum

9. See note 2.

10. Sumaya, I. C., Rienzi, B. M., Deegan II, J. F., and Moss, D. E. (2001). Bright light treatment decreases depression in institutionalized older adults: A placebo-controlled crossover study. *Journal of Gerontology: Medical Sciences,* 56A-6, M356–M360.

11. Lutgendorf, S. K., Reimer, T. T., Harvey, J. H., Marks, G., Hong, S. Y., Hillis, S. L., and Lubaroff, D. M. (2001). Effects of housing relocation on immunocompetence and psychosocial functioning in older adults. *Journal of Gerontology: Medical Sciences,* 56A-2, M97–M105.

12. See note 2.

13. See note 5.

14. See note 14.

15. Kaplan, S., and Kaplan, R. (1989). *The Experience of nature.* Cambridge University Press.

16. Morgan, D. G., and Stewart, N. J. (1999). Multiple occupancy versus private rooms on dementia care units. *Environment and Behavior, 30-4,* 48–503.

17. Day, K., and Cohen, U. (2000). The role of culture in designing environments for people with dementia: A study of Russian Jewish immigrants. *Environment and Behavior, 32-3,* 361–399.

18. See note 2.

19. See note 2.

20. See note 11.

21. Whitehouse, S., Varni, J. W., Seid, M., Cooper-Marcus, C., Ensberg, M. J., Jacobs, J. R., and Mehlenbeck, R. S. (2001). Evaluating a children's hospital garden environment: Utilization and consumer satisfaction. *Journal of Environmental Psychology, 21-3,* 301–314.

22. Ulrich, R. S. (1984). View from a window may influence recovery from surgery. *Science, 224,* 420–421.

23. Larsen, L., Adams, J., Deal, B., Kweon, B., Tyler, E. (1998) "Plants in the workplace: The effects of plant density on productivity, attitudes, and perceptions." *Environment and Behavior 30(3):* 261-281.

24. Friedrich, M. J. (1999). The arts of healing. *JAMA Medical News & Perspectives, 281 (19),* 1779–1781.

25. See note 5.

26. Young, C. A., and Brewer, K. P. (2001). Marketing continuing care retirement communities: A model of residents' perceptions of quality. *Journal of Hospitality & Leisure Marketing, 9-1/2,* 133–151.

27. See note 5.

28. See note 26.

29. Passini, R., Pigot, H., Rainville, C., and Tetreault, M. H. (2000). Wayfinding in a nursing home for advanced dementia of the Alzheimer's type. *Environment and Behavior, 32-5,* 684–710.

30. See note 5.

31. Eshelman, P. E., and Evans, G. W. (2002). Home again: Environmental predictors of place attachment and self-esteem for new retirement community residents. *Journal of Interior Design, 28-1*, 3–9.

32. Sugihara, S., and Evans, G. W. (2000). Place attachment and social support at continuing care retirement communities. *Environment and Behavior, 32-3*, 400–409.

33. Kari, J. A., Donovan, C., Li, J., and Taylor, B. (1999). Teenagers in hospital: What do they want? *Nursing Standard, 13-23*, 49–51.

34. Haq, S., and Zimring, C. (2003). Just down the road a piece: The development of topological knowledge of building layouts. *Environment and Behavior, 35-1*, 132–160.

35. Persad, C. C., Giordani, B., Chen, H. C., Ashton-Miller, J.A., Alexander, N.B., Wilson, C. S., Berent, S., Guire, K., and Schultz, A. B. (1995). Neuropsychological predictors of complex obstacle avoidance in healthy older adults. *Journal of Gerontology: Psychological Sciences*, 50B-5, P272–P277.

36. See note 6.

37. See note 29.

38. Passini, R., Rainville, C., Marchand, N., and Joanette, Y. (1998). Wayfinding and dementia: Some research findings and a new look at design. *Journal of Architectural and Planning Research, 15-2*, 133–151.

39. See note 34.

40. See note 29.

41. See note 38.

42. See note 29.

43. See note 17.

44. See note 38.

45. Logsdon, R. G., Teri, L., McCurry, S. M., Gibbons, L. E., Kukull, W. A., and Larson, E. B. (1998). Wandering: A significant problem among community-residing individuals with Alzheimer's disease. *Journal of Gerontology: Psychological Sciences*, 53B-5, P294–P299.

46. Dickinson, J., and McLain-Kark, J. (1996). Wandering behavior associated with Alzheimer's disease and related dementias: Implications for designers. *Journal of Interior Design, 22-1*, 32–38.

47. See note 46.

48. See note 46.

49. See note 29.

50. See note 38.

51. See note 29.

52. See note 45.

53. See note 46.

54. See note 29.

55. Zeisel, J. (2000). Environmental design effects on Alzheimer symptoms in long-term care residences. *World Hospitals and Health Services, 36-3*, 27–31.

56. Ziesel, J. Information on Alzheimer's disease presented 11 Feb 2005 at NewSchool of Architecture and Design, San Diego, CA.

57. See note 46.

58. Cohen, U., Weissman G., (1991). *Holding on to home: Designing environments for people with dementia*, Baltimore: John Hopkins University Press.

59. Maslow, A. H. (1970). *Motivation and personality* (2nd ed.). New York: Harper & Row.

60. See note 31.

61. See note 5.

62. See note 31.

63. See note 31.

64. See note 29.

65. See note 46.

66. See note 29.

67. See note 55.

68. See note 17.

69. See note 17.

70. See note 34.

71. See note 5.

72. See note 55.

73. See note 17.

74. See note 29.

75. See note 17.

76. See note 10.

77. La Garce, M. (2002). Control of environmental lighting and its effects on behaviors of the Alzheimer's type. *Journal of Interior Design, 28-2*, 15–25.

78. Sloane, P. D., Mitchell, C. M., Weisman, G., Zimmerman, S., Long-Foley, K. M., Lynn, M., Calkins, M., Lawton, M. P., Teresi, J., Grant, L., Lindeman, D., and Montgomery, R. (2002). The Therapeutic Environment Screening Survey for Nursing Homes (TESS-NH): An

observational instrument for assessing the physical environment of institutional settings for persons with dementia. *Journal of Gerontology: Social Sciences*, 57B-2, S69–S78.

79. See note 29.
80. See note 78.
81. Chu, L. W., Pei, C. K. W., Chiu, A., Liu, K., Chu, M.L., Wong, S., and Wong, A. (1999). Risk factors for falls in hospitalized older medical patients. *Journal of Gerontology*, 54A-1, M38–M43.
82. See note 55.
83. Marsden, J. P. (1999). Older persons' and family members' perceptions of homeyness in assisted living. *Environment and Behavior, 31-1,* 84–106.
84. See note 83.
85. See note 29.
86. See note 38.
87. See note 55.
88. Chen, H. C., Schultz, A. B., Ashton-Miller, J. A., Giordani, B., Alexander, N. B., and Guire, K. E. (1996). Stepping over obstacles: Dividing attention impairs performance of old more than young adults. *Journal of Gerontology*, 51A-3, M116–M122.
89. See note 29.

90. Osterberg, A. E., Davis, A. M., and Danielson, L. D. (1995). Universal design: The users' perspective. *Housing and Society, 22-1/2,* 92–113.
91. See note 29.
92. See note 17.
93. See note 29.
94. See note 16.
95. See note 29.
96. See note 38.
97. See note 29.
98. See note 34.
99. See note 38.
100. See note 29.
101. See note 56.
102. See note 17.
103. See note 55.
104. See note 21.
105. See note 21.
106. See note 22.
107. See note 6.
108. See note 31.
109. See note 16.
110. See note 31.
111. See note 55.
112. See note 5.
113. See note 38.

TWELVE

stress, anxiety, depression, and low self-esteem.[23] Although every job and every workplace has stressful elements, people who are dissatisfied with their jobs experience higher levels of negative stress, which may be related to the early onset of cardiovascular disease.[24] Sources of work-related stress can be physical (e.g., repetitive movements, such as typing and lifting; ambient environmental conditions, such as noise, temperature, and indoor pollutant levels; or the lack of suitable furnishings, tools, or illumination), psychological (e.g., pressure created by time clocks, deadlines, or budgets and fear of being reprimanded or fired), and/or social (e.g., embarrassment, harassment, or exploitation by supervisors or coworkers).[25]

Computer technology may be considered a mixed blessing for office workers. More work can be done by fewer people, which can increase production levels as well as reduce the need for new or expanded facilities for workers or archive storage. However, when we work with computers, we do it sitting down, and decreased physical activity contributes to the decline of our overall health status—as do a range of other computer-related worker ailments (e.g., strained eyes, necks, shoulders, and backs; headaches; carpal tunnel syndrome) that result in thousands of disability and workers' compensation insurance claims around the world each year.

Workplace culture is strongly affected by the moods of the individuals who make up the organization. We naturally compare our moods with those of others around us, which we unconsciously assess through many media (e.g., "reading" facial expressions, body postures, gestures, and levels of eye contact); and consistently bad moods negatively affect others' overall satisfaction and stress levels.[26] People who have a need for absolute control are usually highly stressed and often frustrated; their constant dissatisfaction can easily spread up or down the corporate structure until it affects an entire office, department, or company. To illustrate, a clerk's chronic bad mood irritates a secretary, who then is rude to the manager, who then argues with the owner, who then decides to cancel the company picnic.

The consequences of physical and psychological workplace stress cost millions of dollars annually in insurance payments deriving from company-funded workers' compensation and government-funded disability programs. Employers and government agencies around the world are concerned about the growth in workplace stress and the decrease in worker satisfaction[27] and are taking proactive measures to overcome these challenges—many of which can be alleviated or ameliorated by design initiatives. For example, planners and designers can proactively apply the principles of **ergonomics** (the fit between people, their work activities, equipment, work systems, and environment to ensure that workplaces are safe, comfortable, and efficient and that productivity is not compromised) to eliminate or minimize, as much as possible, other cumulative- and repetitive-stress injury factors that are intrinsic to the office workplace (Box 12.1).

Box 12.1 Ergonomics in Office Design

Ergonomics is an important design consideration, especially in the workplace. When workers are uncomfortable or in pain, their productivity and morale decline; worse, an acute discomfort can lead to a chronic or permanent affliction that negatively affects a worker's overall quality of life. Employers pay millions annually in workers' compensation benefits (including rehabilitative training) for employees who have sustained injuries as a result of poor ergonomics. Figure 12.3 illustrates an ergonomic sitting position. As greater numbers of employees work with computers, the ergonomic design of office workstations, including proper distance and placement of computer monitors and keyboards, becomes increasingly important.

Figure 12.3: The proper ergonomic sitting position

Sick Building Syndrome

Sick building syndrome is a serious health problem. Thousands of people each year report a host of illnesses related to respiratory problems, headaches, and fatigue; chronic coughing and overactive sinuses; and chronic eye, nose, and throat irritations.[28] Many workplace environments display circumstances and attributes that cause SBS. Poor indoor air quality results from air-conditioned rooms, sealed windows, limited ventilation, and lack of natural light, and these conditions seem to promote symptoms related to SBS.[29] Research indicates that carbon dioxide (CO_2) levels, in combination with other indoor pollutants—such as volatile organic compounds (VOCs) released by building materials, office machines, and cleaning products and equipment, human *bioeffluents*, formaldehyde found in carpets and furniture, and dust—are responsible for symptoms related to SBS.[30]

One research team noted that women's tendency to report SBS-related symptoms more often than men may be related to differences in biology, work patterns, or gender roles (e.g., men are taught not to show vulnerability by expressing discomfort) or to a combination of these factors.[31] In their study, three types of employees were more likely to complain of SBS-related symptoms: professional, educated women who shared office space with many other people, experienced allergy-related symptoms, and smoked; men who had an *external locus of control*, were younger than 31 or older than 50 years of age, and suffered from an acute illness; and employees who had less education, suffered from an acute illness or allergies, and had low job satisfaction.

Some symptoms associated with SBS can be attributed to psychological rather than physiological factors. Such cases tend to be related to low job satisfaction, high job-related stress, and beliefs or expectations that some environmental factor will make the individual sick. For example, many people believe that they will get sick from air-conditioning. This notion is supported by a research team whose test subjects experienced more symptoms related to poor indoor air quality when they were stressed from work than when engaged in nonwork-related activities.[32] Thus, the question remains: Is it the air conditioning that is making them sick, or is it their belief that they will get sick from air-conditioning?

Research supports the idea that more SBS symptoms occur in air-conditioned buildings than in those that are mechanically ventilated.[33] The problem lies not with air-conditioning, per se, but rather with the mechanical systems and the air itself, especially in buildings that are tightly sealed. When we breathe, we take in oxygen and release CO_2, and oxygen levels cannot be replenished by re-circulated air. Increased CO_2 levels are associated with sore throats, nasal irritation, inflamed sinuses, tight chests, and wheezing, and decreased oxygen levels are related to higher levels of fatigue.[34] Air-conditioning systems re-circulate indoor air that is already contaminated by various pollutants; and worsen indoor air quality throughout the space by adding dust and bacteria from dirty ducts[35] (Figure 12.4).

Figure 12.4: Many copy rooms in corporate settings are small spaces that house many pieces of equipment and have poor, if any, ventilation; in such spaces, the concentration of environmental pollutants derived from the surface materials and the office equipment can easily reach toxic levels.

Figure 12.5: In this idealized office space, a large aquarium takes up much of the far right wall. The cubicle walls have smooth leather surfaces and are enhanced by glass extensions, which increase levels of audial privacy and natural light. The plants dispersed around the space not only add natural elements but also increase oxygen levels while decreasing CO_2 levels. Note that there are no ventilation ducts blowing directly into the work spaces.

Carpeting, draperies, upholstered furniture and seat cushions, and fabric-covered partitions are significant sources of known allergens (e.g., dust, dust mites) and increased static loads. Replacing carpeting with vinyl flooring may not improve indoor air quality because vinyl can be a significant source of VOCs; therefore, consider using ceramic tile or simulated wood flooring composed of nontoxic materials (e.g., wood particles or other cellulose products) as well as nontoxic adhesives.

DESIGN APPLICATION. Planners and designers can help reduce concentrations of indoor pollutants by utilizing better designs, building materials, and ventilation systems, thus reducing SBS-related symptoms.[36] Tall, leafy plants liberally distributed throughout an office space will help to reduce CO_2 levels while increasing oxygen levels; leather surfaces on partitions are easily cleaned and provide less surface area to which bacteria and allergens can adhere; and use of antimicrobial paint inside air ducts along with routine cleanings of air filters will reduce levels of re-circulated matter. However, few organizations are willing to incur the additional expenses of installation and upkeep inherent in such designs (Figure 12.5).

The Corporate Environment

The corporate environment is complex and serves multiple functions. In one regard it is a place to conduct business transactions and, as such, should provide a level of comfort and convenience appropriate to successful work performance. In another regard it is a reflection of the company's image (e.g., attention to detail, organization, competency) and therefore necessitates a high degree of order and efficiency. Still another of its functions in hierarchical organizations is to establish rank and support the corporate structure; through placement and design, both insiders and outsiders are made aware of an employee's status within the organization. As such, the spatial organization of an office environment not only affects how people communicate and collaborate within the corporate environment but also serves to support and reinforce an organization's desired social climate or workplace culture.

Office Layout

Within the traditional hierarchical workplace, it is common to see the lower ranking employees working in a large area with small cubicle-type office space. As rank increases, offices become larger and more private, with the pinnacle being the proverbial "corner office." It is understood in this traditional structure that with rank comes the more prestigious and pleasant office type and location. This visible separation of employees by rank enforces the hierarchical mores of such environments and lends itself well to the autocratic style of corporate management. Little doubt is left in the minds of employees and customers as to corporate status when they enter this domain. The design of this workplace environment lays out an unwritten statement about the type of conduct that is acceptable in the different office areas and serves as a type of societal control mechanism.

Every group of persons associated in work is technically a "team," but workplace structures cannot support truly collaborative efforts when the "goal" of the game is to get the corner office with the best view. Although many corporations strive to develop team approaches, working as a team can be a challenge for team members and within supervisor–subordinate relationships, especially when office designs support the power hierarchy by giving the persons in charge private offices and the support staff cubicles or open workstations. A case study of an organization that pursued greater teamwork values through environmental modification found that, although the workstations had been arranged to promote collaborative production, workers did not function as teams when the project managers were given private offices and the su-

pervisors were placed in offices near windows, therefore reinforcing a hierarchical power structure.[37]

New trends in workplace design are more focused on the notion of teamwork and interpersonal communication. Although cubicles of some sort are provided, along with individual offices to allow for private meetings as necessary, more communal spaces are being included in office layouts.[38] In these more open office plans, people of varying ranks work in the same environment to facilitate communication. The offices of Pacific Sunwear of California, in Anaheim, California, provide an example. Their design, by H. Hendy Associates, incorporates an isle between cubicles that is furnished with long tables to encourage dialogue between employees and teamwork on projects.[39] Also included in many facilities catering to collaborative workplace environments are communal areas for discussions and work breaks. These communal spaces encourage office-wide communication and diminish hierarchical relationships. Often the design of these areas is based on input from the employees who will be using the spaces, which gives workers a sense of ownership and territoriality.[40]

Open Office Plans

Many organizations use open office plans, which are based on the concept that, due to the minimization of physical barriers, employees will be more likely to increase communication and collaborative efforts. Open office plans can provide both financial and spatial conservation (i.e., portable, modular furnishings are less expensive and occupy less floor space than constructed partitions) and are popular with organizations that are highly dependent on creativity; walls and work spaces can be easily reconfigured, which facilitates adaptability and competitiveness. The use of open office spaces allows flexibility in office layout, which can easily meet the changing needs of an organization, and is often associated with increased teamwork; however, research findings are mixed.[41] Open office designs are insufficient to meet privacy needs, and visual and aural distractions—consequences of a lack of privacy—both decrease worker productivity and increase the frequency of errors.[42] Although open office plans were promoted as being a cheaper way to build, they have been scientifically

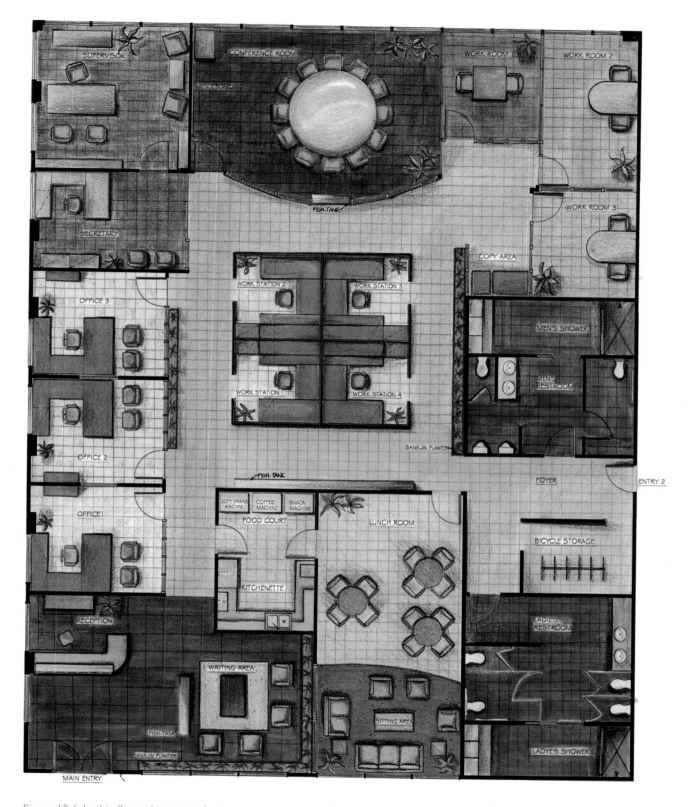

Figure 12.6: In this floor plan, two private rooms can be used by any employee who needs audial privacy to meet with a client, write a report, or participate in a teleconference. The locker room equipped with a shower serves workers who cycle to and from work or exercise during lunch breaks. The indoor storage space protects bicycles from the elements (both natural and criminal).

demonstrated to have inherent costs that offset these initial savings.

People associate psychological privacy with architectural privacy (i.e., physical barriers), and common complaints regarding open offices are related to disturbances and lack of privacy among employees.[43] Because of the greater *social density* and the lack of modifiers (i.e., walls), employees' moods are more likely to affect others; however, shared feelings can lead either to positive outcomes, such as a strong team spirit, or negative outcomes, such as low employee morale and satisfaction levels.[44] Studies of open plan offices have shown increases in worker interaction and problem solving, but also more instances of interruptions and privacy violations.[45]

DESIGN APPLICATION. Limited visual and aural privacy can cause employees to limit their communication with other employees, which reduces overall communication; therefore, consider providing break or conference rooms for private conversations and telephone calls, meetings, and specific tasks requiring concentration.[46] Privacy needs within the workplace vary depending on the work and the needs of the individual;[47] therefore, before opting for an open office plan, consider the privacy needs of the employees.[48] Figure 12.6 shows one approach to meet privacy needs and enhance worker satisfaction.

For more information about the Hawthorne Studies, see Chapter 1.

Personalization

Workplace personalization serves to signify individuality and identity, mark territories, and regulate social interactions, and leads to a positive workplace culture, higher employee morale, and less employee turnover.[49] Some employers believe that office "clutter" is a mark of inefficiency and chaos, and therefore their company policies prohibit employees from personalizing their workstations, whereas others allow or even encourage personalization as an expression of individuality and a symbol of the individual's contribution to the corporation. Unfortunately, the ability to work more efficiently in an apparently haphazard work space is of little concern to many employers who gladly opt for reduced production in exchange for the illusion of better organization and a stronger public image.

Personalization can positively affect not only the individual's environmental satisfaction, well-being, and overall job satisfaction, but also the corporate culture.[50] Women personalize their work spaces more than men; whereas men traditionally have personalized their work spaces with items associated with status, such as diplomas, awards, and trophies, women's workplaces are more expressive of their identity, individuality, and emotions.[51] This difference in office personalization represents a shift from competition to personal relationships. However the personalization of office work space is perceived, employee satisfaction with the physical environment correlates to how much employees are allowed to personalize in relation to how much they would like to personalize and to what extent they can influence the work space arrangement.[52]

Office Design and Décor

In the 1920s, a group of researchers theorized that improved environmental conditions would positively correlate to increased worker productivity (e.g., the Hawthorne studies). Although this theory was never proved, the study did reveal that social factors influence employee satisfaction and efficiency.[53] The physical environment is a setting for social interactions,[54] but whereas physical design of the workplace has historically been used to establish social control over employees, recent studies have been examining the workplace as a means of promoting employee empowerment.[55] From this perspective, the ideal work environment supports high levels of performance and job satisfaction by enabling employees to conduct their work in distraction-free environments, receive support from unplanned interactions, and engage in uninterrupted meetings and group projects.[56]

Cornell University's International Workplace Studies Program (IWSP) concluded that a successful collaborative work environment possesses these criteria: It reflects the team's sense of identity, facilitates communication and task accomplishment, is adaptable to changes in the team and the organization, and enforces rules and policies that support the other four criteria.[57] How and to what degree each of these criteria is incorporated into the overall design affects the end result. Workplace designs provide not only opportunities to build allegiances between workers and the organization, but also ways for outsiders to glimpse the values and norms of the organization's constituency.[58]

A person's satisfaction with the work environment is directly related to job satisfaction and indirectly related to productivity[59] and is influenced by perceived levels of privacy, freedom, and control. Although personal territories are an important aspect of all environmental settings, the workplace engenders many ambiguities related to territorial control. On the one hand, the employer controls the territory; therefore, many supervisors believe this gives them the right to enter or occupy a subordinate's territory at will (i.e., commit *territorial violation*). On the other hand, employees often feel free not only to utilize work spaces that are temporarily unoccupied, but also to leave behind vestiges of their occupation, or *territorial contamination*. Not surprisingly, doors and locks provide the greatest degree of territorial control, while cubicles and open office designs afford the greatest opportunities for *territorial infringement*. In cubicle layouts, employees often establish their spaces through décor and the treatment of boundaries, signs, colors, and artwork. These items serve as territorial markers that provide a sense of identity, control, and purpose among workplace occupants.[60] If employees cannot make their environment their own, they are less likely to "bond" with the company and more likely to seek employment elsewhere.

Research demonstrates that people are more comfortable in interior spaces that are decorated than in those that are not.[61] Employees in work spaces with little or no architectural detail feel deprived, and compensate for feelings of embarrassment, loss of prestige, and vulnerability with behaviors ranging from social withdrawal to quitting and filing suit for damages.[62] Incorporating details, such as privacy spaces, can facilitate employee feelings of "being special," which typically translate into higher morale and job satisfaction. Even a low level of visual stimulation, such as that provided by variation in table and desk shapes, is vital to worker satisfaction. In one study, researchers showed that aesthetics, privacy, furniture, communication, temperature control, and lighting were related to job performance, quality communication, and satisfaction with the environment.[63]

A company's social environment also has a strong impact on worker satisfaction. Social expectations (e.g., attending the company picnic), enculturation (e.g., being a liberal among a majority of conservatives), and expected behavioral norms (e.g., working 60-hour weeks) are subtle variables that can lower employee satisfaction levels.

DESIGN APPLICATION. Design professionals must understand the nature of work to be conducted (e.g., creative development versus repetitive tasks) before they can develop supportive workplace designs. One group of researchers asserts that a physical work environment can promote creativity when it facilitates positive social-psychological conditions such as freedom, sharing, trust, support, and respect. Contending that dynamic environments facilitate creativity, these researchers suggest creating settings that inspire intensity and vigor.[64] Another research team concludes that more stimuli (e.g., brighter or warmer colors, increased visual and aural stimuli) should be incorporated into work spaces in which routine or low-demand tasks are performed, and fewer stimuli (e.g., cooler or darker colors, artwork depicting nature scenes) for those settings in which creative or high-demand tasks are performed.[65] Their study found that the beat of music or repetitive sounds (such as water from an aquarium or fountain) can help to establish a rhythm and may increase productivity levels for routine tasks; participants whose work spaces were designed in blue appeared calmer, perceived more privacy and lower temperatures, and were more focused on their tasks.

To facilitate work space privacy, incorporate conference rooms that will accommodate worker interaction without distracting others, as well as floor-to-ceiling walls, solid doors, and sidelights (e.g., partition windows) with window treatments; be aware that five-foot partitions provide limited visual privacy whereas seven-foot partitions provide both visual and audial privacy[66] (Figure 12.7).

Consider providing attractive, comfortable, nonwork related areas within the work facility.[67] An ideal work space will have provisions for people who cycle or jog to work; a place where meals can be stored, prepared, and eaten; and

Figure 12.7 (above): Many open office environments, including those with cubicles, provide private rooms that can be used by employees on an as-needed basis to ensure their audial privacy.

Figure 12.8 (right): This cafeteria space affords employees comfortable chairs, large windows that allow for natural light and views, and lots of open space for impromptu gatherings.

quiet, relaxing places where people can escape the stressors associated with the job. Locker rooms, shower facilities, sitting rooms, kitchenettes, and cafeterias go a long way toward increasing job satisfaction and reducing job-related stress (Figure 12.8). Planners and designers can help to increase workers' perceptions of spaces by incorporating large, unobstructed windows to bring in more natural light; enhancing artificial lighting with full-spectrum, diffused ceiling lighting, which will enable people to move about the room safely; incorporating task lamps at each desk to illuminate the task at hand; and using lighter and brighter colors as well as furnishings with smooth, simple lines. Also consider the use of indoor atriums in which offices may be organized.

For more on the attention restoration theory, see Chapter 2.

Windows

Views of nature are fundamental to human satisfaction and well-being, and windows can help by providing opportunities for *prospect-refuge*.[68] Workers increasingly are being housed in artificially illuminated office spaces where they spend a significant amount of time using computers, TVs, and other video display screens, all of which have been shown to cause mental and physical fatigue.[69] Mental fa-

tigue can lead to other negative side effects, including irritability, anxiety, depression, and obesity (i.e., if a person is mentally exhausted, he or she is less likely to exercise and more likely to slip into bouts of depression).

Mental fatigue caused by excessive *directed attention* can be reduced or eliminated via methods based on *attention restoration theory* (ART).[70] Copious research has determined that window views of nature positively affect the health and well-being of building occupants, and views have a restorative value in relation to stress at work; one research team contends that it is primarily the presence of windows and the penetration of sunlight into the workplace that are related to increased worker satisfaction and well-being[71–73] (Figure 12.9).

DESIGN APPLICATION. Access to natural light is highly desirable for office workers and positively influences worker satisfaction.[74–76] Designers must consider the quality and amount of sun exposure, as well as the ability to reduce or enhance sunlight penetration in developing designs that provide views of natural environments.[77] Design initiatives that incorporate sunlight and views of nature can provide brief *restorative experiences* that, if ac-

cumulated over time, can forestall the need for long breaks and reduce emotional and mental fatigue.[78]

Illumination

Illumination is simply a measure of visible light striking a surface. The purpose of a lighting system is to place light and shadow where they are needed, but only high-quality lighting responds to its space and provides good visibility, comfort, and safety.[79] **Luminance** is the brightness of an object, whereas **illuminance** is the amount of light seen on a surface.[80] *Ordered* lighting results when the layout of the light source is proportional to that of the space; *coherent* lighting produces even modeling or shading across the space.[81] Every interior space is unique, and every lighting system should meet the requirements of not only the owner and the occupants, but also the space itself; systems that provide too much or too little light are wasteful, and our understanding of a space and the appearance of it can be diminished if the lighting conflicts with the architectural structure.[82]

Lighting affects our well-being on many levels—visibility, activity, communication, mood and comfort, health and safety, and aesthetic judgment—and interior lighting design, utilizing natural or artificial lighting, must respond to all of these needs.[83] Although sunlight has greater beneficial effects than does artificial illumination, the general level of interior sunlight is less important than the size of the sunlit area.[84]

Overhead fluorescent fixtures are the most common sources of workplace lighting. The component of a fluorescent **luminaire** (light fixture) that provides the starting voltage and operating current is called the *ballast*. Whereas high-frequency ballasts supply current electronically, conventional ballasts supply current electromagnetically and usually cause light flicker and audible hum. Fluorescent-light flicker is not always visible to the human eye, but even at very low levels, it can be detected by the central nervous system and lead to physiological arousal; it has a greater impact on people who suffer from headaches, stress, and visual discomfort and can become especially stressful in spaces that lack natural light.[85] This flicker frequency has been known to negatively affect women and children, in particular.

In one study, the light from fluorescent lamps

Figure 12.9: Courtyards strategically placed in large buildings serve to increase window space and allow more natural light to penetrate. Those that are well landscaped and maintained provide green spaces, which give employees opportunities for *attention restoration* amid plants and flowers during breaks. However, enclosed courtyards can become echo chambers; reverberation enhances noise levels and may require that designers make sound-absorption modifications to the overall design.

powered by high-frequency ballasts was perceived as more pleasant than light powered by conventional ballasts, and subjects who were sensitive to flicker exhibited a sharp contraction of EEG-alpha waves (an indication of arousal), increased performance speed, and decreased performance accuracy when exposed to the conventional-ballast condition.[86] Other researchers have cited numerous early studies that demonstrated that luminous flickering affects neural activity, visual performance (including reading ability), and headaches; their findings reveal that the use of high-frequency ballasts reduces the negative effects of fluorescent light flicker on performance and physiological arousal.[87, 88]

Manufacturers of full-spectrum fluorescent lamps (i.e., those that mimic daylight) assert that their use improves people's performance, vision, and mood, but existing research only confirms improved accuracy in distinguishing colors. Reports of beneficial effects on performance and mood are likely influenced by personal beliefs and expectations rather than the lamps' actual characteristics.[89]

DESIGN APPLICATION. Consider designing lighting systems so that indirect lighting accounts for 60 percent or more of total horizontal illuminance because direct (downlight) illumination casts more shadows and makes rooms seem smaller and less spacious than does indirect (uplight) illumination, and direct-to-indirect lighting ratios affect brightness, shadowing, visual comfort, uniformity of light distribution, perceptions of spaciousness, and overall workplace satisfaction.[90] Inadequate or improper lighting can result in glare or shadows; light from general, ambient, and indirect lighting is often more suitable for working horizontally with paper documents than for working vertically with computers; and glare can cause eyestrain and headaches as well as contribute to accidents and stress.[91] It is important to note that computer monitors and other video display terminals (VDTs) or screens produce glare and also reflect light from other sources.

Home Offices

Telecommuters, small business owners, independent contractors, freelance consultants, and artists of all sorts make up the home-based workforce, and a growing number of people are opting to work from home.[92] Worker benefits include increased job satisfaction related to greater flexibility and control over the work itself, as well as freedom from the constraints of corporate life (e.g., commuting issues, standard work hours and dress codes, office politics, and so on); corporate benefits include the retention of valued employees, increased production rates and work quality, and a reduced need for new or larger facilities.[93] Environmental benefits include reduced commuter congestion and improved air quality.

Working from home may seem like an ideal situation, but it can create conflict between work, family, and free time; and home offices offer very few opportunities for social interaction. Therefore, it is important to design the residential environment so as to support both professional and personal activities without sacrificing either. One researcher, noting that spatial boundaries seem to be more effective than temporal boundaries in delineating home-work environments, recommends both the physical separation of work space from the rest of the home and the restriction of work-related equipment and materials to the work space.[94] The greater the distance from the residence, the fewer distractions for the worker.

The addition or incorporation of a home office will affect both spatial and personal relationships within the household, which will lead to necessary changes in social and physical configurations of territorial boundaries.[95] Designers must work with clients to identify the best locations for home office space, particularly in smaller residences. One team's study revealed that home-based creative writers worked most commonly in home offices, but also in kitchens, basements, bedrooms, and dining and living rooms, and women used nature, memorabilia, and color to identify their work spaces, whereas men used their desk area, privacy, and size to create theirs.[96] Another study of home-based workers found that their work space selection was based on availability (90 percent), seclusion and separation (84 percent), overall size (40 percent), and views and the presence of natural light (27 percent).[97]

DESIGN APPLICATION. A home office housed in a separate building outside of the house or in a designated area of a separate space (e.g., in the garage, basement, or attic) is ideal. If this is not feasible, place the home office as far as possible from central living spaces and provide doors that will ensure privacy (Figure 12.10). For those who live in apartments, condominiums, or other smaller residences, consider the use of roll-top desks, computer armoires, or folding screens that serve as temporal boundaries by concealing the work area when the "office" is closed. For those who have the luxury of a dedicated office in a separate area of the home, provide spaces in which memorabilia and natural objects can be displayed, add a couch or easy chair to provide an alternative work position that can enhance cognitive stimula-

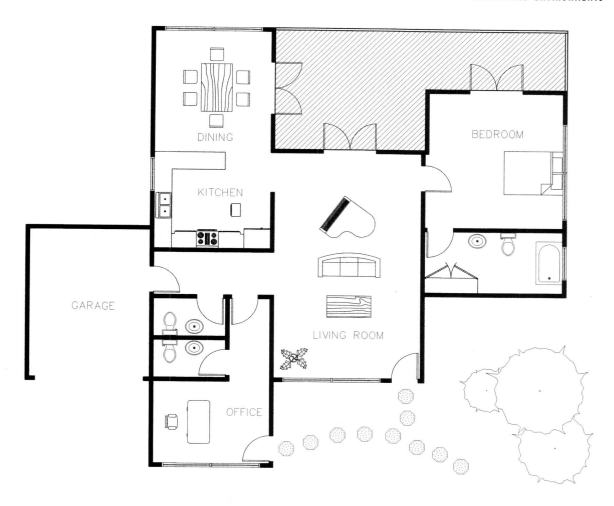

Figure 12.10: To ensure maximum productivity, home offices should be separated from the main residence as much as possible. The home office pictured here has two entryways: one exterior door and one interior door leading from the residence. This setting, with its private bathroom and dual entryways, creates an ideal home office.

tion, and incorporate general and task lighting to enhance the overall work environment.[98]

Neighborhood Work Centers

A neighborhood work center (NWC)—a cooperative facility shared by employees of different organizations—can increase employee satisfaction, reduce corporate expenses, and support the community in which it is located. Some research suggests that the concept lacks practicality, noting that confidentiality may be easily breached, particularly if one fax machine or printer serves several office spaces.[99] However, NWCs can be successful if they are designed and equipped to meet the needs of their constituency, are made available to independent contractors and consultants (i.e., freelancers) and owners of small businesses, and are conveniently located near other businesses and facilities that support the workforce (e.g., office supply stores, post offices, eateries).

NWCs reduce "main office" crowding as well as commuting times and distances, which not only decreases rush-hour traffic and air pollution levels but also allows workers more time for both work projects and home life. A nearby NWC can be a blessing for individuals who cannot cope with long commutes or who are expanding small businesses.

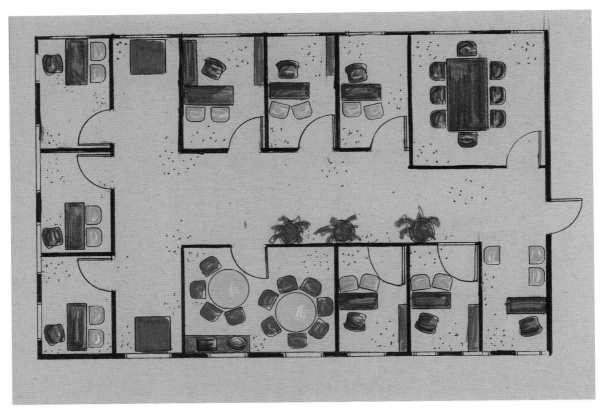

Figure 12.11: In this plan for a neighborhood work center, eight work spaces are taken care of by one receptionist (bottom right). The reception area includes a fax machine available to all occupants. The slightly larger offices on the left accommodate private fax and copy machines for occupants who deal with confidential materials and as such are precluded from communal services. Two copy machines for general use are located in front of the offices on the left. The conference room (upper right), which can be scheduled for use by any of the occupants, should have telephone, video, and conferencing access as well as accommodate modern electronic and technical equipment. Note the break area (bottom center); this communal space should be equipped with a sink, stove, refrigerator, and microwave.

Most NWC users live in the immediate or surrounding area, and the presence of an NWC can contribute to greater community cohesion, especially if the facility's design is compatible with the community's image.

In an ideal NWC, a front-office receptionist would serve as the facility's communications manager by directing visitors, mail, and deliveries; scheduling the use of conference rooms; and coordinating supply orders and maintenance activities. This person's salary and operations budget would be factored into leasing arrangements or derived from dues payments. Individual offices would be furnished with desks, shelving, and storage cabinets. In some neighborhood work centers the organization that develops the center supplies furnishings; in others, the individual corporations or entrepreneurs provide their own furnishings and are responsible for issues such as ergonomics.

Because privacy and security are of critical importance, each lease space would be provided with locking doors and equipped with a fax machine, printer, and independent phone line. The NWC would have conference rooms of different sizes that could be reserved for use by any of the occupants. These rooms would be outfitted with state-of-the-art video conferencing equipment and TVs with VCR/DVD capabilities. There would be a copy center with a keypad entry system and social rules prohibiting entrance when the room is in use, and the occupant would turn a switch that would illuminate a "Copy Room Occupied" sign in each of the other offices. Figure

12.11 illustrates many of these features in a floor plan for an NWC.

Summary Review

Today's workforce consists of men and women of varying ages, cultures, and physical abilities whose environments require many special considerations. During the past three centuries changes to the workplace environment have been fueled by historic revolutions: political, industrial, sexual, and, most recently, technological. The evolution of computer and telephone technology has remade the workplace landscape, and the future possibilities seem endless.

All work spaces have a culture that is formed and reinforced through social systems and physical conditions. Although there are myriad of ways in which the social culture can influence the overall workplace culture, perhaps the most profound is that of the physical environment, which serves as a symbolic representation of the working conditions and the social hierarchy. Every organization has an organizational structure that is either hierarchical or collaborative and promotes a management style that is either autocratic or participative.

Perhaps the most consistent element of the social workplace, regardless of its size, site, or time period, is the hierarchical organizational structure (commonly referred to as the chain of command). This "top-down" structure was advocated as a business model early in the 20th century by Frederick Taylor and can be conceptualized as a pyramid with one or more decision makers at the top, the least influential group members at the bottom, and the workload distributed throughout the hierarchy of directors, organizers, or overseers (i.e. managers and supervisors) and producers (subordinate workers). This structure has been the backbone of nearly every organization in Western society. In a corporation with a strong hierarchy, higher-level employees will have better furnishings and surroundings than will the subordinate staff. A more recent approach to workplace organization is the team approach, epitomized by the collaborative structure. Working as a team can pose challenges for both employees and supervisor–subordinate relationships, especially when office designs support the power hierarchy by giving the persons in charge private offices and the support staff cubicles or open workstations.

People's satisfaction with their jobs is determined by how well the jobs meet their work expectations. Physical work environments that meet the expectations of workers are positively associated with their level of job satisfaction. Although every workplace has stressful elements, people who are dissatisfied with their jobs experience higher levels of negative stress. Common workplace stressors include physical demands, ambient issues, social conflicts, and indoor pollutant levels. The consequences of physical and psychological workplace stress cost businesses millions of dollars annually. Ergonomic office design can reduce the physical stress experienced by employees, which includes such problems as strained eyes, necks, shoulders, and backs; headaches; and carpal tunnel syndrome.

Thousands of people each year report a host of illnesses related to respiratory problems, headaches, and fatigue; chronic coughing and overactive sinuses; and chronic eye, nose, and throat irritations related to the workplace environment. Termed sick building syndrome, this combination of symptoms has been linked to levels of carbon dioxide (CO_2), added to other indoor pollutants such as volatile organic compounds (VOCs). Although some symptoms associated with SBS can be attributed to psychological rather than physiological factors, research supports the idea that more SBS symptoms occur in air-conditioned buildings than in those that are mechanically ventilated.

The corporate environment serves as a place to conduct business, but it is also a reflection of the company's image and, in hierarchical organizations, a means to enforce rank. Through design of the corporate environment, business can be conducted more efficiently, provide a reputable image to outsiders, and support the existing hierarchy. Many organizations have opted for the open office plan, based on the idea that communication and collaborative efforts will increase among employees. The use of open office plans allow for greater flexibility in space planning and can easily meet the changes of the company. Although the open office plan has been promoted as being a cheaper way to build, science has demonstrated that it is not successful.

Workplace culture, job satisfaction, and overall employee well-being are positively linked to the ability to personalize workstations. Women tend to personalize their work spaces more than men. When men do personalize their work spaces, they tend to do so with items associated with status, where as women tend to personalize their work spaces with items that reflect their identity, individuality, and emotions.

Although personal territories are an important aspect of all environmental settings, the workplace engenders many ambiguities related to territorial control. In cubicle layouts, employees often establish their spaces through décor and the treatment of boundaries, signs, colors, and artwork. These items serve as territorial markers that provide a sense of identity, control, and purpose among workplace occupants.

Incorporating architectural details (e.g., privacy spaces) and views of nature increase employee satisfaction, morale, and well-being. Although not every interior space can have a window view, every interior space should meet the illumination requirements of the occupants. Research has shown that lighting affects our well-being on many levels, including visibility, activity, communication, mood and comfort, health and safety, and aesthetic judgment. Overhead fluorescent fixtures are the most common sources of workplace lighting, and the flicker from poor-quality fluorescent lights has been known to cause eye strain and headaches, two of the symptoms associated with sick building syndrome.

A growing number of people work from home, enjoying greater flexibility and control over the work itself, as well as freedom from the constraints of corporate life. Many corporations have embraced this trend, which can increase retention of valued employees, production rates, and work quality and decrease the need for new or larger facilities. Although working from home may seem ideal, it can create conflicts between work, family, and free time. It can also reduce social interaction. In designing the home office, it is important to establish spatial boundaries rather than relying on temporal boundaries to delineate the home work environment. The greater the distance from the office to the primary living spaces, the fewer the distractions to be incurred by the worker will be.

Therefore, designers must work with clients to identify the best locations for home office space, particularly in smaller residences.

If the home-based office poses more problems than it solves, the neighborhood work center (NWC) may provide a solution. NWCs are cooperative facilities that, when designed successfully, can meet the needs of people who telecommute but still need a physical separation between home and work. NWCs can reduce "main office" crowding as well as commuting times and distances, which not only decreases rush-hour traffic and air-pollution levels but also allows workers more time for both work projects and home life. An ideal neighborhood work center would have a front-office receptionist who would serve as the facility's communications manager by directing visitors, mail, and deliveries; schedule the use of conference rooms; and coordinate supply orders and maintenance activities. Individual offices would be furnished with desks, shelving, and storage cabinets. It would also have conference rooms of different sizes that could be reserved for use by any of the occupants, and there would be a copy center for communal use.

Our levels of job and workplace satisfaction and stress are often directly related to our expectations and perceptions. Work for one person may be a pleasure for another, but regardless of what we do and where we do it, the environment will affect our attitude and mood, and, therefore, our work performance. Our notions of work have been shaped by shifts in societal norms, and the still-evolving changes wrought by the industrial, sexual, and technological revolutions affect workplace environments on many levels. Industrial pollution and land-use issues; behavioral and physical differences as a result of gender, age, culture, and ability; and the various physical and psychological afflictions arising from the use of technology that requires repetitive actions and excessive directed attention continue to create workplace issues and circumstances yet to be resolved.

Discussion Questions

1. Define what a work space is to you. What equipment is necessary for you to work?

What environmental factors do you prefer for optimum work performance?

2. Give an example from your own experience of a work space that illustrates a hierarchical structure. How might this workplace design have affected the workers involved? How did the design affect the way you responded to your coworkers?

3. How can design encourage team camaraderie? What examples can you find?

4. Discuss how workplace design directs the attitudes of employees and visitors.

5. How could ambient music and sounds be used to improve worker mood and efficiency? How can design be used to enhance this improvement?

6. How can color be used throughout an office to subtly direct moods and behaviors?

7. What methods can be utilized to give workers privacy without isolating them from each other?

8. Discuss the role of illumination in a typical office. What can be done during the design process to create flexible lighting that will allow multiple users to perform various tasks?

9. What techniques and equipment can be used to modify an existing space to help prevent SBS?

10. Discuss the benefits and liabilities of working from home or from NWCs.

Learning Activities

1. Design your interpretation of an ideal office space.

2. Visit a local office (preferably with fewer than 25 employees) and ask for a tour of the facility. Sketch the office layout, noting how the office is designed and the structure of the organization. Indicate which areas receive natural daylight (and at what times) as well as all other environmental features.

3. Research the types of injury, illness, or stress related to work done on computers. What percentage of the American workforce spends most of their time at work on a computer? What percentage of these workers has devel-

oped injuries? What is the annual cost of treating these injured employees? Compare and contrast current U.S. and European standards for workplace design. Create a presentation using this information as well as any other research and data you can find that illustrates the current trends in worker care and needs. Be sure to cite all sources.

4. Create a survey that will help you redesign a client's work space. Assuming that the current office arrangement is based on the traditional hierarchical structure, what questions would you need to ask to ascertain the overall mood of the company's employees as well as their perceived effectiveness and job satisfaction?

5. Locate articles in architectural and design magazines about "smart building." How are new technologies being used to empower workers and free them from their desks?

6. Design an office space for 50 employees that maximizes natural daylighting, natural air supply, ease of access, privacy, and socialization.

7. Design a setting for a large office building that will be leased by several large companies. Create outdoor areas that encourage activity and social interaction as well as create pleasant views from inside the offices. How can these common areas be used to increase the satisfaction of the majority of the occupants?

8. Design a single workstation that allows the employee total flexibility. Incorporate concepts relating to personalization as well as territorial behaviors.

9. Research the prevalence of telecommuters. What percentage of the American workforce is currently telecommuting, either from home or from a NWC? How does this compare with countries in Europe, Asia, and South America? How does this drive business practices? Research one company that encourages telecommuting. What effect has this had on their efficiency and employee satisfaction? What effect has this had on the company's profits? If possible, contact the company and get quotes from their corporate officers. Cite all sources.

Terminology

collaborative structure   In this environment team roles, goals, and operating principles are an important part of the joint problem-solving and innovative ideas.

ergonomics   Applied science concerned with designing and arranging the things we use so as to ensure both efficiency and safety; also called *human engineering* or *human factors psychology*

hierarchical structure   Traditional imperial organizational structure, characterized by bureaucracy and a chain of command of power and control

home office   Designated space in a private residence that can support either household record keeping or a home-based business or can serve as a telecommuting site

illuminance   Lighting level or amount of illumination; measured in lux

illumination   Quantity of light striking a surface, which is measured in foot-candles

luminaire   Complete lighting unit: fixture, light source, electrical hookup, and parts that help control the light

luminance   Brightness of an object, which is measured in lumens

neighborhood work center   Fully furnished and equipped cooperative facility shared by employees of different companies and/or by entrepreneurs

nonterritorial office   Work spaces are not dedicated (assigned) but are available as needed for employees who work part-time or spend most of their time out in the field

satellite office   Remote workplace location controlled by an organization; form of telecommuting

telecommuting   Working for a company as an employee, but away from the company's organizational workplace (does not apply to independent contractors and consultants); use of computer technology to transfer information from remote locations to the "main office"

virtual office   Mobile workplace supported by a portable computer and telephone; form of telecommuting

workplace culture   Desired social climate within a business organization; the way in which personnel interact

References

1. Kupritz, V. W. (2001). Aging worker perceptions about design and privacy needs for work. *Journal of Architectural and Planning Research, 18-1*, 13–22.

2. Becker, F. D. (1986). Loosely-coupled settings: A strategy for computer-aided work decentralization. In B. Staw and L.L. Cumming (Eds.), *Research in organizational behavior.* Greenwish, CT: JAI Press.

3. McCoy, J. M. (2002). Work environments. In R. Bechtel and I. Churchman (Eds.), *Handbook of environmental psychology*, New York: Wiley, pp. 443–460.

4. Taylor, F. W. 1985 (originally 1911). *The Principles of scientific management*. Easton, Md: Hive Publishing.

5. Rehm, R. (2000). Workplace design paradigms. *People in charge*. Retrieved June 28, 2005, from www.peopleincharge.org/paradigms.htm

6. McHugh, M., O'Brien, G., and Ramondt, J. (2001). Finding an Alternative to Bureaucratic Models of Organization in the Public Sector. *Public Money & Management, 21*, 35-43. Retrieved June 29, 2005, from http://search.epnet.com/login.aspx?direct=true&db=bsh&an=4325388

7. Williamson, S. (2001). Design Principles for Engaged Workplaces. *The Nonprofit Quarterly, 7*. Retrieved June 28, 2005, from www.nonprofitquarterly.org/section/1773.html

8. See note 7.

9. See note 6.

10. See note 7.

11. See note 7.

12. Bryant, G. (1991). The Oregon experiment after twenty years. *Rain Magazine, XIV*. Retrieved June 28, 2005, from www.rainmagazine.com/architecture/origonexperiment.html

13. Cabana, S. (1993). Participative design works, partially participative doesn't. *New Mexico State University, Las Cruces, International Institute For Natural, Environmental & Cultural Resources*

Management. Retrieved June 28, 2005, from www.nmsu.edu/~iirm/articles/cabana2.html

14. See note 5.

15. See note 12.

16. See note 13.

17. See note 6.

18. See note 13.

19. See note 6.

20. Cruz, S. (2003, June 30). Workplace design: Companies want space designed for collaboration post-boom. *Orange County Business Journal*, pp. 22, 26.

21. See note 5.

22. Heslop, P., Smith, G. D., Metcalfe, C., Macleod, J., and Carole Hart, C. (2002). Change in job satisfaction, and its association with self-reported stress, cardiovascular risk factors and mortality. *Social Science and Medicine, 54-10*, 1589–1599.

23. Wells, N. M. (2000b). Office clutter or meaningful personal displays: The role of office personalization in employee and organizational well-being. *Journal of Environmental Psychology, 20*, 239–255.

24. See note 22.

25. Donald, I., and Siu, O. L. (2001). Moderating the stress of environmental conditions: The effect of organizational commitment in Hong Kong and China. *Journal of Environmental Psychology, 21-4*, 353–368.

26. Totterdell, P., Kellett, S., Teuchmann, K., and Briner, R. B. (1998). Evidence of mood linkage in work groups. *Journal of Personality and Social Psychology, 74-6*, 1504–1515.

27. See note 25.

28. Apte, M. G., Fisk, W. J., and Daisey, J. M. (2000). Associations between indoor air and CO_2 concentrations and sick building syndrome symptoms in US office buildings: An analysis of the 1994 BASE study data. *Indoor Air, 10-4*, 246–257.

29. Brasche, S., Bullinger, M., Morfeld, M., Gebhardt, H. J., and Bischof, W. (2001). Why do women suffer from sick building syndrome more often than men?—Subjective higher sensitivity versus objective causes. *Indoor Air, 11-4*, 217–222.

30. See note 28.

31. See note 29.

32. Pejtersen, J., Brohus, H., Hyldgaard, C. E., Nielsen, J. B., Valbjorn, O., Hauschildt, P., Kjaergaard, S. K., and Wolkoff, P. (2001). Effect of renovating an office building on occupants' comfort and health. *Indoor Air, 11-1*, 10–25.

33. Seppanen, O., and Fisk, W. J. (2002). Association of ventilation system type with SBS symptoms in office workers. *Indoor Air, 12-2*, 98–112.

34. See note 28.

35. See note 33.

36. See note 28.

37. Birk, T. A., and Burk, J. E. (2000). Communication and environmental design: Analyzing organizational culture to improve human performance. *Performance Improvement Quarterly, 13-3*, 137–152.

38. See note 20.

39. See note 20.

40. See note 12.

41. COPE Project (2003). Open-plan office lighting environment. Ottawa, Canada: Institute for Research in Construction/National Research Council (IRC/NRC). Retrieved 15 August 2004 from website http://irc.nrc-cnrc.gc.ca/ie/cope/04-Lighting.html.

42. Kupritz,, V. W. (1998). Privacy in the work place: The impact of building design. *Journal of Environmental Psychology, 18-4*, 341–356.

43. Brennan, A., Chugh, J. S., and Kline, T. (2002). Traditional versus open office design: A longitudinal field study. *Environment and Behavior, 34-3*, 279–299.

44. See note 26.

45. Vithhayathawornwong, S., Danko, S., and Tolbert, P. (2003). The role of the physical environment in supporting organizational creativity. *Journal of Interior Design, 29-1/2*, 1–16.

46. See note 43.

47. See note 42.

48. See note 43.

49. See note 23.

50. See note 23.

51. See note 23.

52. See note 23.

53. Cairns, G. (2002). Aesthetics, morality and

power: Design as espoused freedom and implicit control. *Human Relations, 55-7*, 799–820.

54. Goodsell, C. T. (1993). Architecture as a setting for governance: Introduction. *Journal of Architectural and Planning Research, 10-4*, 271–272.

55. See note 53.

56. Brill, M., Weidemann, S., Alard, L., Olson, J., and Keable, E. (2001). *Disproving widespread myths about workplace design.* Jasper, IN: Kimball International.

57. See note 3.

58. Brill, M., Margulis, S., and Konar, E. (1984). *Using office design to increase productivity* (Vols. 1–2). Buffalo, NY: Workplace Design and Productivity.

59. Carlopio, J. R. (1996). Construct validity of a physical work environment satisfaction questionnaire. *Journal of Occupational Health Psychology, 1*, 330–334, C1, 11.

60. Becker, F., and Steele, F. (1995). *Workplace by design.* San Francisco: Jossey-Bass.

61. Campbell, D. E. (1979). Interior office design and visitor response. *Journal of Applied Psychology, 64*, 648–653.

62. Mazumdar, S. (1992). Sir, please do not take away my cubicle: The phenomenon of environmental deprivation. *Environment and Behavior, 24-6*, 691–722.

63. See note 3.

64. See note 45.

65. Stone, N. J., and English, A. J. (1998). [Effects of] Task type, posters, and work space color on mood, satisfaction, and performance. *Journal of Environmental Psychology, 18-2*, 175–185.

66. See note 42.

67. See note 45.

68. Kaplan, R., and Dana, S. T. (2001). The nature of the view from home: Psychological benefits. *Environment and Behavior, 33-4*, 507–542.

69. See note 3.

70. See note 68.

71. Ulrich, R. S. (1984). View from a window may influence recovery from surgery. *Science, 224*, 420–421.

72. See note 3.

73. See note 68.

74. Wineman, J. (1982). The office environments as a source of stress. In G. W. Evans (Ed.), *Environmental stress.* New York: Cambridge University Press.

75. Leather, P., Pyrgas, M., Beale, D., and Lawrence, C. (1998). Windows in the workplace: Sunlight, view, and occupational stress. *Environment and Behavior, 30-6*, 739–762.

76. See note 1.

77. See note 75.

78. See note 68.

79. See note 41.

80. Veitch, J. A., and McColl, S. L. (2001). A critical examination of perceptual and cognitive effects attributed to full-spectrum fluorescent lighting. *Ergonomics, 44-3*, 255–279.

81. Jay, P. (2002). Subjective criteria for lighting design. *Lighting Research and Technology, 34-2*, 87–99.

82. See note 41.

83. See note 41.

84. See note 75.

85. Kuller, R., and Laike, T. (1998). The impact of flicker from fluorescent lighting on well-being, performance, and physiological arousal. *Ergonomics 41-4*, 433–447.

86. See note 85.

87. See Note 3.

88. See note 80.

89. Veitch, J. A. (1997). Revisiting the performance and mood effects of information about lighting and fluorescent lamp type. *Journal of Environmental Psychology, 17-1*, 253–262.

90. Houser, K. W., Tiller, D. K., Becker, C. A., and Mistrick, R. G. (2002). The subjective response to linear fluorescent direct/indirect lighting systems. *Lighting Research and Technology, 34-3*, 243–263.

91. See note 3.

92. Magee, J. (2000). Home as an alternative workplace: Negotiating the spatial and behavioral boundaries between home and work. *Journal of Interior Design, 26-1*, 35–47.

93. Karnowski, S., and White, B. J. (2002). The role of facility managers in the diffusion of organizational telecommuting. *Environment and Behavior, 34-3*, 322–334.

94. See note 92.

95. See note 92.

96. Zavotka, S. L., and Timmons, M. A. (1996). Creative writers' psychological and environmental needs in their home interior writing environments. *Housing and Society, 23-3,* 1–25.

97. See note 92.

98. See note 96.

99. Becker, F. D. (1984). Loosely-coupled settings: A strategy for computer-aided work decentralization. In B. Staw and L. L. Cumming (Eds.), *Research in organizational behavior.* Greenwich, CT: JAI Press.

THIRTEEN

Hospitality Environments

Tourists spend approximately 25 percent of their vacation budget on accommodations and food,[1] and the hospitality industry is expected to be one of the fastest-growing markets.[2] Hotels, motels, bed-and-breakfasts, resorts, cruise ships, theme parks, and more recently timeshares, private residence clubs, adventure excursions, ecotourism, and agritourism are among the strategies used to entice travelers. These environments are designed to capitalize on *environmental meaning*, which, in hospitality settings, is most often related to fantasy, an ideal, or an expectation and must be supported and enhanced by architectural and design elements. As an example, consider the city of Las Vegas, which is comprised of many themed resorts that resemble notable cities and landmarks throughout the world. Above all, hospitality environments must elicit positive associations and feelings from guests and visitors to endure and prosper.

To evoke positive feelings in patrons, the hospitality environment must provide a "home away from home." Travelers bring with them expectations concerning privacy, territoriality, and access to features and amenities such as television sets, toiletries, telephones, and more recently Internet access. Today's travelers include people within all walks of life, including the elderly and disabled persons, who require special features from their environments (e.g., roll-in showers, grip bars in bathrooms, and places for companion pets and service animals to relieve themselves). In addition, because many hospitality environments, particularly themed resorts and cruise ships, are so large, designers need to be creative in developing and incorporating wayfinding methods into the environment. This is important not only for elderly and disabled populations, but also for fully functioning patrons to easily locate themselves in relation to their rooms.

The hospitality environment consists of many and varying forms that attract their own unique clientele. Included in these environments are motels, hotels, inns offering lodging and breakfast (commonly referred to as bed-and-breakfasts), resorts, and cruise ships. Other hospitality environments may include aircraft and trains, but the special design considerations of these forms of transportation are beyond the scope of this chapter. The specificity of each environment enables patrons to select from a variety of hospitality settings the one that supports their needs. Recently, because of a desire on the part of many people to reconnect with nature, a new category of hospitality environment has emerged: the nature resort. These environments, which include ecotourism and agritourism, range from settings that provide a total connection with nature to those that offer an environmentally friendly facility.

Timeshares and private residence clubs are another form of hospitality environment. These facilities are open to people who become members, thus enabling them to have access to that environment during specified times of the year. The main feature that separates this type of environment from other hospitality settings is the removal of the element of fantasy. People who seek these kinds of environments often seek ownership, and these facilities are more likely to be viewed as a second home and serve as a place for stress reduction.

Hospitality Patrons

Tourists have more travel and destination options than ever before, and as the global population increases, so do the possibilities for new and different experiences. Some individuals seek restorative refuges where they can "get away from it all"; some crave the stimulation of unusual, adventurous, or even dangerous settings; others may indulge in once-in-a-lifetime extravagances or simply drive their home-like settings to new locations; and still others focus on exploring or preserving foreign cultures and landscapes. Business travelers, however, share virtually universal needs: convenience, reliability, connectedness, and specific services relative to the necessities of both the work and the person. Design can easily support and enhance each of these purposes.

Patrons' perception of value is often influenced by the purpose of their visit;[3] and a working knowledge of the target population will enhance the design of any ideal environment. Singles, couples, families, and groups utilize hospitality settings for a variety of personal and professional reasons, including cultural or family traditions or celebrations (e.g., holiday, honeymoon, anniversary, reunion, vacation, school break), business meetings and conventions, and pure entertainment according to their interests and finances.

Travelers' requirements for convenience, image, services, and amenities vary according to their needs. For example, business travelers seek convenient environments that provide separate working and living areas, dry-cleaning services, dining convenience, and high-speed fax, computer, and Internet connections or secretarial services.[4] Vacationing families need child-friendly settings that include care and activity facilities and age-appropriate, in-room movie and video game options; whereas newlyweds require little more than ensured privacy, a pleasant outdoor view, and discreet room service. Younger travelers seem to have a greater regard for luxury items and amenities, whereas older travelers appear to focus on convenience.[5] People who travel for pleasure are more likely to select hotels based on personal knowledge, prior experience, or others' recommendations, whereas business travelers tend to base their selections almost entirely on previous travel experiences and the hotel's amenities and reputation for customer service.[6]

Both the notion and the perception of luxury are influenced by culture, heritage, and personal values and experience. If the design goal is to establish a luxurious setting for an elite clientele, it is imperative to understand how travelers from various countries perceive luxury.[7–9] Comprehending the relationship between luxury hotel attributes and business travelers' personal values, as well as the role of culture in defining service, will help planners and designers to better meet the needs of global customers, maintain a competitive edge,[10] and incorporate design elements that will meet the distinct needs of all travelers.[11]

Design Issues in Hospitality Settings

When designing hospitality settings, the totality of the environment—purpose and function, patrons, location and climate, style and theme, services and amenities, and so on—must be considered. Careful attention must be paid to all design components, from general architecture, landscaping, and layout to finishes, furnishings, and amenities.[12] For example, luxury hotels are patronized to a greater degree by international clients[13] and require not only superior services and amenities but also décor and signage appropriate to their clientele's tastes and languages. The physical environment influences the perception of value, but different cultures have different notions of beauty and value and therefore different design expectations. Planners and designers must understand cultural attributes that affect viewers' perceptions of design. For instance, in most Western cultures, the color white symbolizes new beginnings and purity, but in most Asian cultures, it symbolizes death and mourning. Addressing each of the variables associated with preferences and design of hospitality environments can positively affect the overall image and subsequent success of that environment.[14]

Resorts, cruise ships, and some large hotels are microcommunities; they contain restaurants, nightclubs, theaters, shops, art galleries, libraries, emergency care facilities, and other amenities common to community districts. Like communities, they consist of multiple *behavior settings* that require the careful consideration of transition zones and material selection during the space-planning process. For example, many cruise ships have libraries and Internet stations, and placing a bar or dance club

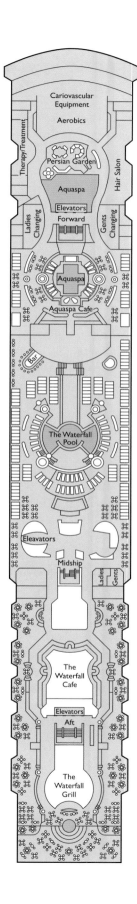

near either of these areas clearly would be poor planning. Therefore, understanding Roger Barker's notion of **synomorphy**, the contributing elements of a behavior setting that create an operational setting when they are compatible,[15] is important for planners and designers of the hospitality environment (Figure 13.1).

"Home Away from Home"

Motels, hotels, resorts, bed-and-breakfasts, and cruise ships are temporary, often high-density residences and social communities—"a home away from home" for guests—and planners and designers must creatively mitigate negative perceptions of certain inherent design components. For example, long corridors serve to maximize the use of space, yet research has demonstrated that long residential corridors increase feelings of crowding,[16–18] whereas greater architectural depth (i.e., more spaces to pass through in going from room to room) results in less psychological distress and social withdrawal.[19] Designers can lessen the negative psychological effects of long hallways by placing lounges or cluster suites intermittently along corridors, changing color schemes, or modifying hallway widths; these measures encourage segmentation bias, the process of mentally breaking a route into separate segments that alters people's perception of distance.[20] Guests can use these segments to "count down" the distance to their rooms (e.g., "Only two more bulges to go").

Generally speaking, guest room designs should be distinctive enough to delineate them from other guest rooms and environments yet not be excessively complex.[21] Windows positively influence perceptions of spatial density: Rooms with windows have more appeal,[22] and people tend to prefer windows in smaller rooms to be proportionately larger.[23] Ceilings that are higher than usual are also preferred,[24] as are rooms that are more square than rectangular.[25] These design elements contribute to perceptions of greater spaciousness and lessen feelings of being crowded. Many guests better experience a sense of place when residential elements

Figure 13.1: It is important to consider the locations of amenities in the space planning of a cruise ship. This layout keeps high-stimulation activities clustered together so as not to interfere with low-stimulation activities.

common to the location's cultural or historical heritage are used in the design; but whether those elements are down comforters, bamboo chairs, or handwoven rugs, they should be durable enough to withstand heavy use.[26]

Wayfinding

The ease with which people can navigate a space or structure influences their overall perceptions of that space, and greater *environmental legibility* facilitates greater exploration. In hospitality environments this translates to greater guest knowledge of the amenities and services available, which can positively affect guests' level of satisfaction with the overall environment. Orientation or *reference points* common to hospitality settings include lobbies, landmarks, particular amenities, and décor elements such as floor and wall treatments. Tall, multistoried structures such as cruise ships, however, can seldom use ceiling and landmark height to support wayfinding and must rely on using wall artwork; varying the colors, patterns, or materials used for flooring and wall coverings; and perhaps creating wall niches to display information or *objects d'art*.

The psychological process of wayfinding is facilitated by spatial organization: The more intricate the layout, the more problems people have finding their way. However, increasing visual access to an environment enhances wayfinding within it. For example, if a large hotel were to host a product convention in its grand ballroom, wayfinding would be well facilitated via numbered or color-coded vendor booths delineated by four-foot-high partitions, directional signage with arrows located at the entrance, clearly visible booth signage atop the partitions or suspended from ceilings, and printed reference maps handed out to vendors and attendees.

Features and Amenities

The entrance and lobby are two of the most influential spaces in a hospitality setting. Their design is critical for visitors who are unfamiliar with the environment; they must not only be functional but also laid out so that patrons can easily locate their intended destinations (e.g., guest rooms, elevators, restaurants, gift shops). [27] The lobby is a **strategic junction node** (a point where activity converges for different purposes) in that it is the point of en-

> For more information about navigating through a space and environmental legibility, see Chapter 5.

trance and departure to the hospitality environment. It also serves as a **dual concentration node** (an area in which people gather for a common purpose). The lobby is the center of guest travel and activity; and, as the first space a person experiences upon entering, its characteristics establish the environment's image (e.g., luxurious, rugged, fantastic). This image sets a mood and ideally will inspire patrons' positive emotions (Figure 13.2).

Creating a positive image can be a challenge for designers because people's appraisals of beauty are highly subjective and change according to trends, culture, and personal experiences.[28] Consider the use of materials and designs that elevate the grandeur of the environment, such as gilt or coffered ceilings, because such design initiatives better prepare patrons for a luxurious experience.[29] One way that designers can influence patrons' perceptions is to design the public spaces within the hospitality environment using interesting and significant pieces of artwork with descriptions.[30] Early studies from museums reveal that the lower right-hand corner of artwork is the best location for placards and descriptions because humans tend to have a **right-side bias**: People will better see and remember those items placed on the right side.[31] Later studies of exhibitions indicated that the addition of sound, smell, or touch to displays helps to attract attention to them and adds another dimension of stimulation to the hospitality patron.[32] For example, rather than having placards describe the work, a button could be pressed to initiate a recorded description and a hint of scent could also be released.

A restaurant located within the hospitality environment is an important amenity that can strongly affect guest preferences, but it can suffer if its only clientele comes from the hotel or resort, especially in smaller settings with shorter tourist seasons. Placing the restaurant close to the entrance enables it to attract patrons from both the hospitality environment and the local community.[33] Consider giving patrons a choice by providing two dining rooms with different ambiences.[34] Be aware, however, that most people will perceive the restaurant and the hospitality environment as one entity, and dissatisfaction with the restaurant's food or service will lower overall satisfaction levels and may deter guests from returning to the hospitality setting.[35]

Figure 13.2: This hotel lobby will evoke different feelings in different types of patrons. Businesspeople who are traveling together may be put off by the outdated lobby, whereas a married couple on holiday may consider it romantic and enticing.

Alternatively, "name-brand" restaurants (i.e., chain, franchise, or chef-owned eateries with corporate financing and geographical or epicurean renown) can provide stabilizing elements—an independent image with positive associations, a sense of familiarity for guests, and consistency in food, service, and customer attraction—that can increase overall customer satisfaction and reduce capital costs[36] (Figure 13.3).

Special Accommodations

More families are engaging in a variety of recreational opportunities, including fine dining, cruises, and trips to foreign countries, and more individuals with physical disabilities are engaging in mainstream types of recreation. Although these trends are positive steps toward the consideration of diverse needs and restrictions among the population, an unintended consequence may be a negative response on the part of other patrons (e.g., people who are offended by hearing a baby wail in

an elegant restaurant, seeing a service dog defecate on a private beach, or being in close proximity to people who are disabled or deformed).

Design can correct the first scenario by incorporating dedicated space for children within guest rooms and utilizing solid concrete and precast materials for sound reduction.[37] The other scenarios can be minimized by incorporating behavioral zoning, a concept that is related to behavior setting in that it restricts certain behaviors to certain locations (e.g., game rooms, cocktail lounges). Many hotels already implement a basic form of zoning by reserving certain rooms for wheelchair users or smokers. Expanding this concept to include the designation of specific zones (e.g., for young families or persons with service dogs) will not only provide spaces that can accommodate specific needs and accoutrements (e.g., high chairs and playpens or food and water bowls), but also give other patrons the opportunity to distance themselves if they so desire.

Figure 13.3: Restaurants within hotels or resorts should be located either near primary entrances or have separate entryways at the fronts of the buildings. Many locals avoid patronizing restaurants located farther inside hotels for fear of being restricted, but such concerns can be allayed by providing greater lines of separation by way of design initiatives.

The senior tourist population, with longer life spans and more discretionary income and free time, represents a significant force within the hospitality market,[38] especially during off-season times.[39] The relative convenience and sense of security provided by hotels may have advantages for senior or disabled guest populations.[40] However, it is important to develop environments that support autonomy, reduce pressure, and increase self-esteem and trust for these individuals.[41]

Special population travelers have unique desires

For more information about ADA requirements see Chapter 9.

and needs that include safety and security relative not only to potential invaders, but also to the environment itself.[42,43] The Americans with Disabilities Act (ADA) addresses many of these concerns as issues of *universal design*; however, as previously noted, trying to meet all ADA requirements can be problematic.

DESIGN APPLICATION. When designing public spaces, consider the various circumstances that could arise relative to their use. For example, a ballroom or restaurant may be used for award ceremonies or events in which one person may rise to offer a toast or the audience may be moved to a standing ovation. The ADA Guidelines require that wheelchair seating be liberally dispersed throughout public arenas to allow seating and viewing choices and that designated wheelchair locations provide wheelchair-bound persons with unobstructed lines of sight comparable to those provided for the general public, regardless of whether others are seated or standing.[44]

Guests with impaired vision can be accommodated with ample lighting, contrasting color schemes that minimize glare, and room accessories (e.g., telephones, TV/CD remote controls, alarm clocks) having large-character display panels, as well as Braille signage.[45,46] Directional and location signs should have large lettering in sharp contrast to the background, along with Braille markers. Provide pedestrian-friendly throughways in public spaces to enhance mobility and accessibility, and consider the use of auditory navigation aids, such as elevators that announce floor stops and floor panels that trigger recorded announcements (e.g., "Welcome to the lobby; the front desk is located to your right").[47]

Design must not only serve to compensate for various human limitations but also make provisions for different means of disability support. For example, mechanical and electronic assistive devices occupy space and may require power sources; all types of service animals require both living spaces and exercise facilities.

Themes

Recent hospitality industry practices have created an interesting paradox: While many hospitality settings employ unique themes related to environmental meaning, many of the larger hotel chains pursue a level of standardization in their designs, and some utilize the same design throughout the chain (Figure 13.4). Homogeneous design rationales include the development of brand recognition and cost savings; however, such consistency may alienate guests who desire a unique experience,[48] and uniformity among luxury hotels can lead to a loss of potential patrons.[49] For example, if you were to visit Budapest, would you rather stay in an environment that looks the same as it would in any other part of the world or in one that is distinctly Hungarian?

Themes work well for many bed-and-breakfasts, resorts, and cruise lines. The primary purpose of a theme is to create an illusion or fantasy experience, which can range from childhood dreams to a former time period to a pampered life of luxury. Many people visit themed hospitality environments to relieve the stress associated with everyday life and to form life-long memories. Let's take a moment to examine these ideas. Sociologist Norbert Elias suggests that as society becomes more structured, people will desire a method of escapism through items such as fantasy books, games, and movies,[50] and through other contrived experiences such as themed hospitality environments. Although the traditional hospitality environment fulfills this desire to some extent, in recent years there have been significant increases in the numbers of themed resorts, cruise ships, and adventure resorts that promise a fantasy. The intent of these fantasy experiences is to instill long-lasting memories in patrons that will prompt a return visit or verbal recommendation to a friend. Hospitality environments, because of their main purpose of fulfilling fantasies, are created for the purpose of forming memories. This is because patrons tend to have preconceived ideas of what the experience will be like. If these expectations are either not met or are surpassed, there is a high probably that the memory will be encoded into long-term memory.[51]

Some cruise themes are based on popular amusement parks, others on guest commonalities such as age (e.g., senior citizens, 35 and under, and young families), and shared interests (e.g., film, music, and sports). Popular resort themes include dude ranches, ski lodges, and island getaways. Fantasy theme settings can range from life in Colonial

Figure 13.4: Many large hotel chains opt for a cookie-cutter approach to design for reasons of expense (production costs), branding (consumer identification), and quality control (product consistency). Chains spend less by buying construction and design materials in bulk. They want consumers to instantly identify their hotels as links in their chain; they want consumers to feel confident that their hotels will provide similar accommodations from Los Angeles to Bangladesh.

America (depicted by authentic or replicated designs and period costumes) to a modern ski lodge where comfortable shelter is provided but not necessarily the slopes or skis.

DESIGN APPLICATION. When designing themed resorts, be aware of the implications and associations of different architectural styles to avoid misusing them.[52] Native vegetation will help to integrate structures into the landscape, enhancing perceived authenticity.[53]

Types of Hospitality Environments

There are several different types of hospitality environments designed to meet the diverse needs of a wide range of patrons. For example, the motel is designed to meet the needs of the road warrior who travels from destination to destination in an automobile. Hospitality environments require special design considerations to meet the unique needs and desires of those who patronize the different hospitality environments.

Motels

In 1925, Arthur Heinman, a Los Angeles architect, decided to capitalize on the growing connection between San Francisco and Los Angeles by erecting the first "mo-tel" (a hybrid of the words *motor* and *hotel*) between the two cities. Unlike hotels, which were predominantly located in urban areas, motels were specifically designed to be automobile friendly. The idea gained popularity for two reasons. One was America's growing love affair with the automobile; the other was the reluctance of many travelers to walk through the elegant lobbies of hotels after spending long hours traveling in a car. Motels appealed to weary motorists who could park their cars next to their rooms and would not have to be seen in a disheveled state.

Because motels offered convenience for cross-country travelers, they had unique design needs. To attract travelers, they needed to be located near popular roadways and surrounded by complimentary services such as gas stations and diners. The original layout of motels contributed to their uniqueness in the hospitality environment. Many took the form of a single-story building with connected rooms and doors that faced the parking lot, often in an "I," "L," or "U" configuration.

By the 1960s and 1970s, the uniqueness of motels began to vanish as large chain franchises gained dominance, replacing privately owned operations. Many motels began to resemble hotels: multistoried and with a homogeneous exterior and interior designs. By the 1980s, many of these franchises took the motel to another stage by replacing the word *motel* with terms such as *roadside inn*, *suite*, and *lodge*.

The expectations of today's motel patrons do not differ much from the patrons in the early to mid–20th century. Most are not interested in fancy décor and simply want a clean, comfortable bed and a hot shower. Although not usually stated, other expectations of what a motel should provide are privacy and quiet.

DESIGN APPLICATION. When designing motels, consider layouts that utilize the bathroom and solid partitions to offer a buffer between each room. Heavy window treatments will not only block out light, but also insulate against sound. The interior design should be comfortable and accessorized with warmer colors and items that can endure wear and tear. Remember, unlike hotels, motel rooms are usually accessed from the outside, meaning that rain, snow, dirt, and debris will be tracked directly into the room.

Although the original design features of motels have all but vanished among the big-chain franchises, the original one-story facility has experienced a resurgence among those seeking the nostalgia of a bygone era. Many of these travelers spend their leisure time motel hopping across the United States. For these people, the enduring symbols of the motel are an important part of the experience.

When renovating and designing original motels, it is important to gain in-depth knowledge of their historical designs. Much like patrons of fantasy-themed resorts, travelers who seek to replicate the mid–20th century motoring experience will likely be aware of the intricacies and detail of original motels, such as neon signs depicting the pop culture iconography of the day. Poorly designed replicas will not only damage the illusion but also negatively impact the value given to the motel.

Hotels

Hotels, in one form or another, have been part of human civilization for millennia. Although they once simply offered the traveler a place to stay on a short-term basis, hotels have evolved to provide the short-term guest with a variety of services such dining, recreation, fitness, and child care. There are two distinct types of hotel guest: the business traveler who is looking for comfort and convenience; and the vacationer who is interested in an experience and the formation of memories with friends and family. To attract business travelers, many hotels offer facilities that can accommodate large and small conferences, along with business services centers that provide copy, fax, and other business-related devices.

Many people have preconceived expectations about hotel settings. The most basic of these expectations is the provision of a room with a bed, closet space, and bathroom facilities. In hotels touting more luxurious accommodations, other items such as a television, telephone, Internet capabilities, coffee maker, alarm clock, and blow dryer are often expected. Because patrons' expectations of a hotel can greatly vary, systems for ranking hotels have been implemented. The most well known is the star system, which associates specific characteristics with a designated number

Table 13.1 Five-Star Hotel Rating System[54]

STAR RATING	ACCOMODATIONS AND SERVICES
One star (Economy)	Accommodates the basic needs of budget travelers. Tends to be located near major attractions or thoroughfares. Usually located within walking distance of dining establishments.
Two stars (Moderate)	Offers moderate aesthetic enhancements in the property grounds, room décor, and quality of furnishings. May offer limited restaurant services with no provisions for room service.
Three stars (First class)	Provides a high level of service with basic amenities, features, and facilities. Décor emulates a sense of style and class. Contains restaurants serving breakfast, lunch, and dinner. Offers room service, valet parking, pool, and fitness center.
Four stars (Superior)	Offers a high level of and a wide variety of amenities. Comfort and convenience are the primary concerns of staff. Facilities are upscale and with a highly stylized décor. Higher-end restaurant facilities are available. Grounds are well landscaped and manicured.
Five stars (Deluxe)	Luxurious property with original design styles and elegant room décor. Provides an exceptionally high degree of service by meeting all conceivable needs for comfort and convenience. Offers outstanding dining facilities. Grounds are meticulously kept.

of stars (Table 13.1). A similar ranking system, developed by the American Automotive Association (AAA), uses a five-point system of diamonds instead of stars.

DESIGN APPLICATION. Most people who visit hotels have preconceived notions of the facility's accommodations and services. Many of these expectations will be confirmed or denied based on an initial impression of the design. If the design matches or exceeds patrons' expectations, they will likely be more tolerant of any deficiencies. The converse may also be true. Design styles that do not meet patron expectations may prejudice them and lead the patrons to feel that other services are also deficient.

Bed-and-Breakfasts

Country travelers in Colonial America often spent the night at small inns or private houses. This custom continued into the 1800s and today lives on in the form of bed-and-breakfasts that serve as temporary housing for travelers and are usually operated out of large, single-family residences. Guests have private bedrooms, which may or may not include a private bathroom. As indicated by the name, the principal amenity of bed-and-breakfasts is the provision of a freshly cooked breakfast, which is often based on regional norms or particular themes. Many bed-and-breakfasts consciously seek to re-create an historical atmosphere.

Travelers who choose bed-and-breakfasts generally seek to immerse themselves in an experience by sampling local cuisine, sleeping in authentic environments, perusing local shops and galleries, and establishing a personal connection with local inhabitants.

DESIGN APPLICATION. In designing bed-and-breakfasts, authentic renovations of older homes should be considered, along with furnishings and décor that compliment the particular culture, region, or heritage. If at all possible, try to accommodate guests by providing them with their own bathrooms, as well as keys to enter and exit the building at their leisure. The most important aspect that a bed-and-breakfast should provide is a home-like atmosphere so that the guest feels as if he or she is experiencing the local life.

Resorts

The word *resort* can be used to describe towns in which tourism or vacationing accounts for a significant part of the local industry (e.g., Aspen and Vail, Colorado) as well as large properties owned by a single company usually incorporate some type of theme (e.g., Disney themed resorts). These hospitality environments are generally high in quality and strive to fulfill all of their patrons' wants and needs so that they never have to leave the resort. As such, a common denominator between resort towns and single-owner resorts is that they tend to be all-inclusive, providing a host of dining opportunities, lodging, entertainment, and shopping within their confines.

DESIGN APPLICATION. A major focus of resorts is the creation of fantasies. Designers can assist in this endeavor by developing memorable interiors that are creative and whimsical. The goal of the design should be to capture a particular illusion so that when guests arrive, they are immediately transported to another place. There are many ways in which this can be accomplished: the use of architectural detail, finish materials, types of artwork, and even lighting levels can go a long way to reinforce an illusion.

Cruise Ships

Cruise ships began as a form of transportation; however, with the advent of the jet plane, the appeal of cruise ships as a mode of travel declined. Today, cruise ships are essentially floating resorts where people go to have an experience. Many cruise ships provide unique experiences (e.g., Disney's Big Red Boat), but most simply pamper their guests. The profit margin for cruise ships derives mostly from onboard purchases, which include all alcoholic beverages, poolside snacks, and duty-free shops, as well as special events such as art auctions. To maximize these expenditures, cruise ships open a running tab for each patron upon boarding the ship, and that tab remains open until the patron is ready to leave. Without conscious thought of the flow of money, people are more apt to spend.

DESIGN APPLICATION. Like resorts, cruise ships rely on their ability to create fantasies as a means of attracting and satisfying patrons. One important difference is that cruise ships

depend on the sale of alcohol more so than resorts. Because alcohol is a depressant, designers may need to emphasize features in the design that increase stimulation (e.g., shiny, sparkling things). Another important consideration in design for cruise ship interiors is the limitation of space. Designers must use their creativity to enhance the illusion of space. For example, removing risers from stairs allows for the passage of more light into an area, making it appear both brighter and larger.

Back to Nature

It is important to remember that when travelers reach their destinations, they are simply entering places that are someone else's home[55] and that *Homo sapiens* are only one of millions of species on the planet. An increasingly popular international tourism trend serves those environmentally conscientious travelers who wish to experience, explore, or simply enjoy a site or region's natural or cultural resources. **Nature tourism** encompasses an eclectic range of recreational and cultural activities and experiences, from bird and whale watching to mountain trekking to nudism to *artesania* (locally produced crafts) to surfing, cycling, climbing, diving, and driving adventures. Whereas traditional resorts are frequently luxurious and generally self-contained, nature-tourism settings range from communal lodges and one-room cabins to primitive survivalist camps, and the pursuit of leisure and exploration activities usually involves travel into the surrounding environment (Figure 13.5).

Ecotourism

Ecotourism can be considered a specialized segment of the nature tourism market. Also called *environmentally friendly*, *sustainable*, and *nature-*, *culture-*, or *community-based tourism*, ecotourism is designed to support and conserve local or indigenous cultures, economies, traditions, and landscapes while promoting ecologically sustainable development.[56] The International Ecotourism Society[57] defines ecotourism as "responsible travel to natural areas that conserves the environment and improves the well-being of local people," noting that those who implement and participate in ecotourism activities should follow these principles:

- Minimize impact
- Build environmental and cultural awareness and respect
- Provide positive experiences for both visitors and hosts
- Provide direct financial benefits for conservation
- Provide financial benefits and empowerment for local people
- Raise sensitivity to host countries' political, environmental, and social climate
- Support international human rights and labor agreements

Although no standards currently exist for certifying the environmental friendliness and sustainability of ecoresorts (or ecolodges), ecotourism projects must provide for environmental conservation, include meaningful participation from the host community, and be profitable and able to sustain themselves.[58] Unfortunately, the smaller the setting, quite often the smaller the profit margin.

Ecotourism settings and experiences range from the primitive to the luxurious, according to host location and visitors demands. Some ecotourists relish "the simple life" (e.g., sleeping on dirt floors in huts or tents, sharing traditional meals with the indigenous population, bathing in streams or lakes), whereas others demand all the amenities and services of a grand hotel (Figure 13.6). Some settings may not meet all or even most of these guidelines, particularly those that offer extravagant accommodations and services in otherwise pristine environments. For example, one ecoresort makes up a 375-acre compound situated on a barrier island off Queensland, Australia, which accommodates 1,300 guests in 357 units ranging from well-appointed studios to luxurious four-bedroom villas and provides a full range of amenities and services, including RV parking, a private marina, a resort train, and a stellar observatory.[59]

Perhaps the least environmental impact is created by ecoretreats, such as the 92-acre Spring House

Figure 13.5: Many ecoresorts use indigenous building materials and distressed woods to provide patrons with a more authentic experience, which can include residing in trees. A universal notion within the ecoresort industry is that facilities should never detract from but always complement their natural settings. For example, guest huts may combine modern building materials (e.g., glass doors) with natural elements (e.g., straw rooftops and wooden walls).

Figure 13.6: Although ecotourism is often equated with a lack of comfort, many ecoresorts have rustic exteriors but provide various modern amenities within. This guest hut provides electricity, a comfortable bed, and modern conveniences such as room service as well as elements to enhance the natural ambience.

Farm in North Carolina, which provides only five guest cottages. These sanctuaries are carefully designed, constructed, maintained, and utilized to preserve and protect the natural environmental balance while providing ample opportunities for leisure, recreation, and solitude for guests who seek peaceful refuge in quiet, secluded settings.

Agritourism

Agritourism is a subset of a larger industry called *rural tourism* that includes resorts, off-site farmers' markets, nonprofit agricultural tours, and other leisure and hospitality businesses that attract visitors to the countryside. The primary goal of agritourism is to preserve the traditional way of farming while conserving rural historic buildings.

For many travelers, agritourism provides a necessary educational bridge between urban and rural lifestyles. It is in essence a form of nature tourism that offers outdoor recreation opportunities, educational experiences, access to rural forms of entertainment (e.g., harvest balls, winter festivals, or barn dances), and direct sales of agricultural products.[60] The main features of an agritourist destination is that the owners are farmers, the primary source of income is derived from farming, and guest accommodations account for no more than 50 percent of the total farm.

The typical agritourist seeks peace and tranquility, shares an interest and curiosity in rural and natural environments, and wishes to escape overcrowded urban and suburban areas.[61] Accommodations at agricultural destinations are diverse and can range from simple rustic campgrounds to four-star luxury accommodations. However, the majority are restored historic country farmhouses or holiday villas that function as bed-and-breakfasts or vacation apartments.[62]

DESIGN APPLICATION. People who are attracted to agritourist destinations are looking for an experience beyond what they are used to. Appropriate designs for this type of environment might seek to evoke an idealized image of rural life. Rustic furnishings, flooring, and wall coverings, combined with hand-sewn or embroidered linen, crocheted blankets, and sewn quilts, can promote and enhance the experience. Additional features could include artwork featuring local landscapes and barnyard images or even a duck pond located within sight of guest accommodations.

Shared Real Estate

Shared real estate is a vacation alternative that attracts a group of people who are well educated, married, and enjoy luxury items. Two predominant forms of shared-ownership real estate are available to consumers for vacation and recreational purposes: timeshares and private residence clubs. While these two forms of vacation ownership are fundamentally the same, public residence clubs tend to be larger units with more floor space, have many more services available to guests, and require substantially higher annual maintenance fees.[63] Whereas public residence clubs are more appealing to affluent vacation-home buyers who do not want to own or be responsible for a second or third home,[64] timeshares tend to be more popular with middle-income vacationers who are looking for a less-expensive place to relax.[65, 66]

As the shared real estate industry grows in response to a sophisticated and demanding consumer market, it must consider additional amenities to enhance "resident guest" experiences and establish a competitive market edge.[67] Consumers who invest in timeshares and public residence clubs consider such properties their homes and may feel safer in fully self-contained or exclusive complexes and compounds.

DESIGN APPLICATION. More hotel guests are looking for home-like elements in their rooms and, given that shared ownership properties require a much greater investment, it can be inferred that resident guests have similar expectations. Designs for shared real estate facilities should include two separate restaurants so that resident guests can dine and socialize conveniently within secure boundaries. One restaurant should be formal to allow for fine dining. The other restaurant should be casual with opportunities for play to accommodate families with small children as well as to provide home delivery or take-out service.

The design of shared real estate should satisfy the unique needs of its users: people who seek a more familiar environment but still want to experience the sense of being on vacation. It should combine familiar and unusual elements so as to evoke feelings both of home and of being special; for example, home-like furnishings juxtaposed against an exotic view. Most shared real estate vacation destinations strive to highlight their locale through specific marketing images (e.g., surfers in Hawaii and California, ranchers in Texas and Oklahoma). Regions and cities also strive to develop their own images, and design professionals must ensure that their designs are in accordance with the image that the consumer is attracted to. For example, visitors to Martha's Vineyard, an island off the coast of Massachusetts, expect archetypically quaint New England villages, and a modern, steel-and-glass structure would be incongruent with the region's marketed image.

Summary Review

The hospitality industry is expected to be one of the fastest-growing markets in the coming years as hotels, motels, resorts, cruise ships, theme parks, timeshares, private residence clubs, and eco-tourism enterprises offer an increasing range of travel and vacation enticements. Today there are more opportunities for travel and destination options than ever before. With the increased globalization of the world, the possibilities for new and different experiences continue to grow. However, guest satisfaction is often influenced by the purpose of the visit. Therefore, hospitality environments must gain a working knowledge of their intended target population and what these patrons deem as an "ideal" environment. For example, the notion of luxury is influenced by culture, heritage, and personal values and experience. This means that travelers' requirements for convenience, services, and amenities will vary according to their needs and expectations of service.

When designing hospitality settings, the totality of the environment—purpose and function, patrons, location and climate, style and theme, services and amenities, and so on—must be considered because the physical environment influences the perception of value. Important components of the hospitality environment include guest-room designs that are distinct from other guest rooms. Many guests experience a sense of place when residential elements common to the location's cul-

tural or historical heritage are used in the design. Likewise, guests tend to dislike designs that are excessively complex.

The ease with which people can navigate a space or structure influences their overall perceptions of that space. The entrance and lobby are two of the most influential spaces in a hospitality setting. They must be not only functional but also navigatable. The lobby is the center of guest travel and activity and provides the first impression. Creating a positive first impression can be a challenge for designers because people's appraisals of beauty are highly subjective and change according to trends, culture, and personal experiences. The presence of a restaurant is an important amenity that can strongly affect guest preferences. However, satisfaction with the restaurant often affects satisfaction with the hospitality.

Some hospitality settings employ themes in their design, while others opt to pursue a level of standardization in their designs. Homogeneous design rationales include the development of brand recognition and cost savings. Bed-and-breakfasts, resorts, and cruise lines are well suited for themes. The primary purpose of a theme is to create an illusion or fantasy experience, which can range from childhood dreams to a former time period to a pampered life of luxury. Popular resort themes include dude ranches, ski lodges, and island getaways. The intent of these fantasies is to instill long-lasting memories that may lead to a return visit or verbal recommendations to friends.

Whether designs are themed or standardized, resorts, cruise ships, and many large hotels are micro-communities; they contain restaurants, nightclubs, theaters, shops, art galleries, libraries, emergency care facilities, and other amenities common to community districts. Like communities, they consist of multiple behavior settings that require the careful consideration of transition zones and material selection by designers and planners during the space-planning process.

A growing number of elderly and people with disabilities participate in many mainstream types of recreation. The senior-tourist population, with longer life spans and more discretionary income and free time, represents a significant force within the hospitality market. These populations have unique physical and cognitive needs that include restroom safety and security from potential invaders. To accommodate the needs of all travelers, it is important to develop environments that support autonomy, reduce pressure, and increase self-esteem and trust for these individuals.

An increasingly popular trend is nature tourism, which encompasses an eclectic range of recreational and cultural activities and experiences. These types of hospitality environments differ from traditional resorts, which are commonly luxurious and self-contained. Nature resorts can range from communal lodges and one-room cabins to primitive survivalist camps. Ecoresorts and agriresorts are two common types of nature resorts. Ecotourism is a specialized segment of the nature-tourism market that is environmentally friendly, sustainable, and nature, culture, or community based. It is designed to support and conserve local or indigenous cultures, economies, traditions, and landscapes while promoting ecologically sustainable development. Agritourism offers access to rural settings as well as to entertainment such harvest balls, winter festivals, and barn dances. Like the ecotourist, the agritourist seeks peace and tranquility and shares an interest and curiosity in rural and natural environments. The primary goal of agritourism is to preserve the traditional way of farming while conserving rural historic buildings.

Shared real estate is another form of hospitality environment that is marketed as a vacation alternative to people who are well educated and married and who enjoy luxury items. The two predominant forms of shared ownership are timeshares and private residence clubs. Although similar to the shares, public residence clubs are larger, have many more services, and require substantially higher annual maintenance fees. These environments fill a need for people who would like a second home but are unable to afford one or do not want to be responsible for the upkeep. The primary expectations of patrons for these environments are home-like elements in their rooms.

People travel—both literally and metaphorically—in search of satisfaction, and their luggage includes their expectations, fantasies, ideals, and hopes. Whether people seek to withdraw and create or restore, engage with others for purposes of business or pleasure, or investigate and discover the new world around them, people need places to call home when they travel to other places that are, in fact, someone else's home.

Discussion Questions

1. Compare examples of travelers who prefer unique culinary and lodging experiences based on locale with those who opt for a homogenous experience irrespective of geography.

2. Discuss what makes a community. What features of a resort setting are necessary to make guests feel they need not leave the resort community?

3. Discuss the possible development of the lobby. Imagine a medieval castle; what area might be considered a lobby? What was the true function of this area? (Hint: strategic junction node.) How does this compare to the designs of the Renaissance or the Victorian era, and what was the significance of the "lobby" then? Now consider these different functions in modern structures. What buildings or settings use a "lobby" in a similar fashion to these historical counterparts?

4. Discuss the importance of food and mealtime in different cultures. How might this knowledge affect your design of a hotel or resort in different areas of the world? Considering that smell is the sense most strongly tied to memory, how might a hotel or resort exploit this fact and utilize an eating establishment to increase patron satisfaction?

5. Discuss different wayfinding techniques that work well across ethnicities and religions. How would you design a hotel so that guests are not bombarded with signs and maps, but can still easily find their destinations? How can technology be used to enhance directional communication?

6. Discuss how you would approach the research aspect of designing a new hotel. What information is essential to ensure proper design layout, décor, and amenities? How would you gather the information necessary to begin your design?

7. In your opinion, can any permanent structure have a positive or net zero impact on an envi-

Retail and Service Environments

People's experiences with retail or service environments begin long before they step inside the buildings. The experience begins with a desire or need for a particular product or function (the objective); it involves the amount of time, effort, and expense required to achieve it (the process); and it results in the feelings evoked before, during, and after the fact (the outcome). This process is illustrated by the comic strip in Figure 14.1.

Retail and service environments include, but are not limited to, convenience stores, gas and service stations, banks, restaurants, bars and clubs, specialty shops, department stores and emporiums, shopping malls, bulk warehouses, booths and kiosks, and vending carts. These establishments sell products or services no matter how different and need customers. They are *public territories*, open to the community at large and therefore subject to the specific perceptions of individuals based on their personalities, ages, gender, status, and experiences. They are affected by periodic *crowding* that is contingent on the time of day and season, the weather, and events such as sales, specials, and holidays. And they are at constant risk for criminal activity.

To be successful, industries that serve the general public must ensure the satisfaction of their customers and their employees. Because many services lack physical (tangible) properties to which people can relate, service industries are beginning to value their physical spaces as sources for positive effects on customer behavior and satisfaction. The retail and service environment, or **servicescape**, can be viewed according to three predominating factors—ambience, layout, and signage—each of which can influence customers' satisfaction or dissatisfaction with the service or product.[1] For instance, the use of mannequins representative of a plus-size clothing store's target market will engender more of a positive emotional response from overweight shoppers than thin mannequins. Conversely, if a restau-

Figure 14.1: We look at every environment with an objective in mind, and the environment dictates a process by which we may obtain our goal. In this comic strip, the *objective* is the acquisition of a purse; the *process* involves maneuvering through hordes of people to reach it; and the *outcome* clearly is satisfaction.

275

Figure 14.2: When we enter a *public territory* such as a restaurant, the surrounding environment provides us an impression from which we form an evaluation of the quality of the product or service. Many attributes contribute to a positive dining experience, including acoustics, lighting, cleanliness, ambience, and natural views.

rant is not as clean as patrons expect, then no matter how good the food is, the environment will foster negative perceptions (Figure 14.2).

This chapter discusses the effects of these variables on the retail and service industry. It examines designs that mitigate undesirable behaviors and foster desirable ones. It discusses crowding and density as they relate to public spaces and applies those concepts to banks and convenience stores, restaurants and cafés, retail facilities, and malls.

Shoppers and Consumers

People often shop as a social or recreational activity and are more likely to become consumers if a setting's external attributes are compatible with their beliefs and values and stimulate the consumer behavior process by arousing potential shoppers' interests, curiosity, or desires.[2] Recreational shoppers seek entertainment, whereas utilitarian shoppers seek accomplishment; therefore, design should focus on enticement for the former and convenience for the latter, and it should provide an attractive, spacious setting for both.[3] When products are intangible, as is the case in many service environments, the physical environment becomes more influential, and pleasant surroundings will help to diffuse negative reactions when mistakes are made or accidents occur.[4] In other words, when we are satisfied and comfortable within an environment, we will be less critical of the services delivered.

One way to mitigate negative environmental associations is to lower the setting's level of stimulation. For example, in a restaurant, design elements to reduce environmental noise levels may include variations in ceiling height and the use of wall partitions, which provide more surface area to diffuse sound as well as a greater degree of privacy for diners at tables; soft materials on the chairs to absorb sound; and soft lighting and a muted color scheme, which relax dining patrons. The addition of soft, soothing background music helps patrons to pass the time pleasantly while they await their orders.

The entertaining or pleasure-seeking shopping experience is most enjoyable when the shopper gains intrinsic satisfaction, perceived freedom, and involvement.[5] Utilitarian or purposive shoppers share the first two needs, but prefer simplicity to involvement; they desire convenient, coherent, well-organized settings in which they can complete their tasks as quickly as possible. One study, which noted two main merchandise categories—social identity products (e.g., jewelry, fine china, and gourmet foods) and utilitarian products (e.g., toothbrushes, duct tape, and groceries)—found that subjects who evaluated social identity products were significantly affected by store atmosphere, whereas those who evaluated utilitarian products were not. The study also found that a more prestigious store atmosphere created an impression of higher-quality products.[6]

Even after we have left an environment, our behavior affects that of others by way of **implicit cues** we leave behind that indicate what we have done. This is an essential concept for planners and designers of servicescapes to understand because shoppers are often influenced by the buying behaviors of other shoppers, especially regarding products with which they are unfamiliar. For example, shoppers often take the items they want from shelves and leave gaps or incomplete stacks of merchandise that imply their behavior (i.e., someone bought those items because they are valuable). Incomplete product displays can lead other shoppers to make positive assumptions about missing items and therefore purchase the same items. One research team found that customer purchases can be stimulated by **virtual modeling** (i.e., the use of implicit cues to modify behavior) even though retailers assume near-empty shelves discourage sales. By maintaining incomplete product displays, especially for new and slow-moving items and for private-label brands retailers encourage customers to purchase.[7]

There are unintentional consequences of the Hawthorne studies, which analyzed the effects of lighting on workers' performances. The following are three important concepts from the Hawthorne studies:

1. The effect of the physical environment is buffered by perceptions, beliefs, preferences, experiences, and personality. In these studies, participants' performance levels improved in response to increased and decreased lighting levels. Their perceptions of any change as being better or an improvement therefore influenced their work behaviors.
2. By focusing on one group of employees (those involved in the study), researchers inadvertently promoted the belief among these employees that they were special.
3. The physical environment created a change in social dynamics, and the increased social contact had a positive effect on performance.

Apply the three concepts to a department store. How can we modify the environment to elicit feelings related to these concepts without redesigning the entire facility? One possible way is to introduce comfortable seating areas in each department. Because most stores have no such areas, patrons may view the change as an improvement. They may consider it a privilege to relax in a pleasant setting with nice furniture, and if more than one person uses the space, there is bound to be social interaction. The secondary outcome is that patrons may spend more time in the store, which will likely lead to more sales. As these patrons discuss the merchandise, they may help to reassure others that their purchases are good ones and therefore reinforce positive perceptions about the store.

Crowding and Density

Crowding is subjective, whereas *density*, the number of individuals per unit area, is objective. Conditions of crowding are affected by other people, objects, and structures,[8] whereas feelings of crowding are mitigated by a person's perception of personal control[9] as well as the levels of *stimulation* and *arousal* that person experiences. Many retail environments try to display as many products as possible, which often results in narrow aisles that limit distances between merchandise displays. Issues such as temperature, odor, noise, and density can exacerbate or alleviate feelings of crowding.

If people believe that they have options or that they can control a given situation, they are less likely to experience stress related to crowding. For example, if you want to go to a popular restaurant that you know is always busy, you can exert some control by making a reservation. People's perceptions of control are also influenced by the amount and quality of information available to them. Large department stores have cash registers dispersed throughout the individual departments, and busy salespeople are responsible for many duties besides customer service. When customers are rushed and cannot locate a register or salesperson, they become stressed by just trying to make a purchase. The use of ceiling-suspended signs to indicate open registers and handbells for customers to ring when they are ready to make a purchase, can greatly reduce checkout confusion, stress, and potential feelings of crowding for both customers and employees.

Crowding, a source of psychological stimulation and arousal, can be related to stimuli other than density, including unpleasant situations or people. **Density-intensity theory**, as it relates to

For more information on the Hawthorne studies, see Chapter 1.

For more on crowding and density, see Chapter 4.

urban versus suburban areas, suggests that density itself is not harmful, but that it can be amplified by co-variables. If a clothing store is having a sale and many people are rifling through the merchandise, the competition for a certain size and color is a co-variable that can lead to positive arousal (excitement) or negative arousal (crowding). Environmentally based co-variables influence people's experiences of environments. In a department store, these co-variables can include **atmospherics** (i.e., environmental cues that contribute to overall ambience), such as scents from salespeople who spray perfume samples, the smells of new fabrics and leathers, and odors emanating from the shoppers themselves; lighting that is either too bright or too dim and the reflected glare from various surfaces; intentional sound, such as background music or unintentional sound such as the clamor of many people talking at once; and climate, which can be too hot, cold, dry, or damp.

Gender

Most men shop for utilitarian rather than entertainment purposes, whereas most women do both. Men tend to respond more negatively to high-density situations than women,[10] who tend to approach high-density more cooperatively.[11, 12] Numerous studies have demonstrated that men generally require more personal space than women.[13–15] Women choose more complex routes,[16] and men require more personal space when ceilings are low.[17] Apparently, men are more susceptible than women to feelings of crowding in environments where social and spatial density are high; however, their feelings of cognitive control can be easily enhanced with information and organization.

DESIGN APPLICATION. Planners and designers can optimize the male shopping experience by creating simple, well-organized floor plans and large open spaces that offer maximum visual range and minimal clutter in environments where men typically shop. For example, position clothing racks far apart in men's departments; provide wide aisles at hardware, automotive, and home improvement stores; and ensure ample open spaces at sports equipment and convenience stores (Figure 14.3). One research team noted that most men prefer shopping for clothing in department stores (although their age influences their expectations and needs) and recommended the use of display kiosks in department stores to provide information about and directions to the merchandise.[18] This information can be encoded with numbers, symbols, colors, or any combination of these; however, encoding by color alone is not recommended, as approximately 10 percent of the male population has some form of colorblindness.

Men and women experience and respond to crowds and crowding differently, as do members of different cultures; therefore, physical layouts and merchandise displays should be designed to accommodate these variables. Small sitting areas in women's departments can enhance the shopping experience for couples; they serve not only as rest-

Figure 14.3: Planning and designing retail spaces for a multitude of users requires consideration of the target populations' particular preferences and needs. In this hardware store, note the wider aisles and spaces between displays in areas where men typically shop, which accommodate men's needs for larger personal spaces.

ing places for people who aren't shopping at the moment (i.e., they afford *refuge*), but also as vantage points from which to contemplate purchases (i.e., they afford *prospect*). By anticipating the constituency of the shopping population and expected levels of consumer traffic, designers can instigate many proactive initiatives to help minimize stress and maximize consumer satisfaction in retail and service environments.

Image and Setting in Retail and Service Environments

Many factors contribute to the design of a successful retail or service facility. Each establishment has an image to project, and location contributes to this image; consider that a boutique in Beverly Hills can offer the same items as one on Chicago's South Side yet charge substantially higher prices simply because many consumers associate Beverly Hills with higher value. The facility's design also affects consumers' environmental perceptions; the architecture, exterior design elements (e.g., façade, entryway, window displays, and signage), and interior design elements (e.g., layout, color scheme, organization, and atmospherics) contribute to the perceived value of the items or services offered. Unfortunately, in attempting to advertise or to defend against territorial violation and contamination, owners often implement methods that may do more harm than good.

Image

A store's image—its appearance and ambience—is an intangible commodity that has both physical and psychological impact. Image can serve not only to differentiate a store from others, including the competition, but also to attract and keep consumers who may rely on the image to communicate information about the quality and value of products and services, especially those with which they are unfamiliar.[19] The external physical attributes of a retail or service setting—the structure itself plus the street and sidewalk, landscaping, doors and windows, signage and symbols, displays and decoration, and so on—provide *external stimuli* that can trigger the consumer behavior process.[20] For example, some shops use constant streams of fragrance outside the door as a means to entice customers inside.

Although customers may take no conscious notice of a pleasant environment, a poor atmosphere can easily create a negative impression.[21]

Citing the original *pleasure–arousal–dominance theory*, which holds that emotion is a mediator between people's environments, personalities, and behaviors, one research team demonstrated that positive shopping behaviors resulted when store designs induced pleasure and arousal.[22] Other researchers noted that all three emotional states can be used to predict and modify customer behavior and that meeting the needs of all three will result in customer satisfaction.[23] These pleasurable emotions can be stimulated by the business itself and aroused by an integrated servicescape (i.e., consumers may first be interested by the goods or services offered, and subsequently drawn into the store by its image).[24] The reverse is also true; a physical image can induce shoppers to investigate an unknown business. In other words, both the business and the building can attract customers and even more so when they function in a cohesive, coherent combination. A clean and attractive store draws more customers,[25] but high densities can lead to negative perceptions and cognitions.[26, 27] In short, a visually appealing facility can stimulate consumer interest and ensure continued patronage.[28] Using design and decoration to communicate and reinforce a store's image, improving the store atmosphere instead of relying on promotional techniques to attract customers, and matching the merchandise's functions to the store's atmosphere will create an effective sales environment[29] (Figure 14.4).

Service delivery was once limited to face-to-face interaction, but technology now allows service industries to interface with consumers in many ways. Banking transactions can be conducted at drop-boxes; by telephone, computer, or automated teller machines; or with human tellers at branch offices and drive-through windows. Many eateries offer in-house or take-out dining, curbside and home delivery, and even catering services. Environments that allow flexibility in the delivery of services can accommodate a wider range of individual preferences;[30] greater appeal to more potential consumers can easily translate into greater sales. We all are drawn to stimulating environments, and we all enjoy places that make us feel good; however,

Read more about the pleasure–arousal–dominance theory in Chapter 2.

Figure 14.4: This setting obviously caters to the outdoor enthusiast. The resemblance to an outdoor environment appeals to the target market's adventurous nature. When consumers investigate the store's inventory, this setting enables them to better understand the purpose and function of various items.

we mostly want to be in places that are very pleasurable and moderately arousing.[31]

Location

The proliferation of catalog and Internet shopping options has made the question "Is it worth the trip?" important for many consumers. More than ever, an establishment risks losing customers if it is hard to find or get to or if parking is problematic. A business's location is often essential to its success, and planners and designers can assist those in the service and retail industries to meet their sales goals by first establishing appropriate site evaluation criteria.

A team of researchers who conducted a study of restaurants in Taiwan[32] recommends using the following criteria to determine site selection:

1. Availability of transportation
2. Compatibility of the commercial area
3. Comparable economic climate
4. Limited direct competition
5. A suitable environment

The researchers also advocate including input from prospective patrons, marketing professionals, and city planners, among others, noting that customers' internal and external proceedings will affect their perceptions of a location. *Internal proceedings* include factors such as a person's background and decision-making processes; *external proceedings* include cost, neighborhood quality, availability of parking, and ease of locating the site.

Exterior Design

The servicescape exterior is made up of the building façade, means of entry and exit, window displays, and parking accommodations.

Building Façade

The building itself can serve as a form of branding or name recognition; consider the golden arches of McDonald's and orange roofs of Howard Johnson hotels. Although this use of branding is easily recognizable to passersby and foreign visitors, a visual menagerie of façades in a confined area can appear disorganized. Some communities have ordinances mandating or restricting the use of specific designs within designated zones to create coherence among and a sense of order in the community. For example, Santa Barbara, California, allows only Spanish colonial designs in certain areas.[33] Clearly, a designer's challenge is to incorporate designs associated with branding and name recognition with appropriate styles that complement community branding.

Means of Entry and Exit

The primary purpose for entrances and exits is to provide individuals with a way to enter or exit a building. Many of these points of entry or exit contain a provisional barrier in the form of a door. Throughout the years these doors have been used as means to promote status, such as the use of heavy double doors and doors that are more than seven feet high. Oftentimes the primary purpose of these oversized doors is to create the illusion of grandeur. Another common type of door is the revolving door. This version is typically seen in larger office buildings and is often associated with elegance and sophistication.

For the average person, most variations on the door have little to no impact on entering or exiting the building. However, for those who rely on a cane, walker, or wheelchair, the style of door used will determine whether the person can access the building. Revolving doors are often too small for the wheelchair user and move too fast for those with canes or walkers. As such, the most accessible doors for people with limited mobility are double doors that slide open once triggered via a sensor. Because of the symbolism often associated with entry and exit ways, many designers have opted to retain the elegance and sophistication associated with revolving doors, or the grandeur associated with tall heavy doors. However, to promote accessibility, these primary entry and exit ways have been augmented with the more traditional automated doors often located to one side of the primary door.

Window Displays

R. H. Macy devised a plan in the 1870s to attract customers to his Manhattan department store. He used window displays as an advertising medium. Because of the quality and friendly competition among New York's emporiums, such window displays not only provided advertising to passersby but also generated free publicity because of media coverage (Figure 14.5). Unobstructed window displays should always be used along pedestrian routes, not only to provide a positive first impression and visual entertainment for those passing by but also to entice pedestrians inside.

Flaws common to many servicescapes include excessive exterior window bars and excessive window signage. The proprietors of many small boutiques and salons who subscribe to the belief that "the more advertising, the better" often have an array of competing signs, many in neon, in their windows. This *environmental load* precludes many potential customers from seeing any one message; instead, they often see only a chaotic mass of color and shape. For storefronts to be effective advertising mediums, messages must be kept simple and to the point, and displays should be changed and updated regularly. Heavily barred windows indicate risk and danger; a profusion of messages cannot be comprehended by the average person in the time it takes to pass by; and dust, cobwebs, and outdated goods imply lack of quality and care. Window displays should be coherent and colorful, on the cutting edge of fashion, not too busy, and above all, updated regularly.

Access and Parking

Transportation access should be as accommodating as possible: wide roads, few barriers to navigation, limited funneling of traffic, and multiple

Figure 14.5: Window displays often entice shoppers to visit a store; for example, viewing Macy's window displays during the Christmas season is an event unto itself. Casual observers, however, often become active consumers when their initial attraction becomes curiosity and leads them to investigate the possibilities.

entrances and exits. Consumers often must walk considerable distances from their cars or homes to shopping areas, whether along a boulevard or through a large parking lot. Ideally, parking lots and structures should be designed along with the main building. Placing pedestrian paths strategically throughout parking areas not only facilitates navigation but also sets the mood for incoming consumers.[34] Parking structures, although often intrinsic to large commercial centers and undeniably convenient, can also be problematic: Being relatively isolated while surrounded by stark concrete walls and columns can evoke feelings of anxiety and apprehension, especially for women and elderly or disabled people. These structures also tend to be drab places with many dark areas that inspire fear. Incorporating well-lit displays throughout adds light and makes the overall setting more inviting, affords merchants additional advertising space, and affords all users opportunities for *attention restoration*.

DESIGN APPLICATION. Designers can help to reduce feelings of anxiety by providing adequate lighting and visually appealing attributes on which users can focus, such as artwork, nature displays (e.g., aquariums, terrariums, and arboretums), and raised cobblestone or slate walkways lined with indigenous, shade-tolerant vegetation. When designing the exteriors of servicescapes, particularly those that are accessible from parking lots or structures, consider developing causeways lined with native landscaping, statuary, and display kiosks that highlight the products or services offered and are constructed so as to complement the façade of the main structure. Such kiosks afford retailers additional display venues, which can increase consumer interest and profits.

Interior Design

Atmospherics can affect consumer spending patterns.[35] In the 1970s, certain department stores introduced the "blue-light special." When the blue light flashed in a particular department, shoppers headed for the limited-time sale offer. Atmospherics, however, are much more than *operant conditioning*. Both the physical environment and the service quality affect customers' tendencies toward pleasure or avoidance, but research into the aggregated

Figure 14.6: The interior design of this men's boutique is reminiscent of the gentlemen's rooms popular in 19th-century homes. Most men consider clothes shopping to be a chore, and the darker colors, comfortable seating, and soft lighting serve to decrease the negative stimulation associated with the shopping experience. When designing retail settings for men, clothing stores in particular consider how a man will perceive the environment as well as how he will feel in it.

affects of both variables occurring concurrently has been limited[36] (Figure 14.6).

Quality and type of merchandising displays are crucial selling factors; therefore, consider the perceived differences of two products placed adjacent to each other in product displays.[37] Because lighting is most important when visual acuity and color discrimination are needed,[38] designers should ensure they get the most natural illumination possible in establishments where color and texture are important (e.g., art stores and galleries). Although one researcher noted that there are several contradictory studies regarding the effects of lighting on mood, cognition, and social relationships,[39] the work of other teams[40, 41] supports earlier studies that equate lower lighting with greater intimacy. Therefore, a business that provides a service based on a personal relationship (e.g., physical therapy) or a location for a personal encounter (e.g., an intimate restaurant) will be enhanced by dimmer lighting.

Research emphasizes the importance of engaging multiple senses within the retail environment, contending that music in particular can motivate customers to make purchases.[42] Music influences our perceptions and behaviors; a fast rhythm and tempo increases psychological arousal,[43] and the tempo of background affects the speed at which shoppers move through supermarkets.[44] Music can facilitate a comfortable atmosphere by masking unpleasant background noises, reducing the negative effects of silence, and promoting social interaction; but be aware that background music should not attract attention, but rather entice customers to linger.[45] Highly complex music causes high levels of activity in the displeasure centers of the brain, which can neutralize positive activity in the pleasure centers, whereas music of moderate complexity will produce the maximum level of pleasurable arousal.[46] One researcher noted that retailers do not take advantage of positive associations that can be formed between products and people through the use of background music, which can serve as a "brand trigger" (i.e., facilitate consumer recall of an experience with a particular product or brand).[47] However, it should be noted that some genres of music appeal to specific populations; for example, teens tend to find classical music unappealing.

Greater consumer approachability, more impulse buying, and a more positive evaluation of the environment may be achieved through the congruent use of music and scent.[48] For instance, a woman who shops for pajamas may instead buy a negligee because the soft music and delicate perfume-scented air make her feel sexy; feeling good about her experience will increase the likelihood of her returning to that store. However, negative effects will occur if the scent does not relate to the merchandise,[49] and it must be noted that individuals vary greatly in their responses to scent—to some, scent is a turnoff.

Defensible Space

Most servicescapes are conveniently accessible *public territories* that contain money, goods, or both and have open, relatively uncontrolled contact with the general populace. These factors attract a variety of criminals who steal, damage, or destroy. Environmental attributes and *virtual modeling* of *implicit cues* can be used to deter crime. Designers must be acutely aware of a multitude of defensible space measures that can be utilized to protect retail and service workers.

The U.S. Occupational Safety and Health Administration (OSHA) cites the following statistics:[50]

- Robbery and other crimes motivated 80 percent of workplace homicides across all industries in 1996
- A large proportion of retail sector homicides are associated with robberies and attempted robberies
- The largest share of such homicides occurred in convenience and other grocery stores, eating and drinking places, and gas stations
- The risk of sexual assault for women is equal to or greater than the risk of homicide for retail employees in general

Numerous studies have confirmed that experienced criminals consider environmental factors in their selection of targets, and that robbers are most attracted to facilities that have large amounts of cash on hand, obstructed views, poor outdoor lighting, and easy escape routes.[51–53] Criminals prefer locations that afford them visual control (i.e., allow them to be either seen or remain concealed, as they so choose).[54] Therefore, the least attractive environments to criminals are those that provide the occupants with full surveillance capabilities throughout their premises. Businesses in disorganized or high-crime locations that offer easy escape (e.g., on a corner, in a low-traffic area, or near a freeway on-ramp) are particularly susceptible to criminal activities.

Both workers and customers must be protected in retail and service environments. Security systems, devices, and signage may deter criminals, but will also inform customers that they are at risk. Planners and designers must not only consider the unintended causes of their designs, but also devise creative strategies for employing defensible space measures without making the general public feel they are at risk.

DESIGN APPLICATION. OSHA provides the following design recommendations for the late-

night retail industry, many of which can be applied to other servicescapes, especially those located in areas with high crime rates:[55]

- *Improve visibility* so that employees have an unobstructed view of the street and passersby can see inside. Minimize window signage. Design work areas to prevent entrapment of employees and to minimize the potential for assault incidents. The interior layout should ensure that both clerk and cash register are visible from outside of the establishment, employees have two or more clear escape routes, and the area behind the counter is slightly elevated, affording employees greater visual range of the premises.
- *Maintain adequate lighting* inside and outside the establishment after dark. Interior lighting at floor level will cast shadows high onto walls, allowing for easy detection of criminal behavior by police or passersby.
- *Use fences and other structures* to control and direct ingress and egress of customer traffic to areas of greater visibility. Wrought iron fences, for example, allow for surveillance of the store from inside and limit possible escape routes for criminals—and they are harder to climb than chain-link fences.
- *Use drop safes* to minimize available cash, and use signage that indicates that little cash is kept on hand.
- *Install video surveillance equipment* and a closed-circuit TV to maintain surveillance of interior and exterior activities. Post signs indicating the use of such equipment at front doors and cash registers.
- *Install self-locking doors or door buzzers* so that entrances can be controlled, but always ensure unimpeded egress in case of emergency. For banks and convenience stores, consider the use of metal-detection systems to identify possible weapons.
- *Use door detectors* to alert employees when persons enter the store. Consider that hi-tech electronic movement detectors can be disabled by a power loss (accidental or deliberate), whereas glass or metal chimes or bells hung just above door height will sound at the slightest breeze, and cannot be disabled silently.
- *Height markers* on exit doors will help witnesses provide more accurate descriptions of assailants.
- *Use silent and personal alarms* to notify police or management in the event of a problem.
- *Install physical barriers* such as bullet-resistant enclosures with pass-through windows to protect employees from customer assaults.

Banks and Convenience Stores

The primary functions of and the design issues relevant to convenience stores and banks are not dissimilar. Efficiency is intrinsic to their success, as they each compete for a customer base that clearly prefers to transact business as quickly as possible—with or without human interaction, since we can obtain cash, pump gas, and make purchases with just the swipe of a card. Perhaps the most profound commonality between banks and convenience stores is their vulnerability to crime; both are known to contain large quantities of cash, and many are ideally located for quick criminal getaways.

Banking is a service industry that has changed tremendously since the early 1900s, when transactions were conducted through holes lined with bars that were set into solid walls. This design maximized the separation between tellers and customers. Later, high countertops with niches denoted individual teller stations; the counters prevented surveillance by those nearby, and the niches provided customers with usable counter space and privacy for their transactions. Some of the banks located in more disorganized neighborhoods replaced the bars and walls with bulletproof glass as a means of crime prevention.

The overall interior of banks changed very little until recently, except that much of the elegant dark wood and leather have been replaced with cost-effective furnishings and décor. Today, however, some banks are opting to place individual teller stations on the floor of the bank; in these designs, the teller and the customer can stand side-by-side throughout the transaction. We can assume that removing the traditional barrier between teller and customer will facilitate warmer social interaction and subsequently strengthen customer loyalty.

Convenience is a top priority for most bank customers. Drive-through teller windows were popular until the mid-1970s, when they were replaced by automated teller machines (ATMs). Interestingly, the first ATM, located outside of New York City's Chemical Bank in 1971 with little concern for design, was often damaged by the area's diverse weather patterns. Today, ATMs are found just about everywhere, and financial transactions can be completed without human interaction in most urban areas. ATMs are part of the servicescape, and, as such, deserve the same attention to location, convenience of use, and safety as larger settings.

The safety of patrons and employees in all public territories must be ensured. Convenience stores with smaller parking lots and those that do not sell gas are more susceptible to robbery because their interiors are less visible to passersby—including the police.[56] Banks with smaller, compact, square lobbies are more likely to be robbed than those with larger, rectangular lobbies that place tellers farther apart.[57] In both settings, greater chances for surveillance equates to less vulnerability.

DESIGN APPLICATION. The development of a safe and convenient banking environment is dependent on factors that include the site, neighborhood, physical design, landscaping, and security measures. The principles of crime prevention through environmental design (CPTED) can help banks remain safe while thwarting potential crimes. CPTED principles include the following recommendations:[58]

- **Allow for natural surveillance and observation points from inside and outside the bank.**
- **Avoid placing furnishings and promotional signs in areas that impede surveillance.**
- **Locate exterior signs in places where important sight lines are not compromised.**
- **Use a uniform white light source that minimizes glare inside and out.**
- **Select and arrange landscaping so that visual surveillance is not compromised. Examples include trees with high branches and low ground cover.**

- **Install surveillance cameras on the interior and exterior.**
  - **Be sure to orient cameras so they are not aimed at the rising or setting sun.**
  - **Strategically post signs around the perimeter of the property advising visitors that that the property is under video-taped surveillance.**
- **Include large windows with clear (not tinted) and nonreflective glazing.**
- **Avoid window treatments, blinds, or window covers. In certain situations a window awning or tint can be used to help shade the upper third of the window**
- **Avoid the inclusion of formal or informal seating areas or other types of public amenities (e.g., information kiosks) outside of the bank.**

When selecting a site for a convenience store, consider placing it close to a freeway, but not next to an on-ramp. An optimal site would be about a block away from the off-ramp and situated so that traffic would have to be crossed to get back onto the freeway. Ensure maximum visibility of the interior from the exterior, provide ample lighting both inside and out, and install visible video surveillance equipment in the parking lot and inside of the store.

Restaurants and Cafés

Many local economies are finding value in the food service industry as families struggle to balance their domestic and professional duties. More people are eating out.[59] As such, restaurants and casual eateries serve as places for people to conduct business or recreational meetings[60] and are playing an increasingly important role in the economy.[61] Restaurants prosper in part because of customer loyalty, and attaining that loyalty involves attitudinal, emotional, and behavioral commitments on the part of all staff members.[62]

The quality of food, service, and atmosphere are the top reasons for selecting a food service setting; expense and location are important only to those customers who are not bonded to particular restaurants through personal recognition, feelings of familiarity, or memorable experiences.[63] If customers favor an eatery because of its overall serv-

See Chapter 6 for more on CPTED.

ice, or that of a particular staff member, employee turnover can result in customer loss. An enjoyable work environment is critical to employee morale, and pleasant settings support both employee and customer loyalty.[64]

Sociologists have classified bars, restaurants, and many stores into three different levels, with differing clienteles: the smallest, at the local level, with a constant local clientele who, in bars or restaurants, usually have their own seats; weekenders, which have a local clientele during the week but draw outside customers on the weekend; and large establishments that always appeal to an outside crowd. The quality of a restaurant's physical space is as important to overall customer satisfaction as that of the food and service.[65] The amalgamation of environmental features (e.g., shapes, colors, noises, odors, and temperature) influences consumers' perceptions of service quality and performance.[66]

DESIGN APPLICATION. Designers can enhance a restaurant's environment so as to give customers an enjoyable experience and create a sense of place. Consider incorporating unique features, handmade or signature objects, nostalgic features, and opportunities to dine alone[67] (Figure 14.7). Of course, ensuring comfortable seating is an obvious way to increase positive perceptions and satisfaction among customers.

An environment's overall design style facilitates the social atmosphere within it by affecting the occupants' expectations and their expected and actual behaviors. Therefore, an elegantly appointed restaurant (e.g., dark woods; subtle illumination and music; and rich fabrics, colors, table settings, and artwork) becomes a *behavior setting* in which customers expect a more sophisticated level of fare, service, and atmosphere than that of an eatery incorporating bright lights and colors, inexpensive place settings, and louder, faster-paced music.

Customer loyalty can be destroyed by a constant point of dissatisfaction, such as always having to wait for a table, and most customers with service complaints will simply take their business elsewhere.[68] Having a combination of table sizes can decrease wait time for customers and maximize seating capacity, but combining tables leads to a decrease in overall available seating.[69] For example, three tables seating four people at each will lose four seats when combined. Business losses can also result when too few combinable tables are available to accommodate larger groups.[70] One research team, finding that the tolerance for waiting is highly contingent on age and culture (e.g., individuals ages 25 and younger are more tolerant of longer waiting periods than older people), advocates including space for pre–dining activities to modify customers' perceptions of waiting times and prevent their leaving in frustration.[71]

The food-service industry provides much more than just places to eat. Restaurants afford us the privilege of being catered to amid pleasant surroundings wherein we may relax and socialize, consume culturally specific or diverse foods, experience a different lifestyle, and hold parties and meetings. Successful eateries occupy settings that promote satisfaction and enjoyment for all parties concerned.

DESIGN APPLICATION. Planners and designers can ensure unique and memorable experiences by creating supportive environments that provide owners and managers with appropriate structural images and good locations that are easily accessible and are perceived as being both safe and attractive; provide employees pleasant, efficient, and safe workstations and restorative break areas; and afford customers enjoyable settings that mini-

Figure 14.7: Many restaurants have become successful through the use of design themes. Patrons of this 1950s-style diner expect to be engulfed in an idealized version of that era.

mize negative variables and distractions (e.g., *ambient stressors* **such as noise, odor, and temperature and** *environmental pollutants* **such as vehicular traffic noises and emissions). Such environments promote the development of** *place meaning* **and** *place attachment* **for management, staff, and patrons alike and can serve as** *fourth environments* **for those who appreciate them most (Figure 14.8).**

Retail Spaces

In the past few decades retailers have begun to value environmental psychology as a means of enhancing sales, developing store loyalty, and creating pleasing environments.[72] Specific environmental features serve as **descriptors** that help us to understand and connect with or respond to our environments; these features, which include sights, sounds, and scents (individually or in combinations), can provide us with instant information or stand out in our minds after we have left an environment. Descriptors affect consumer perceptions and preferences, but because overall appeal is created by a combination of elements—overall design, appearance, ambience, circulation, and parking areas—it can be difficult to determine the influence of each.[73]

From a proprietor's perspective, the primary purpose of retail and service design is to support and increase sales. Customers are unlikely to return to an environment that they perceived negatively; therefore, enhancing shoppers' experiences with the environment will increase both customer satisfaction and company profits. However, some design principles are contrary to increased sales. For example, good wayfinding mechanisms ensure that consumers will be able to locate their desired goals with relative ease but can decrease impulse buying; whereas poor wayfinding mechanisms may increase impulse buying but will not induce shoppers to return.

Recreational and social shoppers engage in more leisurely and impulsive buying than purposive or utilitarian shoppers (consumers having specific needs and goals). Therefore, planners and designers of retail establishments must understand the primary source of their sales (e.g., tourists, locals, trade and businesspeople, and students). A popular mall in downtown San Diego, located near the

Figure 14.8: Coffee shops and cafés appeal to many people who prefer to go places and be among others, rather than read the paper or drink coffee at home.

convention center and other tourist destinations, has been historically more popular with tourists than with the local population. Whereas many locals (purposive shoppers) seldom come downtown to shop, and contend that the mall is confusing and that they routinely get lost, tourists (recreational shoppers) tend to comment on the mall's beauty, uniqueness, and convenient access. Once design practitioners understand the primary constituency, they should gather and use information about customers' perceptions to improve mall designs.[74]

The proliferation of **megastores** (or *hypermarkets*) has changed the retail industry almost as dramatically as the supermarket did in the 1930s. These huge facilities, which attract and serve populations from outside of the community, offer consumers an expansive variety of goods and services that were once limited to specific retail outlets (pharmacies, groceries, clothing and shoe stores, and so on). Because many communities lack the population to support these megastores and the smaller retailers, who cannot match their prices or product ranges, local populations may cease using their local retailers, and this negatively affects the local economy.[75]

Shopping Malls

The largest retail facility in the United States, the Mall of America in Bloomington, Minnesota,

Figure 14.9: Malls, resorts, hospitals, cruise ships, and even some airports are *microcommunities*, one of the fastest-growing segments of our society. As in the development of full-scale communities, architects and designers must keep abreast of the most efficient methods to move pedestrian traffic, maintain security, support wayfinding, and develop places that people will want to visit time and again. Warmer climates allow for open-air facilities that capitalize on natural views.

houses more than 400 stores as well as a small indoor amusement park. Many other shopping malls offer consumers the widest possible range of recreational, dining, and shopping opportunities. Planners and designers of such large public spaces must consider initiatives that were once the sole domain of city planning, such as monitoring the flow of traffic to keep it moving steadily and to minimize bottlenecks wherever possible (Figure 14.9). One difficulty in designing attractive shopping malls lies in the need for spaces that allow for adequate circulation during peak hours and seasons but that don't feel empty at off times.[76]

Enclosed or open-air mall environments provide reasonably safe places for people to shop,

browse, socialize, dine or snack, play arcade games, relax, or be entertained by movies, concerts, and art exhibitions in relative freedom. Bargains are usually available, as are one-of-a-kind specialty items. In some malls, people can pay bills, get haircuts or see doctors or dentists and still have time to grab a sandwich. Many malls serve as both early-morning walking tracks for seniors and after-school hangouts for teens, in effect functioning as centers of social and cultural interaction. Therefore, malls by their very nature meet the needs of the recreational shopper: intrinsic satisfaction, perceived freedom, and involvement.[77]

For young people, malls often serve as a **fourth environment** (i.e., a place to hang out that is not their home, playground, or other site developed specifically for them).[78] Teens have a strong impact on the economy and retail market; because this group makes up a large population segment and has a great deal of disposable income, designers and marketers should understand what motivates and satisfies this population.[79]

Although the stereotypical "mall rat" is a teen with plenty of spare time and disposable income, one study of two large malls counted more elderly men than teens hanging out (relative to overall population percentages).[80] One reason may be users' perceptions of greater security among more people in a public place. Youngsters usually hang around malls after school and on weekends, whereas older people often gather at malls during early mornings and afternoons to exercise (seniors are often allowed to use malls as walking tracks before business hours) or to meet for socializing and people watching. Therefore, when designing malls, designers should consider both the primary purpose of retail sales and the secondary functions of exercising and socializing, all of which serve to enhance the community.

One research team's study, exploring earlier findings that consumers' shopping mall preferences are affected by overall design, circulation, parking areas, appearance, and atmosphere revealed that people prefer shopping centers that are well maintained, have attractive window displays, and offer more greenery and street activities.[81] Another researcher noted that people tend to prefer building façades with ornate or elaborate surfaces that seem to invite touch and exploration and that express a sense of the past more than the future.[82]

Environmental legibility is critical within shopping malls, which are extremely complicated public environments.[83] Both the overall design plan and individual design elements play important roles in a facility's overall legibility, but it is important to note that design elements can actually inhibit wayfinding, even for those with experience in an environment.[84]

DESIGN APPLICATION. Planners and designers of mall environments must consider the needs of a diverse clientele in striving to create simplicity, organization, and convenience to meet utilitarian shoppers' needs;[85] rest areas for adults and play areas for young children; and ex-

citement that stimulates adolescent and young adult consumers,[86] who tend to prefer exotic, wild, or risky scenes.[87, 88] Consider incorporating community centers that will host programs for lonely teens and seniors (e.g., fashion shows, stage performances, or exhibits) and designing food courts and other areas so as to facilitate social gatherings and people watching.[89] Provide logical and consistent organization within mall directories ("you-are-here" map displays); include *pictographs* for people who speak other languages or have reading disabilities; and incorporate clear store numbering systems using a logical sequence that corresponds accurately to the various stores and levels.[90] Keep in mind, however, that a poorly positioned "you-are-here" map is worse than no map at all.

Summary Review

The retail or service environment offers customers an experience stimulated by a desire or need for a particular product or function that results in time, effort, expense, and emotional response. People who enter retail or service environments tend to do so to satisfy either a utilitarian or a recreational need. The utilitarian shopper seeks accomplishment, and the recreational shopper seeks entertainment. Because shopping and dinning are recreational activities for some people, the level of satisfaction and comfort in the environment will most often correlate to the perception of quality and service.

In most cases, men shop for utilitarian rather than entertainment purposes, and women do both. Men also tend to respond more negatively to high-density situations and have greater personal space demands. Therefore, the physical layout of the retail or service environment intended to attract the male shopper should be designed to accommodate these gender variables.

Violation of personal space is likely to lead to feelings of crowding. Crowding is a source of psychological stimulation and arousal caused by excessive stimuli, density levels, and unpleasant situations or people. In the retail environment aisles are often tightly packed with product displays, which can evoke a feeling of crowding in shoppers. However, variables such as temperature, odor, noise, and density can help to alleviate shoppers' perceptions of crowding. In addition, when people believe they have options, or that they have control in a given situation, they are less likely to experience stress related to crowding.

A particular aspect of human interactions within the retail or service environment is that one person's behaviors and actions within this environment are likely to influence another person's experience. Shoppers leave behind implicit cues that reveal their behaviors (e.g., the purchase of a certain brand of coffee leaves a gap or incomplete stack in the product display, which may prompt another customer to purchase that same brand of coffee). This action is called *virtual modeling*.

Many factors contribute to the design of a successful retail or service facility. A retail establishment's image, for example, is made up of the physical appearance and ambience, which is an intangible commodity that has a physical and psychological impact. This image has the power to attract and keep consumers who rely on such information to discern the quality and value of products and services. The external physical attributes of a retail or service setting serve as the first point at which the establishment's image it determined. These attributes include the structure itself along with the quality of street landscaping and sidewalks. Keep in mind that while customers may not take notice of a pleasant environment, a poor atmosphere can easily create a negative impression.

A business's location is often essential to its image and ultimate success. Planners and designers can assist those in the service and retail industries to meet their sales goals by first establishing appropriate site evaluation criteria. These criteria include not only the neighborhood or servicescape, but also the availability of parking. Whenever possible, parking lots and structures should be designed along with the main building, and pedestrian paths included not only to facilitate navigation but also to also set the mood for incoming consumers.

Through its façade, the building itself can serve as a form of branding to promote image or name recognition. However, the visual menagerie of façades that results from the juxtaposition of many different image-specific buildings can appear disorganized. For this reason, some communities have passed ordinances restricting the use of specific designs as a means of creating coherence and a sense of order in the community.

Window displays are another part of the building façade that can serve as a form of branding. Unobstructed window displays provide a positive first impression, visual entertainment for those passing by, and a means to entice pedestrians inside. Among the common flaws in many servicescapes, however, are excessive exterior window bars and window signage. For a storefront to be an effective advertising medium, messages must be kept simple and to the point, and displays should be changed and updated regularly.

The atmospherics of a service or retail environment derive from both the physical environment and the service quality. This quality depends, in part, on lighting, particularly when visual acuity and color discrimination are needed. Music is another component by which people measure quality; it can serve to facilitate a comfortable atmosphere, mask unpleasant background noises, reduce the negative effects of silence, and promote social interaction. Although both lighting and music can enhance the service environment, they can also detract from it. Lighting that is too bright can be unflattering particularly in a clothing store, and music that is too complex has been shown to cause high levels of activity in the displeasure centers of the brain.

Included in the retail and service environment are banks, convenience stores, restaurants, cafes, megastores, and malls. Banks and convenience stores are particularly vulnerable to crime, and the development of a safe and convenient environment for these establishments is dependent on factors that include the site, neighborhood, physical design, landscaping, and security measures. CPTED is one method that has been shown to assist in the deterrence of crime.

Restaurants and cafés have become environments that serve more than a utilitarian function by offering a place for people to conduct business or recreational meetings. Restaurants prosper because of customer loyalty, the quality of food, service, and atmosphere. The quality of a restaurant's physical space, or its atmosphere, is just as important to overall customer satisfaction as the food and service; it is the amalgamation of environmental features that ultimately influences consumers' perceptions of service quality and performance.

A recent trend in the retail and service environment is the proliferation of megastores (or *hypermarkets*). Because smaller retailers cannot match their prices or product ranges, many people cease to use their local retailers when a megastore opens in an area, which has a negative impact on the local economy.

Shopping malls differ from megastores in that they house many different types of stores, typically under one very large roof. Planners and designers of such large public spaces must consider initiatives that were once the sole domain of city planning, such as monitoring the flow of pedestrian traffic to keep it moving steadily and minimize bottlenecks wherever possible. Shopping malls represent much more than places where we can obtain goods, refreshments, and even repair, grooming, and health-care services; for many people, a mall is a secure fourth environment in which to spend time and socialize or simply observe others. Mall environments can be enclosed or open and offer a reasonably safe place for a host of activities, serving, for example, as an early-morning walking track for the elderly. Therefore, malls by their very nature meet the needs of recreational shoppers by providing satisfaction, perceived freedom, and multiple ways to interact with the environment.

Retailers have begun to value environmental psychology as a means of enhancing sales, developing store loyalty, and creating pleasing environments. Through optimal site selection and enhancement of an establishment's physical images and settings, designers and planners using the principles of environmental psychology can create a retail and service setting that attracts consumers, enhances sales, and strengthens customer loyalty. Atmospherics can facilitate a positive behavioral response in people and serve to turn shoppers into consumers.

An understanding of the primary shopping or consumer constituency is crucial to the success of retail and service businesses. Research on crowding has shown that planners and designers must make proactive decisions when creating servicescapes. Defensible space measures will enhance shoppers' experiences while minimizing risks of violent crimes. Efficient wayfinding mechanisms are crucial to the design of all retail and service establishments, especially large-scale sites (e.g., malls, hypermarkets, and bulk warehouses). The overall design plan and the individual design elements play an important role in a facility's overall environmental legibility, even for those who have experience in the space.

Discussion Questions

1. Discuss the effects of store appearance (e.g., cluttered, dirty, bright, organized, and well stocked) on your interest in a store's merchandise.

2. Discuss the needs and wants of different types of shoppers. How can customer surveys be used to help improve the efficiency and efficacy of a design?

3. Discuss the concepts of *crowding* versus *density*. What design characteristics affect a person's sense of space and control?

4. During your last shopping outing, what factors would be considered relative to the *pleasure–arousal–dominance theory*? What was the combined effect of these factors?

5. Discuss the relevance of store location in an Internet economy. Is location still important to a retail store's success? Why or why not?

6. Discuss the increasing impact of and need for parking structures. How does this affect the exterior design and presentation of shopping areas? Discuss design solutions that would improve the appearance and functionality of parking structures.

7. Discuss the types of music played in different types of stores. What does the music tell you about the target clientele?

8. Discuss the effects softened versions of advertising jingles might have on consumers in a grocery store. How might scent play a part in improving store sales?

9. Discuss important design characteristics of a restaurant known for exceptional service. What features support the efficiency and quality of customer service?

10. Discuss ways in which urban planning is affecting the layout and traffic flow of new malls. What methods are being used to encourage exploration and increase universal comfort in large shopping centers?

Learning Activities

1. In groups or on your own, develop a floor plan that identifies the placement of department store merchandise.

2. Visit a local department store and map out its floor plan, paying particular attention to where each department is located in relation to the others. Measure the distances between clothing racks and aisles. Note any differences between areas where men and women typically shop.

3. Design a window display along a community sidewalk, noting any special circumstances to be considered (e.g., window breakage or socioeconomic status).

4. Design parking facilities that are supportive of both vehicles and pedestrians, and analyze your designs with your classmates.

5. Using what you've learned about crowding, preferences, gender influences, and issues germane to restaurants, develop a restaurant design for a private country club catering to either male or female patrons.

6. Visit a local mall or shopping center and select a store you've never been in. List the visual cues you receive about the store; do they entice you to purchase or wander deeper into the store? Why or why not? How can you use information like this to inform your design decisions?

7. Visit a local grocery store during a busy shopping period and, in an aisle displaying similar products with different brand names, spend time observing how individuals choose between the products. How do one shopper's selections influence those of another? Gather data regarding the quantity of each brand selected over a set period of time. Next, manipulate the setting: Remove a noticeable number of slower-selling products from the shelf (be sure to replace or purchase them after this experiment). Does this change alter shoppers' selection patterns?

8. Compare and contrast the layout of a department store (recreational shopping) versus that of a grocery store (purposeful shopping). Draw sketches that illustrate typical floor plans, traffic patterns, and merchandise locations; provide at least one sketch that illustrates the view from a shopper's perspective.

9. Visit a local store that carries both men's and women's fashions, and sketch the layout of the spaces. Analyze the current layout relative to this chapter's information about gender. What improvements could be made based on this information?

10. Visit your favorite retail store and analyze its location based on the five criteria listed on page 280. Next, visit a store you've never entered and conduct the same analysis. Which site would you choose for your location?

11. Create a photo album showing six different storefront styles. Explain the positive and negative aspects of each style.

12. Sketch an interior elevation of your favorite retail store. Focus on types of display fixtures as well as lighting and décor. What aspects of this layout and design improve your shopping experience or leave you with positive memories?

13. Visit three different kinds of convenience stores and make quick sketches of the locations and surroundings. What similarities and differences are there relative to the defensibility of the spaces? How are the employees protected? How is theft deterred?

14. Visit a local shopping mall and interview three different store managers about their typical customer (develop a list of ten questions that can be answered quickly). Use this information to create a basic profile of the mall's target consumer group. Evaluate the facility's features and problems based on this demographic data.

15. With the traditional town square designs of smaller towns in mind, design a mall floor plan that incorporates many features of a town square. Be sure to consider activities that appeal to people of many age ranges and ways to allow several activities to occur simultaneously.

Terminology

atmospherics   Cues, such as sights, sounds, or scents, that contribute to the overall ambience of an environment

density-intensity theory   Premise that density itself is not harmful but rather that it amplifies everything else

descriptor   Environmental feature that helps us to understand and respond to a place

fourth environment   Place where individuals congregate other than their primary, secondary, and tertiary territories or spaces (i.e., not their residences or sites specifically developed for them)

implicit cue   Indicator of our behavior that we leave behind when we leave an environment

megastore   Large retail facility that offers consumers an expansive variety of goods and services; also called *hypermarket*

servicescape   Physical setting that is made up of a retail or service environment

virtual modeling   Practice of using implicit cues to modify behavior

References

1. Ang, S. H., Leong, S. M., and Lim, J. (1997). The mediating influence of pleasure and arousal on layout and signage effects. *Journal of Retailing and Consumer Services, 4-1,* 13–24.

2. Thang, D. C. L., and Tan, B. L. B. (2003) Linking consumer perception to preference of retail stores: An empirical assessment of the multi-attributes of store image. *Journal of Retailing and Consumer Services, 10-4,* 193–200.

3. Jones, M. A. (1999). Entertaining shopping experiences: An exploratory investigation. *Journal of Retailing and Consumer Services, 6-3,* 129–139.

4. Leong, S. M., Ang, S. H., and Low, L. H. L. (1997). Effects of physical environment and locus of control on service evaluation: A replication and extension. *Journal of Retailing and Consumer Services, 4-4,* 231–237.

5. See note 3.

6. Schlosser, A. E. (1998). Applying the functional theory of attitudes to understanding the influence of store atmosphere on store inferences. *Journal of Consumer Psychology, 7-4,* 345–369.

7. Razzouk, N.Y., Seitz, V., and Kumar, V. (2002). The impact of perceived display completeness/incompleteness on shoppers' in-store selection of merchandise: An empirical study. *Journal of Retailing and Consumer Services, 9-1,* 31–35.

8. Machleit, K. A., Eroglu, S. A., and Mantel, S. P. (2000). Perceived retail crowding and shopping satisfaction: What modifies this relationship? *Journal of Consumer Psychology, 9-1,* 29–42.

9. Schmidt, D. E., and Keating, J. P. (1979). Human crowding and personal control: An integration of the research. *Psychological Bulletin, 86-4,* 680–700.

10. Aiello, J. R., Thompson, D. E., and Brodzinsky, D. M. (1983). How funny is crowding anyway? Effects of room size, group size and the introduction of humor. *Basic and Applied Social Psychology, 4,* 193–207.

11. Karlin, R. A., Epstein, Y., and Aiello, J. (1978). Strategies for the investigation of crowding. In A. Esser and B. Greenbie (Eds.), *Design for communality and privacy* (pp. 71–88). New York: Plenum.

12. Taylor, R. B. (1988). *Human territorial functioning: An empirical, evolutionary perspective on individual and small group territorial cognitions, behaviors, and consequences.* Cambridge, MA: Cambridge University Press.

13. Barnard, W. A., and Bell, P. A. (1982). An unobtrusive apparatus for measuring interpersonal distances. *Journal of General Psychology, 107,* 85–90.

14. Gifford, R. (1982). Projected interpersonal distances and orientation choices: Personality, sex, and social situation. *Social Psychology Quarterly, 45,* 145–152.

15. Bell, P. A., Kline, L. M., and Barnard, W. A. (1988). Friendship and freedom of movement as moderators of sex differences in interpersonal distancing. *Journal of Social Psychology, 128,* 305–310.

16. Hill, M. R. (1984). Walking, crossing streets, and choosing pedestrian routes: A survey of recent insights from the social/behavioral sciences. *University of Nebraska Studies, new series no. 66,* 1984.

17. Savinar, J. (1975). The effect of ceiling height on personal space. *Man-Environment Systems, 5-5,* 321–324.

18. Torres, I. M., Summers, T. A., and Belleau, B. D., (2001). Men's shopping satisfaction and store preferences. *Journal of Retailing and Consumer Services, 8-4,* 205–212.

19. Bell, S. (1999). Image and consumer attraction to intraurban retail areas: An environmental

psychology approach. *Journal of Retailing and Consumer Services, 6-2,* 67–78.

20. See note 2.

21. See note 3.

22. Donovan, R. J., and Rossiter, J. R. (1982). Store atmosphere: An environmental psychology approach. *Journal of Retailing, 58,* 34–57.

23. See note 1.

24. See note 1.

25. Patricios, N. N. (1979). Human aspects of planning shopping centers. *Environment and Behavior, 11-4,* 511–538.

26. Harrell, G., Hutt, M., and Anderson, J. (1980). Path analysis of buyer behavior under conditions of crowding. *Journal of Marketing Research, 17,* 45–51.

27. See note 8.

28. See note 19.

29. See note 6.

30. See note 1.

31. Mehrabian, A., and Russell, J. A. (1974). *An approach to environmental psychology.* Cambridge, MA: MIT Press.

32. Tzeng, G. H., Teng, M. H., Chen, J. J., and Opricovic, S. (2002). Multicriteria selection for a restaurant location in Taipei. *International Journal of Hospitality Management, 21-1,* 171–187.

33. Easton, R., and McCall, W., Eds. (1995). *Santa Barbara architecture.* Capra Press: Santa Barbara, CA.

34. van Asperdt, A. (1999). BOOGIE-WOOGIE: The suburban commercial strip and its neighborhood. *Landscape Journal, 18-1,* 41–53.

35. Turley, L. W., and Milliman, R. E. (2000). Atmospheric effects on shopping behavior: A review of the experimental evidence. *Journal of Business Research, 49,* 193–211.

36. See note 1.

37. See note 7.

38. Galer, I. A. R., Ed. (1987). *Applied ergonomics handbook.* London: Butterworths.

39. Knez, I. (1995). Effects of indoor lighting on mood and cognition. *Journal of Environmental Psychology, 15,* 39–51.

40. Gergen, K. J., Gergen, M. K., and Barton, W. H. (1973). Deviance in the dark. *Psychology Today, 7,* 129–130.

41. Butler, D. L., and Biner, P. M. (1987). Preferred lighting levels: Variability among settings, behaviors and individuals. *Environment and Behavior, 19,* 695–721.

42. Fulberg, P. (2003). Using sonic branding in the retail environment—An easy and effective way to create consumer brand loyalty while enhancing the in-store experience. *Journal of Consumer Behaviour, 3-2,* 193–98.

43. Mattila, A. S., and Wirtz, J. (2001). Congruency of scent and music as a driver of in-store evaluations and behavior. *Journal of Retailing, 77-2,* 273–289.

44. Milliman, R. E. (1982). Using background music to affect the behavior of supermarket shoppers. *Journal of Marketing, 46,* 86–91.

45. Areni, C. S. (2003). Examining managers' theories of how atmospheric music affects perception, behaviour and financial performance. *Journal of Retailing and Consumer Services, 10-5,* 263–274.

46. North, A. C., and Hargreaves, D. J. (1999). Can music move people? The effects of musical complexity and silence on waiting time. *Environment and Behavior, 31-1,* 136–149.

47. See note 42.

48. See note 43.

49. See note 43.

50. OSHA (1998). *Recommendations for workplace violence prevention programs in late-night retail establishments* (OSHA #3153). Washington, DC: U.S. Department of Labor: Occupation Health and Safety Administration.

51. Crow, W. J., and Bull, J. L. (1975). *Robbery deterrence: An applied behavioral science demonstration.* La Jolla, CA: Western Behavioral Sciences Institute.

52. Athena Research Corporation. (1981). *Robber interview report.* Presented to the Crime Committee of the Southland Corporation, Dallas, TX.

53. Jeffery, C. R., Hunter, R. D. and Griswald, J. (1987). Crime prevention and computer analysis of convenience store robberies in Tallahassee, Florida. *Security Systems, 1-4.*

54. Archea, J. C. (1985). The use of architectural props in the conduct of criminal acts. *Journal of Architecture and Planning Research, 2,* 245–259.

55. See note 51.

56. D'Allesio, S., and Stolzenberg, L. (1990). A crime of convenience: The environment and

convenience store robbery. *Environment and Behavior, 22*, 255–271.

57. Wise, J. A., and Wise, B. K. (ca. 1985). *Bank interiors and bank robberies: A design approach to environmental security.* Rolling Meadows, IL: Bank Administration Institute.

58. Crowe, Timothy D. (2000). *Crime prevention through environmental design: Applications of architectural design and space management concepts* (2nd Edition), Stoneham, MA: Butterworth-Heinemann.

59. Dermody, M. B. (2002). Recruitment and retention practices in independent and chain restaurants. International *Journal of Hospitality and Tourism Administration, 3-1*, 107–117.

60. Satler, G. (2003). New York City restaurants: Vernaculars of global designing. *Journal of Architectural Education, 56-3*, 27–39.

61. See note 4.

62. Mattila, A. S. (2001). Emotional bonding and restaurant loyalty. *Cornell Hotel and Restaurant Administration Quarterly, 42-6*, 73–79.

63. See note 62.

64. See note 60.

65. See note 60.

66. See note 4.

67. See note 60.

68. Wildes, V. J., and Seo, W. (2001). Customers vote with their forks: Consumer complaining behavior in the restaurant industry. *International Journal of Hospitality and Tourism Administration, 2-2*, 21–34.

69. Thompson, G. M. (2002). Optimizing a restaurant's seating capacity. *Cornell Hotel and Restaurant Administration Quarterly, 43-4*, 48–57.

70. Thompson, G. M. (2003). Optimizing restaurant-table configuration: Specifying combinable tables. *Cornell Hotel and Restaurant Administration Quarterly, 44-1*, 53–60.

71. Becker, C., and Murrmann, S. K. (1999). The effect of cultural orientation on the service timing preferences of customers in casual dining operations: An exploratory study. *International Journal of Hospitality Management, 18-1*, 59–65.

72. See note 22.

73. Oppewal, H., and Timmermans, H. (1999).

Modeling consumer perception of public space in shopping centers. *Environment and Behavior, 31-1*, 45–65.

74. See note 73.

75. Moreno-Jimenez, A. (2001). Interurban shopping, new town planning and local development in Madrid metropolitan area. *Journal of Retailing and Consumer Services, 8-5*, 291–298.

76. See note 73.

77. See note 3.

78. Van Vliet, W. (1983). Exploring the fourth environment: An examination of the home range of city and suburban teenagers. *Environment and Behavior, 15-5*, 567–588.

79. Kim, Y. K., Kim, E. Y., and Kang, J. (2003). Teens' mall shopping motivations: Functions of loneliness and media usage. *Family and Consumer Sciences Research Journal, 32-2*, 140–167.

80. Brown, D., Sijpkes, P., and MacLean, M. (1986). The community role of public indoor space. *Journal of Architecture and Planning Research, 3*, 161–172.

81. See note 73.

82. Frewald, D. B. (1990). Preferences for older buildings: A psychological approach to architectural design. *Dissertation Abstracts International*, 51-1B, 414–415.

83. Dogu, U., and Erkip, F. (2002). Spatial factors affecting wayfinding and orientation: A case study in a shopping mall. *Environment and Behavior, 32-6*, 731–755.

84. Weisman, J. (1981). Evaluating architectural legibility: Way-finding in the built environment. *Environment and Behavior, 13-2*, 189–204.

85. See note 3.

86. See note 79.

87. Sonnenfeld, J. (1966). Variable values in space and landscape: An inquiry into the nature of environmental necessity. *Journal of Social Issues, 22-4*, 71–82.

88. Bernáldez, F. G., Gallardo, D., and Abello, R. P. (1987). Children's landscape preferences: From rejection to attraction. *Journal of Environmental Psychology, 7*, 169–176.

89. See note 79.

90. See note 84.

FIFTEEN

Community Environments

The word *community* can refer not only to an environment but also to a cognitive and emotional state; it can be as much a feeling as a place. The physical community influences the psychological community it contains and vice versa. Physical design affects social relationships in that it affects proximity (i.e., more opportunities for meeting others will result in more opportunities for social interaction and friendship); however, people prefer to associate with those who are like-minded, and no amount of physical closeness will offset this social distance.[1]

Physical or social communities arise when many individuals share a single geographic area. Built communities make up more than cities, towns, and neighborhoods; they include localities such as city blocks, office complexes, and apartment buildings. Those that are relatively self-sufficient (e.g., large healthcare and educational settings, resorts and cruise ships, and even some hotels and shopping malls) are microcommunities. Geographic communities such as precincts, districts, counties, boroughs, states, and so on are usually determined by political policy, whereas localized built communities are determined by public policy; the communities will prosper or fail as a result of the needs, attitudes, behaviors, and goals of the occupants and users.

Feelings of community are based on the sharing and commonality of space, attitude, and behavior. Community spirit, or **sense of community**, is a form of *place attachment* that begins when people share with others a physical space or environment (e.g., a neighborhood or workplace). This feeling deepens according to the number of physical or psychological attributes (e.g., race, age, gender, religion, status, purpose, principle, and vision) people have in common with other members and their

levels of comfort relative to the spaces themselves. The idea of fitting in or belonging are both comfortable and comforting; people derive the most satisfaction and, as a result, the greatest community spirit from sharing spaces with others who are similar to or at least compatible with them. Therefore, it is not surprising that cultural activities, aesthetics, and physical amenities are becoming increasingly important to residents of urban communities[2] (Figure 15.1).

Physical communities are made up of numerous *behavior settings* and require the careful consideration of transition zones, but they also are and encompass territories. Even microcommunities contain primary, secondary, and tertiary territories. For example, resorts, cruise ships, and some airports offer private quarters that serve as temporary *primary territories* for travelers; temporary *secondary territories* such as meeting rooms, bars, and gyms where people gather for a particular purpose; and temporary *tertiary territories* such as shops, eateries, and sitting areas that anyone of good standing in the microcommunity may utilize.

The planning, design, organization, safety, and management of spaces can have political, social, and cultural implications.[3] For example, culture influences the practice of everyday activities (such as cooking, washing, and shopping), and different groups may demand different qualities from the same built environment.[4] Designers have the goal to plan, design, create, or restore successful physical communities and must ensure the support of the psychological communities and constructs (such as safety) within them. Designers can enhance the actual and perceived safety of an environment through a host of measures, some of which come from defensible space.

297

Figure 15.1: Immigrants arriving in a new country tend to be unsure or unaware of local customs and social rules, and being unable to speak the new language exacerbates their feelings of insecurity. As a result, many newcomers cluster in immigrant enclaves. Such enclaves are commonly found in many U.S. cities; they can be large and famous (e.g., Little Italy in New York and Chinatown in San Francisco) or much smaller and known only to the local population.

Defensible Space

Defensible space theory holds that environmental attributes can be used to establish preventive controls against *territorial infringement*. Defensible space measures, both substantive and symbolic, can be applied to single structures and landscapes, as well as the various community contexts: blocks, neighborhoods, developments, centers, and districts. There is a direct correlation between community involvement and the likelihood of crime, and two of the most effective—and least expensive—crime-prevention controls are a sense of community and human surveillance. Neighbors tend to watch out for, or at least be aware of, one another, and they know who does and does not belong in their spaces at different times of the day or year. Numerous studies have demonstrated that fewer incidents of territorial infringement occur in neighborhoods

For more on the direct correlation between the community and the likelihood of crime, see Chapter 6.

where residents have more social interaction (Figure 15.2).

Crime can have a devastating impact not only on a person's sense of place attachment but also on the local economy. Urban planner Mitchell Rycus of the University of Michigan put it bluntly: "People won't live where they don't feel comfortable, and investors won't build where people don't live."[5] The ability to keep surveillance is a critical factor for burglars when they select their targets,[6] and feelings of environmental safety are often correlated to ease of navigation, the amount of natural landscaping, and street illumination.[7] One way to reduce neighborhood crime is to use high-intensity street lighting; however, this measure also increases light pollution (artificial light in the night sky).[8] Consider the use of motion-sensor lighting systems, which can be effective in terms of cost and crime deterrence and also eliminate unnecessary constant illumination.

DESIGN APPLICATION: Excessive light pollution is a problem highlighted by the 1994 Northridge (Los Angeles) earthquake when many standing outside noticed the beauty of the night sky for the first time.

Pedestrian activity and neighboring may be the best defense against crime, but the other defensible space measures are psychologically valuable as well. What appeals to law-abiding community members (because it makes them feel safer) also serves to deter criminals (for the opposite reason)—structures and spaces that are well defined, maintained, and illuminated and that offer clear lines of sight from inside and out. Many defensible space components have artistic value that can support overall design concepts, and incorporating them will not only enhance building, landscape, and neighborhood design but also serve to minimize potential concealment and entrapment and therefore increase occupants' feelings of safety and security. Examples range from a two-foot picket fence, which is essentially a *territorial marker*, to a six-foot-tall wrought-iron fence topped with spikes, which would deter most would-be criminals. Many cities, high-density housing developments, and homeowners employ surveillance cameras to prevent criminal activity. They based this on the premise that their presence alone is often enough to dissuade potential criminals.

Gated Communities

In many parts of the United States, a growing trend is the development of gated or walled communities. Although this method of defense dates back to the first human settlements, walled communities are a redundant method of fortification in societies that have public police and social order.[9] Gated communities have regained popularity as a result of perceived higher levels of crime and the fear of crime in affluent communities. As this perception and fear have grown, gated communities have become more comprehensive; some communities not only control access through gates or a security station but also offer their residents a range of nonresidential amenities, such as schools, offices, shops, and golf courses, becoming, in essence, urban fortresses.[10]

Figure 15.2: Outdoor seating areas not only afford resting places but also support increased community surveillance and thus help to prevent *territorial infringement*. The defensible space practice called *eyes on the street* is based on the idea that criminal activity is deterred when groups of people are nearby. City planners, architects, and designers should strive to incorporate outdoor seating within a variety of climates and situations.

The City

Throughout the past half century, increased global trading, advanced communication technologies, improved education rates, and workforce changes have altered the structure and composition of cities.[11] City planning has traditionally been based on the principle of dispersion (people moving away from the city) rather than on the provision of high-quality, high-density living spaces.[12] According to the U.S. Census Bureau, in 1999 more than 75 percent of U.S. housing units were located in metropolitan areas (i.e., cities and suburbs), almost half of the country's 115 million total housing units were located in the suburban parts of metropolitan areas, 30 percent were located in central cities, and the rest were located outside of metropolitan areas.[13]

A current trend affecting many U.S. communities is the exportation of blue-collar jobs to other countries. This trend is shifting our society toward a workforce that is made up of a higher percentage of white-collar workers, which is typically urban based. Demographic factors also play a role in the popularity of urban areas. Long commutes and the property maintenance associated with suburban life lack appeal for younger and older populations;

therefore, urban areas tend to have high concentrations of both groups.

Gentrification

Increased urban population growth is accompanied by a process called **gentrification**, which is the renewal and rebuilding of deteriorating areas. Unfortunately, the word has become synonymous with the displacement of the poor in many areas. Research has linked gentrification with spatial, economic, and social restructuring due to a shift toward a service-based society.[14] My experience has led me to distinguish three types of gentrification. The first, *public gentrification*, tends to be the most disruptive; it results when city officials seize properties through eminent domain and raze areas for redevelopment. The second, *private gentrification*, occurs when one or more people decide to redevelop an area by donating large sums of capital for specific development projects with the hopes of encouraging further development in the area. The third, *community gentrification*, occurs when community members act for the greater good of the community at large by frequenting local businesses almost exclusively and by reinvesting in their property. For example, gays and lesbians have revitalized the districts of Capitol Hill in Seattle, Castro in San Francisco, West Hollywood in Los Angeles, Hillcrest in San Diego, and many other areas throughout the nation. In these areas, gentrification began when gays and lesbians opted to live in one area so they could live freely without fear of retribution; it expanded as young heterosexual women moved in, followed by young heterosexual men. The overall process can be broken down into the following stages:

Go to Chapter 3 for more information about the five basic continual elements that lead to the image of a city.

1. Rundown community is adopted and renovated by gays and lesbians.
2. Young heterosexual women move into the community because they feel safe.
3. Young, progressive heterosexual men move in to be near the young women.

Pedestrian and Automobile Cities

There are two distinct types of cities, each with its own specific issues and circumstances. Cities that bristle with skyscrapers and appear to have grown up rather than spread out (e.g., New York, Boston,

and San Francisco) are **pedestrian-friendly cities**; their higher *density intensity* makes driving and parking a challenge and, as such, they are more walkable than **automobile cities**, which typically sprawl across hundreds of square miles (e.g., Dallas, Phoenix, and Los Angeles). Issues such as noise, density, and crowding are more problematic in pedestrian cities than in automobile cities, where problems arise from behavioral constraints caused by freeway and street traffic, inadequate public transportation, and the general inconvenience created by the multitude of maintenance operations required for vast amounts of public territory (e.g., streets, highways, and schools, parks).

Elements of Legibility

In his classic text *The Image of the City*, Kevin Lynch described how people imagine the city (i.e., how they create and remember mental images). His focus was on how people conceive of the structure found within their cities. Yielding to the reality that the mental images people form are individualistic, Lynch concluded that there are five basic continual elements that lead to the image of a city. These elements are listed below as follows:[15]

- *Paths* are identifiable and continuous channels of movement (e.g., streets, walkways, transit lines, canals, and railroads). Paths with clear origins and destinations have stronger identities, help tie the environment together, and strengthen users' senses of orientation when they are crossed. In communities, for example, paths are created through the use of gravel and concrete walkways (Figure 15.3).
- *Edges* are linear breaks in continuity that may serve as boundaries, borders, isolating barriers, uniting seams (e.g., walls, shorelines, railroad cuts, and edges of developments), and even paths. The strongest edges are visually prominent, continuous, and impenetrable; design features such as a row of buildings and sea walls can serve as edges.
- *Districts* are regions (relatively large sections of an environment) that have a common and distinctive character recognizable from within, without, and in passing. Districts are determined by thematic continuities (e.g., space, form, color, texture, detail, symbol,

building type, use, activity, level of upkeep, inhabitants, and topography); their physical boundaries may be definite, ambiguous, or nonexistent. Districts contain, and are therefore related to, paths, nodes, and landmarks, all of which structure the region internally and intensify its identity. For example, a theater district is made up of various facilities that have different décor and behavioral norms.

- *Nodes* are conceptual anchor points: strategic spots that people can enter or focal points to and from which people travel. Nodes may be junctions (e.g., path crossings and convergences or shifts between structures or transportation channels); similar decision points (e.g., traffic intersections, subway stations, and airports); or thematic concentrations of some characteristic and/or activity (e.g., a street-corner hangout or an artists' colony). Concentration nodes that are district centers—the focus and symbol of important regions—are appropriately called cores. Form is not essential to node recognition but does strengthen the space's impact (Figure 15.4). For example, a busy intersection and a popular city center would be considered nodes.

- *Landmarks* are highly visible geographic identity clues that serve as reference points for ori-

Figure 15.3 (top): Pedestrian paths should be lined with trees, provide areas for rest, and provide sources of entertainment. The path in this illustration resembles a park in that it has plenty of shade trees, a commemorative monument, and a large water fountain with ample bench seating. For pedestrians to feel safe and utilize walking paths, they must believe themselves safe from automobile traffic. Nearby and adjacent roadways should be narrowed to slow traffic, and lines of trees should be used to further separate them from pedestrian paths.

Figure 15.4 (middle): Perhaps the most famous transportation node in the United States is Grand Central Station in New York City. However, nodes are not limited to transportation; they may be junctions, thematic concentrations, or both.

Figure 15.5 (bottom): Landmarks may be large and famous like the Coit Tower in San Francisco, pictured here, or less imposing elements or structures (e.g., a huge tree, a statue, or a particular retail outlet), but they should be instantly recognizable across linguistic and cultural barriers.

entation and usually singular (unique or memorable), yet simply defined physical objects (e.g., mountain, building, sign, or tree). Landmarks, as with most visual stimuli, are more easily identifiable and more likely to be chosen as significant if they have high figure background contrast and clear form and are located in prominent locations, especially when they are located at junctions involving path decisions. For example, many town and city squares have landmarks that include large trees, fountains, or statues. (Figure 15.5)

Urban planners and designers have found these five elements to be useful as starting points from which to design urban communities and even larger microenvironments, such as resorts, schools, and hospitals, because they help to form a distinctive and legible environment that not only offers security but also heightens the human experience.

Cities are conglomerations of districts that interconnect[16] and are often hierarchical relative to prestige (i.e., image, property values, and available goods and services). Desirable city districts have features related to naturalness, good upkeep, orderly appearance, openness, and historical or social significance,[17] as well as distinct characteristics or qualities that distinguish them from other parts of the city. Metropolitan areas consist of freestanding retail stores among public areas such as roads and parking areas.[18] Simply stated, people need stores and stores need people, and this symbiotic relationship creates districts. Such districts are often called **urban villages** because the residents share a common culture, ethnicity, or lifestyle within a relatively self-sufficient area. In pedestrian cities, such as New York, the physical boundaries of individual communities that have greater *density intensity* may be ambiguous, but social boundaries often form distinct delineations (e.g., Soho). Conversely, conglomerations of suburban districts make up the sprawling automobile cities, such as Los Angeles, and are conceptualized as cities unto themselves (i.e., Century City). Having such districts within the greater context of the city is often a source of pride and part of an individual's identity and provides a sense of connection.[19] The residents of La Jolla, a community at the far northwest end of the sprawling city of San Diego, developed such a strong sense of *place identity* that they successfully petitioned the U.S. Post Office for the right to use the district's name as its legal address, and today most San Diego–area residents regard La Jolla as a separate city.

For city dwellers, even everyday activities are accompanied by a flood of stimulation deriving from pollution, noise, traffic, crime, *density intensity*, excessive *directed attention*, the demands of others, goal obstacles, frequently small living spaces, and uncomfortable commutes. This stream of stress-inducing stimuli can be overwhelming and result in *cognitive overload*. Planners and designers of urban environments and settings need to be acutely aware of these challenges and strive to minimize stimulation by creating relaxing sanctuaries, optimizing the use of available space, creating the illusion of larger spaces, and incorporating natural elements wherever possible.

Commercial Communities

Commercial communities make up more than just business districts (i.e., regions having a specific commercial focus, such as financial, industrial, and theatrical); they include high-rise office buildings, trade centers, business plazas, and *neighborhood work centers*, as well as shopping centers, malls, and even swap meets and farmers' markets. As urban population levels and property values continue to escalate, more commercial communities are being subjected to gentrification as developers strive to improve existing environmental images and increase their profit margins. One research team recommends the provision of daily simultaneous activities, such as shopping and business centers placed together in commercial areas, contending that this action will strengthen pedestrian accessibility to both sectors.[20] Streets, walkways, landscaping, building exteriors, signage, lighting, and upkeep all contribute to a commercial area's image, and consumers' feelings about an area will affect their willingness to shop there.[21]

Districts

Many districts encompass commercial and residential constituencies (i.e., serve as **mixed-use communities**), and planners and designers of such areas must be sensitive to this interrelationship. Design can convey many messages, and if they are incongruent with the rest of the landscape or scene, people will respond negatively.[22] Those who favor tearing down old buildings and erecting avant-garde structures often assume an entire area will be similarly redeveloped. However, because such a massive undertaking is unlikely to be completed in a single lifetime, design elements that soften the juxtaposition of old and new structures and provide continuity should be incorporated into the redevelopment area

Whether it involves a boutique, an apartment building, or a large mixed-use complex, design should ensure coherence within the community (i.e., be legible as to what the building is), maintain design congruency (i.e., maintain similar lines, styles, and building heights), and make provisions to include elements of nature wherever possible. Architectural designers can create continuity between old and new buildings by using common roof lines and similar or complementary materials for the façade and by replicating the existing design elements and ornamentation (e.g., gables or cornices) in new construction.[23]

Traditional community environments in which residents gather and socialize (e.g., coffee shops, cafés, and similar establishments that serve as venues for the development of social bonds and community formation) also function as districts. Architects and planners need to recognize this function and allow for the provision of common gathering spaces, which include sidewalk patios and eateries. However, planners and designers must also consider that the overall environment often determines the success of such places and must be suitable for the services that will be offered. For instance, a sidewalk café setting should offer patrons a pleasant view; protect them from seasonal elements such as rain, snow, and bright sunlight; and minimize their exposure to the noise and pollution generated by vehicular traffic.

In the past, many village streets were lined with business establishments that were owned by families who lived upstairs. One of the challenges of developing a city district into an urban village today is that modern districts usually are made up of single-storied structures built along commercial corridors. As a result, in residential neighborhoods that are adjacent to commercial areas, many homes

face the rear of stores where deliveries are made.[24] Excessive traffic noise is known to detract from neighborhood satisfaction;[25] however, bringing in necessary goods and services to a central area surrounded by residential property, and strengthening access to public recreational areas, can reduce dependence on automobiles and create a more cohesive and pleasing environment for pedestrians.[26] Another challenge is that of people who want to own a detached home with some land, which is in direct conflict with the high-density living usually associated with urban villages.

A commercial area's overall attractiveness and the number, diversity, and quality of its shops determine a district's ability to attract shoppers.[27] Price and proximity are relatively minor factors in many consumers' decisions about where to shop;[28] and time constraints may lead some to seek a single location in another district that has numerous retail establishments.[29] Ultimately, consumers rely on their images of an area to assess the quality of goods and services as well as the value of products sold.[30] If jewelry stores in Beverly Hills and a working-class community, respectively, offer identical diamond rings, which location would command the highest retail price?

DESIGN APPLICATION. When designing a commercial area, consider how it will be used. Consumers will use it to acquire goods and services, younger and older people will likely use it for socializing, and local officials may use it to stimulate community solidarity. How the area is designed and the features and services that it contains will affect its viability. For example, older people are sensitive to intense sunlight and glare and will likely avoid unshaded areas, parents of small children will avoid high-traffic areas that lack visual surveillance, and people who are fearful of crime will likely avoid areas that suggest even the slightest possibility of criminal activity. Providing outdoor furniture, decorative planters, healthy vegetation, water features, outdoor sculpture, ample lighting, and banners on lampposts will not only attract more pedestrians but also increase their perceptions of safety.[31]

Consumers will be attracted to prominent chain outlets that serve as anchors in commercial centers, but designers should carefully select such anchor

Figure 15.6: Many smaller urban parks can serve as nodes to and from which people travel. These can take the form of plazas or small areas along walking paths.

stores so they don't compete with smaller local shops. Name-brand clothing stores, for example, appeal to particular market segments yet do not overshadow other specialty stores, and their corporate status provides staying power; department stores, however, should be avoided because of the wide variety of goods and lower prices they offer compared with independent merchant stores. Designers should include a significant number of popular shops to aid in attracting customers.[32]

Design can enhance *environmental legibility* with coherent layouts, interconnecting sidewalks, and limited directional signage. Commercial complexes should not resemble residential or retail settings, nor should zones or buildings be separated by walls, landscaping, or other barriers that force pedestrians to go out of their ways to reach their destinations. Signage is often overused, creating excessive stimulation and eventually leading to *environmental numbness*. Studies show that people dislike streets with obtrusive signs,[33] and that the most pleasant streets have signs of moderate complexity and high coherence.[34] The strategic placement of a few well-designed signs within a legible environment will have greater positive effects than signs posted at every turn and intersection; therefore, signage should be kept to a minimum and used only when other forms of environmental communication cannot be utilized.

See Chapter 4 for more information about the prospect-refuge theory.

The *prospect-refuge theory* is based on the evolutionary concept that people prefer environments on the edges between open and closed areas.[35] Design can compensate to some degree for feelings of crowding due to high spatial density or vulnerability due to low spatial density by developing plazas that resemble parks, dispersing urban parks among commercial centers (Figure 15.6), and establishing behavioral zoning in larger recreational parks throughout the village (e.g., one park for adult sports, one for children's activities, and one for peaceful contemplation).

"Main Street"

The core of many small towns and city districts is "Main Street," where retail stores, service areas, religious buildings, and government offices are located. Many main streets in small towns are composed of small one-story buildings that house specialty shops and eateries, and include a common, often central gathering place, the frequent use of which promotes community solidarity. Main streets promote a sense of community not only by providing places for people to meet, socialize, rest, or watch others, but also by facilitating local events such as art exhibitions and holiday celebrations—and all within walking distance.

Many main streets were originally the primary commercial areas of the first suburbs of older communities that slowly engulfed their suburbs as they grew; some were integrated into cities while others became districts or urban villages. In some parts of the United States, population shifts caused by people fleeing rural areas in search of better jobs in cities have depopulated small-town main streets. Contributing to their decline is the rise of superstores that can offer products at a fraction of the cost offered at smaller stores. These and other factors have left many main streets in states of decay, with empty streets and boarded-up shops. Today, however, there is growing interest in the revitalization of such areas that have been neglected or abandoned.

DESIGN APPLICATION. Main streets, in both large and small settings, provide people with opportunities to shop and be entertained, as well as open areas where residents and visitors can congregate, such as town squares, urban parks, and plazas. Briefly, a town square is a larger piece of land in a central area of a dis-

trict, urban parks are small green spaces intermittently dispersed throughout commercial corridors, and plazas are areas in front of large business complexes and high-rise buildings. Although the terms for these open public spaces differ, many of the same design principles apply to each. They should be designed with social interaction in mind[36, 37] and be pedestrian-friendly[38] and aesthetically pleasing. Scenes containing natural features, green areas, open spaces with pathways, and water features are universally liked;[39] if designers add suitable seating areas and shady trees, they will have a template for designing plazas and urban parks.

"Walking Distance"

The maximum distance the average person will walk to reach a particular destination, commonly referred to as **walking distance**, is approximately a quarter of a mile or 400 meters.[40–42] This quarter of a mile should contain attractive features and well-landscaped walking areas, which not only will be aesthetically pleasing but also will help to promote a sense of security.[43] Consider invoking segmentation biases by incorporating meaningful intersections and landmarks, without which people may perceive the distance as being longer than it actually is. Good overall visual stimuli (e.g., attractive signs, awnings, and plants in front of shops) will encourage both pedestrian and shopping activity in the environment.[44]

Traffic Calming

Traffic-calming strategies reduce traffic flow and speed, which benefits children who play outside, pedestrians, and cyclists[45] during days and evenings and enhance nighttime neighborhood surveillance. Figure 15.7a–k illustrates various traffic-calming strategies. Traffic calming can be accomplished by means of speed bumps or humps, circuitous intersections such as roundabouts or traffic circles, sidewalk bump-outs (i.e., paved sidewalk areas that extend into the roadway), T-configuration roadway alignments, street closures, island narrowing, winding curves called *chicanes*, and raised walkways.[46, 47] Sidewalk bump-outs (also called *bulb-outs* or *pop-outs*) at intersections serve to visually separate driving and parking lanes, provide clear areas of shorter distances for pedestrian crossing, and accommodate

decorative features such as vegetation or statuary.[48] Incorporating a T-configuration not only reduces vehicle operating speeds within intersections, as well as the likelihood of the roadway becoming a bypass for other roads, but also creates a focal point that can be used as a park.[49]

Residential Communities

As populations increase and society continues to evolve, interest in how neighborhoods affect the physical and mental health of their residents is growing. Residential environments are not simply physical spaces in which people live; they are the aggregate of what people think about them and how they interact within them[50] and can influence residents' behaviors, attitudes, values, and opportunities.[51] Neighborhood characteristics may influence children directly through the availability of resources (e.g., libraries, schools, and suitable recreation areas) or indirectly through their parents' experiences.[52]

The landscape in which people live plays a major role in people's perceptions of themselves and the images they present to society. Complexity (with a degree of order) and open spaces contribute to greater visual richness, and chaotic scenes, excessive complexity, too many nuisance elements (e.g., vehicles, noise, glare, and foul odors), atypical and illegible scenes, and inconsistent lighting all contribute to disorder.[53]

In an Australian study of the notion of town character from a community's perspective, residents of a coastal town reported that a positive character image was strongly supported by landscape features associated with naturalness, beauty, pleasantness, and interest created by landmarks and other built features.[54] Residents identified other landscape features associated with negative meanings, such as boredom, ugliness, lack of charm and stimulation, monotony, unpleasantness, and being ordinary as incompatible with local character.

Neighboring may be loosely defined as a set of social relationships based on shared locales. Different types of neighboring are dependent on the amounts and levels of spaciousness within neighborhoods, including physical density, structured and unstructured open space, and the quality of buildings. One recent study's subjects linked spacious-

Street Closure

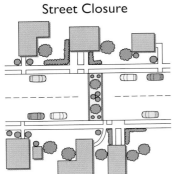

a

Traffic Redirection

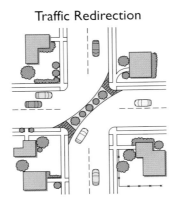

b

Cross Traffic Closure

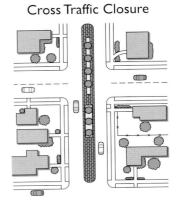

c

Single Direction Closure

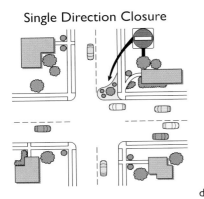

d

Raised Intersection

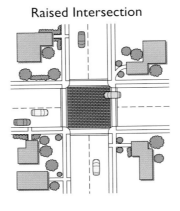

e

Speed Table

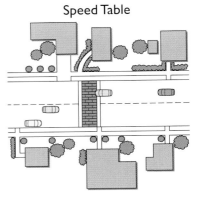

f

Speed Hump

BUMP

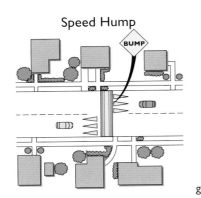

g

Island Narrowing

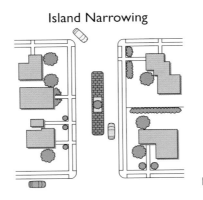

h

Choker

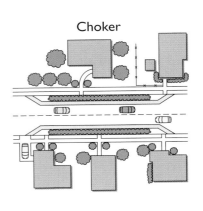

i

Traffic Circle

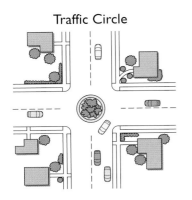

j

Chicane

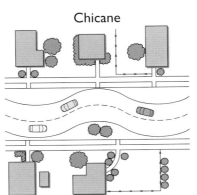

k

for ingress, egress, socialization, and relaxation? How do the different uses relate to one another? Using tracing paper, overlay your zoning map with a diagram showing pedestrian and vehicular traffic flow.

7. Visit different local neighborhoods, including at least one that has been revitalized, one that is mixed-use, one that is not well cared for, and one that is high-rent but single-use. Without focusing on the design details, sketch massing diagrams and traffic diagrams that illustrate the overall impression and feeling of these neighborhoods. Pay particular attention to the spacing of buildings, how the roof lines relate to one another, how pedestrians access residences and businesses, and the social areas.

8. Photograph a town square, plaza, and park, making sure your images capture the spaces' intended uses and also highlight critical safety and navigational features. Are these spaces being used as intended? Provide photographic evidence to support your answer.

9. Ask ten friends to list the areas they consider to be *walking distance* from their homes and plot these locations on a map. How do these distances relate to the standard quarter mile or 400 meters?

10. Using a preexisting neighborhood (no larger than three square blocks) developed before 1980, draw a detailed map or a current organizational layout. Then, using the information in the text, redesign the neighborhood to incorporate mixed-use areas, park settings, controlled traffic, retail and business spaces within walking distance, social areas, and areas suitable for people of different ages. Be sure to consider issues of *defensible space* and security.

Terminology

automobile city   City that typically sprawls across hundreds of square miles (e.g., Los Angeles)

gentrification   Process of renewing deteriorating urban areas so as to encourage social and economic growth

mixed-use community   Structure or district that encompasses a variety of uses such as housing, retail, and restaurants.

pedestrian-friendly city   City that appears to have grown up rather than spread out (e.g., New York)

sense of community   Emotional bond to a place based on feelings of belonging relative to the occupants, environment, or both; form of *place attachment*

urban village   City district where residents share a common culture, ethnicity, or lifestyle within a relatively self-sufficient area

walking distance   Maximum distance the average person will walk to reach a particular destination; approximately a quarter of a mile or 400 meters

References

1. Abu-Ghazzeh, T. M. (1998). Housing layout, social interaction, and the place of contact in Abu-Nuseir, Jordan. *Journal of Environmental Psychology (1999), 19-1*, 41–73.

2. Clark, T. N., Lloyd, R., Wong, K. K., and Jain, P. (2002). Amenities drive urban growth. *Journal of Urban Affairs, 24-5*, 493–515.

3. Haar, S. (2002). Location, location, location: Gender and the archaeology of urban settlement. *Journal of Architectural Education, 55-3*, 150–160.

4. Rapoport, A. (1998). Using "culture" in housing design. *Housing and Society, 25-1/2*, 1–20.

5. Savitskie, J. (1996). Downtown: Sense of security vital for neighborhood growth. *The Detroit News* [Online]: www.detroitnews.com.1996/menu/stories/67591.htm.

6. MacDonald, J.E., and Gifford, R. (1989). Territorial cues and defensible space theory: The burglar's point of view. *Journal of Environmental Psychology, 9*, 193–205.

7. Hanyu, K. (2000). Visual properties and affective appraisals in residential areas in daylight. *Journal of Environmental Psychology, 20-3*, 273–284.

8. Painter, K. A., and Farrington, D.P. (2001). The financial benefits of improved street lighting, based on crime reduction. *Lighting Research and Technology, 33-1*, 3-12.

9. Landman, K., & Schönteich, M., (2002). Urban fortresses: gated communities as a reaction to crime. *African Security Review, 11*, 4.

10. See note 9.

11. See note 2.

12. See note 1.

13. U.S. Bureau of the Census (13 October 2003). "Housing: Physical Characteristics." Retrieved 06 Sept. 2004 from http://factfinder.census.gov/jsp/saff/SAFFInfo.jsp?_pageId=tp13_housing_physical.

14. Satler, G. (2003). New York City restaurants: Vernaculars of global designing. *Journal of Architectural Education, 56-3*, 27–39.

15. Lynch, K. (1960). *The Image of the City*. Cambridge, MA: MIT Press.

16. Bonnes, M., Mannetti, L., Tanucci, G., and Secchiaroli, G. (1990). The city as a multiplace system: An analysis of people-urban environment transactions. *Journal of Environmental Psychology, 10*, 37–66.

17. Nasar, J. L. (1990b). The evaluative image of the city. *Journal of the American Planning Association, 56*, 41–53.

18. Bell, S. (1999). Image and consumer attraction to intraurban retail areas: An environmental psychology approach. *Journal of Retailing and Consumer Services, 6-2*, 67–78.

19. Proshansky, H. M., Fabian, A. K., and Kaminoff, R. (1983). Place-identity: Physical world socialization of the self. *Journal of Environmental Psychology, 3*, 57–83.

20. Filion, P., McSpurren, K., and Huether, N. (2000). Synergy and movement within suburban mixed-use centers: The Toronto experience. *Journal of Urban Affairs, 22-4*, 419–438.

21. See note 18.

22. Wohlwill, J. F. (1982). The visual impact of development in coastal zone areas. *Coastal Zone Management Journal, 9-3/4*, 225–248.

23. Schmandt, M. J. (1999). The importance of history and context in the postmodern urban landscape. *Landscape Journal, 18-2*, 157–165.

24. Van Asperdt, A. (1999). BOOGIE-WOOGIE: The suburban commercial strip and its neighborhood. *Landscape Journal, 18-1*, 41–53.

25. Higgitt, N. C., and Memken, J. A. (2001). Understanding neighborhoods. *Housing and Society, 28-1/2*, 29–46.

26. See note 20.

27. Dennis, C., Marsland, D., and Cockett, T. (2002). Central place practice: Shopping cen-tre attractiveness measures, hinterland boundaries and the U.K. retail hierarchy. *Journal of Retailing and Consumer Services, 9-4*, 185–199.

28. See note 18.

29. Moreno-Jimenez, A. (2001). Interurban shopping, new town planning and local development in Madrid metropolitan area. *Journal of Retailing and Consumer Services, 8-5*, 291–298.

30. See note 18.

31. See note 23.

32. See note 27.

33. Nasar, J. L., and Hong, X. (1999). Visual preferences in urban signscapes. *Environment and Behavior, 31*, 45–65.

34. Nasar, J. L. (1987). The effect of sign complexity and coherence on the perceived quality of retail scenes. *Journal of the American Planning Association, 53*, 499–509.

35. Appleton, J. (1975). *The experience of landscape*. New York: Wiley.

36. Whyte, W. H. (1980). *The social life of small urban spaces*. New York: The Conservation Foundation.

37. Nasar, J. L. (1990a). Patterns of behavior in public spaces. *Journal of Architecture and Planning Research, 7*, 71–85.

38. See note 24.

39. Fenton, D. M. (1985). Dimensions of meaning in perception of natural settings and their relationships to aesthetic response. *Australian Journal of Psychology, 37*, 325-339.

40. Aultman-Hall, L., Roorda, M., and Baetz, B. W. (1997). Using GIS for evaluation of neighborhood pedestrian accessibility. *Journal of Urban Planning and Development, 123-1*, 10–17.

41. See note 24.

42. Pikora, T., Giles-Corti, B., Bull, F., Jamrozik, K., and Donovan, R. (2003). Developing a framework for assessment of the environmental determinants of walking and cycling. *Social Science & Medicine, 56*, 1693–1703.

43. See note 20.

44. Zacharias, J. (2001). Path choice and visual stimuli: Signs of human activity and architecture. *Journal of Environmental Psychology, 21-4*, 341–352.

45. Auld, J. W., (2001). Consumers, cars, and communities: The challenge of sustainability. In-

ternational *Journal of Consumer Studies, 25-3*, 228-237.

46. Wolshon, B., and Wahl, J. (1999). Novi's main street: Neotraditional neighborhood planning and design. *Journal of Urban Planning and Development, 125-1*, 2–16.

47. See note 45.

48. See note 46.

49. See note 46.

50. Popay, J., Thomas, C., Williams, G., Bennett, S., Gatrell, A., and Bostock, L. (2003). A proper place to live: Health inequalities, agency and the normative dimensions of space. *Social Science & Medicine, 57*, 55–69.

51. Brooks-Gunn, J., Duncan, G. J., Klebanov, P. K., and Sealand, N. (1993). Do neighborhoods influence child and adolescent development? *American Journal of Sociology, 99*, 353–395.

52. See note 25.

53. See note 7.

54. Green, R. (1999). Meaning and form in community perception of town character. *Journal of Environmental Psychology, 19-4*, 311–329.

55. See note 42.

56. See note 7.

57. Skjaeveland, O. (2001). Effects of street parks on social interactions among neighbors: A place perspective. *Journal of Architectural and Planning Research, 18-2*, 131–147.

58. Levine-Coley, R., Kuo, F. E., and Sullivan, W. C. (1997). Where does community grow? The social context created by nature in urban public housing. *Environment and Behavior, 29-4*, 468–494.

59. See note 7.

60. Hanyu, K. (1997). Visual properties and affective appraisals in residential areas after dark. *Journal of Environmental Psychology, 17-4*, 301–315.

61. Case, D. (1996). Contributions of journeys away to the definition of home: An empirical study of a dialectical process. *Journal of Environmental Psychology, 16-1*, 1–15.

62. Nasar, J. L. (1983). Adult viewers' preferences in residential scenes: A study of the relationship of environmental attributes to preference. *Environment and Behavior, 15*, 589–614.

63. Stamps, A. E. (1999). Physical determinants of preferences for residential façades. *Environment and Behavior, 31-6*, 723–751.

64. See note 62.

65. Gaster, S. (1991). Urban children's access to their neighborhood: Changes over three generations. *Environment and Behavior, 23*, 70–85.

66. See note 45.

67. See note 42.

68. See note 42.

69. See note 40.

70. See note 42.

APPENDIX

11. A Behavioral Game Methodology for the Study of Proxemic Behavior by William J. Ickinger

http://sharktown.com/proxemics/gfx/media/RESEAR1.pdf

Ickinger's thesis on behavioral models deals specifically with the manner in which people define personal space during interactions.

12. Approach—Avoidance Conflict Revisited by Christine Hyde for the British Stammering Association

www.stammering.org/approach-avoidance.html

Hyde explores an example of approach-avoidance conflict.

13. Assessing Your Approach-Avoidance Tendencies, presented by Rollins College

www.rollins.edu/communication/wschmidt/approach_avoidance.htm

This is a very brief self-survey to determine approach-avoidance tendencies.

14. Urban Forests and Parks as Privacy Refuges by William E. Hammitt for the *Journal of Arboriculture*, 28(1): January 2002

www.treelink.org/joa/2002/jan/03Hammitt.pdf

Hammitt makes a convincing argument for urban green spaces as settings for privacy and rejuvenation with heavy emphasis on the role of privacy in healthy living.

15. Intimate Relationships: Vitally Linked to Health from the Pfizer Journal—Perspectives on Health Care and Biomedical Research

www.thepfizerjournal.com/default.asp?a=article&j=tpj15&t=Intimate%20Relationships%3A%20Vitally%20Linked%20to%20Health

This is a panel of experts who offer information and advice in this article about the necessity of intimacy for human well-being.

16. The Impact of Density and the Definition and Ratio of Activity Centers on Children in Child-care Classrooms by Randy White for the White Hutchinson Leisure & Learning Group, Kansas City, Missouri

www.whitehutchinson.com/children/articles/ratio.shtml

White writes about the negative effects of high-density classrooms and crowding on young children. This article includes design cues to assist students and professionals design classroom areas more conducive to learning and happiness.

17. Danger on the Dance Floor: A Study of Interior Design, Crowding, and Aggression in Nightclubs by S. Macintyre, V. Police, and Ross Homel of Griffith University, Australia

www.popcenter.org/Library/CrimePrevention/Volume%2007/03%20McIntyre.pdf

This detailed study examines the correlations between poor interior design, crowding in nightclubs and increased incidence of violence. Suggestions are made for relieving the perception of crowding and thereby reducing potential for violent outbursts.

18. Crowding and Violence on Psychiatric Wards: Explanatory Models from the Canadian Psychiatric Association

www.cpa-apc.org/Publications/Archives/CJP/2001/June/crowding2.asp

This article is a detailed observation of causes and effects of overcrowding in psychiatric wards and why the crowding often results in violence. Suggestions are given to avoid the sense of crowding through better design principles and other methods.

19. Excerpt from *The Impact of Density: The Importance of Nonlinearity and Selection on Flight and Fight Response* by Wendy C. Regoeczi. Social Forces article review by George H. Conklin for *Sociation Today*

www.ncsociology.org/sociationtoday/v22/crowding.htm

The excerpt from the book *The Impact of Density* outlines effects of density and overcrowding, the resulting potential for social withdrawal, as well as lack of privacy, on people in urban environments.

20. The Effects of Prison Overcrowding from the John Howard Society of Alberta, Canada

www.patrickcrusade.org/EFFECTS_OF_OVERCROWDING.html

This article discusses the problem of prison overcrowding, a significant concern in Canada and the United States. The cyclical nature of adverse reactions to overcrowding and its effects on the entire prison population is discussed.

Chapter Five

1. Evolutionary Psych Strikes Back by Sarah Blustain for *Psychology Today*

http://cms.psychologytoday.com/articles/pto-129.html

APPENDIX

Blustain presents the debate between two seemingly opposed schools of thought with regard to gender roles and evolution. The debate has been ongoing for decades and continues to grind forward unresolved.

2. Staying Alive: Evolution, Culture, and Women's Intra-Sexual Aggression by Anne Campbell of Durham University, North Carolina

www.bbsonline.org/documents/a/00/00/04/40 /bbs00000440-00/bbs.campbell.html

Campbell gives a detailed report on the evolution of gender differences, specifically the different externalization of aggression by women compared with the violence of men.

3. Evolutionary Psychology: A Defense—Sort of! by Ken Taylor for Philosophy Talk . . . The Blog

http://theblog.philosophytalk.org/2005/05 /evolutionary_ps.html

Taylor writes in response to a discussion dismissing the evolutionary theory as having no merit at all. Although not exactly a defense of the evolution theory, this entry offers some insight into both sides of the story in a thought-provoking manner.

4. The New Sex Scorecard by Hara Estroff Marano for *Psychology Today*

http://cms.psychologytoday.com/articles /pto-2832.html

Estroff Marano explores the biological and physiological similarities and differences between males and females with the outcome of discussing why women and men process information differently.

5. Bimbos and Rambos: The Cognitive Basis of Gender Stereotypes by Margaret W. Matlin, SUNY at Geneseo, for the National Honor Society in Psychology

www.psichi.org/pubs/articles/article_112.asp

This article is a review of a lecture given by Margaret Matlin on gender stereotypes and cognitive processing by males and females. Matlin is especially focused on how the stereotypes lead to trends in cognitive processing.

6. Influence of the School Facility on Student Achievement by E. Jago, and K. Tanner at the University of Georgia; Dept. of Educational Leadership

www.coe.uga.edu/sdpl/researchabstracts/visual.html

This article discusses the impact of lighting, color, and aesthetics in classrooms on instructors and students. The information covered includes effects on absenteeism, performance, health, and behavior.

7. The Meaning of Color for Gender by Natalia Khouw for Color Matters Research

www.colormatters.com/khouw.html

Several studies are examined in this paper regarding the effects of color by gender. Although findings are ambiguous they are thought provoking.

8. The Psychology of Color presented by San Diego State University, California

http://coe.sdsu.edu/eet/Articles/wadecolor/start.htm

This simple page gives the basics of color theory and serves as a starting point for studies into the effects of color on mood.

9. Color, Value, and Hue from Art, Design and Visual Thinking, An Interactive Textbook by Charlotte Jirousek of Cornell University

http://char.txa.cornell.edu/language/element/color /color.htm

Jirousek gives a detailed view of color concepts including explanations of hue and value, as well as an introduction to color psychology.

10. Wayfinding Textbook Project from the Institute for Innovative Blind Navigation

www.wayfinding.net/iibnNECtextbook.htm

This constantly evolving e-text contains a multitude of information on wayfinding techniques and design options for people with visual disabilities.

11. Spatial Aspects of Task-Specific Wayfinding Maps: A Representation-Theoretic Perspective by Christian Freksa, Department for Informatics, University of Hamburg, Austria

www.arch.usyd.edu.au/kcdc/books/VR99/Freksa.html

Freska gives an in-depth look into the ways of assisting in wayfinding and designing useable signage options.

12. Wayfinding is Not Signage by John Muhlhausen for Signs of the Times magazine

www.signweb.com/ada/cont/wayfinding0800.html

Muhlhausen gives concise information about signage and wayfinding techniques that are suitable in combination or independently to suit the needs of the site and the population who would be using the wayfinding markers.

13. Creating Park Signage: Some Helpful Hints from Project for Public Spaces, Inc., Lebowitz & Gould Design, Inc. and Lance Wyman Design, Ltd

www.pps.org/upo/info/design/Signage

This clear and easy-to-read Web page shows some options for clear, easily understood signage. Although it focuses primarily on signage for parks, the guidelines given can be developed to suit other projects.

Chapter Six

1. The Effects of Stressors, Learning Module 2 from the University of Virginia School of Nursing

www.nursing.virginia.edu/centers/research/wait/psyched/stressors.html

This is a clear study guide with information on stressors, stress responses, coping behaviors, and relationship of stress to anxiety and depression.

2. What Stress Does to the Body. Presented by Indiana University, adapted from R. C. Engs, *Alcohol and Other Drugs: Self Responsibility*

www.indiana.edu/~engs/hints/stress1.htm

This article explains the effects of stress and stressors on the body. Easy-to-read tables are included to break down the information in point form.

3. Stress from Nidus Information Services

www.reutershealth.com/wellconnected/doc31.html

This is a succinct explanation of stressors and stress-related ailments. Also included on the site are links to further research and holistic treatments.

4. A Hassle a Day May Keep the Doctor Away: Enhancing Versus Suppressive Effects of Stress on Immune Function by Firdaus S. Dhabhar, Ph.D., Ohio State University, for the National Center for Complementary and Alternative Medicine

http://nccam.nih.gov/news/upcomingmeetings/abstracts_mt/stress.htm

Dhabhar presents a study on acute stress and its beneficial effects on health, as opposed to chronic (long-term) stressors, which have a negative health effect.

5. When Buildings Don't Work: The Role of Architecture in Human Health by Gary Evans and Janetta Mitchell McCoy of Cornell University, for the *Journal of Environmental Psychology*

http://web.media.mit.edu/~intille/teaching/fall03/readings/EvansMcCoy98.pdf

This article regards the potential beneficial effects of sensitive design in interior design and architecture. Stress is the ailment used as the example for prevention in this paper.

6. Who Decides What Constitutes a Pollution Problem?: Barriers to Community Organizing Around Small Source Polluters in Low-income Communities by Raquel Rivera Pinderhughes, San Francisco State University

http://bss.sfsu.edu/raquelrp/pub/1997_july_pub.html

Rivera Pinderhughes expresses the concerns about how pollution is dealt with and whose responsibility it is to remedy the problem. A case study in a low-income area is used to outline the issues and suggest possible action.

7. Promote Health and Well-Being by the Whole Building Design Guide Committee

www.wbdg.org/design/promote_health.php

This is a series of simple guidelines offered to aid designers in creating healthy buildings through use of natural light, ventilation, and reducing indoor air contamination through well-designed ventilation systems.

8. The U.S. Environmental Protection Agency Air Pollution subtopic menu

www.epa.gov/ebtpages/airairpollution.html

The EDA provides up-to-date, accurate information on air pollutants and the results of pollution. Topics are sorted alphabetically by type in easy to browse sections. Each subtopic is described succinctly with access to legal restrictions on the materials, if applicable.

9. Cause and Effects of Noise Pollution by Daniel G. Nunez at the University of California, Irvine

http://darwin.bio.uci.edu/~sustain/global/sensem/S98/Nunez/Noise.html

This is an in-depth paper into the causes and effects of noise pollution. Discussed are scenarios that are common to most people, physiological information about the potential harmful effects of noise pollution, and unexpected sources of potentially damaging sounds.

10. Health House

    www.HealthHouse.org

    The Health House is a website maintained by the American Lung Association. People can easily find information on improving and maintaining indoor air quality at this site.

11. Indoor Air Pollutants

    www.simpsonpowervac.com/commserv.htm

    Simpson Power Vac commercial website gives information on removal of indoor air pollutants in air ducts, such as bacteria, fungi, and fiberglass particles.

12. Sick Building Syndrome

    www.epa.gov/iaq/pubs/sbs.html

    The U.S. Environmental Protection Agency website gives extensive details on Sick Building Syndrome, including causes, symptoms and solutions.

13. Decibel Levels

    www.lhh.org/noise/decibel.htm

    The Noise Center of the League for the Hard of Hearing provides a useful list of disruptive sounds along with their decibel level. Also included for the sake of reference are other levels of sound we hear routinely, such as normal breathing, rain falling, and whispering.

14. CPTED Crime Prevention Through Environmental Design (CPTED) for the Isle of Wight Crime & Disorder Partnership

    www.iowcrime-disorder.org/design.html

    This is a brief discussion of the ideas behind defensible design and how the objectives can be reached through thoughtful barrier design.

15. Security: By Design and Decree by Robert A. Gardner, CPP

    www.crimewise.com/library/lr&a.html

    Gardner presents a look at how defensible design has been proven through studies to reduce crime rates. Covered in this article are topics such as history of crime prevention, security ordinances, settings for negligence, and a guide on where to begin with defensible design strategies.

16. Protecting Against Transit Crime: The Importance of the Built Environment by Robin Liggett, Anastasia Loukaitou-Sideris, and Hiroyki Iseki of University of California, Los Angeles

    www.spa.ucla.edu/calpolicy/files04/Liggett_ChapterAz.pdf

    The authors discuss the persistent problem of transit crime, specifically in Los Angeles. The authors suggest why these crimes occur and how the built environment influences these types of activities, as well as how improvements or area development can prevent crime.

17. Review and Critique of Defensible Space and Crime Prevention Through Environmental Design (CPTED) by Dawn Einwalter

    http://web1.greatbasin.net/~lupine/portfolio/files/cpted.pdf

    Einwalter discusses the advances in CPTED as a field and as a profession, as well as an overview of Defensible Space Principles. The author also discusses territoriality, perceptions of being unsafe, influences of the design professions, symbolic barriers, and surveillance.

18. Exploring the Relationship Between Sense of Community and Territoriality in Rural Neighborhoods by Shannon van Zandt of Arizona State University

    www.asu.edu/caed/proceedings97/vanzandt.html

    Van Zandt's documentary discusses the sense of community and territoriality discovered in the rural and poverty stricken *colonias* that have arisen on the Texas-Mexico border. Despite dismal living conditions, researchers have discovered a sense of union among the residents of these camp towns.

19. Creating Defensible Space by Oscar Newman for the Institute for Community Design Analysis

    www.huduser.org/Publications/pdf/def.pdf

    Newman's online book is about the principles of defensible space and how to institute them using his work in troubled areas as examples.

20. Environmental Barriers to Crime by Randall Atlas and William G. LeBlanc of Atlas Safety & Security Design, Inc., published in *Ergonomics in Design*, October 1994.

    www.cpted-security.com/barricad.htm

    The authors discuss the need for barriers and defensible design in today's society along with suggestions on how to implement the design tenets. The article goes through the process of installing barriers in a residential neighborhood.

Chapter Seven

1. Newsbreak January 24, 2000, *Relocation Journal & Real Estate News* Volume 6, Number 4

    www.relojournal.com/nbarchive/nbn216.htm

    This website has brief overviews of relocation trends and discussions of political motivations and restrictions.

2. Women's Roles and the Presence of Gender Equity in Utopian Societies by Gwen Bedford for The University of Louisville, Kentucky

    http://athena.louisville.edu/a-s/english/subcultures /colors/red/g0bedf01

    This is the start page for a series of articles on gender roles and Utopian sociological experiments.

3. The Home Of Man: Chapter XXI from the Council for Research in Values and Philosophy (RVP) by Aviezer Tucker

    www.crvp.org/book/Series04/IVA-9/chapter_xxi.htm

    This highly in-depth chapter of Aviezer Tucker's book explains the different notions of what makes a home, as opposed to the characteristics of a permanent or temporary residence.

4. No Place Like Home by Ann Webber for Toledo Blade on HGTV.com

    www.hgtv.com/hgtv/ah_real_estate_other /article/0,1801,HGTV_3163_3056541,00.html

    Webber discusses the importance of a sense of permanence in a home. The article discusses an example of a permanent home's effect on the people who are raised there and the relevance of the concept of home in childhood development.

5. Ham and Eard: Ideas of Home—Toh Hsien Min Goes Digging for Roots by Toh Hsien Min in the Quarterly Literary Review Singapore, Volume 1, Number 4, July 2002.

    www.qlrs.com/essay.asp?id=213

    Hsien Min discusses the concept of home, or lack thereof, in modern-day Singapore and the way the government there is attempting to encourage young residents to remain in the area. Also discussed are the foundations of the word home and how we came to understand it.

6. End Trip by Jan Rosenberg from Southern Journey

    www.ariga.com/southernjourney/endtrip.htm

Rosenberg discusses the folkloric and emotional features of home and how they are incorporated into daily life. He discusses the effects of experience and emotion on concepts of home over time, as situations and perceptions change.

7. Social and Environmental Gerontology: Housing and Relocation by Dr. Frank Oswald and Dr. Hans-Werner Wahl for Deutsches Zentrum fur Alternsorschung

    www.dzfa.uni-heidelberg.de/english_version/asoeg /w_zuhause.html

    This article details findings in an empirical study on the meaning of home for elderly people. Facets taken into consideration through studies from numerous schools of thought include social, emotional, cognitive, physical, and behavioral effects.

8. Outreach to People Experiencing Homelessness. Module 6A: The Meaning of Home by Ken Kraybill for the National Health Care for the Homeless Council (NHCHC.org)

    www.nhchc.org/Curriculum/module6/module6A /module6a.htm

    This is an activity designed to aid in learning and understanding about the meaning of home. The simple educational activity should take approximately 15 minutes to complete and requires very simple tools. This is a useful learning tool as well as a helpful study guide.

9. Personal Utopia: Technology's Effect on the Meaning of Home by James Mitchell, for Viable Utopian Ideas: Shaping a Better World

    www.utopianideas.net/1st_edition/Mitchell.htm

    This article regards the meaning of home and its cultural context. The writer juxtaposes Bill Gates home to that of the Natomos family from Mali, West Africa, to exhibit the similarities and differences in meaning of home.

10. For Better or Worse: Exploring Multiple Dimensions of Place Meaning by Lynne C. Manzo for the Department of Landscape Architecture, College of Architecture and Urban Planning, University of Washington, Seattle

    www.caup.washington.edu/larch/people/faculty/lynne /docs/For_better_or_worse.pdf

    Manzo discusses research on the meanings of place, both positive and negative, for a group of residents in New York City. The goal was to discover the emotional relationships people have with the places in which they reside and the roles of meaningful places in life.

11. Big Ideas Behind Not So Big Houses by Sarah Susanka for ArchitectureWeek

    www.architectureweek.com/2000/0726/design_1-2.html

    Susanka focuses on a building resident's sense of home and place rather than size of a residence. She brings to light some ideas about designing residences for modern families based more on the use of the building than the dimensions of it.

12. Contributors to Student Satisfaction with Special Program (Fresh Start) Residence Halls by Yan Li, Erin McCoy, Mack Shelley II, and Donald Whalen for the Journal of College Student Development, March/April 2005

    www.findarticles.com/p/articles/mi_qa3752/is_200503/ai_n13616615

    This article discusses student feelings regarding satisfaction in college residence facilities, focusing on how the environment impacts emotional and academic performance.

13. The Determinants of Neighbourhood Dissatisfaction by Alison Parkes, Ade Kearns, and Rowland Atkinson for the University of Bristol, England

    www.bristol.ac.uk/sps/cnrpapersword/cnr1sum.doc

    This study was conducted to examine the factors that influence the satisfaction levels of residents in specific neighborhoods. The study took into account ethnic and gender concerns as well as income level and location type.

14. Hope VI: A Study of Housing and Neighborhood Satisfaction by John Gilderbloom, Michael Brazley, and Zhenfeng Pan for the University of Louisville, Kentucky

    www.louisville.edu/org/sun/articles/HopeVI0706.pdf

    This study discusses the overall satisfaction of residents in the pioneering Hope VI public housing neighborhood. The study focuses on general satisfaction of the residents about the environment as a whole, including amenities, schools, transportation, and so on rather than discussing the residents' feelings on their individual homes.

15. Assisted Living Facility as a Home: Cases in Southwest Virginia by Youngjoo Kim for

Virginia Polytechnic Institute and State University

http://scholar.lib.vt.edu/theses/available/etd-05242002-000656/

Kim's dissertation provides in-depth researched information on residences for the elderly.

16. Pathways to Life Quality: Residential Change and Well-Being Among Older Adults: Summary of Findings 1998–2002, a research project of Ithaca College and Cornell University

    www.pathwayslifequality.org/pdf/final%20pathways_2003.pdf

    This case study of more than 1,100 elderly adults examines residential satisfaction with special emphasis on gender and social roles.

17. Toward Gender-Sensitive Architecture by Diana Lee-Smith

    www.unhabitat.org/HD/hdv5n2/forum2.htm

    Lee-Smith's essay discusses cultural and gender issues, and how to consider them, in residential design. The author writes from experience in a Kenyan city where the unique social and behavioral norms posed unexpected issues in residential design.

Chapter Eight

1. Safe Kids Worldwide

   www.safekids.org

   This is an international community of organizations that seek to prevent childhood injury, a significant cause of accidental childhood deaths. The website provides information on prevention of injury, safety guidelines, news, and facts relevant to the cause.

2. U.S. Consumer Product Safety Commission

   www.cpsc.gov

   This website can be used as a resource to find recalled products, household and neighborhood safety alerts, safety standards, and regulations. Extensive research is available through the CPSC library on the above-mentioned subjects and related topics.

3. National Institute of Environmental Health Sciences

   www.niehs.nih.gov

   This institution is one of the National Institutes of Health in the U.S. Department of Health and

Human Services. The website provides information from researchers, scientists, and doctors on all aspects of environmental health sciences. A library of sources is available online.

4. **A Schematic for Focusing on Youth in Investigations of Community Design and Physical Activity by Kevin Krizek, Amanda Birnbaum, and David Levinson**

www.ce.umn.edu/~levinson/Papers/Youth.pdf

This is a paper on how well thought-out communities can be designed to encourage youths to keep physically active. This type of design aids in bettering general health of young people as well as developing a more livable community.

5. **Children, Youth, and Environments Journal**

www.colorado.edu/journals/cye/

This website is a juried source of information specifically directed at researchers, professionals, designers, and teachers. Detailed journal articles can be accessed through the website, including articles from current and archived issues.

6. **Creative Environments for Learning Organisations**

www.edspace.school.nz/

This New Zealand–based website features a number of color photographs depicting advanced design in school facilities. Links to related articles are provided for deeper research, findings, and design cues.

7. **Architects Seek Safer Schools: Shootings and Teen Violence Inspire New, Safer School Design from About.com**

http://architecture.about.com/od/socialconcerns/a/safeschools.htm

This article briefly outlines ways in which school designers and architects can develop attractive, stimulating, and safe environments in schools. Also included are links to related articles and information.

8. **33 Principles of Educational Design by Jeffery Lackney for the University of Wisconsin-Madison**

http://schoolstudio.engr.wisc.edu/33principles.html

Lackney provides detailed descriptions of ideal designs for educational facilities. The authors encourage designers to work with users of the institution when preparing their designs.

9. **Child Development Institute**

www.childdevelopmentinfo.com/

This website provides numerous resources and detailed information on developmental stages in children from prenatal through teenaged years. Some of the topics include childhood diseases, parenting issues, mental disabilities, and developmental stages.

10. **Development, Child from Encarta Encyclopedia**

http://encarta.msn.com/encyclopedia_761557692/Development_Child.html

This detailed article discusses the psychological and cognitive development in children from prenatal stages through young adulthood. Topics covered include physical development, social and behavioral changes, scientific discoveries, and historical perspectives on childhood.

11. **Physical Development: Infancy Through Preschool by Parenting—MissouriFamilies.org and the University of Missouri**

http://missourifamilies.org/features/parentingarticles/parenting11.htm

This article describes the physical developmental stages of childhood from infancy through preschool age. Information in the article includes physical abilities by age group, psychological abilities by age group, and steps parents can take to encourage greatest development in their children.

12. **Adolescent Growth and Development by Angela Huebner for Virginia Polytechnic Institute and State University**

www.ext.vt.edu/pubs/family/350-850/350-850.html

This publication offers information on the stages of physical and psychological development in adolescents, and how parents and teachers can best deal with children in this age group. The document is presented in point form, which makes it quick to read and comprehend.

13. **Inside the Teenage Brain: What's Going on in There? How Science May Help to Explain the Mysteries of the Teen Years from PBS**

www.pbs.org/wgbh/pages/frontline/shows/teenbrain/

This resource provides detailed information on teenagers. Much of the information is presented in the form of interviews with medical experts along with diagrams and scientific studies.

Chapter Nine

1. National Association of the Deaf

   www.nad.org/infocenter/infotogo/legal/ada3aux.html

   This comprehensive website features detailed information on legal rights, advocacy issues, current news, and political implications relative to people with auditory disabilities.

2. Alzheimer's Association

   www.alz.org

   This website can be accessed to find resources for people with Alzheimer's and their families. Also available, and easily searchable, through the association are research findings, articles, and news on potential treatments or new discoveries related to Alzheimer's.

3. Understanding Stages and Symptoms of Alzheimer's Disease adapted from Caring for People With Alzheimer's Disease: A Manual for Facility Staff by Lisa Gwyther, for the Alzheimer's Disease Education & Referral Center.

   www.alzheimers.org/pubs/stages.htm

   This article describes the stages leading up to and appearing throughout the progression of Alzheimer's disease. The information is provided in point form for quick and simple reading.

4. The Center for Universal Design: Environments and Products for all People presented by North Carolina State University

   www.design.ncsu.edu/cud/index.html

   This website provides detailed information geared toward designers and housing manufacturers regarding universal design principles and applications. In-depth articles are available along with research findings, design cues, searchable publications, and a general outline of universal design principles.

5. Accessible Design/Universal Design Resources from Makoa.org by Jim Lubin

   www.makoa.org/accessable-design.htm

   This comprehensive website provides multiple resources for information on accessibility and universal design. The site is developed with significant sensitivity to disability needs as the creator is a C2 quadriplegic. Resources include pertinent articles, the seven principles of universal design, resources for people with disabilities and those who work with them, and house plans developed through universal design, among other informative links.

6. A Comparative Analysis of Barrier-Free Housing: Policies for Elderly People in the United States and Canada by Peter A. Dunn of Wilfrid Laurier University, Canada

   www.independentliving.org/docs5/dunn1997b.html

   Dunn discusses current policies regarding barrier-free housing in Canada and the United States. He writes about human rights legislation, building codes, government housing, and more. The paper is concluded with the discussion of a new, comprehensive model.

7. Blueprint for Aging transcript from a conference held by the University of California at Berkeley

   http://socrates.berkeley.edu/~aging/Blueprint1.html#Introduction

   The transcript covers the perspectives of numerous academics and professionals in gerontology, architecture, and design. The purpose of the conference was to bring together these disciplines to design appropriate, accessible, warm environments for the elderly and disabled.

8. Designing Facilities for the Elderly: Mobility presented by Providence Health Systems, Oregon

   www.providence.org/oregon/programs_and_services/research/center_on_aging/mobility.htm#mobility

   This simple list provides guidelines to assist designers and professionals to create the most unrestrictive environment for the elderly with mobility concerns. Attention is given to stairs, entries and exits, restroom facilities, and other important features.

9. Domestic and Foreign Urban Continuing Care Retirement Communities of Today and Tomorrow by Jae Seung Park and Joseph Sprague for the American Institute of Architects

   www.aia.org/static/journal/ARTICLES/v3/Continuing_Care_Retirement_Communities.pdf

   The authors discus trends in aging and the development of long-term care facilities for the aged in developed countries. Charts are supplied for quick reference. Discussion focuses on advanced design concepts to promote mobility and independence in housing for the aged, especially people with age-related disabilities.

10. From Sheltered Housing to Lifetime Homes: An Inclusive Approach to Housing by Julienne Hanson for University College, Bartlett School of Graduate Studies, London

www.lifetimehomes.org.uk/library/UCL_2001.pdf

Hanson discusses how residential environments impact the elderly and how these environments can meet their special needs. Emphasis is placed on independence, inclusion in society and mobility for the elderly.

11. Assisted Living for Deaf Elderly Is Longtime Dream for Woman for The Oregonian, presented by Concepts In Community Living, Inc

http://ccliving.com/news/20030318.html

This article describes a landmark design project geared especially for the deaf and deaf-blind elderly in Gresham, Oregon. The facility described can be used as inspiration for future designers, and the article gives some insight into the needs and wants of the elderly who reside in this type of facility.

12. Creating a Comfortable Environment for Older Individuals Who Are Visually Impaired, from the American Foundation for the Blind

www.afb.org/Section.asp?SectionID=44&TopicID=188&DocumentID=1417

This simple-to-read series of guidelines will assist designers in creating environments conducive to independent living for people with visual disabilities, specifically the elderly. Suggestions are given on lighting, use of color and furniture, elimination of hazards, and other vital points.

13. Treating the Failing Mind by Beverly Russell for Interior Sources Design Network

www.isdesignet.com/Magazine/Oct'97/Install_Huron.html

Russell discusses the Huron Woods Residence and how the design of this facility is specifically suited to the needs of the Alzheimer's patients in residence. Special attention is given to the architectural layout and interior design features.

14. Group Living for Elderly with Alzheimer's Disease: The Importance of Environmental Design presented by *Stride Magazine*

http://stridemagazine.com/node/14

This article discusses developing concepts in design for people with dementia-type diseases. The focus of this article is group housing that is comfortable and homelike for the long-term residents and caregivers. Special attention is given to pilot projects started in the 1980s in Sweden, which now serve as models for facility design internationally.

15. A Role for Institutional Care?: The Nursing Home, a seminar by David Fey for the Resource Center on Aging, University of California Berkeley

http://ist-socrates.berkeley.edu/~aging/blueprint5.html

A registered architect gave this seminar, and it focused on long-term care facilities for the aged who suffer from dementia. The information given is a guideline for real-world applications and deals with important design concepts in successful dementia care environments.

Chapter Ten

1. Herff Jones Academic Degree Colors

www.herffjones.com/capgown/college/index.cfm?at=7&con=7

This website from the academic regalia supplier gives a listing of the lining colors for academic robes and the fields to which they are related.

2. The Sound Learning Environment? Acoustics in School Design, by Bridget Shield for the Royal Institute of British Architects

www.architecture.com/go/Architecture/Debate/Forums_2808.html

Shield presents this article in point form for easy and quick reading. Information covered includes studies on effects of noise in classrooms on students and instructors, discoveries from noise surveys, types of noise, and design/material options to reduce noise interference.

3. Design of Child Care Centers and Effects of Noise on Young Children by Lorraine Maxwell and Gary Evans of Cornell University

www.designshare.com/Research/LMaxwell/NoiseChildren.htm

This presentation discusses the primarily negative effects of noise on children within the context of child-care centers. Examined are the findings of research on the subject and an outline of the role of design with regard to noise in these environments.

4. Classroom Design for Good Hearing by Ewart Wetherill for Quiet Classrooms

www.quietclassrooms.org/library/goodhearing.htm

Wetherill gives descriptions and diagrams to illustrate the effects of noise on learning as well as classroom layouts to dampen noise. Information is given on how to control unwanted noise and enhance the sounds necessary for proper learning.

5. Classroom Acoustics and Learning, presented by the League for the Hard of Hearing, New York, and Florida

www.lhh.org/noise/children/acoustics.htm

This brief but informative document discusses the effects of noise on students and instructors, how noise can be mitigated, and how quiet a classroom should actually be.

6. New Standards Should Help Children in Noisy Classrooms by Diane Weaver Dunne for Education World

www.educationworld.com/a_issues/issues073.shtml

This detailed article expresses the findings from studies conducted on the effects of noise in the classroom. Discussed are topics such as costs involved in retrofitting classrooms to reduce noise, research findings, retrofitting options, and links to additional resources.

7. Children, Youth, and Environments Journal

http://colorado.edu/journals/cye

This website is a juried source of information specifically directed at researchers, professionals, designers, and teachers. Detailed journal articles can be accessed through the website, including articles from current and archived issues.

8. Building a Safe Outdoor Environment by Heather Olson, Susan Hudson, and Donna Thompson for School Planning & Management

www.peterli.com/archive/spm/695.shtm

This insightful article focuses on the multiple aspects of playground design that need to be taken into consideration. Detailed information is provided on surface materials, current norms in playgrounds, heights and materials used for equipment, and maintenance schedules.

9. Why Our Playgrounds are Boring to Today's Wired Child by Jay Beckwith for the Minnesota Recreation and Parks Association

www.bpfp.org/PlaygroundDesign/WiredChild.htm

Beckwith gives a brief history of playgrounds to illustrate how much childhood play has changed over time. He explains how children are bored with the old style play equipment and require a different type of stimulation. In this article he gives brief ideas on what equipment could be incorporated into new playgrounds for greater use and enjoyment by the intended target group.

10. A Playground With a Difference: It's Designed for One and for All by Michelle Murphy

www.bpfp.org/PlaygroundDesign/PlaygroundWithDifference.htm

Murphy explains how one mother came up with concepts for a new playground design based on the needs of her disabled son. The accessible concepts expressed could provide valuable inspiration for playground designers.

11. When Child's Play Is Too Simple; Experts Criticize Safety-Conscious Recreation as Boring by Janny Scott

www.bpfp.org/PlaygroundDesign/WhenChildsPlay.htm

Scott brings forward both sides of the debate regarding safety features in playgrounds. In the article, the perspectives of children who use playground facilities are considered in the suggestions for good design.

12. Playground Magic: 6 Hot Topics in Playground Design by Craig Bystrynski

www.ptotoday.com/0303playground.html

Bystrynski discusses six aspects of playground design that should be considered in new play areas. Bystrynski suggests incorporating the ideas of children in playground design to keep the environment interesting and stimulating. Also covered are accessibility and safety issues.

13. The Work of the Child by Lauri Puchall for the American Institute of Architects, San Francisco

www.techstrategy.com/lineonline/dec02/puchall.html

Puchall discusses the psychosocial and physiological needs of children in regards to the appropriate design of preschools. The author writes about her observations of existing schools, how they do and do not meet the requirements of the children, and how to design safe, enriching preschool environments.

14. Adults Are from Earth; Children Are from the Moon—Designing for Children: A Complex Challenge by Randy White

www.whitehutchinson.com/children/articles
/earthmoon.shtml

White includes anecdotes in this article to express the unexpected ways children engage their environment. As designers, he suggests that these behavior patterns be understood when designing environments for young children.

15. Landscape for Learning: The Impact of Classroom Design on Infants and Toddlers, by Louis Torelli and Charles Durrett

www.spacesforchildren.com/impact.html

This article exposes problems in poor classroom design for young children, which can impede optimal learning and create safety concerns. Torelli and Durrett use their experiences and observations to provide guidelines for good classroom design geared specifically for the infant and toddler age groups.

16. Oasis for Children by Michael Crosbie for *Architecture Week*

www.architectureweek.com/2003/0924/design
_1-1.html

Crosbie focuses on the design of a child-care center for homeless and previously homeless children in San Francisco. Socioeconomic concerns were integrated into the design along with standards for childhood stimulation and play.

17. Peace of Mind by Janet Wiens

www.isdesignet.com/Magazine/May'00/peace.html

Wiens uses an urban child-care center at the Pfizer headquarters in New York City as a case study in modern day-care design. The facility is intended to reflect the urban nature of its environment while incorporating nature as well. The innovative design can be used as inspiration for future designers of centers catering to children in the preschool age group.

18. The Relationship Between Environmental Quality of School Facilities and Student Performance by Jeffery Lackney for School Design Research Studio

http://schoolstudio.engr.wisc.edu/energysmartschools
.html

Lackney explores many aspects related to good school design, including lighting, noise reduction, air quality, classroom size, and more. Information offered in this article is useful to designers who wish to focus on creating the healthiest schools possible where the greatest opportunities for learning abound.

19. Classroom Organization: The Physical Environment, an excerpt from Learning to Teach ... Not Just for Beginners by Linda Shalaway

http://teacher.scholastic.com/professional/fu-
tureteachers/classroom_organization.htm

Initially geared toward teachers, designers could find this article to be useful when deciding on placement of desks and necessary classroom equipment in their proposals. Shalaway discusses how the placement of desks affects the behavior of students' learning and interactions within the classroom.

20. Classroom Design and How It Influences Behavior by Judith Colbert

www.earlychildhood.com/Articles/index.cfm?A
=413&FuseAction=Article

Colbert offers detailed information for designers and teachers on how to encourage learning through the environment. She discusses the benefits of play areas, organized spaces, and classroom design.

21. Schools Our Kids Would Build by Catherine Burke and Ian Grosvenor for *Architecture Week*

www.architectureweek.com/2005/0119/culture
_3-1.html

This article includes graphic illustrations by children and expresses how the ideas of children can be incorporated into school design. It is suggested that the children who use the facility can have valuable insights. The article begins with a brief history of school design and concludes with ideas on combining traditional and nontraditional design concepts to make better school environments.

22. Designing the Future University by Zack Pinchover, Edan Razinovsky, and Talya Shaulov

http://noar.technion.ac.il/scitech2003/architecture1
.pdf

This paper discusses the three archetypal designs historically used for colleges and universities and how these archetypes are flawed. Through their research, Pinchover, Razinovsky, and Shaulov explore more modern concepts in university design.

23. The Architect/Librarian Team: Ensuring Excellence in Library Design by Janine Schmidt and Hamilton Wilson

www.library.uq.edu.au/papers/the_architect
_librarian_team.pdf

Schmidt and Wilson discuss how library design is changing as new needs must be met. The discussion explains the benefits of combining the knowledge of the architect and the librarian to design better, more functional libraries for the future.

24. **Current Issues in College Libraries by John Ruble for** *Architecture Week*

    www.architectureweek.com/2003/0611/design_1-1.html

    Ruble discusses the needs and constraints on college library design with regard to modern requirements including technology. Also discussed in the article are issues such as wayfinding, storage space for mixed media, and computer terminals.

25. **Learning Curve: Today's Student Housing Rivals the Best Market-Rate Apartments by Cheryl Weber for** *Residential Architect*

    www.findarticles.com/p/articles/mi_m0NTE/is_1_7/ai_106914127#continue

    Weber uses a number of new and retrofitted residence halls at prominent universities in case studies describing design implications and influences. Each team of architects approached the situation differently resulting in user-friendly, modern dormitories for the school residents.

26. **CPTED on College Campuses: Guidelines for Implementation by Christ Lipnickey**

    www.ifpo.org/articlebank/cpted.htm

    Lipnickey discusses how incorporating environmental design to prevent crime, along with modern technologies and campus police, can create a beautiful and safe collegiate environment.

Chapter Eleven

1. **Evidence-Based Hospital Design Improves Healthcare Outcomes For Patients, Families and Staff by Kari Root and Mary Darby for the Robert Wood Johnson Foundation**

   www.rwjf.org/newsroom/newsreleasesdetail.jsp?id=10298

   This article's broad scope covers many vital topics for consideration in good healthcare facility design. Subjects explored include stress mitigation, wayfinding, interior design, and employee-friendly environments.

2. **Ergonomic Principles in the Design of Healthcare Environments by Herman Miller for** *Healthcare*

   www.hermanmiller.com/hm/content/research_summaries/wp_ergodesign0503.pdf

Miller describes the stresses on employees in healthcare facilities, focusing primarily on physical stress and potential injury. He discusses how ergonomic design can be used to reduce occurrence of stress in the healthcare workplace and provides illustrations and photographs for easy comprehension.

3. **Therapeutic Environments by Ron Smith for** *Whole Building Design Guide*

   www.wbdg.org/design/therapeutic.php?print=1

   Smith presents the information in this article in point form for quick, easy reading. He discusses the role and design objectives in modern healthcare facilities, including stressors and means of reducing environmental stress. Information is also given on operational models, research findings, and photographic examples of the applications presented.

4. **Environments That Support Healing: Design Works Hand in Hand with the Technology of Healing by Beth Frankowski Jones**

   www.isdesignet.com/Magazine/J_A'96/EnvSupHeal.html

   Jones details the types and effects of stress on patients and employees in healthcare facilities. Solutions to the problems include giving people a sense of control, social support, and using color and light to aid in mood enhancement.

5. **What Is at Stake in the Sound Environment? by Susan Mazer for Healing Healthcare Systems**

   www.healinghealth.com/d-resources/sound_environment.php

   Mazer explores the effects of noise and disruptive sounds as stressors in healthcare facilities on employees, patients, and visitors. She discusses how sound can be mitigated and how designers can reduce noise stress through thoughtful design and use of technology.

6. **Evidence-based Design Could Help Quality of Care: Literature Review Shows Impact on Outcomes by Craig Zimring for** *HealthCare Benchmarks and Quality Improvement*, **August 2004**

   www.findarticles.com/p/articles/mi_m0NUZ/is_8_11/ai_n6191084#continue

   Zimring discusses how evidence-based design can reduce stress for patients and staff in healthcare facilities. Research has shown the negative effects of stress on healing and employee satisfaction but has also revealed ways that thoughtful design can reduce the problems.

7. Building Places for Children by William Mead for *Children's Hospitals Today*, Summer 2003.

www.childrenshospitals.net/Template.cfm?Section
=Home&CONTENTID=2376&TEMPLATE=
/ContentManagement/ContentDisplay.cfm

Mead introduces the concept of designing children's hospitals to give the patients a sense of place, or place attachment, in the facility. The Hasbro Children's Hospital in Providence, Rhode Island, is used as a case study for this article.

8. Holistic Design: Designing for the Mind, Body, & Spirit by Barbara Huelat

http://iidexneocon.com/2004/conf_Proceedings
_2003/T1.pdf

Huelat outlines the history and modern applications of holistic design in healthcare settings. She asserts that developing place attachment through holistic design aids in healing for patients in healthcare facilities.

9. Beyond the Lab: 8 Tips for a Dynamic Research Building by Herbert Baker for *Laboratory Design*

www.labdesignnews.com/LaboratoryDesign
/LD0408FEAT_3.asp

Place attachment can result in better employee retention and satisfaction in all industries, including medical research. In this article, Baker describes how a sense of place can make laboratory settings less sterile and more welcoming for employees and visitors. Examples are explored and presented through photographs. Concepts discussed in this article can be easily adapted for use in healthcare environments.

10. Wayfinding by Design by Randy Cooper and Roger Smith for *Healthcare Design*

www.healthcaredesignmagazine.com/Dispstpg.htm?ID
=2925

Cooper and Smith explore the multitude of circumstances that need to be addressed in healthcare wayfinding such as patients' language abilities, visibility, and cultural influences. The authors explore various options to meet the facility and patients' needs using examples and photographs.

11. Way-to-Go: Getting Around At HCMC presented by the Hennepin County Medical Center, Minneapolis, Minnesota

www.hcmc.org/general/waytogo.htm

This article about modernized wayfinding techniques was initially intended for the employees of HCMC. However, it provides useful information from the viewpoints of people who use hospital environments and how new wayfinding techniques were developed through an interdisciplinary approach.

12. Wayfinding in Health Facilities by Janet Carpman

www.muhc-healing.mcgill.ca/english/Speakers
/carpman_p.html

Carpman presented this lecture on wayfinding in healthcare facilities for the Healing By Design: Building for Health Care in the 21st Century conference in 2000. Although this is the abstract of the lecture, Carpman offers valuable advice and information on wayfinding in medical facilities, as well as questions designers should ask of themselves and clients when designing an appropriate wayfinding system.

13.. Memorial's Wayfinding Project: Creating the Memorial Experience Memorial Medical Center, Springfield, Illinois

www.memorial-health.net/info_desk/wayfinding.htm

This article discusses the redesign of wayfinding and orientation cues at the Memorial Medical Center. The information provided can be used as a case study for designers as features such as color-coding, landmarks, art installations and noticeable entrances/exits are discussed.

14. Wander Gardens: Expanding the Dementia Treatment Environment by Mark Dtweiler, David Trinkle, and Martha Anderson, for the *Annals of Long-Term Care*

www.mmhc.com/altc/displayArticle.cfm?articleID
=altcac157

This comprehensive article discusses the need for wandering regions for people with dementia and how these types of areas are beneficial. Specific information is given on wandering behavior, the risks of wandering, and how sensitive design can mitigate these risks creating a welcoming and healthy environment.

15. Engaging Wanders by Bradford Perkins for *Architecture Week*

www.architectureweek.com/2004/1208/design_3-1
.html

Perkins discusses the causes of and need for wandering in healthcare settings in this article. He gives special consideration to designing for people with dementia, and explains the use of properly planned design for wandering paths/circuits. Photographs, successful designs, and footprints are included.

16. Lost and Found by Michelle Gardner for *Assisted Living Success*

   www.alsuccess.com/articles/251feat3.html

   Gardner explores the various causes and effects of wandering behavior in day-care and long-term care facilities. Some information is given on design objectives to prevent elopement and to successfully allow for wandering activities reducing or eliminating the need for medication or sedation.

17. Beyond the Basics of Health Care Design: Getting Down to Specifics with Jain Malkin by Diane Wintroub Calmenson for *ISDesigNet.*

   www.isdesignet.com/Magazine/Jan'96/Cover.html

   Calmenson bases this article on a discussion with healthcare interior design expert Jain Malkin and describes how specific materials and design elements can positively or negatively effect patients in healthcare facilities depending on their ailment.

18. Lighting Design for Healthcare Facilities: A Common-Sense Approach presented by the American Institute of Architects

   www.aia.org/nwsltr_print.cfm?pagename=aah_jrnl _lighting_102704

   This detailed article features information on the effects of good lighting design in healthcare facilities. Lighting can be used to assist in wayfinding, to create mood, and to enhance the space. Many photographs and diagrams are included to assist designers in making informed decisions in lighting implementation.

19. RTKL: Designing for the Consumer Revolution in Health Care by Leeza Hoyt for ArchNewsNow.com.

   www.archnewsnow.com/features/Feature21.htm

   Hoyt describes how patients in healthcare facilities have become consumers who drive the modern designs of these facilities to be more user-friendly. She discusses how changing facility layout, interior design, wayfinding devices, and amenities leads to better overall design and user satisfaction.

20. Turning Healthcare Green: A Case For Sustainable Healthcare by Greg Roberts for *Interiors Sources*

   www.isdesignet.com/Magazine/oct02/feature _turning.html

Roberts explores the benefits of sustainable design and "green" materials in this review of materials used in healthcare facilities. The article focuses on materials that create an aesthetically appealing as well as healthy environment and how these selections aid in patient satisfaction and employee retention.

21. Ceilings: Popular Design Element by Ann Miller for Buildings.com

   www.buildings.com/Articles/detail.asp ?ArticleID=2021

   Miller discusses emerging trends in ceiling treatments. Materials and design elements discussed focus on varied environments and produce a number of interesting visual and acoustic effects.

22. New Design Technologies: Healing Architecture—A Case Study of the Vidarkliniken by Gary Coates and Susanne Siepl-Coates for the *Journal of Healthcare Design*

   www.antroposofi.org/vidar/healthcare.htm

   Coates and Siepl-Coates discuss the architect Asmussen's attention to detail, and incorporation of inspired design elements, at the Vidarkliniken healing center in Sweden. Some of the features of this facility include a sewage treatment garden, seating nooks, integrated art works, and landscaping.

23. Understanding the Client's Clients: Patients Inform Design by Sara Malone for the *AIA Journal of Architecture*

   www.aia.org/nwsltr_aiaj.cfm?pagename=aiaj_a _0404_clientsclients

   Malone describes in this article how the requirements of patients and their loved ones should influence design of healthcare facilities. She discusses inclusion of design elements such as religious centers, private patient rooms and waiting areas, interior design, staff relaxation areas, and healing gardens to enhance employee satisfaction and patient wellness.

24. Psychologically Accessible by Brian Libby for *Architecture Week*

   www.architectureweek.com/2005/0119/design _1-1.html.

   Libby explains how designing healthcare facilities for children with autism has special concerns. Using case studies, observations and research, Libby shows how design features in facilities for this special constituent group can benefit patients and their families as well as create greater employee satisfaction and retention.

25. Healing by Design: Healing Gardens and Therapeutic Landscapes by Jean Larson and Mary Jo Kreitzer for *Implications Newsletter* from InformeDesign.umn.edu

    www.informedesign.umn.edu/_news/nov_v02-p.pdf

    The authors of this article explain how healing gardens have been used historically and how the use of nature in modern healthcare environments can aid in health recovery.

26. Providing a Safe Harbor: What Senior Living Communities Need for True Security by Kelli Donley, for *Assisted Living Success*

    www.alsuccess.com/articles/341feat2.html

    Donley uses numerous case study references to illuminate the importance of security features in assisted living and healthcare environments. Attention is given to design features, security systems, and employee training for the safety and potential rescue assistance required for residents of the facility.

27. Architectural Showcase: Emergency Center/NICU presented by *Healthcare Design Magazine*

    www.healthcaredesignmagazine.com/Past_Issues.htm?ID=1062

    This case study examines the design features of NICU, which include innovative flooring designs to direct circulation patterns, functional and attractive materials usage, and art installations. Also examined are architectural features such as bright, large entryways to draw attention, and corridor layouts to direct patients and visitors.

28. BI Design Awards 2005—A Healthy Dose of Design by Leah Garris for *Buildings Magazine*

    www.buildings.com/Articles/detailbuildings.asp?ArticleID=2342

    The award-winning Monroe Carell Jr. Children's Hospital in Nashville, Tennessee, was examined in this case study. The spectacular children's hospital was designed with advanced architectural features such as themed levels, easily interpreted wayfinding mechanisms, and a more homelike/ less sterile feel to make the stay of the child patients and their families more comfortable and stimulating.

29. Promote Health and Well-Being presented by Whole Building Design Guide

    www.wbdg.org/design/promote_health.php

    This brief article describes how interior design can enhance healthcare facilities by giving optimal light, views to outdoor spaces, comfort and sense of place to patients.

30. What Is a Healing Environment? Understanding The Components of a Healing Environment

    http://patientexperience.nhsestates.gov.uk/healing_environment/he_content/healing_environment/introduction.asp

    This series of articles provides valuable information on how interior design features supporting the senses can result in improved healing facilities.

31. Interior Design: Not "Just Colors" Anymore by Judy Klich and Ben Bahil for *Healthcare Design Magazine*

    www.healthcaredesignmagazine.com/Dispstpg.htm?ID=4149

    This article discusses the importance of interior design in healthcare environments. Klich and Bahil describe specific products and uses as well as design concepts appropriate for medical facilities.

32. Choosing Artwork for Healthcare Projects by Diana Brady Spellman for *Healthcare Design*

    www.healthcaredesignmagazine.com/Dispstpg.htm?ID=3223

    Spellman explains the importance and significance of art in healthcare facilities. Spellman explains how selection of appropriate artwork can be done and how the art is not an afterthought but should be designed with the overall project in mind.

33. Interior Design: Making the NICU an Attractive Place by Anne Marshall-Baker for Pediatrix Medical Group

    www.pediatrix.com/documents/intdes.pdf

    Marshall-Baker answers specific questions relative to the pediatric unit at NICU. This article, and the design information therein, can be used as inspiration or a case study for designers who are interested in healthcare settings.

Chapter Twelve

1. The Ergonomics of Economics Is the Economics of Ergonomics by H. W. Hendrick for the University of Southern California

    www.hfes.org/Web/PubPages/Hendrick.pdf

    Hendrick examines the interactions of ergonomics and economics in this article. He explores the effects of ergonomics in employee satisfaction with special focus on a variety of workforce categories.

2. Building Healthy Organizations Takes More Than Simply Putting in a Wellness Program by Graham Lowe for the National Quality Institute, Canada

www.nqi.ca/articles/article_details.aspx?print=yes&ID=469

Lowe discusses how remedying negative underlying working conditions such as stress, injury, and poor working conditions can enhance people's workplace satisfaction. He explains how change can be undertaken to improve the workplace, as well as what steps a company can take for overall employee health improvement.

3. Office Environments: The North American Perspective presented by Herman Miller

www.hermanmiller.com/hm/content/research_summaries/wp_Office_Environ.pdf

Various corporate models are examined along with traditional and nontraditional frameworks. The article includes diagrams and graphs for quick comprehension.

4 Easing the Stress by Stephen Minter for *Occupational Hazards*

www.occupationalhazards.com/articles/6893

Miller discusses the ill effects of stress on employees and how this stress can be mitigated. He includes information on how stress can be managed and the sometimes-blurred distinction between stress and challenge.

5. Do Work-Site Exercise and Health Programs Work? by Roy Shephard for *The Physician and Sports Medicine*

www.physsportsmed.com/issues/1999/02_99/shephard.htm

Shephard explores the effects on employee satisfaction and health with regard to workplace health programs. He includes case studies and research reviews to support his arguments.

6. Daylight Dividends Case Study for the Lighting Research Center by Rensselaer Polytechnic Institute, Troy, New York

www.lrc.rpi.edu/programs/daylighting/pdf/TomoTherapyCaseStudy.pdf

This research study examines an occupied medical facility and the effects of incorporating daylight into the design scheme of the office areas and general facility spaces.

7. High-Tech Windows Could Save Energy by B. J. Novitski, for *Architecture Week*

www.architectureweek.com/2000/1011/building_2-1.html

Novitski examines how the careful selection of windows for corporate environments can affect employee satisfaction and well-being while also reducing the costs associated with heating, cooling, and lighting office facilities.

8. Indoor Air Facts No. 4 (revised): Sick Building Syndrome (SBS) presented by the United States Environmental Protection Agency

www.epa.gov/iaq/pubs/sbs.html

This introductory article discusses the causes, symptoms, and hazards of Sick Building Syndrome to employees. Tests for Sick Building Syndrome and rehabilitation information are also offered.

9. Sick Building Syndrome by Joe Heimlich for Ohio State University

http://ohioline.osu.edu/cd-fact/0194.html

This detailed paper explains the history, causes, effects, and treatments for SBS.

10. Avoiding Sick Building Syndrome: A Checklist for Identifying Problem Areas by Marcia Sawnor for ISDesignNet

www.isdesignet.com/Magazine/Jun'95/SickBuilding.html

Sawnor describes the ways to check for, and eliminate, the causes of SBS. She explains trouble signs to look for during examinations of facilities such as problems with HVAC systems and high noise levels.

11. Is Good Design Good Business? by Attilla Lawrence for *Architecture Week*

www.architectureweek.com/2000/0830/building_3-1.html

Lawrence explores the effects of good design on corporate environments. Special attention is given to the performance of employees in sensitively designed corporate offices.

12. Office Design Gets Personal by Marion Hudson for OfficeSolutions

www.findarticles.com/p/articles/mi_m0FAU/is_1_21/ai_113309740#continue

Hudson discusses the value of workplace personalization. She explores the effects of personalization on goals such as employee satisfaction, sense of ownership, and effects on productivity.

13. Space Planning: How Much Space Do You Really Need? by Ned Fennie, Jr. for *The Space Place*

www.thespaceplace.net/articles/fennie200501a.htm

Fennie discusses the manner in which designers and corporations can establish the space requirements for their offices. Informative diagrams and office layouts are included.

14. More Staff in Less Space by Kristin Hill for *Architecture Week*

www.architectureweek.com/2001/0725/design_3-1.html

Hill examines how corporations have utilized progressive office designs to fit large numbers of employees into smaller spaces without compromising the quality of the environment or communal spaces such as cafés.

15. Using Interior Design to Convey Corporate Identity by Al D'Elia for *Real Estate Weekly*

www.findarticles.com/p/articles/mi_m3601/is_31_51/ai_n13500133

D'Elia discusses how companies can use interior design to express corporate goals and attitudes. He explains how style can make a lasting impression to the benefit or detriment of the business, depending on whether good design choices were made.

16. The Home Office presented by Rona

www.rona.ca/webapp/wcs/stores/servlet/ContentServlet?storeId=10001&langId=-1&assetId=210

This article is directed to the professional who has decided to open a home office. However, the guidelines given for room arrangement, entrance and exit options, and general décor are useful to design professionals as well as home-based business owners.

17. Please, Do Not Disturb! by Gail Gabriel for *Home Office Computing*

www.findarticles.com/p/articles/mi_m1563/is_n1_v12/ai_15035374#continue

Gabriel examines the home office of J. Richard Taft as a case study in successful design. This space offers the convenience of working from home with all the necessary amenities and features for a fully operational business.

18. Designing a Home Workplace by Neal Zimmerman for *Architecture Week*

www.architectureweek.com/2002/0123/culture_2-1.html

The author examines actual home office environments as examples to understand good home office design. Zimmerman's unique perspective stems from the fact that he works from a workplace at home. Benefits of working from a home office are expressed, as well as design cues including photographs.

19. Practice Brief: Extablishing a Telecommuting or Home-based Employee Program (Updated) for *Journal of AHIMA* 73, No. 7.

http://library.ahima.org/xpedio/groups/public/documents/ahima/pub_bok1_013767.html

Nontraditional working environments such as working from home or from neighborhood work centers are discussed in this article. The authors examine the effects on productivity and economics in these work environments.

20. Smart Valley Telecommuting Guide

www.cisco.com/warp/public/779/smbiz/netsolutions/find/telecommuting/p03.html

This brief article explains the various options for telecommuting locations, such as working from home, hotels, satellite offices, neighborhood work centers, and virtual offices. Telecommuting is also explained.

21. "The Telework Concept" Saving You Time and Money for *Hispanic Times Magazine*

www.findarticles.com/p/articles/mi_m0FWK/is_5_20/ai_58359151#continue

The author explains telecommuting by giving a brief history and the benefits of this system and points out the types of community services that assist in telecommuting, such as neighborhood work centers and guidelines for successfully implementing telecommuting into a business.

Chapter Thirteen

1. Hotels: Differentiating with Design by Stephani Robson and Madeleine Pullman, for *Implications Newsletter* by InformeDesign

www.informedesign.umn.edu/_news/june_v03r-p.pdf

This article focuses on the changing face of hotels as design issues become increasingly varied. The discussion touches on stylistic cues as well as the effects of site restrictions, renovation, and target demographic on hotel design.

2. Strategies for Designing Effective Restaurants by Stephani Robson for *Implications Newsletter* by InformeDesign.

www.informedesign.umn.edu/_news/dec_v02-p.pdf

Robson explores the sometimes dissimilar needs of restaurateurs and guests. She discusses how the roles of staff and diners are intertwined and how good design can accommodate the needs of all parties while still allowing the facility to be profitable.

3. Trends in Hotel Design: Lifestyle-Branded Hotels Give New Meaning to "Home Away from Home" by Roger Hill and Ron Swidler

www.gettys.com/news/Trends%20in%20The%20Hotel%20Indusdry%20PKF.pdf

Hill and Swidler examine emerging trends in hotel design and guest expectations in this article. They discuss various scenarios, using existing examples and photographs, and how the design implications to create a home away from home were handled.

4. One Person's Opinion: Ventilation Without Representation? by Elia Sterling

www.esmagazine.com/CDA/ArticleInformation/features/BNP___Features___Item/0,2503,97998,00.html

This article focuses on the issues involved in designing effective HVAC systems for hospitality settings.

5. Hotel Bars: Getting Trendy & Profitable in *Federation of Hotel and Restaurants Associations of India Magazine*

www.fhrai.com/Mag-News/magArchtDesign.asp

This detailed article focuses on hospitality design in bars, hotel bars, and nightclubs. Special attention is given to design cues that are attractive to patrons as well as the hospitality industry.

6. Participatory and Holistic Approaches in Ecotourism Planning and Design by Hitesh Mehta for the American Planning Association 2001 National Planning Conference

www.asu.edu/caed/proceedings01/MEHTA/mehta.htm

This detailed article explains the value of specialized design for ecotourism. Included are case studies on existing ecotourism facilities as well as discussions on Feng Shui and other holistic approaches to design.

7. Scenic Tahoe: Building a Private Residence Club in Tahoe Vista, California by Deanna Fryer for the *Magazine of the Western Architect*

& Specifier

www.architecturalwest.com/cover_story/may_june_04/cover_may_june_2004.htm

Fryer focuses on the issues surrounding the design and construction of a private residence club in Tahoe Vista, California. Photographs of the project are included in the article.

Chapter Fourteen

1. Form Follows Function ... or the Store Dies by J'Amy Owens for the *Seattle Daily Journal of Commerce*

www.djc.com/special/design97/10032223.htm

Citing specific well-known stores and brand names, Owens discusses the importance of market-driven design. The article covers the important aspects of retail sales and consumer requirements and how these should be implemented in design.

2. Scripting Today's Retail Experience by David Gester

www.rtkl.com/docs/retail_experience.pdf

Gester discusses how the understanding of complex consumer wants can lead to the design of outstanding retail facilities. He discusses various styles and features such as thematic design, community-driven design, and active spaces where shopping is not the single-minded objective.

3. Retail Design Trends: Real Simple by Janet Groeber for *RetailTraffic*

http://retailtrafficmag.com/design/trends/retail_retail_design_trends/

Giving another perspective on retail design, Groeber suggests that uncluttered simplicity is the key to good design. The focus on this article is less about experiential qualities and more about efficiency in design.

4. A Theoretical and Empirical Study of Retail Crowding by Delphine Dion for Rennes University, France

http://perso.wanadoo.fr/pvolle.net/sitedelphine/fichiers/dion_eacr_crowding_1999.pdf

Dion and other researchers propose new methods to study the effects of crowding and recording density in retail environments. Designers can use the information given in this document to develop a means of reviewing the effects of the environment on potential shoppers, thereby creating a maximally dynamic and profitable shopping experience.

5. The Power of the Purse by Marti Barletta for *Photo Marketing*

www.trendsight.com/article-photomarketing.php

Barletta examines gender differences in the shopping habits of men and women. She discusses how the expectations of males and females differ in retail environments giving designers the information necessary to design successful shopping facilities.

6. Environmental Graphics: Way-Finder, Image-Maker, Mood-Enhancer by Sarah Huie for *RetailTraffic*

http://retailtrafficmag.com/mag/retail _environmental_graphics_wayfinder/

Huie discusses the value of environmental design in retail environments for today's shoppers. When the design is thoroughly considered prior to implementation, the facility can have a unique image and feel to it, which can lead to greater profitability.

7. Outfitting Retail: Design an Experience by Michelle Collins for *CanadaOne Magazine*

www.canadaone.com/ezine/jan02/retailing.html

Collins asserts in this article that designers should create shopping environments that become all-encompassing image settings with thematic design elements. She discusses using creative models to enhance the overall shopping experience and places heavy emphasis on dealing with budget constraints.

8. Retail Site Selection presented by Business for Social Responsibility

www.bsr.org/CSRResources/IssueBriefDetail.cfm ?DocumentID=50964

In this article, site selection is discussed with primary focus on bringing new business to low-income areas. This article explores the societal and financial impact of bringing new shopping centers into impoverished areas with the intention of bettering the social and economic climates.

9. Six Design Lessons From the Apple Store by Jesse James Garrett for *Adaptive Path Publications*

www.adaptivepath.com/publications/essays/archives /000331.php

Garrett uses the Apple Store, opened in San Francisco in 1994, as a case study for good interior design of a retail space. He discusses six major design

concepts as guides to designers for other facilities regardless of their target constituency.

10. Expert Analysis: A Second Look at Hardscapes by Darrell Pattison for *RetailTraffic*

http://retailtrafficmag.com/mag/retail_expert _analysis_second/

Pattison encourages a multidisciplinary approach to the exterior design of retail centers and describes how all the facets of the hardscape, from architecture to external graphics, should be designed and developed for best integration at the beginning of the project.

11. Environmental Design That Prevents Crime by Randall Atlas

www.cpted-security.com/cpted11.htm

Atlas describes the ways in which CPTED design methodology can be utilized to create defensible space in retail and other environments.

12. Introduction to Crime Prevention Through Environmental Design (CPTED) presented by Safer Auckland City

www.aucklandcity.govt.nz/auckland/introduction /safer/cpted/7.asp

This informative article explains the proper use of CPTED with descriptive photographs and information. Features that are examined include lighting, sightlines, mixed land use, and natural surveillance.

13. Hipper Banking in Portland by *Architecture Week*

www.architectureweek.com/2003/0604/design _1-1.html

This article explores emerging trends in bank design, using the Umpqua Bank in Portland, Oregon, as the case study. New attention is given to comfortable customer service areas and artworks rather than the conservative styles previously favored.

14. Lebanon's Master Architect: A High Tech Bank by Victor Khoueiry

www.architectureweek.com/2002/0724/design _3-2.html

This excerpt from Khoueiry's article focuses on the design features of the extraordinary Banque du Liban et d'Outre-Mer (BLOM) in Beirut. The inclusion of unusual architectural forms and green spaces makes this bank an excellent source of inspiration for other designers.

15. C-Stores: Breaking the Mold: Design Firms Reinvent the Convenience Store for a New Generation of Shoppers by RoxAnna Sway for *DDI Magazine*

    www.ddimagazine.com/displayanddesignideas /magazine/article_display.jsp?vnu_content_id =1000928738

    Sway describes some of the developing concepts that are being brought forward through competitions on convenience store design.

16. C-Store Design Pitfalls presented by *Australian Convenience Store News*

    www.c-store.com.au/magazine/archive/2000/topten.html

    This article lists and explains the ten major failing points in convenience stores. If designers are aware of the issues that may arise, modern convenience stores can serve their community more appropriately, and therefore be more profitable.

17. Delicious by Design: Creating an Unforgettable Dining Experience by Sarah Smith Hamaker for *Restaurants USA*

    www.restaurant.org/business/magarticle.cfm ?ArticleID=131

    Smith explores techniques used in modern dining facilities to enhance the experience and draw diners in. The author discusses use of thematic design elements to give eateries an appropriate atmosphere, which sophisticated clients have come to expect.

18. Sydney Bistro by *Architecture Week*

    www.architectureweek.com/2004/0609/design _3-1.html

    This article describes the innovative design of the Sydney Bistro. The use of lighting and attention to design details can serve as inspiration to designers of restaurants and cafés. The article includes numerous photographs.

19. Café Boulud Palm Beach: Interior

    http://danielnyc.com/cafeboulud_palmbeach /interior.html

    This Web page discusses the interior design of Café Boulud in Palm Beach, Florida. The influences of the head chef as well as surrounding buildings are strongly reflected in the design of this café.

20. Is Japan Becoming a "Café Society"? for Japan Information Society

    http://web-japan.org/trends01/article/010820soc _r.html

Current design trends in cafés are being explored with special regard to the selective tastes of Japanese women who are in their twenties and thirties. It is proposed that cafés have become a culture unto themselves with heavy Parisian influence. The article discusses design cues and includes photographs.

21. Design Factors and Retail Space Types for Lighting Design Lab

    http://lightingdesignlab.com/articles/retail/design _space.htm

    This article discusses the three types of retail spaces as outlined by the Illuminating Engineering Society of North America. Through these three types, lighting goals are explored to aid designers in selecting the most appropriate fixtures for retail space.

22. Green Tips: A Basic Guide for Commercial Designers by Lucinda Jennings and Victoria Schomer for the American Society of Interior Designers

    www.asid.org/resource/Green+Tips+A+Basic+Guide +for+Commercial+Designers.htm

    Jennings and Schomer outline the fundamentals in sustainable design for commercial and retail spaces in this article. The suggestions they provide stem from the LEED (Leadership in Energy and Environmental Design) Building Ratings System.

23. Uncommon SPACES by Joy Armstrong for *Retail Traffic Magazine*

    http://retailtrafficmag.com/design/trends/retail _uncommon_spaces/index.html

    Armstrong discusses how leading edge retailers use design themes to draw in more consumers. She presents a number of examples ranging from sporting goods megastores to department stores and designer fashion retail outlets.

24. Double Duty by Patricia Kirk for *Retail Traffic Magazine*

    http://retailtrafficmag.com/design/trends/retail _double_duty/

    Kirk compares retail megastores, such as Wal-Mart, with shopping malls and smaller individual retail spaces with regard to design and shopping trends. To compete with super centers like Wal-Mart, designers are creating more dynamic and interesting spaces to draw people into individual stores despite current consumer leanings toward saving money and time.

25. How to Jazz Up Mediocre Malls by William Gallo for *Retail Traffic Magazine*

www.findarticles.com/p/articles/mi_m0OUH/is_10_33/ai_n6272103

Gallo explores how developing shopping malls to feel more like town squares and main streets brings in consumers, especially when the shopping center is competing with megastores. Trends in design are explored and discussed through use of modern examples.

Chapter Fifteen

1. A Defensible Space Project: Deterring Crime and Building Community in Rogers Park for the Center for Urban Research and Learning, Loyola University, Chicago

www.luc.edu/curl/pubs/defense.shtml

This detailed article explains the steps that were taken to develop defensible spaces and thereby create a sense of community in the Rogers Park area of Chicago. The information provided can serve as useful guidelines for designers on projects of this sort.

2. Safe Community Planning & Design: An Introduction to Crime Prevention Through Environmental Design (CPTED) for *Center Views* for the Planning Center.

www.planningcenter.com/pdf/g.2.8Cpted.pdf

This article explores four basic principles in CPTED and how they can be designed into all aspects of a community to keep crime down and community participation and population satisfaction high.

3. The Freestyle Frisbee Page

www.frisbee.com/freestyle/places/locales_list.html

This website provides information on Frisbee events, articles, and locations around the world. This page is specifically dedicated to United States Freestyle Jam Zones.

4. City of Vancouver Community Services, Planning: Current Planning

www.city.vancouver.bc.ca/commsvcs/currentplanning/urbandesign/

This website provides articles that focus on the continuing city planning and development underway in Vancouver, Canada. There is a brief description of urban design and access to a series of informative articles following the growth of Vancouver, which are ideal for case studies and reference.

5. Restoring Community Through Traditional Neighborhood Design: A Case Study of Diggs Town Public Housing by Stephanie Bothwell, Raymond Gindroz, and Robert Lang for the Fannie Mae Foundation

www.fanniemaefoundation.org/programs/hpd/pdf/hpd_0901_bothwell.pdf

The authors focus on the implications of New Urbanism when it is combined with traditional design to try to redevelop an impoverished community. This case study focuses on the restoration of the public housing project Diggs Town in Norfolk, Virginia.

6. What Is Gentrification? by Benjamin Grant for PBS

www.pbs.org/pov/pov2003/flagwars/special_gentrification.html

Grant explores the meaning of gentrification in this article along with how the process comes about and what the effects are on communities. He discusses the positives and negatives of gentrification with heavy consideration given to the consequences.

7. A Tale of Three Cities: Gentrification Made Visible with Interactive Maps of Three Neighborhoods in Flux by PBS

www.pbs.org/pov/pov2003/flagwars/special_tale.html

This exploration of gentrification is arranged as three articles, each focused on a major city. The three cities examined are San Francisco, New York City, and Columbus, Ohio. The studies include interactive maps, photographs, brief histories, and results of gentrification.

8. Influence of Environmental Design on Pedestrian Travel Behavior in Four Austin Neighborhoods by Katherine Shriver

http://enhancements.org/trb%5C1578-09.pdf

Shriver uses four Austin, Texas, neighborhoods for comparative case studies in the effects of automobile and pedestrian traffic on community sentiment.

9. A Pedestrian: The Forgotten Factor in Regional Transportation Planning by Spenser Havlick for the Department for Planning and Infrastructure, Government of Western Australia

www.dpi.wa.gov.au/walking/pdfs/K2.pdf

Havlick discusses the potential for improved walking cities based on case studies of successful examples from around the world. Guidelines are given for urban planners and city designers.

10. Social Legibility, The Cognitive Map, and Urban Behavior by Thierry Ramadier and Gabriel Moser for the *Journal of Environmental Psychology*

www.girba.crad.ulaval.ca/Articles/JEP1998-09 _P307.pdf

The authors discuss the value of social legibility and related spatial understanding in city design. The paper is a scholarly presentation of many vital points for designers and planners to develop into urban planning.

11. DeForest Town Square presented by Keller Real Estate Group of Madison Wisconsin

www.kellerrealtors.com/deforest/apartment _content.html

Keller Real Estate gives a description of the DeForest Town Square apartment homes complex in DeForest, Wisconsin.

12. Commercial Qualities of Montreal by *Architecture Week*

www.architectureweek.com/2004/0818/news _3-1.html

This article reviews the outcome of the Commerce Design Montreal competition. Looking at twenty buildings designed for the competition, the authors relate how they function in the business area of Montreal and enhance the overall community.

13. Talking Sheds by Denise Scott Brown for *Architecture Week*

www.architectureweek.com/2005/0420/design _2-2.html

Brown discusses her experiences as an architect in developing business centers using the model of buildings dealt with as "a shed with communication on the outside." She includes reference to specific buildings and their community position as well as photographs.

14. Walkable Communities: The Commercial Environment by David Kopec for *Realty Times*

http://realtytimes.com/rtapages/20031224 _walkable.htm

Kopec discusses the value of walkability in commercial settings with special emphasis on the demographics of the users. He explores the effects of

the environment on the perceptions of the people who utilize it and how the design can lead to the success or failure of a commercial setting.

15. The Main Street Four-Point Approach to Commercial District Revitalization presented by the National Trust for Historic Presevation

www.mainstreet.org/content.aspx?page=47 &section=2

This organization provides a number of guidelines and articles to assist in main street redevelopment and understanding of design objectives. The information given by the trust is valuable to designers, planners, residents, and city councils.

16. Downtown Revitalization & Streetscape Enhancement for the *St. Croix Valley Development Design Study*

www.metrocouncil.org/planning/stcroixvalley /downtown_rev.htm

The authors discuss how commercial districts can be revitalized and made more appealing to consumers and visitors. Diagrams, maps, and photographs are included to emphasise the points made.

17. Traffic Calming 101 for the Project for Public Spaces

www.pps.org/info/placemakingtools/casesforplaces /livememtraffic

This article introduces the various methods of traffic calming. The easy-to-read concepts are accented with descriptive photographs to accent the important features of traffic calming. The article also includes links to related information.

18. AIA Housing Knowledge Community Honors 8 Residential Designs presented by the American Institute of Architecture

www.aia.org/aiarchitect/thisweek05/tw0318 /0318housing.htm

This article gives eight examples of outstanding residential design. Many people focus on community living and multifamily residences. The award winning designs include photographs and brief summaries of the design objectives.

19. Housing presented by the Local Government Commission

www.lgc.org/community_design/housing.html

With this organization's focus on building livable communities, this article describes the changes that are occurring in today's housing markets and how these changes affect residential design and communities.

20. **A Better Suburbia by Mark Francis for** *Architecture Week*

www.architectureweek.com/2005/0119/building _1-1.html

Francis discusses the extraordinary design of a residential community plan called Village Homes. The goal of the design principles is to create a communal pride and involvement in the residential neighborhood, which includes public use green spaces, attractive edging and less-obvious parking options than most traditional residential areas. Plans and photographs are included.

21. **Housing High and Low by Roberto Perez-Guerras for** *Conceptual Architecture*

www.architectureweek.com/2004/0310/design _2-1.html

Residential designs by Perez-Guerras are examined in this article. His designs foster a sense of community whether he is designing a residential high-rise building or smaller housing facilities.

22. **Residential Street Pattern Design for Healthy Livable Communities by Fanis Grammenos and Julie Tasker-Brown**

www.cardinalgroup.ca/nua/ip/ip02.htm

Grammenos and Tasker-Brown examine historic and commonly used modern models of street patterns in residential environments to develop the most appealing road layouts possible without sacrificing efficiency or safety.

GLOSSARY

abstract representation   Data-based mental image used to perceive, comprehend, and store information about an environment

accessible route   Continuous, unobstructed path that connects all accessible elements and spaces of a building or facility; interior accessible routes may include corridors, floors, ramps, elevators, lifts, and clear floor space at fixtures; and exterior accessible routes may include parking access aisles, curb ramps, crosswalks at vehicular ways, walks, ramps, and lifts

acoustics   Increased sound qualities of an environment; design elements that affect the sound characteristics of a space through transmission, absorption, and reflection

activities of daily living (ADLs)   Routine functional activities such as bathing, grooming, dressing, dining, cooking, light housekeeping, and taking medication

acute care facility   Healthcare environment equipped to deal with emergencies, life-threatening illnesses and injuries, and surgical operations

acute stressor   Sudden and intense bursts of stress

adaptation   The process of adjusting to environmental conditions

adaptation level theory   Premise that individuals adapt to certain levels of stimulation in certain contexts

aesthetics   Characteristics of beauty or pleasure that appeal to the senses as opposed to the logical mind (see *formal aesthetics, symbolic aesthetics*)

affect   A person's emotional reaction to an environment

allergen   Substance, frequently airborne, that compromises the human immune system; source of allergic reactions

ambient noise   Irrelevant sounds mostly derived from exterior sources

ambient stressor   Source of stress that is typically short-term and limited to a particular environment

architectural delineation   Separation of one area from another by way of architectural elements or features

architectural determinism   Theory that there is a direct relationship between the built environment and a particular behavior

area of rescue assistance   Space that has direct access to an exit where people who are unable to use stairs may remain temporarily in safety while they await instructions or assistance during emergency evacuations

arousal   Excitement or stimulation to action or physiological readiness for activity

arousal perspective   Theory that much of human behavior and experience is related to arousal levels

assistive device   Physical mobility aid that assists people's movements, such as a brace, cane, crutch, walking frame, wheelchair (standard or motorized), prosthetic limb, or service animal

attentional deficit   Inability to focus or concentrate; inadequate attentional capacity; caused by mental fatigue due to excessive *directed attention* and can be ameliorated by *restorative experiences*

attention restoration theory (ART)   Premise that mental fatigue is caused by excessive *directed attention* and that attentional capacity and mental balance can be restored by engaging in *effortless attention*

attitude   A belief that tends to follow the values of an era and vice versa; predisposition

atmospherics   Cues, such as sights, sounds, or scents, that contribute to the overall ambience of an environment

auditory learners   People who process information by what they hear, and reason through discussion

345

automobile city   City that typically sprawls across hundreds of square miles (e.g., Los Angeles)

behavioral controls   Physical or psychological elements that serve to restrict or encourage specific behaviors

behavioral health facility   Psychological healthcare environment such as a psychiatric hospital or mental health institution

behavior setting   Physical or psychological environment (i.e., place or occasion) that elicits or supports certain patterns of behavior based on the environmental design and learned as a result of *operant conditioning*

bioeffluent   Organic body waste such as carbon dioxide, skin cells, hairs, and microbes (bacteria, germs, and viruses)

birthing center   Facility that allows women to give birth in home-like settings

brightness   Luminance or lightness or darkness of color relative to its intensity

broken windows theory   Premise that a single broken window, if ignored, can lead to the decline and eventual destruction of an entire community

building layout   Logical spatial progression and organization of a built environment

building-related illness   Symptoms of diagnosable illnesses that are found in occupants of all office buildings to some degree

building-specific illness   Symptoms that occur only in air-conditioned buildings

cardinal direction   Compass direction (e.g., north, south, east, and west)

cognitive map   Mental image of *navigational space* based on sensory information, imagination, and language; pictorial and semantic concept of an environment or setting

chronic stressor   Constant or recurring source of stress that slowly erodes our abilities to cope

collaborative structure   In this environment, team roles, goals, and operating principles are an important part of joint problem solving and the brainstorming of innovative ideas

crowd   A large, temporary group of emotional people who may or may not have a common goal or purpose

crowding   Psychological reaction that produces an emotional response based on both personal factors and circumstances; subjective feeling of being unable to control our situations when there are too many people, too little space, and especially both

cognition   Mental analysis or how information is interpreted, stored, and recalled; second phase in overall thought process

cognitive map   Pictorial and semantic (language) mental image of an environment or setting

cognitive truth   Belief that may or may not be factual but is held to be true

commodify   To commercialize; to turn an intrinsic value into a commodity (i.e., a recognizable unit of economic production)

concentration node   Area in which people gather for a common purpose

continuing care retirement communities   Campus-like environment that allows residents to "age in place" as their health deteriorates

culture   The values, norms, and artifacts of a group of people

declarative memory   Recall that uses semantic representations as is related to facts, rules, and concepts (*see procedural memory*)

defensible space theory (DST)   Premise that the appropriation and exercise of *territorial control* reduces both the opportunity for and the fear of crime (i.e., the more a person claims and defends a territory, the less likely that space is to be violated)

defensible space marker   Indicator of an occupant's physical presence in or claim to a space; can be a *physical barrier* or a *symbolic barrier*

density   Objective (mathematical) measure of the number of individuals per unit of area; the term may describe social or spatial ratios

density-intensity theory   Premise that density itself is not harmful, but rather that it amplifies everything else

descriptors   Environmental features or attributes that help us to understand and respond to a place

determinism   Theory that acts of will, occurrences in nature, or social or psychological phenomena are causally determined by preceding events or natural laws

directed attention Intention- or goal-based attention; requires focused mental effort and can cause *attentional deficit*; also called voluntary attention.

ecological perception Theory that much environmental information is conveyed by perceptual patterns that do not require higher-brain processing

ecotourism Specialized type of tourism intended to support and conserve local or indigenous cultures, economies, traditions, landscapes, and ecologically sustainable development in settings ranging from the primitive to the luxurious

effect Resulting state or condition

effortless attention Interest-based attention that can serve to restore attentional capacity; also called automatic and involuntary attention

ethic of care theory Premise that it is women's nature to focus on sustaining relationships and caring for others

environmental cognition Analysis of how we understand, diagnose, and interact within the environment

environmental load State of excessive arousal; also called overstimulation

environmental numbness State of being unaware of the environment until it or something in it changes

environmental perception People's interpretation of the world around them as influenced by their experiences and sensations

ergonomics Applied science concerned with designing and arranging the things people use so as to ensure both efficiency and safety; also called human engineering or human factors psychology

external locus of control The belief that lives are controlled by external forces (e.g., fate, luck, chance, or powerful otherworldly beings)

external proceedings Environmental factors that affect our decisions and behaviors, such as accessibility and organization; our interactions with the physical environment and other individuals that are influenced by our *internal proceedings*.

extraneous noise Type of noise related to speech or vocal tones; linked to negative mood changes

external stressors Sources of stress that derive from variables in the physical environment, such as noise, temperature, crowding, and over- or understimulation

fight-or-flight response An automatic response to stress that is perceived to be a survival threat

formal aesthetics Character of beauty or pleasure relative to dimensions (shape, proportion, scale, novelty, and illumination), enclosure (spaciousness, density, and mystery), complexity (visual richness, diversity, and information rate), and order (unity and clarity) (*see symbolic aesthetics*)

fourth environment Place where individuals congregate other than their primary, secondary, and tertiary territories or spaces (i.e., not their residences or sites specifically developed for them)

gentrification Process of renewing deteriorating urban areas so as to encourage social and economic growth

hard room Room decorated with bare floors, minimal wall and standing artwork, and modern or industrial furnishings

hierarchical structure Traditional imperial organizational structure, characterized by bureaucracy and a "chain of command" of power and control

home office Designated space in a private residence that can support either household record keeping or a home-based business or can serve as a telecommuting site

hospice Specialized environment that provides care and comfort for terminal (dying) patients

hue Attribute of color that allows its identification (e.g., red, blue, or yellow)

human-scale element Design element that is neither oversized nor undersized

illuminance Lighting level or amount of illumination; measured in lux

illumination Quantity of light striking a surface; measured in foot-candles

immunocompetence Ability or capacity for the immune system to respond or function adequately

implicit cue Indicator of our behavior that we leave behind when we leave an environment

implicit behavioral cues Cues that we leave in a setting that indicate our behavior in that environment and imply its acceptability to those who follow, who will be more likely to model their behavior after ours

interactionism Simplest form of *integration theory*; holds that people and the environment are separate but interacting entities (i.e., all or most outcomes can be attributed to either the person or the environment)

internal locus of control Belief that people's actions, choices, and pursuits control their lives and nothing else (e.g., fate)

internal stressors Sources of stress that derive from interpersonal conflict or violence, disorganized daily life, or a combination of these factors

internal proceedings Personal factors that affect our decisions and behaviors; thoughts and feelings that help us to represent, explain, and predict the world around us and that affect our *external proceedings*

integration (integral) theories Theoretical models intended to encompass the complex range of human–environment relationships

interactional territory Space temporarily controlled by a group of interacting individuals (e.g., playing field, conference room, or theater)

irrelevant sound Type of noise related mostly to exterior sources; linked to impaired cognitive performance

kinesthetic learners People who process information by experiencing, doing, and touching

mediator Behavioral variable that influences both the moderator and the individual; operating in a sequence between other variables

long-term care facility Residential environment for (usually elderly) individuals who require routine medical care and assistance with activities of daily living; also called nursing or convalescent home

luminaire Complete lighting unit: fixture, light source, electrical hookup, and parts that help control the light

luminance Brightness of an object; measured in lumens

megastore Large retail facility that offers consumers an expansive variety of goods and services; also called *hypermarket*

mixed-use community Structure or district that encompasses a variety of uses such as housing, retail, and restaurants

moderator A variable that facilitates a desired behavior activity; when one variable interacts with another, the level or intensity of the second variable will determine the change in the first variable

music stream Constant flow or stream of pleasurable, musical background noise

nature tourism Eclectic range of recreational and cultural activities and experiences related to the natural world

navigational space Space we move through and explore that usually cannot be seen all at once

needs assessment Survey conducted prior to construction or occupancy to determine environmental conditions and user needs

neighborhood work center Fully furnished and equipped cooperative facility shared by employees of different companies and/or by entrepreneurs

nonterritorial office workspaces are not dedicated (assigned) but are available as needed for employees who work part-time or spend most of their time out in the field

neurotransmitter Chemical substance that transmits nerve impulses across synapses

occupancy evaluation Survey of a planned development conducted during the formative stages to determine the needs of the intended users

operant conditioning Social process that teaches and reinforces acceptable/desirable behaviors; a form of behavior modification. It is also called *stimulus-response learning*.

organismic theory Form of *integration theory* that focuses on the complex interaction of social, personal, and societal factors

overload The negative mental state that results when one experiences excessive information, stimulation, and arousal

paradigm Philosophical or theoretical conceptual framework

pedestrian city City that appears to have grown up rather than spread out (e.g., New York)

pediatric hospital Specialized hospital dedicated to the exclusive care of infants and children

perception Initial gathering of information through the five senses and subsequent organization of that sensory input; first phase in the overall thought process

peripheral vision Outer part of the field of vision

personal control   The ability of a person to control his or her environment or situation

personalization   Use of physical indicators of personal identity and individuality; serves to mark territories and therefore regulates social interactions

phobia   Irrational fear that is very real to an individual, but is highly unlikely to occur in normal circumstances

physical barrier   Indicator of *territorial control* that is intended to deter or prevent *territorial infringement*; physical barriers include locks, fences, high walls, road closures, and other barricades (*see symbolic barrier*)

place attachment   Emotional bond to a place's social and physical components

place identity   The manner in which a person incorporates a place into the larger concept of his or her own identity or sense of self

pleasure–arousal–dominance hypothesis   Premise that people have three primary emotional responses to an environment: positive feelings, excitement, and a sense of control

postoccupancy evaluation (POE)   Survey conducted after a space is occupied to determine if user needs were met

predesign research (PDR)   See *needs assessment*

primary spaces   Common areas in territories such as residences and workplaces where communication and social interaction take place (e.g., living rooms and conference rooms)

primary territory   Space, generally owned by an individual or primary group and closed to outsiders, that is controlled on a relatively permanent basis and is of high psychological importance to the occupants (e.g., family residence or business establishment)

procedural memory   Recall based on performance, actions, and skills (*see declarative memory*)

prospect   Visual range for detecting food or danger at a distance afforded by open areas

prospect-refuge theory   Premise that humans prefer environments with both open and closed areas because these afford both visual range and safety

psychological construct   Conceptual representation of an environment or idea; a way of thinking about or conceiving of a place or idea

psychological reactance   A person's attempt to regain his or her freedom within or control over an environment stemming from feelings of lack or loss of control; also called *reactance*

public territory   Public space open to anyone in good standing within the community (e.g., library, mall, park, or restaurant)

refuge   Safe haven or shelter afforded by closed spaces

rehabilitation facility   Extended-stay environment that provides multidisciplinary physical restorative services and in which patients work to regain their health after accidents, strokes, and so on

restorative experience   Episode that allows a person to function primarily in the effortless attention mode as a means of restoring attentional capacity and therefore relaxing

right-side bias   Human tendency to better see and remember items located on the right-hand side than on the left

satellite office   Remote workplace location controlled by an organization; form of telecommuting

saturation   Color purity (freedom from dilution with white)

scenographic representation   Picture-based mental image used to perceive, comprehend, and store information about an environment

secondary spaces   Common areas in territories such as residences and workplaces, to and from which communication and social interaction migrate (e.g., kitchens and reception desks)

secondary territory   Space of moderate significance to the occupants; psychological control is likely to change, rotate, or be shared with others (e.g., work space or favorite eatery)

segmentation   Division of a whole space or structure by separation or partition into smaller areas/sections

segmentation bias   Cognitive process of breaking a route into smaller segments that alters our perception of distance (distance estimates)

selective attention   Ability to focus on select stimuli and screen out others

separatism   Belief system that one entity must dominate the other in the human–environment relationship (see interactionism, transactionalism)

self–identify The manner in which people identify themselves according to their personal experiences and the tangible components that represent and symbolize their places in the world

self–regulation Behavioral limitations or boundaries that people set for themselves in either physical or social environments

sense of community Emotional bond to a place based on feelings of belonging relative to the occupants, environment, or both; form of *place attachment*

sense of place A feeling that develops when a level of comfort and feelings of safety are associated with a place

servicescape Physical setting that is composed of a retail or service environment

sick building syndrome (SBS) Acute health and discomfort effects that seem linked to time spent inside a building but for which no specific illness or cause can be identified

sick role Patient role we assume when we are sick or injured that affects our cognitive processes, behaviors, and medical outcomes

signage and numbering systems Displayed wayfinding cues that are matched with cognitive codes

social appropriation Type of physical appropriation of a space; aspects include talking to or spending time with others in that space. It is a form of *territorial control*.

social density Density ratio created by a varied number of individuals occupying a fixed amount of space; ratio of persons per square foot of space (*see spatial density*)

social learning theory Construct that explains human behavior in terms of continuous reciprocal interaction between cognitive, behavioral, and environmental influences

sociofugal Type of seating arrangements wherein people face away from others

sociopetal Type of seating arrangements wherein people face others

soft room Room decorated with carpeting, canvas-based artwork, and overstuffed furnishings

spatial cognition Specialized thinking process used to navigate through environments

spatial density Density ratio created by a fixed number of individuals occupying different-size spaces (*see social density*)

special care unit (SCU) Separate area within a healthcare facility that provides specific services (e.g., emergency, pediatric, and rehabilitation services)

stimulus association Association that develops when a new but similar situation causes the body to reproduce its initial response

stimulation theory Concept that explains the environment as a source of sensory information (stimuli) that leads to arousal

strategic junction node Point where activity converges for different purposes

supports and constraints Environmental elements that facilitate and restrict human actions

symbolic aesthetics Character of beauty or pleasure relative to denotative (e.g., of function or style) or connotative (e.g., either welcoming or forbidding) meaning; sources include naturalness, upkeep, intensity of use, and style (*see formal aesthetics*)

symbolic barrier Indicator of territorial control that is intended to deter or prevent territorial infringement; symbolic barriers include signs, borders, low railings, landscaping, and changes in size, shape, color, and construction materials (*see physical barrier*)

synomorphy Principle that an environment's physical and social aspects should fit together well; also, congruity between the physical, psychological, and social aspects of an environment

telecommuting Working for a company as an employee, but away from the company's organizational workplace (does not apply to independent contractors and consultants); use of computer technology to transfer information from remote locations to the main office

teratogen Environmental agent that causes developmental malformations

territorial appropriation Type of *physical appropriation* of a space; aspects include feelings of ownership, taking care of and monitoring the space, and/or noticing and intervening if destructive or illegal activities occur there; a form of *territorial control*

territorial contamination Intentional fouling of another's territory; sources include vandalism, graffiti, stink bombs, and excessive noise

territorial control   Physical appropriation of the space surrounding a territory; can include *social appropriation*, *territorial appropriation*, or both as means of deterring or preventing *territorial infringement*

territorial infringement   Unwanted or illegal intrusion into another's territory; can involve *territorial contamination*, *invasion*, or *violation*

territorial invasion   Physical entry by an outsider into a territory with the intention of taking control of it

territorial violation   Temporary incursion into another's territory, usually for purposes of annoyance, harm, or power rather than ownership

tertiary spaces   Private or personal spaces or areas where a person goes to be alone

threshold   Point at which too much or too little stimulation has been received

tradition   A custom or practice that has been passed down from generation to generation

transactionalism   Belief system that the human–environment relationship is mutually supportive and that all or most outcomes can be attributed to both the person and the environment (*see interactionism, separatism*)

universal design   Approach to the design of products and spaces that emphasizes usability by people with a wide range of needs; intended to enable people of all ability levels to achieve maximum environmental independence

urban village   City district where residents share a common culture, ethnicity, or lifestyle within a relatively self-sufficient area

virtual modeling   Practice of using *implicit cues* to modify behavior

virtual office   Mobile workplace supported by a portable computer and telephone; form of telecommuting

visual access   Clear line of sight to a destination or reference point

visual learners   People who process information by what they see and think in terms of pictures

walking distance   Maximum distance the average person will walk to reach a particular destination; approximately a quarter of a mile or 400 meters

wayfinding   Process of navigating to or from a particular destination

worldview   Perspective or philosophy that incorporates a general belief; may be held by an entire culture or generation

workplace culture   Desired social climate within a business organization; the way in which personnel interact with on another

FIGURE CREDITS

ONE

1.1a: Dean Conger/Corbis
1.1b: Bryan and Cherry Photography/Alamy
1.2: Illustration by Therese Holt
1.3: Illustration by Karen Blackerby
1.4a: Paul A. Souders/Corbis
1.4b: Macduff Everton
1.4c: John Linden/Beateworks
1.4d: Chris Hellier/Corbis
1.5: Illustration by Susan Day
1.6: Illustration by Paul Norman Reyes
1.7: Illustration by Susan Day
1.8: Faith Saribas/Reuters/Corbis
1.9: Illustration by Katsura Furumi
1.10a: IML Image Group Ltd./Alamy
1.10b: Andrea Rugg/Beateworks

TWO

2.1: Randy Faris/Corbis
2.2: Illustration by Paul Norman Reyes
2.3a: H. Spichtinger/Corbis
2.3b: Gene J. Puskar/AP
2.4: Macduff Everton/Corbis
2.5: Andreas von Einsiedel/Elizabeth Whiting & Associates/Corbis
2.6: Peter M. Fisher/Corbis
2.7a: Illustration by Karen Blackerby
2.7b: Illustration by Sara Harstrom
2.8: Ron Carboni
2.9: Illustration by Katsuri Fumari
2.10: Andre Jenny/Alamy

THREE

3.1: Ron Carboni
3.2a: Illustration by Brandy Beardslee
3.2b: Illustration by Paul Norman Reyes
3.4: Callison Architecture
3.5: Elizabeth Whiting & Associates/Corbis
3.6: Brian Harrison/Elizabeth Whiting & Associates/Corbis
3.7: Alan Levenson/Corbis
3.8: Kevin Fleming/Corbis
3.9: Illustration by Susan Day
3.11a–f: Alan Reingold

FOUR

4.1: Ivan Barta/Alamy
4.2a: Lester Lefkowitz/Corbis
4.2b: Paul Almasy/Corbis
4.2c: Peter DaSilva/New York Times
4.2d: Tim Street-Porter/Beateworks
4.3: LWA-Dann Tardif/Corbis
4.5a, b: Illustrations by Karen Blackerby
4.6: Wolfram Schroll/Corbis
4.7: Illustration by Linda Gram and Helga Kohen
4.8a: G. Rossenbach/Corbis
4.8b: Tim Street-Porter/Beateworks
4.9: Illustration by Paul Norman Reyes.
4.10: Colin McPherson/Corbis

FIVE

5.1a: C. Wilhelm/Corbis
5.1b: Robert Maass/Corbis
5.2: Shannon Stapelton/Corbis
5.3: Illustration by Jimma Alegado
5.4: Roger Antrobus/Corbis
5.5: Adrian Wilson/Beateworks
5.6a: Callison Architecture
5.6b: Adrian Wilson/Beateworks
5.7: Illustration by Brandy Beardslee
5.8: Callison Architecture
5.9: Jeremy Horner/Corbis
5.10a: Matthias Kulka/Corbis
5.10b, c: Corbis

SIX

6.1: Laura Dwight/Corbis
6.2: Roger Ressmeyer/Corbis
6.3: Corbis
6.4: Tony Arruza/Corbis
6.5: Will & Deni McIntyre
6.6: Illustration by Peter Karoll
6.7: Henry Diltz/Corbis
6.8: Macduff Everton/Corbis
6.9: Michael S. Yamashita/Corbi
6.10a: Tim Street-Porter/Beateworks
6.10b: Corbis

SEVEN

7.1a-c: Ron Carboni
7.2: Illustration by Linda Gram
7.3: Corbis
7.4: Alan Schein Photography/Corbis
7.5a: Corbis
7.5b: Richard Hamilton Smith/Corbis
7.6: Scott Van Dyke/Beateworks
7.7: Illustration by Paul Norman Reyes
7.8: Elizabeth Whiting & Associates/Corbis
7.9: Alamy
7.10: J. Scott Smith/Beateworks

EIGHT

8.1: Illustration by Paul Norman Reyes
8.2: Tim Street-Porter/Beateworks
8.3: Andrea Rugg/Beateworks
8.4: Alan Schein Photography/Corbis
8.5: Tom & Dee Ann McCarthy/Corbis
8.6: Paul Norman Reyes
8.7: Corbis
8.8: Paula Solloway/Alamy
8.9: Gideon Mendel/Corbis

NINE

9.1: Corbis
9.2: G. Schuster/Corbis
9.3: Pat Behnke/Alamy
9.4: Craig Holmes/Alamy
9.5: R. Henning/Alamy
9.6: Scott Van Dyke/Beateworks
9.7: Peter Karoll
9.8: Henry Westheim / Alamy

TEN

10.1: Paul Norman Reyes
10.2: Corbis
10.3: Paul Norman Reyes
10.4: Jerry Cooke/Corbis
10.5: Linda Gram
10.6: Jack Sullivan/Alamy
10.7: Elizabeth Whiting & Associates/Corbis
10.8a: David Butow/Corbis
10.8b: Bob Rowan/Corbis
10.9: Linda Gram
10.10: Jeffery Allan Salter/Corbis

ELEVEN

11.1a: Alinari Archives/Corbis
11.1b: LWA-JDC/Corbis
11.2: Corbis
11.3a: Ricardo Miramontes
11.3b: Linda Gram
11.4: Rick Gayle/Corbis
11.5: C. Lyttle/Corbis
11.6: Peter Turnley
11.7: ER Productions/Corbis
11.8: Corbis
11.9: Massimo Listri/Corbis
11.10: Ed Kashi/Corbis

TWELVE

12.1: Illustration by Susan Day
12.2: JG Photography/Alamy
12.3: Ron Carboni
12.4: Blend Images/Alamy
12.5: Alla Carrasco
12.6: Alla Carrasco
12.7: John Feingersh/Corbis
12.8: Adrian Wilson/Beateworks
12.9: David Williams/Alamy
12.10: Paul Norman Reyes
12.11: Lara Jacobs

THIRTEEN

13.1: Ron Carboni
13.2: Tor Eigeland
13.3: Morton Beebe/Corbis
13.4: Thomas A. Kelly/Corbis
13.5: Blasius Erlinger/Corbis
13.6: Tim Street-Porter/Beateworks

FOURTEEN

14.1: Paul Norman Reyes
14.2: Profimedia/Alamy
14.3: Swerve/Alamy
14.4: Andre Jenny/Alamy
14.5: Ed Bailey/AP
14.6: Rupert Horrox/Corbis
14.7: Owaki-Kulla/Corbis
14.8: Sarah Hadley
14.9: Callison Architecture

FIFTEEN

15.1: Oote Boe/Alamy
15.2: Danita Delimont
15.3: Paul Norman Reyes
15.4: Jeff Greenberg
15.5: K. Hackenberg/Corbis
15.6: Alan Schein/Corbis
15.7a-k: Ron Carboni

INDEX

abstract representations, 90, 95, 96, 202, 345

academic programs, 8–9

accessible route, 170–71, 184, 345
See also wheelchair accessibility

acetylcholine, 40, 41

acoustical privacy, 74, 134

acoustics, 174, 184, 192–94, 345
See also under noise

action research, 7

activities of daily living (ADLs), 170, 175, 176
defined, 169, 184, 345

acute care facilities, 211, 226, 228, 345

acute stressors, 102, 117, 154, 345

ADA. See Americans with Disabilities Act (ADA)

adaptation, 13, 16, 23, 26, 345

adaptation level theory, 24, 35, 345

additive primaries (color), 87

administration, workplace, 234, 235

adolescence, 145, 147, 159–60, 161, 216
privacy issues in, 148–49

adrenaline (epinephrine), 23, 40, 41, 108

adventure excursions, 257, 263

advertising, 20, 23, 281, 282

aesthetics, 59, 130, 226, 297, 345
See also beauty
color and, 85, 94
formal, 85, 86, 96–97, 347
symbolic, 64, 85, 97, 350

affect, 13, 16, 26, 345

affiliative-conflict theory, 67

affluence, 125, 299

affordances, 28, 32, 34

age and aging, 137, 138, 169, 233
See also children; elderly populations
independence and, 174–75, 176

agritourism, 257, 268

air
See also ventilation
fresh, 196
perfume-scented, 68, 283
air conditioners, 42, 106, 238

air pollution, 103, 104–6, 153
See also pollution; volatile organic compounds (VOCs)
exterior, 101, 104–5
interior, 105–6, 107

airports, 33, 69, 91, 103, 109, 297

alarms, 108, 284

alcohol and alcoholism, 23, 199, 266

alcoves and niches, 134, 224, 260

allergens, 107, 117, 239, 345
children and, 146, 153, 154, 161

Altman, Irwin, 69

Alzheimer's disease, 40, 42, 170
See also Dementia of the Alzheimer's Type (DAT)

ambience, 85, 260, 278, 279, 290
See also atmosphere

ambient noise, 108, 117, 345

ambient stressors, 103, 117, 287, 345

amenities, 133, 147, 258, 260–61, 297

American Automotive Association (AAA), 265

American Psychological Association (APA), 8

Americans with Disabilities Act (ADA), 170–71, 173, 174, 181, 262

amnesia, 50. See also memory

amusement parks, 288

amygdala (brain region), 40, 103

anger, 103, 108, 169

animal companions. See pets

anonymity, 73

antiseptics, 108

anxiety, 88, 149, 198, 226
See also stress

apartments, 127, 138, 268

approach-avoidance concept, 67

aquariums, 212

architects, 10, 263–64

architectural delineation, 91–92, 96, 345

architectural determinism, 22, 35, 345

architectural identity, 128–29

architectural purpose, 63–64

areas of rescue assistance, 223, 228, 345

Argyle, Michael, 67

Arizona State University (ASU), 131, 132

arousal, 16, 23–24, 26, 30, 277
defined, 13, 345

arousal perspective, 23, 35, 345
See also pleasure-arousal-dominance theory

ART. See attention restoration theory (ART)

art deco style, 6

artwork, 216, 220, 260

Asian cultures, 30, 71, 89, 106, 149, 258

assistive device, 172, 184, 345
See also mobility aids; wheelchairs

atmosphere, 39, 216, 285–86, 290

atmospherics, 278, 282, 290, 292, 345

ATMs (automated teller machines), 285

atriums, 244

attention
directed, 24, 35, 84, 244, 302, 347
effortless, 24, 35, 83, 347
selective, 48, 56, 349

attention deficit, 24, 35, 345

attention deficit/hyperactivity disorder (ADHD), 103, 139, 149–50, 345

attention restoration theory (ART), 5, 24, 32, 200, 244, 245
defined, 35, 345

attitude, 49–50, 56

audial privacy, 239, 241, 244. See also hearing

auditoriums, in schools, 192

auditory learners, 190, 205, 345

Australia, 267, 305

automobile cities, 300, 308, 311, 346

automobiles, 264, 300, 307, 309
See also under motor vehicles; traffic

autonomy, 134, 135, 176, 177, 182

autonomy-supportive environments, 169, 216

Averill, James, 20

background music, 225, 243, 276, 278, 283